D1446185

# The Clinician's Handbook

# THE CLINICIAN'S HANDBOOK

## The Psychopathology of Adulthood and Late Adolescence

**Robert G. Meyer**
UNIVERSITY OF LOUISVILLE

**Allyn and Bacon, Inc.**
Boston London Sydney Toronto

*To my parents, Bob and Ardelle, who gave so much.*

**Library of Congress Cataloging in Publication Data**

Meyer, Robert G.
    The clinician's handbook.

    Bibliography: p.
    Includes index.
    1. Mental illness—Diagnosis.  2. Minnesota multiphasic
personality inventory.  3. Sixteen personality factor
questionnaire.  4. Wechsler adult intelligence scale.
5. Rorschach test.  6. Psychotherapy.  I. Title.
RC469.M46    1982    616.89    82–8901
ISBN 0–205–07792–7

10 9 8 7 6 5 4 3 2    88 87 86 85 84

Printed in the United States of America.

# Contents

# Preface

During my graduate training and internship, I was impressed that no book had integrated the common symptoms, personality styles, test patterns, and treatment recommendations that are associated with the various major psychodiagnostic categories. These data were available, but they were not incorporated in a practical handbook. In the ensuing years, books such as Graham's *The MMPI: A Practical Guide* and Zimmerman and Woo-Sam's *Clinical Interpretation of the WAIS* took steps in this direction. Yet these books have each dealt with only a single test. Also, such texts primarily link expected behavior patterns to particular test results, but results are not related clearly to the diagnostic classifications that clinicians use everyday. Finally, there is seldom any link with the next step, treatment recommendations.

*The Clinician's Handbook* is an attempt to integrate these distinct, but necessarily related, considerations. This book presents updated correlates for the most commonly used objective psychological test, the Minnesota Multiphasic Personality Inventory (MMPI), as well as complementary personality information from the Cattell Sixteen Personality Factor Questionnaire (16 PF) Test. It links this information with data from the two other psychological tests most commonly used with adults, the Wechsler Adult Intelligence Scale (now revised, the WAIS-R) and the Rorschach Ink Blot Technique. The next steps are to integrate common behavioral features (and *Diagnostic and Statistical Manual of Mental Disorders* descriptors in most instances) and the most valid treatment recommendations. This synthesis is based on the assumptions that virtually all theories and schools are useful in some degree and that the biggest challenge to modern treatment is determining the best fit of client type with treatment type. Moreover, the eclecticism (in the best sense of that word) of this view dovetails with a multimodal approach to treatment recommendations. That is, it seldom appears that a single treatment approach is sufficient to treat clusters of disordered behaviors comprehensively, and the use of only one technique is probably not the best approach with any one client.

*The Clinician's Handbook* was designed first for practitioners, since they are likely to encounter the broad variety of emotional disorders in their work. Even practitioners who do not regularly administer the tests noted above should find this book useful, as test responses are tied to various functional aspects of each disorder and to treatment options that might be used. The practitioner can access this information in several ways. Generally, it is most useful to begin with common initial diagnoses and to examine the book's behavioral descriptors, DSM-III requirements, and various personality indices that are detailed for each. The relevant treatment recommendations can then be checked and incorporated into a report or overall treatment program.

Clinicians who prefer to look at MMPI data first, before making a tentative diagnosis, can use this book by going to chapter 2 to locate the particular high score (or two-point code) that is obtained, and then, if desired, use Table B at the end of chapter 2. Table B presents a list of probable diagnoses associated with virtually all of the two-point MMPI codes. These probable diagnoses can then be checked as described above.

Although originally designed for the practitioner—clinical, counseling, educational, forensic, and industrial psychologists; psychiatrists; clinical social workers; and pastoral counselors—it is also potentially useful as a text in graduate level courses. The breakdown of the disorder patterns follows the same schema as that of DSM-III and, in addition, adds material about important allied topics such as the criminal personality, acting-out potential, malingering, central nervous system dysfunction, and legal concepts (insanity, incompetency) as they relate to diagnostic categories. Thus, a full spectrum of adult and late adolescent psychopathology can be studied. Several instructors have used it as a primary text, which they then supplemented with readings on research relevant to the various disorder patterns and with other textbooks. The Clinician's Handbook also can be used to supplement a standard text of abnormal psychology, or in clinical courses and practicums as an adjunct to books on specific tests or test research, or to books on test administration.

As noted in the Introduction, this book incorporates most modern research available on the relationship of disorder patterns to diagnostic indicators and treatment options. Table A (in the Introduction) lists the many standard sources for the general and developing tradition of research studies noted throughout. The Introduction details the long process by which this book evolved; as noted there, the bedrock was the available research information.

However, it is clear that this material, like any other body of information, will change with time. It is hoped that many of these changes will be spurred on by this book itself, that is, that researchers will refine, through more practical, precise studies, the clusters of diagnostic features, test results, and treatment options which are offered in the following pages. Reports of such research and word of the experiences of clinicians as they use these formulations would be most welcome. Please send any information to the author, c/o Department of Psychology, University of Louisville, Belknap Campus, Louisville, Kentucky, 40292, or to the publisher with a request for forwarding.

This author is grateful to the American Psychiatric Association for its permission to convey generally the essence of the DSM-III categories seen in this book. Readers who wish a more detailed description of these categories should consult the DSM-III itself or the *DSM-III Case Book* (Spitzer el al., 1981), which gives one or two paragraph vignettes for each of the DSM-III subcategories. Those wishing a narrative and amplified analysis of the major categories and subcategories of psychopathology can consult *Case Studies in Abnormal Behavior* (Meyer & Hardaway, 1982).

As noted in the Introduction, this book has been significantly aided by the contributions of the many teachers, colleagues, and students whom I have known over the years; each has in some way been helpful. A particular debt is owed to my major professors at Michigan State University, Albert I. Rabin and Bertram Karon, as well as to many other clinicians such as Norman Abeles, Curtis Barrett, Patricia Carpenter, Mary Clarke, Larry Cowan, Dan Cox, Herb Eber, Will Edgerton, Sam Fulkerson, Mitch Hendrix, Bud Jackson, Peter Mayfield, Lovick Miller, Carleton Riddick, Paul Salmon, and Harvey A. Tilker, all of whom have been helpful and instructive throughout the years.

A major acknowledgment also goes to the two people whose time and efforts were most important to the eventual publication of this book, Mike Moll and Darlene Posey. Mike's cogent critiques and diligent efforts were most important in organizing this material, and Darlene's clerical efforts are deeply appreciated. A similar thank you goes to Nancy Davenport, Frances Knox, Kathleen McDaniel, and Donna Smith, who also contributed significantly to this book, and also to Grace Sheldrick, of Wordsworth Associates, for her editorial assistance.

R. G. M.

# Introduction

It would be absurd to expect that any one treatment approach or single pattern of test responses will be specifically relevant to one and only one diagnostic grouping, and conversely, that individual clients in any one category are going to respond only to one type of treatment or show a single pattern on diagnostic tests. Cumulative experience of clinicians bears out these statements. Psychological tests have been a substantial improvement over interview data alone. This is true even when the interview data are obtained in a controlled format, such as the Mental Status Examination, which includes assessment of the following: 1) physical appearance; 2) motor activities; 3) speech activity and patterns; 4) mood and affect; 5) alertness and attention; 6) content and organization of thoughts; 7) perception; 8) the general areas of memory, abstract thinking, and the client's fund of knowledge; and 9) the client's attitude toward the examination and toward his or her condition (Kupfer, 1975).

Some of the questions that commonly appear in the Mental Status Examination are the following: What is this place? Who am I? What day is it? Who are you? Who is the President? Who was the President before he was? What does "don't cry over spilled milk" mean? Would you count backward from 100 by 7s?

Even though there is structure provided to the interview by the Mental Status Examination, the examination contains the weakness of all data obtained from interviews: there are few or no statistical or normative standards for the obtained responses on which to base a communicable inference and an eventual diagnosis. Examiners are too often left to develop their own idiosyncratic notions of what a certain response means. While this procedure may be helpful in developing beginning inferences, these are strengthened significantly (or called into question) when the more objective data of psychological testing are considered as well.

The author saw markedly the potential of idiosyncratic error in the first case conference examination of a patient that he ever witnessed. The senior clinician who was examining the client proceeded with the questions of the Mental Status Examination. The client did generally well on most questions, except that he did not remember what day it was, he had some trouble counting backward from 100 by 7s after he got to 86, and he gave a rather concrete interpretation to the "spilled milk" proverb question. After the client left the room, the examining clinician suggested the diagnosis of schizophrenia, pointing out that 1) the client's lack of awareness of what day it was suggested a global disorientation, 2) the problem in counting backward from 100 by 7 suggested general confusion, and 3) the difficulties with the proverb suggested concreteness.

By this time, this author was uncomfortable since he had missed the day of the week by a full seven days. In actuality, a more parsimonious and better explanation for the client's behavior is available. A lack of knowledge of the exact date, even being off by a number of days, is common. In addition, people who have been in an institution for any period of time easily become confused, if not indifferent, about the date. The problems with the other two pieces of data are explainable by the fact that this client was not very bright.

There are trends, probabilities, and even some hard data to link the categories typically used by clinicians to various patterns. This book presents these relationships to the extent they are known at this time. In that regard, it is hoped that this book will result in more research that relates patterns of responses on several tests (which is what most clinicians use in an individual case) to various syndromes. As in any other area of scientific knowledge, subsequent research may supplant little, much, or all of what is now known.

This book is based on research results (wherever possible) that were then melded with reported consensual clinical experience. The depth or extent of the clinical experience naturally varies, depending on the particular syndrome that is being discussed.

If a single author or study is the source of material leading to a diagnostic or therapeutic recommendation, it will be directly referenced as such. If the recommendation is the speculation of the author alone, it will be so labeled. Where two or more different sources have provided information on which a recommendation is either directly based or inferred, it will be stated in such ways as, "The evidence shows . . .," or "The classic profile for . . .," or it will be put in a direct statement such as "Clients who are low on scale 8 are. . . ." The primary sources for the inferences for each of the four major tests used in this book—Minnesota Multiphasic Personality Inventory (MMPI), Cattell Sixteen Personality Factor Questionnaire (16 PF), Wechsler Adult Intelligence Scale-Revised (WAIS-R), and Rorschach—are presented in Table A.

In the second chapter, the clinical correlates of the MMPI and 16 PF scales are examined. Many researchers and clinicians have carried out

Table A    Primary Sources for Four Test Inferences

| MMPI | Rorschach |
| --- | --- |
| Boerger et al. (1974) | Aronow & Reznikoff (1976) |
| Butcher (1979) | Beck (1951) |
| Carson (1969) | Beck & Molish (1952) |
| Dahlstrom et al. (1972) | Beck & Beck (1978) |
| Dahlstrom et al. (1975) | Exner (1974, 1978) |
| Dahlstrom & Dahlstrom (1980) | Gilbert (1978, 1980) |
| Dahlstrom & Welsh (1960) | Goldfried et al. (1971) |
| Duckworth (1979) | Klopfer & Davidson (1962) |
| Fowler (1976, 1981) | Klopfer & Taulbee (1976) |
| Gilberstadt & Duker (1965) | Lerner (1975) |
| Golden (1979) | Levitt (1980) |
| Graham (1977) | Megargee (1966) |
| Greene (1980) | Ogdon (1977) |
| Gynther et al. (1973) (a) | Peterson (1978) |
| Gynther et al. (1973) (b) | Phillips & Smith (1953) |
| Hedlund (1977) | Rabin (1964, 1968, 1972, 1981) |
| Holland et al. (1981) | Rapaport et al. (1968) |
| Holland & Watson (1980) | Rickers-Ovsiankina (1960) |
| Kelley & King (1979) | Rorschach (1951) |
| Lachar (1974) | Shafer (1948, 1954) |
| Lane & Lachar (1979) | Wiggins (1969) |
| Marks et al. (1974) | Wiggins et al. (1971) |
| Megargee (1966) | |
| Megargee & Bohn (1979) | |
| Newmark (1979) | |
| Spiegel (1969) | |

| WAIS | 16 PF |
| --- | --- |
| Blatt & Allison (1968, 1981) | Cattell (1965, 1973, 1978, 1979) |
| Gilbert (1978, 1980) | Cattell & Warburton (1967) |
| Golden (1979) | Cattell et al. (1970) |
| Guertin et al. (1962) | Eber (1972, 1975) |
| Holland & Watson (1980) | Golden (1979) |
| Klingler & Saunders (1975) | IPAT (1963, 1972) |
| Matarazzo (1972) | Karson (1959, 1960) |
| Rabin (1964, 1968) | Karson & O'Dell (1976) |
| Rapaport et al. (1968) | Krug (1978, 1980, 1981) |
| Shafer (1948) | Megargee (1966) |
| Zimmermann & Woo Sam (1973) | |

similar work in this area, and much is owed to them. This chapter will attempt to integrate and update previous efforts so that the reader has an up-to-date body of information along traditional lines—that is, the various behavior patterns that are associated with the scale patterns. For some readers, much of this information will be new. For others, it will be at least a short refresher and a handy section to which to refer on occasion while using the rest of the book.

The remainder of this book will proceed in a standard sequence for each syndrome, with a number of related syndromes grouped together under an appropriate chapter heading. An overview of the material relevant to the specific diagnostic syndrome that is being discussed is presented first for each syndrome. This is then usually followed by a synopsis of what the *Diagnostic and Statistical Manual-III* (DSM-III) requires so that the clinician may apply this diagnosis to a client. In some cases, where there is little detail in the DSM-III requirements, I incorporate it into the first general subsection rather than having a specific DSM-III subsection for that syndrome.

The next subsection presents the MMPI code types and scale patterns one might expect with a client who exhibits this specific disorder. In most cases, the disorder can manifest itself in a variety of ways, so the text attempts to detail the major possibilities. This same approach is used in the next subsection, the presentation of 16 PF correlates. Following the subsection on the 16 PF, corresponding information from other relevant test sources will be presented, notably from the Wechsler Adult Intelligence Scale–Revised (WAIS-R) and the Rorschach. When referring to the WAIS-R, it should be understood that the research and data from the WAIS research are integrated as the primary sources (the WAIS being the earlier version of the WAIS-R).

For some of the syndromes little information is available. If so, only a short subsection is included based on this limited information and, combined with consensual speculation, it is presented under the heading of Diagnostic Considerations, a designation that supplants the categories usually used; for example, MMPI, 16 PF, and Other Test Response Patterns.

The last subsection, usually entitled Treatment Options, will succinctly present a number of possible treatment methods appropriate for the particular disorder, since the clinician often faces this question. An important point is that I will not consistently mention psychotherapy, chemotherapy, or general schools of therapy as treatment options for the various syndromes. There is good reason to believe that psychotherapy is an appropriate treatment for virtually every syndrome mentioned here, either as the major component or as an adjunct to other techniques (Smith & Glass, 1977; Olbrisch, 1977). Hence, it would be redundant to mention it consistently as an option. On those occasions where psychotherapy is specifically mandated, this fact will be noted. Similarly, the proponents of psychoanalysis and the other major therapy schools often assert that their techniques are valid for the majority of syndromes noted here. Where the literature indicates that a particular theoretical approach is especially efficient, it will be noted. Also, chemotherapy may be a useful adjunct in many of the categories. It will be mentioned only where it is specifically warranted, with no implied assertion that it may be inappropriate in those groupings where it is not specifically listed.

The reader will also note that specific secondary or derived MMPI or 16 PF scales for the diagnosis of a pattern or type of disorder are seldom mentioned. For example, many secondary scales have been derived on the MMPI for almost everything from depression to potential for happiness in marriage (Fowler, 1976). In fact, there are secondary scales derived by researchers for almost every type of personality or affect pattern imaginable. The problem is that these scales are not routinely given in standard clinical assessments, and many are not well validated and/or do not measure what the scale title suggests they do (Fowler, 1981). Marked exceptions are the Ego Strength Scale, which is useful in measuring personal resiliency and potential for response to psychotherapy, and the MacAndrew Alcoholism Scale (MacAndrew, 1965; Schwartz & Graham, 1979). Several others are fine for research purposes, and they may be helpful in assessing a population for a specific concern. However, in the majority of assessments, the clinician may neither score for these scales nor administer any special questionnaires. The reader is referred to the many other sources that provide commentary about these derived scales and specific tests.

The reader might ask why the primary emphasis is on the MMPI, 16 PF, WAIS-R, and Rorschach. The reason is obvious with the MMPI and WAIS-R since they are the most commonly used and researched objective psychological tests. Virtually every clinician, regardless of theoretical orientation or type of training, has some familiarity with the MMPI and WAIS-R. There has also been such an extensive amount of normative data gathered on the MMPI that it is by far the most useful standard objective test among the clinician's diagnostic options. Similarly, even though certain clinicians question the validity of projective tests, they are in common use, there are data to support their usefulness in many situations, and the Rorschach is one of the most commonly used and well known of these tests.

The Cattell 16 PF test is also commonly used. The MMPI is particularly good at assessing severe patterns of pathology, whereas the Cattell 16 PF is used more commonly as a measure of personality patterns. Thus, they dovetail nicely and provide the practitioner with an effective overview of the client. This is not to assert that other tests, such as the Edwards Personal Preference Test, would not be useful as an adjunct to the MMPI as well. However, the validity data on the 16 PF are certainly as impressive as the data on these other tests (Cattell, 1979; Krug, 1981), and the Cattell group has formulated tests for persons in the lower age ranges. Thus, if practitioners use these tests with adults, they begin to develop some facility with a related set of children's tests, and vice versa. Also, it is felt that the motivational distortion scores derived for the 16 PF are more useful (Winder, O'Dell, & Karson, 1975; Krug, 1978) than those in other available tests, when they have them at all. Last, from a personal standpoint, this author has worked consistently with both the childhood and adult forms of the Cattell test since internship and hence has gathered a great deal more data regarding this test. Like numerous clinicians, I have consistently used it in conjunction with the MMPI and have found the combination to be especially effective.

Before proceeding to the description of the correlates of the MMPI and 16 PF in behavior, I will point out the procedure by which the information in this book was gathered and integrated. The following stages were followed to bring research information into coordination with consensual clinical experience.

1. For about fifteen years, the author consistently used these tests, especially the MMPI, 16 PF, and WAIS-R, in a wide-ranging diagnostic practice and kept written records that were cross-checked and compared to the research literature to develop correlations of test patterns with various syndromes. This is in keeping with Arkes's (1981) admonition that too much dependence on memory quickly leads to error in clinical inference. These patterns were also used as a teaching tool in graduate courses in diagnostic testing and clinical psychopathology; thus, the developing concepts were again consistently checked against available clinical research literature and within the case itself (Hayes, 1981).

2. A formal and thorough review of the literature was instituted, and from this and the information collected in step 1, a first draft was written that formally correlated the patterns on the 16 PF and MMPI with the diagnostic categories in the initial draft of the DSM-III.

3. Graduate students in sequential clinical psychopathology courses were each assigned a subset of DSM-III categories. They were asked, independent of the information in the first draft, to find correlates of the DSM-III draft categories on the MMPI, 16 PF, WAIS-R, and Rorschach in the research and clinical literature. Another review of the most recent literature was coordinated with the corrections and suggestions gleaned from the production of these graduate students.

4. As soon as the final DSM-III was published, the work that emerged from step 3 was coordinated with changes from the earlier versions to produce a polished draft.

5. The information derived to that point was presented to a continuing education seminar of twenty practicing clinical psychologists. These people responded via formal feedback procedures as to the reasonableness and accuracy of the findings in this draft. There was substantial agreement between the views of these practicing clinicians and the draft that was produced by the end of step 4. Yet, corrections were noted, and some interesting suggestions were incorporated.

6. After integrating this information, the latest draft was presented to five of the most respected practicing clinical psychologists in the region, all of whom consistently use these tests in their practice. They each carried out a thorough review of the book, and again, although there was general agreement with the material as presented to them, they did offer much helpful commentary.

7. After this material was integrated and amplified in accordance with the publisher's reviewers, there was a last check with the relevant research literature, and the manuscript was again considered and put into a final state.

Through this process, as much research information as possible was gathered and integrated, and then complemented by consensual clinical experience.

In addition to the standard DSM-III categories, this book examines several other topics of interest to practitioners. In particular, these are the issues of Acting-Out Potential (e.g., Aggression and Suicide Potential); the Criminal Personality; Rape; and the legal concepts and psychological correlates of Insanity, Involuntary Civil Commitment, and Competency to Stand Trial. Malingering is included in the DSM-III, but it receives only scant notice, as it does in most diagnostic texts. It is considered by this author to be of considerable importance to the diagnostician, and hence will be dealt with in some depth in this book.

This text contains three major appendices. Appendix A is an outline of topics for conceptualizing diagnostic material and writing a diagnostic report. The author has found this to be a helpful checklist for thoroughness of reports. Similarly, Appendix C offers an organized format for collecting, organizing, and reporting a full neuropsychological examination.

Appendix B is a set of paper-and-pencil test materials that the author has revised and integrated over the past fifteen years. The reader can use the material as a classroom handout with the text without written permission, so long as it is not sold or reproduced for any other reason. The reader may want to insert a drawing test different from the Draw-A-Group Test, add some Bender-Gestalt-like figures (see the section on Central Nervous System Impairment), or otherwise modify it. The four proverbs included were selected because Johnson (1966) found these to be the most efficient in discriminating between cases of central nervous system impairment and schizophrenia.

Aside from the overall chart of DSM-III categories already presented, the following summary of certain aspects of the DSM-III may be useful to some readers who do not yet consistently use the DSM-III.


## DSM-III


The DSM-III is the third edition of the *Diagnostic and Statistical Manual of Mental Disorders* (1980).[1] It supersedes DSM-II (1968) and is different from

---

1. American Psychiatric Association, *Diagnostic and Statistical Manual of Mental Disorders.* Third Edition. Washington, D.C., APA, 1980. The many references to this book in this text are made with the permission of the American Psychiatric Association.

it in many respects. A number of classic categories were eliminated, though several that were absent from the initial drafts of DSM-III were eventually restored.

Even though the DSM-III has been criticized for a number of reasons (Shacht & Nathan, 1977; Garmezy, 1978; Zubin, 1978), it is the official document of the American Psychiatric Association and has received qualified approval from the American Psychological Association. For several reasons—the more thorough and extensive description of categories and criteria for diagnosis, the high and increasing demand of third-party payers for a full diagnosis, its influence on an increasing diversity of types and numbers of health service providers—the DSM-III will likely have more influence than its predecessors. Another major reason is that there is simply no alternative system that has even reached a minimal level of usage or acceptability.

A major change in the DSM-III is the use of a multiaxial diagnostic system, which allows the clinician to provide several different types of information. Though there are five axes that can be potentially used, the first three make up the official DSM-III diagnostic categories. A client may receive a diagnosis on each of the first three axes:

Axis I: Clinical Syndromes

Axis II: Personality Disorders and Specific Developmental Disorder

Axis III: Physical Disorders and Conditions

Axis IV is used to denote the Severity of Psychosocial Stressors that preceded the disorder. They are coded from number 1, which designates no psychosocial stressor, through 7, which is a catastrophic psychosocial stressor, with the numeral 0 referring to an unspecified stressor. Axis V refers to the highest level of adaptive functioning noted in the year previous to the disorder. This is a composite judgment based on three major areas: 1) Occupational Functioning, 2) Social Relationships, and 3) the use of Leisure Time. It is coded: 1—superior, 2—very good, 3—good, 4—fair, 5—poor, 6—very poor, 7—grossly impaired, or 0—designating an unspecified category. Most clinicians will not regularly use Axes IV and V, and their predominant use will be in research situations.

It is interesting that the only conditions that are appropriate for listing on Axis II are the Personality Disorders and the Specific Developmental Disorders. This limits the potential disorders for this axis to less than twenty different categories, as opposed to the substantial number of categories possible for Axis I. However, personality traits rather than disorders may also be listed on Axis II. For example, if the clinician felt the client should be considered paranoid, yet did not feel a formal diagnosis of paranoid personality disorder was warranted, the paranoid trait would be put on Axis II, and no code number would be used along with it, since a code number indicates a formal diagnosis of disorder.

If there is no evidence of disorder on an axis, the clinician should write: "V71.09 No diagnosis on Axis I (or II)," or one of the Conditions Not Attributable to a Mental Disorder (the "V" codes) should be recorded on Axis I. There may also be occasions when it is felt that the principal diagnosis—the one mainly responsible for the diagnosis and treatment—is on the second axis. In that case, the diagnosis listed on the second axis should be followed up with the phrase *Principal Diagnosis*. Otherwise, it is assumed that the principal diagnosis is the one listed on Axis I. When multiple diagnoses are made on any one axis, they are to be listed in the order of importance for attention or treatment. Several diagnoses are followed by a small "x," indicating a place for a further qualifying phrase (see DSM-III).

The clinician should take note of several categories that are available to indicate a questionable level of diagnostic certainty. For example, the clinician may put the term *Provisional* after a diagnosis to indicate a tentative formulation while more data are gathered. This development in DSM-III was undoubtedly spurred by research that indicated problems in diagnostic certainty, such as that by Rosenhan (1973). Incidentally, the numeric designation 300.90 is used where the clinician has obtained enough data to rule out a psychotic disorder but has concluded that further diagnostic specification is not likely to occur.

The diagnosis number 799.90 can be used on either Axis I or II when there is not adequate information to make a diagnostic judgment, and it is thus deferred. Most categories contain a term that is qualified by the word *atypical*. This word is used to indicate that the disorder does not fully meet the required specifications of a more refined categorization.

# 1

## Clinical Correlates of the MMPI and 16 PF Scales

Even though the essential feature of this book is the correlation of various test patterns with standard diagnostic categories, this chapter first presents the classical descriptors and correlates of the MMPI and 16 PF scales. This task has been carried out by numerous authors throughout the years, mainly through an accrual process. Those authors and the present one owe much to those who went before them. In this first part on the MMPI, the author took MMPI material primarily from his own experience and then integrated it with both the classical and recent sources of clinical interpretation of the MMPI, primarily those that were noted earlier in this book in Table A.

### MMPI

The Minnesota Multiphasic Personality Inventory (MMPI) is composed of 556 self-reference statements that cover topics from physical condition through social history, emotional states, social attitudes, and moral belief systems. Clients are encouraged to answer every question, but they often skip a few, and their only option is a true or false answer.

The test was derived by Starke Hathaway and Jovian McKinley, who at the time were working at the University of Minnesota hospitals. They hoped that they could derive a test that would substantially aid in the routine psychological examinations given there. Their efforts culminated in the publication of the MMPI in 1943 by the Psychological Corporation. Hathaway and McKinley accumulated a large collection of self-reference statements from sources such as textbooks, psychological reports, and other tests. They eventually limited their pool of statements to the 504 that they thought were relatively independent of each other. A number of items are repeated on the standard MMPI form.

They first administered the test to groups of normals and also to patients in the following clinical groups: Hypochondriasis, Depression, Hysteria, Psychopathic Deviant, Paranoia, Psychasthenia, Schizophrenia, and Hypomania. They performed an item analysis in order to detect which items significantly differentiated these groups. In the second stage, the scales derived from that item analysis were administered to groups of normals and patients who had those specific clinical diagnoses already assigned, and after adequate cross validation, the scales were accepted into the test. It was only later that the Masculinity-Femininity (Mf) scale was added, with the original purpose of differentiating heterosexual males from homosexual males. The final addition also included the Social Introversion (Si) scale (0). Initially Scale 0 was used to distinguish female college students who were socially retiring from those who were active in a number of extracurricular activities, and only later was this scale generalized to males.

The MMPI can be administered individually or in a group and can be hand- or machine-scored. Many groups provide a computerized interpretation and scoring service; the reader is referred to the excellent introduction to that area by Fowler (1976). The newest and most revolutionary development is to perform the testing at a computer terminal. The client takes the test at the terminal, it is processed in a central program, and the results are quickly provided to the clinician.

Any computerized interpretation of an MMPI protocol should always be first routed through a clinician who has had substantial training in MMPI interpretation, since that clinician can consider the profile in light of the many particulars of an individual case that are not fed into the computer. Also, in the great majority of diagnostic cases, making a report or diagnostic decision based only on one test would be a questionable practice. After any type of initial level of scoring, a K-correction is added to the obtained raw scores for scales Hs(1), Pd(4), Pt(7), Sc(8), and Ma(9). In addition to the four validity scales and ten basic clinical scales, there are a number of derived scales that require special scoring and that vary widely in their validity and reliability.

The raw data from the MMPI are translated into T-scores. T-scores, the scores that are eventually coded onto the profile sheet, were based originally on the responses of the Minnesota normal group (Hathaway & McKinley, 1967). T-scores have a mean of 50, the middle black line on the profile sheet, and a standard deviation of 10 (for the Minnesota normal group; most populations average at least a bit higher on most scales). The T-score is printed on each side of the profile sheet so that T-scores can be obtained visually off the raw data, and separate norms are available for males and females.

Most clinicians refer to profiles in two-point code phraseology (e.g., a

4-9). This only indicates that 4 is the highest scale and 9 is the second highest scale in T-scores. There are also methods by which the whole profile can be coded. Though using this book does not depend on knowing how to code an MMPI fully or read these latter codes, they are occasionally found in the literature, and some clinicians find it very useful to code their profiles, so it is noted here. There are two major coding systems for use with the MMPI. Hathaway's (1947) was the original system, although the more complete system developed by Welsh (1948) is more commonly used. The reader is referred to Graham (1977) for a detailed discussion of these methods of coding. As an example of the Welsh code, the following profile has been coded from the T-scores:

$$7^* \ 2'' \ 1' \ 8- \ 46/ \ /: \ \underline{35\#} \ 0 \text{ to the right of } \#9$$

What this actually says is that:

| | |
|---|---|
| 7* | Scale 7 is 90 T or greater |
| 2″ | Scale 2 is between 80 and 89 |
| 1′ | Scale 1 is between 70 and 79 |
| 8- | Scale 8 is between 60 and 69 |
| 46/ | Scales 4 and 6 are between 50 and 59 |
| /: | The juxtaposition of two break symbols (/ and :) indicates no score was in the T range of the one to the right, in this case 40–49 range |
| 35# | # indicates Scales 3 and 5 are between 30 and 39 T; the underlining states that they are within one T score point of each other |
| To the right of 9 | indicates that Scale 9 is 29 T or less |

Streiner and Miller (1979) find that acceptable interpretations from MMPI single scales and the two- and three-point code types can be made if only 300 items of the MMPI are completed, using a conversion factor from the tables in their article (p. 475). The only marked exception is scale 6, which appears to require 350 items before an adequate interpretation can be made.

Even though there is no inherent upper age level limit for the MMPI, it has been traditionally accepted that only individuals at a sixth-grade reading level and sixteen years of age can validly complete the MMPI. However, there is some indication that the test can be properly scored for individuals under sixteen if they can read adequately and can maintain attention properly. Those with less than a sixth-grade reading level take the test by having someone read the items to them, or by an audiotape.

There is some indication that the estimate of a sixth-grade level of reading ability for the MMPI is a bit low. Ward and Ward (1980) assert that an actual grade level of 6.7 (closer to the seventh-grade reading level) is necessary for the overall MMPI, and that several scales clearly require a seventh-grade reading level.

Ward and Selby (1980) suggest that the readability problem with the MMPI can be helped by the use of what they term the Improved Readability Form (IRF), a 167-item, short form of the MMPI. They provide data that suggest the form is more readable than the overall form or other short forms. It is effective with those clients who are on the edge of ability to read and perform on the MMPI. The authors also assert that the IRF can be orally administered with effectiveness to adults with an IQ of 65 to 85, the group that has the greatest problems with the standard MMPI. Readers who are interested in obtaining the items that make up the IRF can request a reprint of the article and the listing of IRF items from Dr. L. Charles Ward, Department of Psychiatry, Medical College of Georgia, Augusta, Georgia 30901.

Both the normal and abnormal profiles of adolescents differ from those of adults, and when dealing with adolescents, the norms for that group in Marks et al. (1974) should be consulted. Fowler (1981) advises using these norms until the time when persons have started to drop an adolescent lifestyle and are beginning to accept some primary responsibility for taking care of themselves. Thus, adolescent norms would be appropriate for a nineteen-year-old living at home under significant parental controls, whereas adult norms could be used for a street-wise seventeen-year-old who lives away from home. Adolescent norms bring the mean profile of an adolescent clinical population down from one with very high scores on F, 4, and 8, and scores on 6 and 9 around 70 T to a mean profile with F around 70, 4 and 2 as the two highest scores though they are below 70, and 8 and 9 as the next highest scores (Marks, 1974; Fowler, 1981).

Clinicians have often used "critical items" on the MMPI. These are usually single items whose content is used to cue the clinician to further inquiry in that area, or to indicate a problem because of the face validity of the item. A number of sets of these critical items have been used historically. However, most have not consistently predicted the actual behavior that they apparently reflect. Additionally, most that are used are loaded with items to which the deviant response is "true," which leaves them open to a "yes-saying" response bias. In addition, many of them overlap too highly with the F scale, and hence may reflect a tendency to "fake bad." At present, two sets of critical items have improved on most of these criticisms, though there still is little predictability from the item to its face-valid content. If the clinician is interested in using critical items, they are referred to these latter two sets, devised by Koss and Butcher (1973) and by Lachar and Wrobel (1979). At the very least, a perusal by the clinician of critical items marked by the client is worthwhile. For one thing, clients who admit to these face-valid items usually feel that they have communicated directly to the clinician and may be quite surprised if the later content of a therapy contact indicates a lack of awareness about these issues.

Readers who need more familiarity with the administration and scoring of the MMPI are referred to books like Graham (1977) or Dahlstrom and Welsh (1980) that have detailed discussions. In proceeding through the individual scales of the MMPI here, there will be descriptions of each scale, along with overall behavior correlates and correlates of high and low scores on each scale, as well as some patterns the clinician can expect from the scale interrelationships.

In the traditional clinical interpretation approach to the MMPI, authors referred to the scale name rather than to scale number. However, as the years passed, it became clear that the actual behavioral correlates of a scale have not always matched the originally applied scale name. As a result, the scale numbers will be used throughout the text rather than the traditional scale name. The traditional names are included here for the sake of convenience.

| Scale Number | Traditional Scale Name |
| --- | --- |
| 1 | Hypochondriasis (Hs) |
| 2 | Depression (D) |
| 3 | Hysteria (Hy) |
| 4 | Psychopathic Deviant (Pd) |
| 5 | Masculinity-Femininity (Mf) |
| 6 | Paranoia (Pa) |
| 7 | Psychasthenia (Pt) |
| 8 | Schizophrenia (Sc) |
| 9 | Hypomania (Ma) |
| 0 | Social Introversion (Si) |

It is common to hear persons experienced in the use of the MMPI referring to individuals as a "high 4" or a "4-8." These shorthand descriptors take on the meanings associated with them in this text and are helpful as an abbreviated communication of various behavioral descriptions. In general, a high score on the MMPI is one above 70 T, moderately high is a score of from 60 to 75 T, low is below 40 T, and moderately low is from 40 to 50 T.

Although there is good evidence that various groups (blacks, males or females, younger or older persons) differ in their average scores on various MMPI scales, it has been asserted that this is not evidence of bias, and simply reflects actual differences or response set differences that can be accounted for in interpretation (Pritchard & Rosenblatt, 1980; Wadsworth & Checketts, 1980; Graham, 1977). Wadsworth and Checketts (1980) also present evidence that the religion of neither the diagnostician nor the client, or the interaction of the two, significantly influences clinical diagnoses in general. Pritchard and Rosenblatt (1980) present impressive data to support their assertion that there is no significant evidence the MMPI is racially biased, though they and others note that blacks tend to score higher on F, 4, 8, and 9. Females are more likely to show peaks on 3 and 6, and males are more likely to peak on 1, 4, and 7.

## Individual Scale Interpretations

### The ? Scale

On the ? or "cannot say" scale, little significance is usually attached to raw scores of less than 30. This is not actually a scale since it accounts only for the number of items to which the individual has not responded. Of course, one has at least to examine the ? scale, since skipping many items leads to lowered scores on other scales. If a client does obtain a high score, a reading difficulty should be first considered. If this can be ruled out, gross impairment in the decision-making required to give an answer should be considered. If this is not the problem, then obsessive, paranoid, or blatant avoidance issues should be considered. Obsessive clients may feel constrained by the either-or dichotomy allowed in the MMPI; rather than commit themselves, they may skip the item. Paranoids naturally fear the self-disclosure involved in a number of items and may avoid them.

Obviously an ounce of prevention is the most logical cure for this problem. The client should be clearly instructed ahead of time to fill out all the items, or to leave at most only a few blank. One has several options in the face of a high ? score. In most instances where many items have been skipped, the client can be persuaded to answer more questions, which leads to a valid profile. As already noted, scores can also be prorated without great loss. Some clinicians score the items that have been skipped in the direction they feel the client would have answered them, while other clinicians score them in the significant direction. Such scoring reflects the finding that a nonresponse can refer to either controversial content or decisional ambiguity (Fulkerson & Willage, 1980). In either case, the profile should be compared with that obtained by the original scoring.

### The L Scale

The L scale is composed of fifteen items such as, "I do not always tell the truth"; these items in a naïve and open fashion identify people who present an overly idealistic and perfectionistic portrayal of themselves. Sophisticated or well-educated people seldom score high on this scale, as the items are quite transparent. When well-educated clients score high here, they are likely to be repressed and rigid in their personality structure, as well as conforming in behavior.

The clinician should naturally consider possible deception any time a high score is obtained. This is usually true only when the person is not well educated and still obtains a high score. In general, people with high scores are naïve and defensive about their conflicts and are often unable to perceive the effects of their behavior on other people. Persons in occupations where there is a strong demand to present a "good person" image (e.g., a minister) score higher on this scale, in spite of their educational level. A high L score is also associated with a denial of any need for help, and with an unwillingness to be honest about deficiencies or admit guilt about behavior, or to admit alcohol abuse (Hedlund, 1977).

Highly sophisticated individuals who are manipulative and defensive may score low on the L scale, though a low score usually indicates a fairly relaxed and independent individual who has responded openly to the items. A very low score may occasionally be associated with wariness and cynicism, but a moderately low score primarily reflects a person who is not particularly defensive, is willing to admit some deficiencies in the self, and is able to communicate reasonably well with others.

*The F Scale*

The F scale consists of sixty-four items chosen because they were scored by fewer than 10 percent of a normal adult population. Blacks and adolescents consistently score higher on F, and it is best to lower the T-score as many as ten points when dealing with these populations. Very high T-scores, above 80, suggest either marked confusion, significant errors in scoring, inability of the client either to read the items or to understand the directions, hostility toward the examiner, or, for other reasons, a clearly invalid profile. If a reading problem is suspected, simply having the client read the first ten items may give a clue in this regard. If a reading problem is noted, use of a tape-recorded version, e.g., the one available from the Psychological Corporation, is suggested. The clinician should also first rule out organic brain dysfunction as a source of confusion in clients with very high F scores. Gynther et al. (1973) have shown that high F scores in an adult inpatient population may warrant the term *confused psychotic*. In an outpatient population, it is more likely to indicate some form of an invalid profile. Responding with clearer instructions or a confrontation and acceptance of any hostility in an apparently intact client who produces a high F profile usually results in a subsequent valid test.

More moderate T-scores (in the range of 65 to 79) are associated with mild confusion, some significant emotional problems or an attempt to "fake bad" or exaggerate symptomatology. Such scores can also be associated with unconventional thinking, and in adolescents it is commonly and paradoxically associated with both antisocial (acting out) and withdrawn behaviors. If there are other indications of anxiety, a score in this range may be a plea for help.

Moderately low scores on the F scale are associated with normal response sets and conventional behavior patterns. If the score becomes very low, a denial of psychopathology, and even more rigid and conforming personality patterns are likely. "Faking good" should also be considered.

In general, if one can rule out an invalid profile, the F scale is a good indication of overall psychopathology. The higher it is, the more likely it is that there is general psychopathology, although this inference is not as valid in blacks (Smith & Graham, 1981). Conversely, the lower the F scale, the more likely it is that any existing problems are focused.

## The K Scale

The K scale consists of thirty items obtained by comparing the responses of disturbed individuals who had normal profiles with normals who also had normal profiles, and it is now generally used to identify "faking good" cases. These items correlate well with social desirability scales, by measuring more subtle defensiveness than the L scale, and in that sense they function as a suppressor variable on the other scales (Meehl & Hathaway, 1980). The amount of K contributing to the T scores of other scales should always be considered.

There is usually a negative correlation between scores on F and K, though certain clients, especially inpatients, may score high on both. Such persons are likely to have a reason for avoiding responsibility for psychopathology, such as in a criminal case. At the same time, they feel the need to be honest, possibly from the urging of their attorney, or from a need to use an admission of specific psychopathology to excuse behavior. Well-educated and/or sophisticated individuals score higher on this scale, although the positive deviation from the mean is not as marked as it is in the opposite direction on L.

High K scores are generally associated with attempts to deny vulnerability and psychopathology. Such persons are unwilling to admit to psychological or physiological deficit, are inclined to blame others for their problems, and as a result are not likely to cooperate in an intervention attempt. They have little insight into their own patterns and are intolerant toward deviant or disturbed behavior in others. A high K indicates resistance to intervention, whereas a moderate elevation (50–65) indicates a good prognosis for treatment change. In fact, a rise in K is often found with improvement through treatment.

The F-K index, a test popular with clinicians, is discussed later with regard to several of the ensuing diagnostic categories. In particular, the reader is referred to the section on malingering for qualifications of the interpretation of this index. It has been traditionally asserted that when the index (in terms of raw scores) is negative and is greater than 12, it indicates a deliberate effort by the client to be seen as emotionally healthy and without vulnerability, and when F-K is positive and more than 11, "faking bad" should be considered. Most clinicians now feel that wider differences should be allowed, and that the index is more effective in assessing "faking bad" than "faking good."

## Scale 1 (Hs)

Scale 1, traditionally referred to as the Hypochondriasis scale, is comprised of thirty-three items that focus on bodily functions and disorders. The items are reasonably obvious in content, and the complaints embedded in the items are not very specific. Thus, persons with actual physical disorders are more likely with time to score higher on scale 2 as a reaction to the disorder. Scale 1 is a good indicator of overall pessimism—the higher the score, the more pessimistic the view of the world—and it particularly correlates with the channeling of this pessimisim into somatic concerns and complaints. Clients with high 1 scores may be using physical symptoms to focus tension, to express hostility, or to control others. High scores are also associated with clinical depression (usually exogenous rather than endogenous), though this "r" with depression does not usually hold for blacks.

High or low scores on scale 1, unless found in the relatively rare 1–8/8–1 profile, are seldom correlated in a consistent fashion with extreme psychotic processes. Even moderate scores on this scale are likely to be associated with a degree of somatization, and since this is combined with the narcissism, immaturity, and stubbornness that are also characteristic of this group, the clinician's patience is sorely tested. As might be expected, such individuals are demanding and critical regarding intervention attempts and are particularly resistant to psychological interpretations of their disorder. As a result, they seldom respond positively to psychotherapy and instead demand support, attention, and concrete physical explanations for their disorder. Therapists may find it a helpful technique to contract with such clients for a set period of time in the therapy hour during which a focus on physical complaints is allowed (i.e., an "organ recital"). This procedure can facilitate a later uninterrupted discussion of the other critical issues that are often avoided. Shorter sessions are also helpful with such clients (Fowler, 1981). Persons who are low on scale 1 are usually adjusting adequately to their world, though they may have problems with the warmth and sharing demands of intimate interpersonal relations.

## Scale 2 (D)

Scale 2, subtitled the Depression scale, consists of sixty items and clearly measures what it purports to measure—the degree of contentment with the world, self-esteem, and view of the future. People who score high on scale 2 are clearly distressed and usually are depressed and withdrawn, show psychomotor retardation, and may be schizoid. There is a good chance they may harbor suicidal ideation if 2 is elevated above the 80 T mark. Adolescents score somewhat lower than the general population, whereas the elderly score higher on the average, probably reflecting the different range of options available in these age groups, as well as their different sense of optimism about the future. Since a spike (a marked elevation relative to all other scales) on scale 2 particularly taps symptomatic depression, it is unstable on repeat testing, compared to other scales. The spike 2 code type is seldom described in clinical literature, but when found, it is likely to be a reactive depression in response to environmental stress. In some cases, it may be related to an ongoing depressive process that develops out of an inability to deal effectively with aggression, with a concomitant history of rage reaction (Kelley & King, 1979).

Unless they are attempting to "fake bad," persons with a very high score on scale 2 do consistently show a clinical level of depression, and they likely warrant the potentially psychotic depressive diagnosis. If the elevation is moderate, it may reflect either a depressive episode, a neurotic depressive component, or depression from an accompanying maladaptive personality style that cannot cope with changes in the world.

People with high scale 2 scores are at least moderately withdrawn and show a low activity level, whereas persons low on scale 2 are typically comfortable with their world and are reasonably active and alert. In some cases, a very low 2 score may reflect a lack of impulse control and possible conflict with societal mores, yet this has not usually brought the person into legal difficulties. Hedlund (1977) asserts that there is no strong correlation of scale 2 with psychotic symptomatology.

Persons very high on scale 2 initially show a moderate to marked interest in therapy. However, this can be a direct result of their situational distress, and when the crisis passes they may terminate therapy, even though pathological patterns remain. Yet some elevation on 2 is a good prognostic sign for psychotherapy. Contracting for behaviors that increase activity level are helpful here.

Although there is no definitive suicidal profile on the MMPI, it appears that scale 2 is more indicative of suicidal ideation than of actual suicide attempts, and factors tapped by other scales, e.g., scale 9, appear to act as catalysts for actual behavior in this regard.

### Scale 3 (Hy)

Scale 3 is comprised of sixty items that tap two overall constructs: 1) items that deny problems or vulnerabilities in one's emotional or interpersonal world, and 2) complaints of reasonably specific somatic problems. Naïveté, narcissism, and a lack of awareness of intrapsychic issues are characteristic of persons high on scale 3. Like those with the avoidant personality disorder, they may be highly demanding of attention and caring responses, although they avoid committing themselves in this way.

Scale 3 is only moderately correlated with the development of conversion symptomatology, the initial construct that it was thought to tap, and it shows a low correlation with psychotic complaints. Rather than evidencing the hypochondriasis so characteristic of scale 1, scale 3 is more likely to tap depression-generated somatic complaints, as well as ego-alien anxiety and agitation. Thus, sophistication is a factor in the score obtained on scale 3. Those who are brighter or higher in socioeconomic class tend to have lower scores. When Scale 3 scores are quite low, conforming behaviors are likely, and little interpersonal affect is demonstrated.

Persons high on scale 3 are usually still interpersonally adequate, though they may be rather manipulative. The naïveté, anxiety, and need for attention result in an initially high level of apparent interest in psychotherapy. In particular, they love advice; they simply do not follow it. When these persons realize that they cannot manipulate the therapist to feed their ego, they may stop in a huff or attempt to maneuver the therapist into a physical or medical interpretation of their difficulties. Yet they are quite suggestible and usually responsive to hypnosis.

## Scale 4 (Pd)

Scale 4 has fifty items and generally taps these factors: 1) an angry rebelliousness against recognized rules and mores; 2) shallow and often hostile and manipulative interpersonal relationships; 3) inability to profit from experience or to plan effectively for long-term future contingencies; and 4) anger at family and a belief that one was victimized as a child. An examination of three content scales—AUT (authority conflict), FAM (a residue of adolescent family conflict), and HOS (a scale measuring manifest hostility and sadistic cruelty at high levels—may give a more precise idea as to what an overall high 4 score means in an individual case (Fowler, 1981, 1976). Behaviorally, scale 4 shows a high correlation with antisocial behavior, moodiness, characterological patterns, substance abuse, and sexual immorality. A high scale 4 indicates potential for hostile and aggressive outbursts, particularly in whites (Hedlund, 1977), as well as depressive ideation (not necessarily accompanied by psychomotor retardation). Blacks, adolescents, and males score higher on this scale on the average, and this could be adjusted for by subtracting up to 10 T points when interpreting the scale. High scale 4 individuals are usually extroverted; they are also impulsive and lack social poise. They do not usually have blatant psychotic symptoms or high intrapsychically generated anxiety. A spike 4 profile commonly suggests problems with the law.

Persons who are average on scale 4 usually show adequate interpersonal relationships and are perceived by other people as sincere and concerned. If they are very low, they are more likely to be conforming and even rigidly responsive to the dictates of authorities, manipulated by others, and without a great deal of available energy to actuate plans that they have made. Males who are very low may have a deep-seated mistrust of females, similar to the classic concept of castration anxiety.

Whereas persons who are low on scale 4 can become dependent on the therapist's advice and recommendations and will even seek out a therapist who will give such direction, persons high on scale 4 are likely to be manipulative in any quest for or response to therapy. They may seem to be good candidates because they are usually articulate and socially sophisticated. However, at their best they subtly project blame onto other persons or situations and are inclined to use therapy to avoid problems of the real world, such as coercion from legal authorities or from intimate others. They are likely to terminate therapy as soon as they have obtained the goal of their manipulation, or if they perceive the therapist as either unresponsive toward that end or able to confront their manipulations effectively.

### Scale 5 (Mf)

Scale 5 is comprised of sixty items that tap vocational preference, aesthetic interests, sexual role interests, and an activity-passivity dimension. In general, low scores indicate a person who fits closely with traditional role expectations of his or her sex, whereas high scores reflect a person who in some fashion has moved away from the traditional role. Scale 5 is highly correlated with intelligence, with an r of up to .25 with intelligence often being reported.

Men who are low on scale 5 are usually perceived by others as bland, insouciant, and/or macho persons. They are not likely to be introspective, they disdain intellectual and artistic pursuits in favor of active outdoor interests, and they often delight in being coarse and adventurous. They avoid psychotherapy.

Men who are high on scale 5 *may* have a homosexual identification and/or show a lack of identification with activities associated with the traditional male role. They are usually sensitive, higher socioeconomically and intellectually, and likely to have interests in the humanities and arts. They usually do well in therapy, especially group therapy. Ambitious and intrapsychically introspective individuals also tend to score higher on scale 5. A spike 5 profile is usually indicative of transient situational disturbance. If combined with a low 4, it suggests a very passive man, a "Mr. Milquetoast."

Women who score low on scale 5 are likely to be submissive and passive, though petulant. They prefer to be involved in dependent interpersonal relationships, and if they exert any control in the relationship, it is through passivity and stubbornness. A very low 5 suggests masochism.

Women high on scale 5 have rejected many aspects of the traditional female role. They perceive themselves as extroverted and content with their world, although others may see them as aggressive or at least unfriendly. As a result, they easily elicit aggression in others, including therapists. Women with a high 5 more consistently have sports and outdoor interests than do women low on this scale. A high scale 5 score in a hospitalized woman has in a number of cases been associated with underlying psychosis (Graham, 1977).

*Scale 6 (Pa)*

Scale 6 includes forty items, and a high score comes from paranoid or unusual ideas, feelings of being wronged, or complaints about others. At the same time, a low score does not rule out similar ideation. In fact, if the person is a sophisticated, integrated, and defensive paranoid individual, such as an intelligent person with a diagnosis of paranoia, he or she may score quite low on this scale. Very high scores, which are relatively uncommon, are often associated with a diagnosis of paranoid schizophrenia.

As scores drop into the moderate to high range, more integrated paranoid ideation is probable, and sexual deviation or preoccupation is also a significant possibility. Anger toward authority or toward others as a result of a deprived or punitive childhood also elevates this scale into at least the moderate range. However, moderate scores can also be obtained by individuals who are perceived by others as cooperative and intelligent and without any psychological disturbance. As a result, it is worthwhile to examine responses to individual items on this scale. Both adolescents and blacks tend to score higher on scale 6.

As noted, a person with a low score on scale 6 may well be a very sophisticated and guarded paranoid, although more likely to be a generally optimistic, warm, and productive individual. In a psychiatric population, a low scale 6 is associated with subtle defensiveness and stubbornness. In particular, if it is very low, controlled anger and suspicion are likely.

Individuals high on scale 6 seldom become meaningfully involved in psychotherapy. At best, they are intellectualized and rigid. Some success can be attained over time if the therapist is able to give adequate feedback, maintain integrity as a therapist, and gradually develop in them at least a modicum of trust (Barrett, 1981).

*Scale 7 (Pt)*

Scale 7 consists of forty-eight items that include factors of 1) general discontent with one's world, 2) obsessional concerns, 3) anxiety, and 4) indecision and self-devaluation. Scale 7 primarily taps the obsessional features of the obsessive-compulsive disorder, rather than the compulsive aspects, so the compulsive personality is not necessarily high on this scale. People high on this scale anxiously ruminate about problems in their world and have perfectionistic standards of performance that they seldom feel they actually meet. As a result, they show feelings of inferiority in many areas and have a negative self-image. Generalized physical complaints such as fatigue are common. These features not suprisingly lead them into psychotherapy, but the obsessiveness and perfectionism often cause initial problems. They are not likely to give in, so they continue to introspect and ruminate when changes in behavior would be more productive. If the therapist can be patient and keep such clients involved beyond this initial stage of resistance, the prognosis becomes more positive. An abrupt involvement in therapies that quickly knock out repression and denial, such as encounter groups, can be dangerous to high 7 clients, since these clients may be attempting to hold onto control of very high anxiety or self-destructive impulses.

Hedlund (1977) found the presence of phobias to be correlated with a high scale 7 score for white samples only. In female patients, there is a significant negative correlation of irritability and delusions with high scale 7 scores. In general, when a high 7 is found in a psychotic client, it points to a more acute onset. Persons low on scale 7 are perceived by others as contented and satisfied with their lives, self-confident and emotionally stable, and yet also ambitious and seeking of status.

## Scale 8 (Sc)

Scale 8 is the longest subscale on the MMPI, comprising seventy-eight items that focus on factors of 1) confused thought processes, 2) hallucinations and other indications of formal thought disorder, 3) social and interpersonal alienation, and 4) depression and dissatisfaction. Adolescents and blacks both score higher on this scale, and the clinician should subtract up to 10 points from the T score. Black men in particular score high here, possibly reflecting alienation from a society that has traditionally made it difficult for them to actualize themselves as both black and male.

Persons high on scale 8 are usually significantly disturbed, though a subsample of individuals may be "faking bad." As noted, confusion, bizarre thought processes, and social alienation are characteristics of high 8 scorers. It is interesting that a very high score here is not necessarily indicative of schizophrenia, though most who have a high score feel as if they are out of phase with the world, as if they are space cadets in a new world. Schizophrenics are more likely to score between the 70 and 95 T score range. Agitated neurotics and people who are severely emotionally unstable, and yet only borderline with respect to psychosis, are more likely to score extremely high on scale 8. Persons in the T-score range of 60 to 75 are more likely to show problems in attention and staying on tasks, with accompanying agitation and anxiety. They usually have high standards that they feel unable to meet, are inclined toward guilt, and have low self-esteem. When under stress, they are prone to become irritable and stubborn.

Persons very low on scale 8 are perceived as happy and reasonably productive individuals, and are yielding in interpersonal relationships. Yet they have rigid thought patterns and are unable to come up with abstract or creative solutions to interpersonal and vocational problems, particularly if scale M on the 16 PF is also low.

Persons with high scores on scale 8 are enigmatic for the therapist. They are often willing to discuss their problems openly, though it is hard to pin them down into concrete ways of changing their behavior. They are prone to discussions that distract from the focus on the problem and are unstable in their trust of the therapist. Nevertheless, they are likely to remain in some form of contact with the therapist over a long period of time, and if a degree of trust can be generated, modest and steady progress may occur.

## Scale 9 (Ma)

This scale includes forty-six items that focus on a propensity for 1) high energy output, 2) distractibility and lack of persistence on tasks, 3) extroversion, and 4) grandiosity. Persons very low on scale 9 show little energy and may be depressed. A high 2 with a low 9 indicates severe depression. The clinician should note that even when scale 2 is not elevated, a very low score on scale 9 is a cue for underlying depression. As 9 moves up toward the average range, the client is more likely to be quietly productive, reliable in most job situations, and possibly perceived as quiet and withdrawn.

Elderly individuals on the average score up to 10 points lower on scale 9, and adolescents average up to 10 points higher than normal adults. Blacks also tend to score a bit higher here. In females, a high 9 may result from counterphobic attempts to deny dependency and/or passivity.

In general, people very high on scale 9 are likely to be significantly disturbed psychologically and show grandiosity and a high level of distractibility. As they move into the moderate to higher ranges, these tendencies are muted, though the person still has problems organizing tasks. Although they may be creative, they need others to carry the plans to the point of actualization. They tend to be extroverted and perceived by others as gregarious and occasionally pushy. A spike 9 profile is likely to indicate drug abuse and/or antisocial personality disorder and in males is also associated with aggressive acting-out (King & Kelley, 1977).

High 9's are difficult for the therapist to work with as they are distractible, not inclined to view themselves as vulnerable or responsible for problems in their world, and not able to persist introspectively to connect contingencies between their behavior and the difficulties they are encountering. If confronted by the therapist, they are likely to intellectualize their

problems, attempt to distract from the issue by acting out, or simply terminate therapy. Lithium therapy should be considered here.

*Scale 0 (Si)*

Scale 0, subtitled Social Introversion, was developed later than the other
scales and as a result does not have as much consensual clinical experience
or data surrounding it. Scores on this scale are usually quite stable over time
and may represent biological and constitutional factors that contribute to
an introversion-extroversion component. This scale was designed to assess
the propensity for avoidance of social responsibilities and contact with
others. While it seems to assess this factor, it also may tap psychomotor depression, particularly when associated with social insecurity. Such individuals would score high on scale 0 and are usually perceived by others as
oversensitive and touchy. Individuals scoring low on scale 0 are likely to be
seen as happy-go-lucky and extroverted and may occasionally manifest
problems in impulse control.

Both adolescents and elderly individuals score a bit higher on this scale.
Persons high on scale 0 are often initially resistant in therapy as they fear
rejection in interpersonal relationships and are insecure about increased
vulnerability. Yet, if they can deal with this issue in the initial stages of therapy, the prognosis is reasonably positive, as they are inclined to work productively in dealing with their symptoms. Social skills training is useful
here. The spike 0 MMPI profile is suggestive of situational adjustment difficulties such as marital problems and/or a schizoid adjustment and also may
indicate religiously oriented distress, perhaps an abrupt loss of faith in God
(Kelley & King, 1979).

## MMPI Interrelationship Interpretations

The 1–2/2–1 combination is consistently indicative of somatic disturbance,
accompanied by a degree of irritability, agitation, and anxiety. The 1–2
code is relatively infrequent and, without associated elevations, points to
the somatoform disorders. If 7, 8, and F are also elevated, schizophrenia
should be considered. The 2–1 code is a more frequent combination, particularly in males. Men here show somatic tension along with pessimism and
depression, and there is usually little physical basis for their disorders.
Women who score a 2–1 code show more classicial hypochondriacal patterns, with an emphasis on restlessness and tension.

When one is assessing an inpatient sample, particularly male, alcoholism and depression should be considered, particularly episodic forms of alcoholism accompanied by somatic concerns. Persons with the 1–2/2–1 code

are generally passive-dependent in interpersonal relationships and are not likely to take responsibility for their behaviors, especially if 3 and 4 are also elevated. This passivity, combined with a general avoidance of responsibility, makes them at best a moderate risk in therapy. They need very directive and structured therapy targeted at overt symptoms.

Scales 1, 2, and 3 are commonly referred to as the neurotic triad, and elevations on these scales are found in most neurotic disorders. When scales 1 and 3 are elevated, with a valley on scale 2 (the conversion V), the client is prone to use somatic disorder as a projection channel for personal difficulties. The function is hysteroid and/or hypochondriacal rather than classically psychophysiological in nature. Persons with an actual illness tend to have high scale 2 scores, often without remarkable elevations on other scales.

When the 1–3/3–1 profile is accompanied by a marked elevation on scale 8 and an elevation on F, one must look for somatic delusions. The 1–3/3–1 pattern is common in older people and in women, and when other scales are not particularly elevated, it reflects a combination of neurotic symptomatology and psychophysiological concerns. Consistent with the hysteric component, these persons have shallow interpersonal relationships, are narcissistic, and are somewhat Pollyanna-ish or avoidant in reaction to their problem. Males who show these patterns may be feminine in orientation, particularly if this is accompanied by an elevation on scale 5. When elevations on 1 and 3 are accompanied by a high 7, a panic disorder is quite possible.

The 1–3/3–1 codes are common, and if 1 is greater than 3 there is more irritability and pessimism. To the degree that scale 1 is close to the height of scale 3 and 2 is somewhat lower, conversion reactions are more likely. Such complaints as hypertension, low back pain, eating disorders such as anorexia nervosa and obesity, and gastrointestinal disorders are common. Persons who show a multiple personality are also likely to obtain a 1–3/3–1 code. The combination of passivity, resistance to responsibility in a psychological disorder, preference for medical explanations, and the suggestibility and high need for structure all predict problems in psychotherapy with the 1–3/3–1 client. They prefer powerful and magical cures and are inclined to terminate the therapy relationship prematurely if signs of concern by the therapist are not forthcoming.

The 1–4/4–1 code type is relatively infrequent with inpatient groups yet occurs at least moderately often in outpatient clinical settings. In either case, it occurs far more commonly in men, is correlated with severe hypochondriasis, and possibly focused on low back pain or headaches. With inpatients it is more often associated with a combination of somatization symptoms, narcissism, and alcohol problems, and there are correlated problems with the vocational and interpersonal areas, particularly with the opposite sex.

This code type often has a high associated score on the L scale, and, not surprisingly, such persons do poorly in psychotherapy because of their resistance, somatization, and possible problems with alcohol. A very low score on 1, combined with a high score on 4, suggests someone who has truly given up on his or her body and is likely to take high risks physically, possibly as a counterphobic reaction to early anxiety about bodily symptoms (Fowler, 1981).

The 1–8/8–1 code type may be indicative of schizophrenia, particularly if 8 is markedly elevated and F is also elevated. In general, such persons have trouble with expression of aggression and may alternate behaviorally within a classic passive-aggressive pattern. They may show sexual deviate patterns. They usually have some dissociative or schizoid components, especially if Scale 0 is also high.

The 1–9/9–1 profile is marked by a high level of anxiety and distress. Gastrointestinal symptoms and headaches also occur. Such persons may be passive-dependent in actual functioning, yet maintain a gruff exterior. If a number of other scales are moderately elevated, including F, the possibility of brain damage should be considered.

The 2–3/3–2 code type is marked by depression and anxiety, with depression predominating when 2 is higher than 3, and with anxiety and accompanying neurotic and somatic symptoms predominating when 3 is higher than 2. In both codes, there is evidence of passive dependency and shyness, particularly when 2 is high and 9 is low. The emphasis here is more on inadequacy than on somatization, the latter being primary in the 1–2/2–1 code type. Clients with a 2–3/3–2 profile are more likely to have accepted their psychopathology, as opposed to the 2–7/7–2 types, who are usually still struggling to cope with it. When scales 4, 7, and 8 are also moderately elevated in a 2–3/3–2 type, histrionic components are probable. The 2–3/3–2's seem to seek responsibility in vocational and interpersonal situations but then are stressed by and dislike the responsibility associated with such commitments. They are sensitive to rejection, and in that sense are similar to persons with the avoidant personality disorder. Moderate elevations on scales 2, 3, and 7 are characteristic of the phobic disorders and sexual dysfunctions.

To the degree that 2 is greater than 3, success in psychotherapy is more likely. In fact, some elevation on 2 is almost a prerequisite to success of psychotherapy, as it suggests an allowance for vulnerability that the therapist can work with. When 3 is greater than 2, there is more tendency to avoid intrapsychic introspection and more likelihood of projection. Hence, response to psychotherapy is poorer, and directive and dramatic therapies are more helpful.

The 2–4/4–2 code type is relatively common in inpatient populations, though not as likely to occur in outpatients. Since 2–4/4–2's are often consumers of stimulation, alcoholism or other kinds of substance abuse is common, as is impulsivity. Other types of concomitant sociolegal problems (and some situational guilt) also occur. If both scales are quite high, and if scales 8 and 9 are also high, there may be evidence of schizophrenic disorder, and if 6 is also elevated, a possible paranoid component may be present.

Even though 2-4/4-2 types can often present a facade of confident behavior, they easily move into manipulative behaviors, including suicide. In that same vein, they are likely to manifest a cry for help, possibly through manipulative suicide gestures. They verbalize a need for help, then when it is proffered, they terminate therapy before fully dealing with the more basic aspects of the problem. In general, male alcoholics with these patterns show a long history of alcohol abuse that is associated with secondary psychopathic patterns. Female alcoholics in this code type are more likely to have depressive components, situational stress, and physical complaints.

The profile types 2-6/6-2 are rare and are primarily seen in females. They are likely to complain of physical symtoms first, and on further examination indicate a recent interpersonal stress, such as breaking up with a lover or spouse (Kelley & King, 1979). They tend to be more flat than depressed in affect, are likely to have had relatives who have had problems with alcohol, and are concerned about potential alcoholism in their own lives. They are inclined to be dependent and preoccupied with thoughts of suicide and have often made manipulative suicidal gestures in the past. They are significantly disturbed characterologically and thus may earn the diagnosis of borderline personality disorder.

The 2-7/7-2 pattern, if high, is denoted by the presence of agitated depression, difficulty in concentration, somatic complaints, and a high probability of suicidal thoughts. When scales 4, 8, and 9 are also elevated, the probability of acting out these thoughts is raised, and 8 in particular gives a cue as to lack of control. If 0 is high, interpersonal avoidance and fear of rejection can also be expected. Males who show this overall pattern are more likely to have concomitant obsessive compulsive patterns (especially when 7 is higher than 2) as well as vague somatic complaints. Males with some high point combinations of scales 2, 7, and 8 are more likely to be psychotic than females, who are more likely to be neurotic (Kelley & King, 1979).

Persons with the 2-7/7-2 code type are generally passive and dependent, show little anger or hostility, and keep emotionally distant from most people. When scale 1 is also elevated, the agitated anxiety of the 2-7/7-2 profile is channeled into marked somatization. A neurotic diagnosis is probable, and assertive training can be helpful. The scale 7 component points more to anhedonia than to classical depression, and if it is high in the 2-7/7-2 combination, it points more to a lack of ability to experience pleasure than to psychomotor retardation (Gynther & Green, 1980). As a result, the clinician should explore possible suicidal ideation.

When elevations on 2 and 7 are associated with an elevation on scale 3, the tendency toward passive dependency is even more marked. Passive behaviors accompanied by underlying anger and hostility are more likely when the elevation on scale 2 is predominant and associated with elevations on scales F, 8, and 4, and with only a moderate elevation on scale 7 (Carson, 1969). Fowler (1981) notes than when a high 5 is combined with a high 2-7/7-2, there is a paradoxically high probability of sexual acting out. In general, the prognosis for the 2-7/7-2 code type in psychotherapy is positive, though it is less so when both scores are very high.

The 2-8/8-2 code occurs infrequently, particularly in outpatient groups. A sense of having been hurt as a child, confusion, concreteness, and a high level of tension are common, as is depression. If scale 1 is also raised, then somatic delusions are probable. When 2 is markedly high and greater than 8, psychotic depression is likely, whereas when 8 is greater than 2 and particularly high, a schizophrenic or schizoaffective adjustment is more likely. In either case, there is often suicidal ideation, and it is more likely to be associated with a specific plan than in the 2-7/7-2 profile. Even where the 2-8/8-2 code type is associated with only mild elevations, inefficiency and problems in carrying out plans occur, and a sense of having been rejected by others, including therapists, is common. In general, this code type is more indicative of pathology in females, and with females particularly it should be a cue to look for possible substance abuse (Kelley & King, 1979).

The 2-9/9-2 profile incorporates a true paradox, since it is the manifestation of simultaneous manic and depressive components; that is, it represents an attempt through manic defenses to cope with underlying depression, though such a coping pattern is not often successful. If both 2 and 9 are very high, a bipolar affective disorder is suggested, although the possibility of a defense against depression over loss from organic brain damage should also be considered. This pattern is occasionally found in male alcoholics who are defending themselves against depression by increased alcohol abuse. In adolescents, this can reflect separation anxiety and problems in developing a distinct identity.

The 2-0/0-2 profile is obtained by shy individuals who are insecure about their introversion. It is also particularly common in adolescents who are having difficulties socially. In all age ranges, it may manifest itself as a mild, chronic depression. Fowler (1981) reports that this pattern is notably common in parents, especially women, who bring their children to child guidance clinics, and that 2-0/0-2's ultimately often beget 2-0/0-2's. Any training in social skills is helpful, as is psychotherapy to help the shy people adjust to and accept the more stable components of the introverted pattern.

The 3-4/4-3 profile is associated with problems in impulse control, and this control is usually focused on hostility. When 4 is greater than 3, there is a higher probability of acting-out behavior, and the 4-3 profile is often noted in female delinquents. However, as Davis and Sines (1971) suggest, when 3 is greater than 4, the anger is more repressed and more likely to manifest itself in intermittent and episodic fashion. Diagnoses such as a dissociative reaction, intermittent explosive disorder, or passive aggressive personality disorder are common, whereas a diagnosis that focuses on emotional instability and anger is more characteristic when 4 is greater than 3. Denial, combined with the antisocial aspects and the tendency to avoid responsibility for behavior, make high success in psychotherapy improbable.

When this code type is found in females, it often reflects marital problems associated with sexual difficulties and, as already noted, problems in dealing effectively with anger. These persons are overcontrolled most of the time but on occasion fly into rages (Kelley & King, 1979). As a 3–4 client changes to a 4–3, divorce becomes more probable (Fowler, 1981).

The 3–6/6–3 code is characterized by overt anxiety, tension, and rigidity that covers deeply suppressed underlying hostility. There is a denial of this hostility, especially a denial of any of its results as it emerges in a passive or episodic aggressive fashion. The hostility is often directed toward intimate others, so marital problems are common.

People who score moderately high on these two scales are suspicious and hostile, yet overtly promote themselves as naïve and optimistic about the world. They have significant difficulties in interpersonal relationships and perceive their problems as emanating from others. To the degree that these two scales are high, there is more likely to be a clear paranoid disorder. If there is distinct bimodality, paranoia is common, whereas a rise on scales F and 8 suggests paranoid schizophrenia as more likely.

In contrast, the 3–8/8–3 person shows a high probability of anxiety attacks, which are occasionally then channeled into either phobias or acting out (depending on scale 4). If both scales are very high and F is also high, consider possible cognitive dysfunction. When scores are more moderate, consider diagnoses that include dependency and hysteroid defense mechanisms. If 2 is moderately elevated in this pattern, psychotherapy is usually effective. If it is low, a supportive and structured therapeutic orientation is more productive. When an elevation on scale 3 is accompanied by an elevation on K and concomitant low scores on scales F and 8, look for individuals who are conforming, constricted emotionally, and yet dependent on others without acknowledging their dependency since it signifies vulnerability.

The 3–9/9–3 profile is rare and usually found in women rather than men. These persons usually manifest depression as a referral complaint, but on closer examination are likely to show evidence of a histrionic personality disorder, or less frequently, a conversion disorder. They are inclined to distort their perceptions easily and particularly have difficulty dealing effectively with sexual relationships, especially communication in the relationship. At a secondary level, they are likely to show headaches as well as a number of other somatic complaints (Kelley & King, 1979).

The 4–6/6–4 code is mildly similar to the 3–8/8–3, except that there are fewer anxiety and phobic components and the emphasis instead is on narcissism and suspiciousness. A passive-aggressive diagnosis is common, though paranoid schizophrenia must be considered if scales 4 and 6 are very high and accompanied by high scores on scales 8 and F. Persons with a 4–6/6–4 are usually bitter, obnoxious, and difficult to deal with, as they quickly reject responsibility for any problems and may abuse alcohol. Intermittent aggression and a prepsychotic adjustment are also probable (Fowler, 1981). They avoid being involved in any therapy, if at all possible, and seldom make any significant changes even when they are involved.

The 4–7/7–4 combination presents the paradox of the insensitivity and social alienation connoted by scale 4, combined with the moodiness and excessive concern about the effects of one's behavior connoted by scale 7. As a result, such individuals may be involved in cyclical acting-out behavior in which damage to other people is followed by apparent regret—such as the alcoholic who goes on a spree and disrupts friends and family, then follows this with contrite pleas for forgiveness. Yet there is good reason to believe that they are truly insensitive to the feelings of others. Certain sexual deviate patterns that are a counterphobic response to a fear of the opposite sex attain a 4–7/7–4 profile. When the profile has high scores on 2–7 and 4–9, there is often a warring between these somewhat disparate elements. With age, both 4 and 9 tend to diminish, and the more obsessive and depressive elements of the 2–7 profile emerge. Clients with a 4–7/7–4 do indicate a desire for change and will become involved in psychotherapy. At the same time, however, they are concrete in their thinking and not psychologically minded; thus, they do not prove easily responsive to most insight-oriented therapies and they prefer symptomatic support and structure.

The 4–8/8–4 code types are perceived by others as narcissistic, weird, or very peculiar. They are inclined toward antisocial behavior, yet it is usually within a family structure and reflects some underlying dependency and a deteriorating loss of control. If both scales are very high and 8 is greater than 4, the clinician should consider the diagnosis of paranoid schizophrenia. Such persons, especially when there is also a high score on 6, usually had very destructive family backgrounds and appear to feel as if the world is a jungle; they thus perceive their own acting out as a matter of survival (Fowler, 1981). When 4 and 8 are high, such individuals may show consistent antisocial behaviors (e.g., rape), are prone to violence if cornered, and prefer a nomadic and transient existence with few responsibilities. When elevations on 4 and 8 are accompanied by a high F and a low 2, one may find a punitive and interpersonally destructive person who goes about in the guise of a helpful role (e.g., minister, guidance counselor). Punitive aggression, almost to the point of sadism, is directed into a good cause. In spite of an apparent caring role, they are a bit schizoid in their personal life.

The 4–9/9–4 code is a very common one and when high it is frequently found to indicate a behavior disorder. These individuals do not profit from experience, are seekers of high stimulation, often get embroiled in sociolegal difficulties, and show concomitant deficient functioning in the interpersonal and vocational areas. They are narcissistic and impulsive, and even though they do manifest a certain degree of ambitiousness, they have many problems from their transient life style, narcissism, and inability to follow through on plans. A history of alcohol abuse, notably episodic sprees, is common, especially if F is also high. If the profile is distinctly bimodal, these persons are not so consistently aggressive, yet are inclined toward deception. To the degree 8 and 6 are elevated, they are likely to be more directly aggressive.

It is interesting that when women obtain a 4–9 profile that is not markedly high overall, they have been characterized as having high potential for a sales position. If 4 and 9 are only moderately elevated in males or females and there is an indication of psychological distress via scale 2, such persons can respond positively in psychotherapy, though initial sessions are generally replete with resistance. When 4 and 9 are quite high and 6 and/or 8 are elevated, success in psychotherapy is much less probable.

Men with a 4–5/5–4 profile are often Bohemian characters inclined toward various types of nonconformity. They may be overtly homosexual and flaunt this in a passive-aggressive manner. Males with a high 4 and a low 5 show stereotyped macho masculinity. Females with low 5 and high 4 scores, on the other hand, lean toward social masochism. They adopt an overly feminine posture but carry a significant degree of underlying hostility. They often generate hostility and then use guilt and/or legal sanctions to punish the aggressor. Females with both a high 5 and high 4 are those who have adopted behaviors that do not fit with the traditional female role. If these scores are not markedly elevated, they suggest a woman who has developed an independent and competent life style.

The 6–8/8–6 code type is closely associated with a prepsychotic or psychotic adjustment, especially if these scales are substantially elevated. There is much rebellion and anger and other persons are alienated, thereby creating a vicious cycle for their prophecy that they are persecuted. If both of these scales are quite high and 7 is low—the "paranoid valley"—Gynther et al. (1973) suggest looking for further evidence of paranoid schizophrenia associated with auditory hallucinations.

In general, 6–8/8–6's show underlying inferiority and low self-esteem, which seems to be counterphobically defended against by an irritable and hostile veneer. They demonstrate poor judgment in a number of areas and are unstable emotionally. They naturally do not respond well to psychotherapy and, if at all receptive, are inclined toward fad treatments. Significantly elevated 6–8/8–6 profiles, with high L and F scores and relatively low scores on scales 3 and 7, suggest markedly disturbed persons who show paranoid ideation. The available psychological energy, often reflected in an accompanying elevation on scale 9, is a factor in whether or not the underlying hostility evidences itself.

The hallmark of the 6–9/9–6 profile is hostile excitement. A high level of dependency seems to underly this hostile agitation. The clinician needs to consider the possibility of organic brain dysfunction where the manic and suspicious adjustment may be a reaction to loss of functioning in a personality that simply finds loss unacceptable.

The 7–8/8–7 pattern, in the moderate range, shows depressive and/or obsessive-compulsive features. If elevations are marked and accompanied by elevations on scales 0 and 2, severe depression, anxiety, and introverted behavior should be expected, and deterioration into a more blatant schizophrenic adjustment is possible. If so, it is marked by use of neologisms, bizarre speech, depersonalization, and possible catatonic stupor. Even in the more moderate range, these individuals show a low level of social skills, and if they are not diagnosed as schizophrenic, they at least have a borderline personality (Kelley & King, 1979). To the degree that 7 is greater than 8, the individual usually retains a degree of control in behavior adjustment, is less likely to be blatantly psychotic, and is still fighting deterioration in functioning. Unfortunately, a high scale 7 is soluble in alcohol and other drugs.

If both scales 7 and 8 are elevated well above the 70 T mark and 8 is higher, schizophrenia is a strong probability, particularly so if scales 1, 2, and 3 are relatively low. This holds even more for men than for women. Even if no psychosis exists, a significant and pervasive emotional disturbance of some sort is probable.

The 8–9/9–8 code type identifies a person who is narcissistic, hostile, and unable to relate effectively to others. The fear of relating is handled by distractibility techniques and as a result psychotherapy is extremely difficult. It is very hard to keep any issue focused for any significant period of time. In addition, persons with this profile are considered to have a poor prognosis. Even if the scores are only moderately high, there should be much concern about long-term adjustment. Abusers of multiple drugs, particularly adolescents, may show this pattern. In adults it is associated with a schizophrenic adjustment, pressed speech, and confusion, and more likely than not is either a disorganized or agitated catatonic schizophrenic, depending on scales 6, 3, and K. There is often a history of delinquency, or at least of behavioral problems. A high 8–9/9–8 associated with elevation on scales F, 2, and 7 may be a schizoaffective disorder, depressed type.

A high 9 score, associated with moderate elevations on scales 4 and 3 and a moderate or greater elevation on K, denotes a narcissistic and aggressively competitive person. They do not tolerate vulnerability or dependency and raise their own self-esteem by denigrating others. If this pattern is bolstered by real-world support for the narcissism, such as a high level of physical attractiveness or athletic skill, the personality style is reinforced in a vicious cycle. When these people do enter therapy, the therapist hears various fascinating anecdotes and may even be entertained by dramatic self-confrontations. However, marked change cannot be expected unless the cycle of narcissism is broken for some reason, such as aging or trauma resulting in a forced loss of attractiveness.

The 0–2/2–0 and 0–7/7–0 code types are characterized by tension, insecurity, and anxiety, with the trend more toward depression in the 0–2/2–0, and with more insecurity and low self-confidence characteristic of the 0–7/7–0's. This latter group is shy and has substantial difficulties in interpersonal relationships, even with family members, and may be agoraphobic. The social problems noted in the 0–2/2–0 group concern relations with the opposite sex and vocational and academic problems, many in this group having come from a disrupted home (Kelley & King, 1979).

To facilitate the reader's use of the two-point codes, a list of first (not exclusive) consideration diagnoses associated with a specific two-point code is presented in Table B. This table is coordinated with the material in the previous section, as well as with that discussed in the later sections on the various clinical syndromes.

**Table B   First Consideration Diagnoses and the 2-Point Codes**

| Code | First Consideration Diagnoses |
| --- | --- |
| 1–2 | Chronic Alcohol Intoxication, Female Psychosexual Dysfunction, Schizophrenia (rare), Somatization, Hypochondriasis |
| 1–3 | Conversion Disorder, Hypochondriasis, Malingering, Faking Good, Panic Disorder, Psychogenic Pain Disorder, Eating Disorders, Multiple Personality |
| 1–4 | Hypochondriasis, Social Phobia, Chronic Alcohol Intoxication, Somatization |
| 1–6 | Paranoid Schizphrenia |
| 1–7 | Somatization, Eating Disorders |
| 1–8 | Pedophilia, Schizoid Personality Disorder, Schizophrenia (rare) |
| 1–9 | Central Nervous System Impairment (rare), Dependent Personality Disorder (rare), Sexual Masochism (rare) |
| 2–1 | Conversion Disorder, Chronic Alcohol Intoxication, Female Psychosexual Dysfunction, Somatization |
| 2–3 | Female Psychosexual Dysfunction, Generalized Anxiety Disorder, Histrionic Personality Disorder, Panic Disorder |
| 2–4 | Acute Alcohol Intoxication, Schizophrenia, Secondary Psychopath, Antisocial Personality Disorder, Suicidal Potential, Unsocialized Nonaggressive Conduct Disorder |
| 2–6 | Borderline Personality Disorder (rare) |
| 2–7 | Agoraphobia, Avoidant Personality Disorder, Dependent Personality Disorder, Depressive Episode, Dysthymic Disorder, Chronic Alcohol Intoxication, Factitious Disorder, Generalized Anxiety Disorder, Identity Disorder, Obsessive-Compulsive Disorder, Psychogenic Pain Disorder, possible toxic addiction to pain killers, Schizotypal Personality Disorder, Sexual Masochism, Stuporous Catatonic Schizophrenia, Suicidal Potential, Zoophilia |

**Table B    First Consideration Diagnoses and the 2-Point Codes (continued)**

| Code | First Consideration Diagnoses |
| --- | --- |
| 2-8 | Depressive Episode, possible Bipolar or Cyclothymic Disorder, Generalized Anxiety Disorder, Panic Disorder, Schizoaffective Disorder |
| 2-9 | Bipolar Affective Disorder, Central Nervous System Impairment |
| 2-0 | Depressive Episode, possible Bipolar or Cyclothymic Disorder, Schizoid Personality Disorder, Avoidant Disorder |
| 3-1 | Compulsive Personality Disorder, Conversion Disorder, Hypochondriasis, Malingering, Faking Good |
| 3-2 | Depressive Episode, possible Bipolar or Cyclothymic Disorder, Female Psychosexual Dysfunction, Histrionic Personality Disorder |
| 3-4 | Avoidant Personality Disorder, Dissociative Disorder, Intermittent Explosive Disorder, Manic Episode (rare), Passive-Aggressive Personality Disorder, Pedophilia, Psychogenic Amnesia, Voyeurism |
| 3-6 | Paranoia, Paranoid Personality Disorder, Paranoid Schizophrenia, Somatization |
| 3-7 | Depersonalization Disorder, Somatization |
| 3-8 | Multiple Personality, Pedophilia, Schizophrenia (rare), Somatization, possible Psychosis |
| 3-9 | Conversion Disorder, Explosive Personality Disorder (rare), possible Psychosis, Histrionic Personality Disorder (rare), Panic Disorder, Passive-Aggressive Personality Disorder (rare), Somatization |
| 4-1 | Hypochondriasis, Social Phobia, Chronic Alcohol Intoxication, Somatization |
| 4-2 | Acute Alcohol Intoxication, Primary Psychopath, Antisocial Personality, Schizophrenia, Secondary Psychopath, Antisocial Personality, Suicidal Potential, Unsocialized Nonaggressive Conduct Disorder |
| 4-3 | Aggression Potential, Explosive Disorder of Impulse Control, Passive-Aggressive Personality Disorder, Pedophilia, Rapist, Voyeurism |
| 4-5 | Exhibitionism, Homosexuality (males), Opiate Abuse |
| 4-6 | Amphetamine Disorder, Oppositional Personality Disorder, Chronic Alcohol Intoxication, Paranoid Schizophrenia, Passive-Aggressive Personality Disorder, Somatization (rare), Intermittent Explosive Disorder |
| 4-7 | Chronic Alcohol Intoxication |
| 4-8 | Exhibitionism, Pedophilia, Primary Psychopath, Antisocial Personality, Pyromania, Rapist, Schizophrenia, Sexual Sadism, Unsocialized Aggressive Conduct Disorder |
| 4-9 | Amphetamine Disorder, Chronic Alcohol Intoxication, Pathological Gambling, Rapist, Secondary Psychopath, Antisocial Personality, Sexual Sadism, Socialized Nonaggressive Conduct Disorder |
| 5-1 | Transsexualism |
| 5-3 | Egodystonic Homosexuality, Transvestism |
| 5-4 | Egodystonic Homosexuality (males) |

Table B    First Consideration Diagnoses and the 2-Point Codes (continued)

| Code | First Consideration Diagnoses |
|------|-------------------------------|
| 6–1 | Paranoid Schizophrenia |
| 6–2 | Borderline Personality Disorder, Shared Paranoid Disorder |
| 6–3 | Paranoia, Paranoid Schizophrenia, Paranoid Personality Disorder, Somatization |
| 6–4 | Chronic Alcohol Intoxication, Paranoia, Paranoid Schizophrenia, Passive-Aggressive Personality Disorder, Shared Paranoid Disorder |
| 6–8 | Aggressive Acting Out, Polydrug Abuse, Paranoid Schizophrenia |
| 6–9 | Central Nervous System Impairment, Paranoid Schizophrenia |
| 7–1 | Somatization |
| 7–2 | Agoraphobia, Avoidant Personality Disorder, Dependent Personality Disorder, Depressive Episode, Bipolar or Cyclothymic Disorder, Dysthymic Disorder, Chronic Alcohol Intoxication, Obsessive-Compulsive Disorder, Post-Traumatic Stress and Adjustment Disorder, Sexual Masochism, Suicidal Potential |
| 7–3 | Somatization |
| 7–4 | Chronic Alcohol Intoxication |
| 7–8 | Borderline Personality Disorder, Brief Reactive Disorder, Depression, Obsessive-Compulsive Disorder, Schizophrenia, Schizophreniform Disorder |
| 8–1 | Pedophilia, Schizophrenia, Schizotypal, Personality Disorder |
| 8–2 | Depression, Schizoaffective Disorder |
| 8–3 | Multiple Personality, Pedophilia, Somatization |
| 8–4 | Paranoid Schizophrenia, Pedophilia, Primary Psychopath, Antisocial Personality, Rapist, Unsocialized or Socialized Aggressive Conduct Disorder |
| 8–6 | Central Nervous System Impairment, Schizophrenia, Paranoid Schizophrenia, Primary Psychopath, Antisocial Personality |
| 8–7 | Borderline Personality Disorder, Brief Reactive Psychosis, Depression, Obsessive-Compulsive Disorder, Schizophreniform Disorder |
| 8–9 | Acting Out in general, Polydrug Abuse, Agitated Catatonic Schizophrenia, Central Nervous System Impairment, Depression, Schizoaffective Disorder, Disorganized Schizophrenia, Mania, Paranoid Schizophrenia |
| 9–1 | Central Nervous System Impairment (rare), Dependent Personality Disorder (rare), Sexual Masochism (rare) |
| 9–2 | Central Nervous System Impairment, Bipolar Affective Disorder |
| 9–3 | Conversion Disorder, Histrionic Personality Disorder (rare), Panic Disorder, Somatization (rare) |
| 9–4 | Chronic Alcohol Intoxication, Secondary Psychopath, Antisocial Personality |
| 9–6 | Central Nervous System Impairment, Manic Episode, Bipolar or Dysthymic Disorder, Paranoid Schizophrenia |

Table B    First Consideration Diagnoses and the 2-Point Codes (continued)

| Code | First Consideration Diagnoses |
|------|-------------------------------|
| 9–8 | Central Nervous System Impairment, Depression, Schizoaffective Disorder, Disorganized Schizophrenia, Mania, Schizoaffective Disorder, Bipolar or Dysthymic Disorder, Paranoid Schizophrenia |
| 0–2 | Depression |
| 0–7 | Agoraphobia |

## The Cattell 16 PF Test

The Sixteen Personality Factor Questionnaire, developed primarily by Raymond Cattell and Herbert Eber and herein referred to as the 16 PF, was devised to tap a wide range of the client's ongoing personality functioning. It is more designed for personality traits and conflicts as opposed to the MMPI, which is oriented primarily toward categories of psychopathology. The 16 PF gives scores on sixteen different dimensions that Cattell derived through a factor analysis of a huge number of personality descriptors, which were then validated on a wide variety of abnormal and normal client groups.

There are six forms of the 16 PF. The first five are designated by the consecutive letters A through E. The sixth form is a short form (128 items), which is Part 1 of the Clinical Analysis Questionnaire (Krug, 1980). As a result, it is not quite as reliable as Forms A or B. Form A is the one most commonly used. It is composed of 187 items, which means there are approximately 10 to 13 items for each of the 16 scales. The client's response to an item affects only one scale on the 16 PF, whereas in the MMPI a single response may affect more than one scale. The Institute of Personnel and Ability Testing (IPAT) (the present owners of the test) recommend that both Form A and Form B, which are similar in length, be administered to allow for greater validity. In practice, however, most clinicians usually administer only Form A.

Forms C and D are much shorter than Forms A and B and are useful in situations that require quick screening. It takes the average client about thirty minutes to complete forms C and D, whereas it takes about fifty minutes to complete either A or B. Form E is intended for those clients who read below the sixth grade level. Unfortunately, the reliability and validity data on Form E are not as strong as for Forms A and B.

The 16 PF allows three response choices, with *undecided* commonly available as an option. This, along with the fact that it is much shorter and does not ask questions that are so personal, makes the 16 PF more acceptable to most clients than the MMPI. As with the MMPI, it is helpful to encourage the testees to give the most accurate response they can and to answer every question if possible. They should also be warned against spending extensive time mulling over an answer and be asked to give their first clear response.

The 16 PF can be either machine- or hand-scored, and IPAT now provides a service that gives a computer-scored and -interpreted report on the 16 PF. To score the 16 PF by hand, the examiner uses two templates provided by IPAT. If the client's mark appears in the hole on the template, the appropriate number of that hole, either two or one, is added to give a sum that is the raw score for that subscale. These raw data are converted into standard scores, termed *stens*, a shortening of the phrase *standard ten*. These stens, or standard scores, range from 1 to 10 on the answer sheet, have a mean of 5.5 (the middle of the answer sheet), and a standard deviation of two. Thus, a sten score of 1 or 10 is considered quite extreme; scores 2, 3, 8, or 9 are significantly deviant, a score of 4 or 7 is mildly deviant from the norms; and a sten score of 5 or 6 is average. A sten score of 8, 9, or 10 is labeled high in this book, whereas a score of 1, 2, or 3 is low. Moderately high generally refers to a score of 7 or 8, and scores of 3 or 4 are termed moderately low. If the phrase *higher on scale* . . . is used, it simply designates a sten score of 6 or above, *lower on scale* . . . designating a score of 5 or lower. To convert raw data into sten scores it is necessary to use the appropriate Tabular Supplement, based on the demographics of the client. IPAT provides tabular supplements on such groups as college students, general population, and high school juniors and seniors. Along with the 16 personality trait subscales, the 16 PF can be scored for faking good and faking bad, and the reader is referred to the section in this text on malingering for more detail in that regard.

## Cattell 16 PF Factors

### Scale A

Scale A, which Cattell referred to as Cyclothymia versus Schizothymia, generally differentiates between people who are reserved and aloof (low on scale A) and those who are sociable and warm. High A's are more gregarious and trusting, less prone to cyclical moodiness, and less vulnerable to criticism. However, very high A scores may be associated with mania and/or difficulties in impulse control.

Most of the adjectives associated with low A's are fairly negative, although such persons are often more compulsive and precise and therefore more productive in certain areas. They are often more effective in tasks that require working alone and/or generating their own structure. They are self-disclosing and generate rapport only if they feel comfortable in a particular relationship. Persons who are very low are more likely to earn adjectives like schizoid and introverted as well as obnoxious, and frequently display the "burnt-child" syndrome regarding interpersonal relationships (Karson & O'Dell, 1976).

## Scale B

Scale B was originally labeled as High General Intelligence (appropriately enough, the high end of the scale) versus Mental Defectiveness. In actuality, low scores do not necessarily indicate low mental ability. For one thing, there are only thirteen items on this scale, and the scoring is binary rather than the 2, 1, or 0 scoring applied in the other scales, so any precise assertions of validity are unrealistic

Low scores may be associated with random or distorted answering sets, attentional difficulties, impulsiveness, or a lack of ability to persist on a task. Low scores should only be of major concern if there is good reason to believe the person was trying to do well. High scores (8–10) generally indicate at least average intellectual ability, and probably higher ability.

## Scale C

Scale C is labeled as dissatisfied and labile emotionality (the low end of the continuum), as opposed to emotional stability or ego strength. It taps emotional stability, maturity, threshold for irritability and upset, and consequent neurotic fatigue  Overall, C is probably the single most important predictor in the 16 PF for emotional stability. Most neurotics show low C scores; criminals are relatively higher here. Persons low on C may be faking bad, and this should be considered, just as those scoring high may have a high motivation distortion or faking good score (Winder, O'Dell, & Karson, 1975; Krug, 1978).

Low C scores need to have their self-esteem improved and some control over emotional lability generated before they can make any strides with insight therapy. If there is no distortion, a higher C score offers a good prognosis for psychotherapy. There is some evidence that C will rise following a successful therapeutic intervention. In general, high Cs have learned to channel their emotionality into productive and integrated behaviors, as opposed to impulsively dissipating it

## Scale E

The reader might wonder why there is no scale D in the 16 PF. In Cattell's original list of factors, D is referred to as excitability and is not thought to be a major differentiating issue in adults, so it is only found on the Cattell tests for children.

Scale E primarily assesses an assertive or dominance factor, as well as lesser contributions from a willingness to conform to authority. A high score on E would indicate an assertive and tough individual who has strong needs to be independent (which may mask real feelings of inferiority). However, probably because of the conflicts over role expectations, high scores in females have extra factor loadings from attention-getting, social poise, and possible hypochondriacal aspects. High E connotes an assertive personality style, and, though it is not always associated with leadership ability, established leaders do tend to be higher on this score. Persons who are shy are low on E, whereas those who are narcissistic, chronically angry, or inappropriately assertive are higher on E.

## Scale F

Scale F is denoted as Surgency versus Desurgency. This may be better labeled as sober introspective seriousness (the low end of the scale) versus an alert, enthusiastic, and even happy-go-lucky style. Along with scale A, F is an important predictor toward extroversion-introversion. Persons who show bipolar affective disorders may swing markedly on this factor. Success in psychotherapy raises F, and the initial effect of substance abuse is a rise on F. Hysteric individuals and those with sexual, personality, and impulsivity disorders usually score higher on this scale, whereas persons with depression, phobias, and introverted patterns score lower.

The F score drops rather markedly between the ages of eighteen and thirty-five years, and there is even some indication that F rises slightly with metabolic rate within individuals. Although there is a slight correlation of an above average F score with the presence of a leadership position, this does not necessarily connote effective leadership, as the F score may refer to impulsivity as well. Persons in leadership positions who are high on F often need associates who can take the plans they generate and bring them to fruition.

## Scale G

Scale G denotes a person who is demanding, casual in moral standards, and potentially undependable (the low end of the continuum) versus a conscientious and responsible individual. High G individuals are guardians of the moral order, cautious in decisions, and set in their thinking and biases. Markedly low scores are found in self-disclosing psychopaths, and even moderate scores suggest a person who is likely to disregard obligations. However, since this measures adherence to subgroup standards as well, certain criminals do score high here. Rebellious adolescents particularly score low here. Scale G does measure the more overt aspects of morality, and other scores, such as on O, would further indicate whether or not this was a thoroughgoing personality trait. There is a definite correlation with age and socioeconomic class; the older and the higher the socioeconomic status, the higher will be the score on G.

## Scale H

Scale H denotes a person who is shy, constricted emotionally, and threat-sensitive (the low end of the continuum), versus one who is more adventurous, thick-skinned, and friendly. Cattell suggests that this is an innate and genetically determined factor. A low H score indicates a person with an overresponsive sympathetic nervous system, whereas a higher H person is more likely to be seen as lazy, especially during the developmental years. Very low H scores are found in introverted personalities. This is one of the factors that predicts a basic schizoid temperament, as well as a chronic schizophrenic adjustment. Since H connotes threat sensitivity, it should be low in such disorders as agoraphobia and panic disorder. There is some evidence that low H individuals are more likely to suffer ulcers.

## Scale I

Though scale I was labeled by Cattell as Harria versus Premsia, the more common connotations have to do with a person who takes a tough and realistic view of life, is inclined to be self-sufficient, and is not highly responsive to pain or conflict (the low end of the continuum), as opposed to a person who is sensitive, dependent, and possibly effeminate or demanding. Persons who are not introspective and reflective about their self tend to be lower here. Though scale I has not been found to be highly associated with psychopathology, psychotics, on the average, are slightly lower than normals on this factor. One area of pathology in which I is predictive is in the stress-related disorders (such disorders are commonly associated with high scores on both scales E and I).

There are age and sex differences on I, as older people tend to score higher than the very young, and women consistently score higher than men. At the extreme high point the clinician finds women who have stayed within the traditional female role, almost to a stereotypical degree. Macho men score very low on I. In general, this continuum reflects William James's traditional distinction between tough-minded and tender-minded people; those people in the tender-minded subgroup (high on I) generally wish to avoid conflict and have high aesthetic interests. Being low on I does not necessarily help a person adapt to conflict, however, possibly because the tough-minded continuum is a more brittle adjustment and therefore less adaptive to certain types of stress.

## Scale L

Scale L, denoted as Potension versus Relaxed Security, is often interpreted as suspicious jealousy and emotional distancing as opposed to a relaxed trust and openness to the world (the lower end of the continuum). Protension is a combination term from the words *projection* and *inner tension*, and, as is implied, paranoid concerns are often reflected here. Persons high on the scale tend to be cynical, take elitist views, insist on their ideas being heard, and in that sense reflect some of the dominance characteristics also attributed to scale E. Persons high on L are not primarily schizoid, though their personality easily results in rejection by others, so the interpersonal isolation is secondary.

A major issue is how a person channels these traits into vocational and interpersonal interests. For example, eminent researchers often score higher on L, as the characteristics of cynicism, isolation, and confidence in their intellectual superiority serve them well.

The problems of the high L person are that they are often rejected, they may have too high a level of inner tension, their defenses may be too brittle, and they may not have enough access to other persons as emotional resources. Also, high scores predict coronary artery disease and general illness. On the other hand, low L persons in general are emotionally healthy but are subject to interpersonal manipulation, and can get heavily involved in dependency relationships.

## Scale M

Scale M, originally denoted as Praxenia versus Autia, is now more commonly known as conventional practicality versus unconventional imagination (the high end of the scale). Persons high on M have well-developed imaginations, easily consider unconventional options, and more easily dissociate than others. There is some evidence that very high M persons alternate between outbursts of rumination-generated activity and rather placid periods when they seem to be totally wrapped up in themselves. In that sense, this scale is a measure of introversion. High M is also significantly and paradoxically correlated with both creativity and accident proneness (e.g., the absent-minded professor).

Persons with somatoform disorders are lower on M than are those with anxiety-based disorders. The assumed explanation for this difference is that persons with anxiety-based disorders are keeping their conflicts in higher levels of consciousness, thereby experiencing anxiety, whereas the somatoform disorders reflect a denial of inner conflict.

*Scale N*

Scale N is termed the naïveté (lower end of the scale) versus shrewdness continuum. Persons on the high end are socially alert, though a bit calculating and aloof, and may show sophisticated anxiety, or concerns about success in relation to high internal standards. At very high levels, individuals are Machiavellian, whereas if they are too low, they manifest extreme naïveté about other people's motives. People on the low end are socially clumsy, overtrusting, and have rather simplistic interests. Psychotics and neurotics on the average score lower on N.

*Scale O*

Scale O is generally labeled as a placid confidence (the low end of the scale) versus an insecure proneness to guilt. Persons high on this scale are avoidant of stimulation, oversensitive, show a strong sense of morality and duty, and are prone to anxiety-based disorders. A high O score occasionally reflects situational depression. On the other hand, scale O is low in individuals who are psychopathic or who are more likely to act out their conflicts. Along with scale G, O taps what Freudians have referred to as superego.

*Scale $Q_1$*

Scale $Q_1$ denotes cautious conservatism (the low end of the scale) versus a free-thinking and experimenting approach to life. Like the other Q scales, this factor has not been totally validated in all types of data collection, though most clinicians find the Q scores to be extremely helpful. The interested reader is referred to Cattell (1973) for the subtle distinctions he used to discriminate the Q scales from the previously mentioned scales.

Persons high on the $Q_1$ scale are rather critical of others but tend to be analytical and liberal in thought patterns. Depending on vocational and interpersonal situations, the high $Q_1$ person can have difficulties with authority figures or establishment rules and hence can be disruptive in a highly structured environment. A high $Q_1$ person can be viewed as an intellectualized aggressor, with an implicit potential for loss of impulse control. People quite low on this scale are colorless individuals who, rather than being rejected by others, are often simply ignored. Liberal (high $Q_1$) versus conservative political beliefs also affect this scale.

*Scale $Q_2$*

Scale $Q_2$ taps group dependency (the low end of the scale) as opposed to a self-sufficient resourcefulness. Persons low on this scale show little initiative, need much more social approval, and easily move into the dependent role in relationships. In that sense, $Q_2$ reflects a more basic dependency factor than scale G, as G taps more of an adherence to group standards.

## Scale $Q_3$

Scale $Q_3$ is denoted as low self-concept integration (the low end of the scale) versus a controlled approach to life, with an emphasis on a strong will. In clinical terms, high scores on $Q_3$ can reflect a high need to control conflict and anxiety that threaten to break through brittle modes of coping, or, as Karson and O'Dell (1976) so aptly state, there is a high need to bind anxiety into symptomatology or avoidance patterns. On the other hand, a low score may reflect a lack of impulse control or lack of ability to structure one's psychological world effectively. People high on scale $Q_3$ persist on tasks and keep to their commitments, yet are also inclined toward suppression of anger and to obsessive and compulsive concerns.

## Scale $Q_4$

Scale $Q_4$ is generally termed low anxiety and tension (the low end of the scale) versus high tension and anxiety. $Q_4$ is the best 16 PF measure of situational anxiety, and hence there is reasonable fluctuation over time. It measures a person's frustrations in attempting to cope with life. If scale O is also high, it suggests an insecure and anxious quality that persists beyond the situational parameters. Scale $Q_4$ is easily distorted by faking good or bad.

People quite high on $Q_4$ are likely to have experienced rejection by others, have a high level of frustrated sexuality, and be prone to both neurotic and psychosomatic disorders. Once emotional disorder crystallizes into a psychosomatic pattern, $Q_4$ is lower. $Q_4$ is generally higher for the person who has continued with more conscious anxiety, such as neurosis.

## 16 PF Scale Interrelationship
## Interpretations

If a person is high on scale A, it is important also to consider the score on $Q_2$; if that is low, the person has a particularly high need for interpersonal feedback and may be petulant and querulous if it is not provided. High scores on both A and F show a gregarious and friendly extrovert, whereas low scores on A and F with a high score on L are central to the hostile and suspicious introvert pattern.

When a high scale B score is combined with high scores on scales E and $Q_3$, there is likely to be much intellectualized hostility, with consequent rejection by others. It is also worthwhile to look at scale M in relation to scale B, as this suggests to what degree intellectual competence is channeled into imaginative, creative activities rather than into more practical and immediate plans.

If a low scale C is found with a high H and lower G and $Q_3$ scores, a psychopathic quality is likely. But if the low C is associated with a high O and $Q_4$ and a low H, introversion and anxiety disorders are likely. When scales C, F, and A are low, particularly if associated with a moderately low H, look for a withdrawn, shy, and fearful individual. In general, a high O combined with a low C points to a deterioration in competency to adapt to environmental stressors.

As noted earlier, a high I score combined with a high E score predicts the development of stress-based disorders, especially if L and $Q_4$ are also high. A conflict arises in that the individual is both sensitive and dominant at the same time and is torn between the need to look assertive and yet to actuate a desire to reach out emotionally to other people. The competitiveness inherent in the high E blocks the needs of the high I. Where both E and L are quite low, a passive-aggressive personality, with passive-dependent mechanisms, is often noted.

Very low A in combination with low E is characteristic of people who have experienced rejection or abuse in interpersonal or developmental relationships and hence are avoidant of engaging in new relationships. High scores on E, L, and $Q_1$ particularly predict hostility, and the clinician should look to scores on scales B, M, and $Q_3$ to see whether this is likely to be intellectualized aggression or whether it is expected to manifest itself in controlled plans or actualized retribution.

When a high F is combined with low scores on G and $Q_3$, and especially if scores on N and H are high, impulsive irresponsibility is expected. A high F and low G combined with a high $Q_1$ and low $Q_2$ may indicate a young adult in severe conflict over identity development. Analogously, high O combined with low G is found in persons who portray themselves as rebellious and free thinking but who experience much guilt whenever they act out this behavior. This is different from the pattern of low G and low O, consistently found in psychopathic individuals who show little if any guilt.

Persons with high H in combination with high $Q_1$ are critical in interpersonal relationships, yet avoid the risks incumbent on taking responsibility for or acting on their criticism. When the isolated suspiciousness of the high L is combined with low scores on H and A, a paranoid-schizoid component is probable and warrants further scrutiny. As noted, high I and high E are related to stress-based disorders. Conversely, low scores here predict an individual who appears passive yet may be tough at the core and able to resist stress reasonably well.

If L is low and I and M are high, look for a person who avoids interaction with the world by escaping into fantasy, whereas if I and M are low and L and N are high, look for a shrewd, cold, and pragmatically plotting individual. If a low L is accompanied by a low E, one may have an individual who is both very dependent and manipulative—a person who takes on a "poor me" role and yet manipulates other people in a passive-dependent fashion. High N's, particularly when they also score low on $Q_1$, are interpersonally provocative, and, if scale B is also high, this provocativeness may be used in an intellectual manner. Interestingly enough, a high M score generally predicts recidivism in criminal populations.

High scores on N along with a low score on G and high scores on E and H predict a "con man," a person who manipulates others through a combination of assertiveness and shrewdness. The quality of the conning may be predicted by scores on M and B.

Persons high on N, E, $Q_1$, and low on G are particularly difficult to work with and cause a variety of troubles in interpersonal relationships. If they are also high on B and N, their disruption is more difficult to detect. Similarly, high $Q_1$ and $Q_3$ scores, along with a moderately high G score, predict compulsiveness, and this is amplified into obsessive compulsiveness to the degree that B and M are also high.

As already noted, low scores on G and $Q_3$ generally indicate low impulse control and a propensity for characterological disorders, and the problem is confounded if C is also low. In addition, $Q_4$, the measure par excellence of situational anxiety, takes on more ominous connotations if it is found along with high O and low C scores, as this predicts a more long-term disorder. When high $Q_4$ is associated with high M and I, and low G and $Q_3$ scores, substance abuse is probable.

Overall, profiles that clearly slope right (low A through a high $Q_4$) are more indicative of psychopathology. Those that clearly slope left (higher A, B, and C down through lower Q scores) are indicative of psychological health (Krug, 1981).

Before proceeding into the discussion of the diagnostic and treatment recommendations relevant to specific diagnoses, it should be noted that on occasion the 16 PF and MMPI profiles on an individual client may appear to be somewhat contradictory. It is rare that any direct contradictions occur, as the two tests do not measure exactly the same areas. However, if there is an apparent contradiction, the validity scores for each test should be checked. If all is in order, the secondary adjective in the 16 PF scale descriptors should be given more weight to see if that produces a better meld. If there is still no resolution, which is unlikely, greater weight should be given to the MMPI as it has been more thoroughly researched and has more items per scale.

# 2

## Substance Use Disorders

Modern society provides an increasing number of substances that are abused, and this is reflected in the DSM-III. The drugs that are commonly abused, such as heroin, the barbiturates, the amphetamines, cocaine, and marijuana, are given separate subcategories in the DSM-III. Caffeine and tobacco use disorders are also included, so the list covers a great many individuals; this author contends that the term *disorder* is occasionally inappropriate because of its often pejorative connotations. It is interesting that two syndromes that are becoming increasingly common in our society—polydrug abuse and prescription drug abuse—are not specifically delineated in the DSM-III. This is probably due to the responsibility that not only the drug companies but some physicians as well share in the development of these disorders. Naturally, a medical group (the architects of DSM-III) would not be inclined to spotlight these areas (Helman, 1981).

This section will first take note of some overall characteristics of the nonalcohol substance use disorders and then specifically focus on several of the more important individual patterns.

### MMPI

Trevithick and Hosch (1978) have noted that persons with substance use disorders in general are typically elevated on MMPI scales 4, 8, 2, and 7, and others note that 9 is often high (Johnson et al., 1980; Patalano, 1980). These elevations reflect the confusion, distress, and depression that are found in addition to the sociopathic traits of drug abusers. Scores on scale 9 will vary, depending on the person's need to affiliate with others, and whether they are inclined toward the use of depressants or stimulants in response to their own typical physiological patterns. The rare spike 9 profile

48

is indicative of drug abuse associated with antisocial patterns (King & Kelley, 1977).

An MMPI content scale that is particularly useful in diagnosing substance abuse disorders, especially problems with alcohol, heroin, and heavy marijuana and polydrug use, is the MacAndrew Alcoholism Scale (MacAndrew, 1965; Schwartz & Graham, 1979; Fowler, 1976, 1981). This scale is also useful with adolescents in predicting later abuse patterns. Setting a cutoff point (raw scores) at 24 picks up about 80 percent of abusers and potential abusers; a score of 27 very strongly suggests an addiction problem of some sort; and over 30, addiction is nearly certain. Since blacks and obese persons tend to score a bit higher on this scale, adjusting the cutoff points two points higher is suggested for these clients. Streiner and Miller (1981) provide guidelines for prorating short or incomplete MacAndrew scale protocols.

## 16 PF

In the typical testing situation, when disposition is at least one of the considerations, individuals with substance use disorders tend to score high on the M, H, $Q_4$, and I scales, and low on F, which reflects their imagination and their disdain for typical societal standards, as well as their distress. They are likely to be moderately high on scale L, reflecting their concern about arrest and the eventual disposition of their situation. They tend to be moderately low on both scale G and scale $Q_3$, reflecting again their disdain for the standard mores. They are also lower on scales B, C, and E, and if their distress is relatively high, they are also likely to show a lower score on scale F.

### Other Test Response Patterns

Clinicians should of course look for physical signs of substance abuse (needle marks, abscesses over veins, constriction of pupils), and make sure that adequate physiological screening such as urine analysis has been carried out. (Van Hasselt et al., 1981). If the substance abuse has not been long term or if there is little in the way of allied psychopathology, WAIS-R scores are in the normal range and do not show marked subtest deviation (Hewett & Martin, 1980). In some instances, if clients are tested after having ingested low doses of cocaine or amphetamines, they do slightly better on tasks such as digit symbol that require speed and rote learning (Kestenbaum et al., 1978).

If individuals have been abusing drugs for some time, they do poorly on tests that reflect school achievement, such as information and arithmetic, though they still do reasonably well on vocabulary. If they have begun to develop confusion, which occurs in the polydrug abuse syndrome, they are likely to do poorly on the coding and the block design test. They do best in subtests such as similarities, picture completion, and comprehension.

## Treatment Options

A variety of treatment techniques have been used in substance use disorders (Sobell et al., 1982). Aversive conditioning has been favored for working on the specific habits that together form the matrix of substance abuse, as well as in helping develop an aversive response to the drug itself. For example, Duehn (1978) used covert sensitization to develop an aversive response in persons addicted to several drugs, most notably LSD. It is also arguable that relaxation training is helpful for substance abusers, particularly those who look toward the tranquilizers or depressant drugs. Where the disorder appears to be an escape response from fears and phobias, systematic desensitization is helpful. Analogously, assertive training may be included in the treatment package if social inadequacy is evident, as is often the case in substance dependence.

In the initial stages of the treatment, when the persons are being detoxified in a controlled setting, token economies are helpful in getting them to organize their behavior in some effective fashion. With regard to the cognitive behavioral treatments, many feel that covert sensitization is especially useful for the substance abuse disorders (Cautela & Wall, 1980). Within the psychoanalytic therapies, it is felt that the Adlerian approaches have the most to offer for this particular pattern (Belkin, 1980). As the person progresses away from drug abuse, the existential therapies take on a particularly important role. As Krasegnor (1980) notes, the critical issue in treatment success in any substance abuse pattern is the client's decision to change. Since the experience-seeking subfactor of the stimulation-seeking variable particularly characterizes the substance abuser (Zuckerman et al., 1980), the therapist needs to help the client channel this need into more legitimate and constructive pursuits. Family therapy is also usually necessary (Bagarrozzi et al., 1982).

## Chronic Alcohol Intoxication

### DSM-III Considerations

The DSM-III classifies the drug use disorders into the organic mental disorders to reflect their effect on the central nervous system, and at the same time to allow the classification of the behavior as a substance use disorder in order to reflect the maladaptive behavior caused by taking the substances. Thus, a diagnosis from both sections would be appropriate. The initial reaction to this conceptualization has been confusion, and it is possible that this system will be modified over time, if only in the DSM-IV.

The subcategory diagnoses of alcoholism—the organic alcohol disorders and the substance use alcohol disorders—are very specific. The problem is that alcoholics may run the gamut of behaviors appropriate to each of several diagnostic categories in each division, and in a very short period of time. Thus, any particular observed behavior is contingent on when the diagnostician happens to be seeing the alcoholic. It would be absurd to try to detail these subcategories here as it would require an inordinate amount of space, as in DSM-III. However, the important differentiation between substance abuse and substance dependence is presented.

Substance abuse (i.e., Alcohol Abuse, 305.ox) requires that 1) the substance be abused rather consistently for at least one month; 2) there be some type of social complications such as work or interpersonal difficulties; 3) there be either some pathological pattern of use, such as use for several days intensively and then abstinence for a day or so in a repeated fashion, or evidence of psychological dependency. This dependency is indicated when a person cannot stop using the substance, or compelling desire to use it overwhelms any pledges, even when honestly made, to stop using the substance.

Substance dependence (i.e., Alcohol Dependence, 303.9x) requires fulfillment of the above criteria for substance abuse, plus evidence of either tolerance or withdrawal. Withdrawal refers to specific reactions that consistently follow the cessation of the use of the substance, such as the headache and nervousness often associated with withdrawal from caffeine. Tolerance is the need to use higher and higher levels of the substance to gain the anticipated response.

## Other Behavioral Considerations

The psychological euphoria from alcohol is functionally a toxic response. Alcohol is not digested, but absorbed through the stomach and intestinal walls and then metabolized in the liver by the process of oxidation (Seixas, 1981). In this process, alcohol fuses with oxygen, and the resulting pure grain alcohol, or ethanol, is converted by enzymes to acetaldehyde, which is further broken down to acetic acid (vinegar). The vinegar is then broken down by enzymes into water and carbon dioxide, which are passed out of the body. The liver can only break down approximately one ounce of 100 proof whiskey per hour, assuming average weight of the person. Any excess that cannot be broken down directly affects the brain, causing intoxication. Interestingly, even where males and females are of equal weight, this process is still slower in females.

Pharmacologically, alcohol acts as a depressant that first inhibits the higher brain centers, and only later depresses the lower brain centers (Seixas, 1981). As a result, there is a loss of inhibition in overt behavior since the normal censoring faculties of the higher brain centers are inhibited. This has led to the mistaken belief that alcohol is a stimulant. With continued alcohol intake there is a loss of the more complex cognitive and perceptual abilities, and eventually a loss in simple memory and motor coordination.

It is interesting that part of the strength of the effect depends on whether people are getting drunk or sobering up. Those who are sobering up perform better on short-term memory and perception tasks than those who have the same blood level of alcohol but who are getting high.

Long-term alcohol abuse is likely to result in central nervous system dysfunction, or organicity; the reader is referred to that section for relevant diagnostic considerations. Also, most researchers now believe that this dysfunction is not simply a result of B vitamin deficiencies from the overall poor diet that often accompanies chronic alcoholism, but at least in part is caused by the effects of alcohol per se (Seixas, 1981). The reader is also referred to the important work of researchers like Alan Marlatt (e.g., Lang, Goechner, Adesso, & Marlatt, 1975) and Terrance Wilson (e.g., Abrams & Wilson, 1979) who have indicated that the belief that one has ingested alcohol is often more critical than whether one has actually done so or not. These researchers show that both aggression and sexual behavior are highly dependent on the belief system of those individuals who use alcohol, and many times the alcohol is a learned excuse for acting-out behavior in these areas.

## MMPI

Since chronic alcohol intoxication refers to one behavior pattern within an overall personality, and since it can be generated by diverse trains of personality development, what one might expect on various tests is even less clear than with a number of the other disorders that will be discussed later. As noted earlier, the MacAndrew Alcoholism Scale is useful here (MacAndrew, 1965). Holland and Watson (1980) reported elevations above the 65 T level on F, 2, 4, 7, and 8 in their sample of MMPI's from inpatient alcoholics. They compared this group to neurotic, schizophrenic, and brain-damaged groups and found that the only marked differences from the other groups in general were the alcoholics' low scores on L, K, and O. They assert that this is indicative of the introversion, somatization, and depression that are characteristic of this group. The 8–7 alcoholic is most likely to be psychotic and/or depressed (Svanum & Dallas, 1981; Conley, 1981).

The classic high 4–9 pattern that characterizes the psychopath is commonly found in outpatient alcoholics, though in alcoholics it is usually accompanied by a higher F score (Conley, 1981; Svanum & Dallas, 1981). When referring to the more acute alcoholic, people like Conley (1981),

Johnson et al. (1980), Gynther et al. (1973), and Lachar (1974) have noted that the 2–4/4–2 profile is particularly common. The 2–4/4–2, which Fowler (1981) also finds is common here, reflects the depression that the person in the acute state of an alcoholic disorder is naturally likely to experience. Johnson et al. (1980) state that the 4–2 is more common than the 2–4, though the two scores are closer together here than in the 4–2 obtained with other drug disorders. This 4–2 pattern is particularly noted in those arrested for driving under the influence of alcohol.

Gynther and his colleagues have also found that the 1–2/2–1 MMPI profile is common in alcoholics, particularly for males who show an episodic pattern with numerous physical complaints. This usually represents a person who has used alcohol for a significant period of time and who primarily manifests the abuse in episodic sprees. When 3 is also elevated, with 7 one of the next highest scores, a substantial and often severe neurotic component is involved (Conley, 1981). Profiles with an elevation on 4 and 7 frequently indicate persons who manifest a cycle of alcoholic indulgence, regret and remorse, and then repetition of the acting out, while the 2–7/7–2 is noted where remorse is more chronic and has channeled into depression as well.

The 4–6/6–4 profile is commonly found in alcoholics who have a long history of alcohol problems. They are less inclined toward episodic drinking than those with the 1–2/2–1 profile, and they are likely to avoid treatment. The 6–4/4–6 alcoholics usually have very poor work histories (Lachar, 1974) and also have had numerous marital problems, though they do tend to get married repetitively. When the 6 scale is higher, one is more likely to have an abusive individual, with the spouse probably the main target of this abuse. The 4–9/9–4 profile with a high F scale has already been noted. Such persons also tend to be long-term alcoholics.

There is also the 1–4/4–1 pattern where the person is high on scale 9 and at least moderately low on the 0 scale. These individuals are the extroverted social alcoholics who do not have as severe underlying conflicts as those with the other patterns already noted.

## 16 PF

Some of the early research gathered by the people who developed the Cattell 16 PF test has delineated some characteristics on the 16 PF that are common to most alcoholics (IPAT, 1963). They find the alcoholic to be high on the O, $Q_4$, M, and I scales, as well as moderately high on the L and N scales. They expect the alcoholic to be low on the B, C, and F scales, and at least moderately low on scales E and G.

Gross and Carpenter (1971) found somewhat similar results in a study of 266 alcoholics who showed elevation on O and $Q_4$, with slightly elevated scales on M and B. They also found low scores on C, E, G, H, and $Q_1$, with a moderately low $Q_3$. They assert that these profiles characterize the alcoholic as having more imaginative capacity and intellectual ability than the normative group, and also indicate extroversion, passivity, emotional instability, anxiety, and interpersonal undependability.

Costello (1978) found two major subtypes of alcoholics reflected in the 16 PF. The first is characterized by high scores on L, N, O, and $Q_4$, with low scores on C, E, H, I, M, $Q_2$ and $Q_3$. This group, which apparently fulfills the stereotype of the alcoholic, manifests anxiety, introversion, and ambivalent dependency. The second subtype shows high scores on G, N, and $Q_3$, with lower scores on B, C, F, $Q_1$, and $Q_2$. This group is a more aggressive type, is more highly socialized, and has less immediate anxiety.

The score on the O and $Q_4$ scales depend in large part on the degree of anxiety the alcoholic is experiencing at the time of the test. Some alcoholics no longer have immediately intense sources of anxiety and are involved with alcohol in large part out of habit and personality factors. They are not likely to be so high on the $Q_4$ and O scales and could be expected to be lower on the $Q_3$ scale.

## Other Test Response Patterns

In part, the response of the alcoholic to the WAIS-R is dependent on whether or not there has been a development of central nervous system impairment (CNSI), and the reader is referred to chapter 14 on CNSI later in this text. It has generally been assumed that alcoholics do well on such tests as vocabulary, which may be the highest score, and on similarities, information, and comprehension, but do more poorly on tests that tap visual motor coordination and problems in impulsivity. They occasionally miss surprisingly easy items, reflecting a lack of attention and/or CNSI.

Holland and Watson (1980) administered the WAIS-R to alcoholic inpatients, with their subjects obtaining average scores on similarities, comprehension, information, vocabulary, picture completion, and arithmetic. Scores were significantly lower on digit symbol, block design, object assembly, and picture arrangement, which suggests the decrements in visual motor coordination to which others have alluded.

Kish et al. (1980) tested four groups of alcoholics at 6, 15, 21, and 102 days of abstinence from alcohol, using the arithmetic, digit span, block design, similarities, and digit symbol WAIS-R subtests. At the time of the first evaluation (6 days), the alcoholics showed scores that were deficient on all the scales used. Scores improved, however, between 6 and 21 days on digit span, block design, and similarities and this pattern continued, indicating that with reference to the degree of alcoholism they were studying (not markedly severe), "recoveries in short term memory and attention, visual, analytic and synthesizing ability, and abstracting ability" (p. 587) did occur, while the decrements in learning new material or handling arithmetic tasks continued. Others have reported these same continuing deficits in the arithmetic scale and the digit symbol scale.

On the Rorschach, a high percentage of oral responses as well as anatomy responses have been reported. W responses and an increment of Dd responses have been reported by Rapaport et al. (1968) to be associated with addictive tendencies. Others (Gilbert, 1978, 1980) have found a high number of anatomy responses, a low F+ percentage, a number of aquatic animal responses, and color responses to be related to orality. Phillips and Smith (1953) have found an absence and/or decrement of Popular responses in the record. Bug and/or beetle responses are alleged to denote the frustrated dependency commonly associated with alcoholism.

## Treatment Options

A critical first step in the treatment of alcoholics is simply getting them involved in the treatment program (Seixas, 1981). Confrontation type techniques are often useful here. Another helpful approach to this problem was demonstrated by Craigie and Ross (1980). They used videotape to model self-disclosing behaviors and treatment-seeking behaviors with one group of alcoholics who were in a detoxification unit. They compared their subsequent degree of involvement in treatment to those who had only seen general films about alcoholism and found that the modeling for self-disclosure and treatment-seeking significantly improved the probability of staying in treatment.

Many alcoholics who have been chronically imbibing will need an initial period of detoxification. In addition, this period of hospitalization or other controlled structure keeps them from giving in to strong immediate habits that would return them to drinking (Sobell et al., 1982). Drugs such as Antabuse can also be helpful in controlling the immediate impulse to drink, though of course the effects of the Antabuse can be bypassed in short order (Krasegnor, 1980). The implantation of time-release drugs similar in action to Antabuse is a future option, though there are potential legal liabilities if the client would fatally overdose with alcohol and the drug, as is possible. Aversion therapy techniques are also helpful in giving the client additional control over impulses, and aversion by electric shock can be supplemented by videotape replays of the person while he or she is drunk (Krasegnor, 1980).

Many alcoholics, like other persons with impulse problems, are relatively unaware of their physiological reactions as they proceed in their abuse. Analogous to obese individuals, alcoholics are less aware of how much more they drink than normal drinkers, a surprising finding in light of the alcoholic's substantial experience. Lovibond and Caddy (1970) used biofeedback of blood alcohol levels to teach alcoholics to become more aware of the bodily signs associated with increasing blood alcohol levels and in that fashion were able to teach them to be more aware of when they were approaching intoxication. As a result, some were able to return to social drinking. Clients who are able to return to social drinking rather than to rely on total abstinence are usually better educated, have a shorter drinking history, and are more confident of their ability to avoid drinking which goes out of control (Pachman, Foy, & Van Erd, 1978).

Brandsma (1979) found that persons treated with either Insight Therapy or Rational-Emotive Therapy did better than those who received only standard supportive therapy, although the two specific treatment groups did tend to relapse somewhat at a twelve-month follow-up. This points to the important need for continued monitoring, supportive therapy, and work with the alcoholics' social network well beyond the point when they have stopped drinking.

Continued contact is one of the advantages of Alcoholics Anonymous. In addition to the group therapy support structure, AA also forces alcoholics publicly to label themselves as in need of help and gives them a new social network composed of nondrinkers (Mathew et al., 1979; Wolin et al., 1979). Though AA's data that claim high rates of success are strongly flawed methodologically, AA is helpful to persons who have trouble with impulse drinking, who need a new social network, and who are able to work within the somewhat fundamentalistic and rigid demands of the AA belief system.

Marital and family help therapy are most important for dealing with the disruption that has usually been caused in the alcoholic's family life, and most importantly, for helping the family offer positive support to the alcoholic while not reinforcing or subtly encouraging a return to drinking. Such approaches may be extended beyond the nuclear family to friends and associates in order to keep them from subtly encouraging the drinking (Bagarrozzi et al., 1982). Chemotherapy can be helpful in specific instances in weaning the person away from alcohol, though it introduces the paradoxical problems of treating drug abuse with another drug, and the secondary problem of the implicit message in any chemotherapy that the client's own efforts to change are not the critical factor.

## Prescription Drug Abuse

The DSM-III discusses a number of separate substance abuse patterns, and the differentiation between organic and psychological patterns that was mentioned in the alcoholism section is continued in this section. The DSM-III does not discuss a pattern called prescription drug abuse. This author, however, feels that this is an important pattern because it focuses on the common characteristics of clients rather than making a differentiation according to the specific drug that is abused, an approach that often cuts across personality patterns. As Helman (1981) and Meyer and Salmon (in press) point out, physicians and drug companies bear a degree of responsibility for the high level of prescription drug abuse in our society.

While the barbiturates were for many years the most commonly abused prescription drugs, the amphetamines and minor tranquilizers are heavily abused in our present society. For example, Blackwell (1979) notes that during the latter years of the 1970s, more than two billion diazepam (Valium) tablets a year were prescribed in the United States, and diazepam is only one drug in the benzodiazepine family, which, in turn, is only one group of the minor tranquilizers. Valium has long been one of the most frequently used prescription drugs in this country (Blackwell, 1979).

Since this book will discuss some of the ancillary patterns common to amphetamine abuse, the focus will now be on prescription drug abuse involving minor tranquilizers. This latter abuse pattern typically emerges in individuals between the ages of thirty and sixty years of age, predominantly in middle-class and upper-class females. Abusers are rather evenly divided between housewives and those who work outside the home, and they take these prescribed tranquilizers initially for nervousness or insomnia. They gradually decide to increase the dosage, and it is commonly compounded with an increasing use of alcohol.

Interestingly, Schuckit and Morissey (1979) found that out of a large sample of alcoholic women, one-third of them had abused the tranquilizers that had been prescribed for their alcoholic problem. Physicians seem particularly inclined to prescribe mood drugs for women. The likelihood of abuse is compounded because more than 90 percent of the mood-altering drugs taken by women have been prescribed by physicians who have no special training in psychological disorders (Helman, 1981; Meyer & Salmon, in press).

## MMPI

It has already been noted that in substance abuse in general, the clinician can expect elevations on MMPI scales 4, 8, 2, and 7. This would generally hold for the typical prescription drug abuses as well, though I would accentuate the depression reflected in the 2 scale. The 8 and 7 scales are also likely to be substantially elevated, reflecting tension, a sense of being disturbed, and the allied complaints of problems of a vague nature. At the same time, I would expect the 4 scale to be less elevated than one would find in most drug abuse patterns. It will probably be above normal, particularly since these individuals are likely to use the more simplistic defense mechanisms of denial and projection and are also narcissistic in their personality orientation. These factors also predict moderately high scores on scales 1 and 3.

A low score on scale 5 is expected, since these individuals usually identify with the female role, and lower scores on scale 5 are typical of the standard middle-class interest pattern for females. This would vary because of age, and whether or not the woman had a paying job. Since these individuals often feel isolated, and since many of them actually live alone, a moderately high score on scale 6 is not uncommon. The depression and the social isolation also suggest that scale 9 is likely to be lower than average.

### 16 PF

The 16 PF pattern should differ somewhat from the overall substance abuse pattern presented in the last section. Similar to that pattern, a high I score likely reflects a tender-minded and somewhat dependent individual, and the $Q_4$ score, reflecting anxiety, may be somewhat higher than with the standard drug abuse pattern. I expect scale A to be only moderately high at best, and in some individuals, possibly the housewife who is bordering on agoraphobia because of her anxiety, I expect a low A.

The M score, unlike that obtained in many drug abuse patterns, should be no higher than average. In the case of the housewife, particularly the middle-class one, it may tend toward the low end of the scale. Since anxiety is not being dealt with very well, there should be a high $Q_3$ score. I would expect at least a moderately high L scale, in coordination with the high scale 6 on the MMPI. As in most psychological disorders, C should be low. The shyness and social isolation is likely to be reflected in a low H score and low F and E scores. $Q_1$ should be much lower than that of most drug abuse patterns. The B scale, measuring general intelligence, will depend on the social class and education of the individual, as well as on the degree of depression.

### Treatment Options

Persons with prescription drug abuse are oriented toward medical treatment, and often have a middle-class value system, so hospitalization for detoxification fits well with their concept of what should occur. After this initial stage, the clinician has to deal with the tension and depression that often underlie this pattern (Lewisohn & Hoberman, 1982). The development of a relaxation response is important, particularly since it teaches clients that they can exert some control over their lives and thus do not need to be so dependent on external agents such as drugs.

Many of these people have withdrawn socially, so assertive training, as well as any efforts to expand their social network, are most important. Along with this, the therapist can attempt to present the issue of taking drugs as an existential choice (Bugental, 1980) while emphasizing how the clients can determine many of the events that occur in their world and that they must also accept the anxieties and responsibilities concomitant with these choices.

Since insomnia and overweight are common initial problems that lead to prescription drug abuse, it is important to help the person cope with them. With either pattern, any form of relaxation training that emphasizes deep muscle relaxation can help, though the habit control procedures are more important (Sobell et al., 1982). With regard to weight problems, the reader is referred to the treatment options in the section on Amphetamine Abuse.

## Polydrug Abuse

The term *polydrug abuse* is also not included in DSM-III. It reflects an essential feature of our society—the belief that there is a circumscribed remedy for virtually any physical and psychological disorder that occurs (Helman et al., 1981). The polydrug abuser usually combines the expectancy that an external agent will take care of all problems with a high need for new experiences or sensation seeking. Polydrug abusers show a high degree of sensation-seeking behavior (Zuckerman et al., 1980).

The use of a combination of drugs over a period of time is, of course, not new to human society, though in our present culture the pattern is magnified. The epidemic aspects of this pattern are so recent that there are few significant data as to how these individuals will eventually function in later life. These data are important to obtain, since polydrug abusers appear to most clinicians to be more disturbed psychologically than those with other abuse patterns (Penk et al., 1980; Svanum & Dallas, 1981).

Polydrug abusers could be described as psychotics without the loss of reality contact. That is, they show deterioration of behavior in a wide variety of arenas, such as work, school performance, interpersonal relationships, and motivation, especially if they have been abusing for any substantial length of time. Affect is generally flat; or, when emotion is manifest, it is quite labile. Like the alcoholic, there are many protestations of future positive change, and like the alcoholic, the promises are seldom fulfilled. This does not appear to be a manipulative deception, as the person seems intellectually committed to changing, yet the motivation and behaviors necessary to actuate that change cannot be generated.

Polydrug abusers are likely to be late adolescents or young adults. They commonly begin ingesting some mood-altering substance in their early teens and quickly progress through the less potent substances to the point at which they will use practically anything provided to them (Helman, 1981). There are some sex differences in the preferences for drugs; males lean toward the use of alcohol, cocaine, the opiates, and marijuana and hashish, and females are more prone to combine diet pills, tranquilizers, relaxants, sedatives, and, more recently, tobacco.

## MMPI

As with alcoholics, scale 4 is consistently high in polydrug abusers, as is 8, especially with late adolescent polydrug abusers. It is relatively lower in that subgroup of polydrug abusers who tend to be depressed and who therefore have high 2, 7, and 8 scales as well. The more psychopathic 6–8 and 8–9–4 patterns are less likely to show depression and more likely to act out in ways other than simply drug abuse. In those individuals who are high-sensation seekers the F scale is consistently elevated above a T score of 70. Elevations on scales 1 and 3 are not consistently found with polydrug abusers, though when these are at least moderately elevated, some feel it is a better prediction of successful participation in treatment programs. As a person continues in the polydrug abuse pattern, apathy increases and scores on scale 9, and to a lesser degree on scales 6 and 4, will be lowered. The apathy and social problems that accompany this pattern predict a high 0 scale, especially if depression is still present and not diluted by the drug use.

Overall, polydrug abusers have been found to have more MMPI scores elevated over the 70 T level than do heroin abusers. The latter group on the average shows elevations above 70 T on 2, 4, and 8, whereas polydrug abusers show them on F, 2, 4, 7, and 8 (Penk et al., 1980; Savnum & Dallas, 1981). As noted earlier, the MacAndrew Alcoholism Scale is useful here (MacAndrew, 1965).

## 16 PF

Collins et al. (1977) state that the four factors consistently found in drug abusers are high F, low G, high H, and moderately high I. The high H measures their venturesomeness, and more specifically their willingness to try nonapproved consciousness-altering drugs. The moderately high I, in conjunction with the other scores, reflects reliance and yet also the sensitivity and ambivalent dependency found in alcoholics. The low G measures the sociopathy to be expected here. The high F suggests extroversion and even a slightly manic quality; this primarily depends on when the individual is tested.

These persons' lack of a consistent value system, along with an imaginative though nonpersistent problem-solving approach, predicts a higher M score, and the orientation toward experimentation with drugs and disavowal of standard morality systems predicts a high $Q_1$ score. Similarly, emotional lability and a lack of discipline predict a low C score and a low score on $Q_3$. In the early stages of the pattern, one could also expect relatively high scores on A, B, and $Q_4$, but with an increase of apathy and inability to generate new behaviors, these scales should decrease. The lack of adequate social skills usually noted in this group would suggest at least a moderately low N score and a moderately raised $Q_2$ score, though this latter score is then more appropriately interpreted as group avoidance rather than self-sufficiency.

## Treatment Options

In many instances, there is an acute toxic reaction to the drug that must be dealt with first (Cheek & Miller, 1981). For example, in an acute reaction to cocaine the standard stabilization sequence may require the use of 1) oxygen to stabilize respiration, 2) Inderal for any cardiac arrhythmias, 3) a barbiturate to reduce central nervous stimulation, or 4) benzodiazepines to control convulsive reactions. This response must be short-term and very carefully monitored in order to avoid secondary abuse patterns.

Since the typical polydrug abuser is an adolescent or young adult who is showing a deterioration of functions in a wide array of behaviors, the broad spectrum treatment is necessary. The clinician should be aware of the probability that polydrug abusers will attempt to obtain addicting drugs while in the detoxification phase through manipulation of their peer group.

Group experiences that emphasize confrontive techniques are often necessary here, so Reality Therapy (Glasser, 1980) can be an important adjunct to the overall treatment program. Polydrug abusers easily verbalize promises and commitments, but seldom tie commitments to future contingencies. Reality Therapy, of course, emphasizes this linkage. Most importantly, polydrug abusers should be forced to accept responsibility for the abuse behavior, as these persons often promote an implicit message that they were seduced into the drug culture. Aversive techniques can be helpful in dealing with specific habit patterns (Sobell et al., 1982). Since family problems may have been a catalyst for the early drug abuse, this needs to be worked out via family therapy (Bagarrozzi et al., 1982).

## Amphetamine Use Disorder

As we have noted, the DSM-III lists a variety of substances for which abuse can be diagnosed; this includes tobacco and marijuana. For many of these substances, especially for the last two, there is no consistent personality pattern. However, this book will comment on two patterns, use of the amphetamines and of the opiates, because these two are so important in our society today, but are diverse patterns.

The first synthetic amphetamine, a methamphetamine, was compounded in 1919 by the Japanese scientist Ogata (Bertinetti, 1980). Amphetamines were used to combat fatigue in World War II and are used today in treating hyperactive children. They have also been too commonly prescribed as a diet aid in the past, although there are now increasing restrictions on physicians. The use of amphetamines or other similarly acting sympathomimetic substances is often the first step from abuse to dependence (Helman, 1981). Tolerance to amphetamines builds quickly, so abuse easily leads to increased intake and dependence. Continuation of an intake of amphetamines over a significant period of time leads to paranoid and other psychotic symptoms, which may continue for some time after the drug is discontinued.

### DSM-III

All of the DSM-III diagnostic categories relevant to amphetamines include the concept *or similarly acting sympathomimetic agents*, as these are thrown together in the same diagnostic category. In the section on organic diagnosis, there is a term *Amphetamine Intoxication* (305.70), which refers to the toxic effects of a single recent dose. Criteria include 1) evidence of a recent use of amphetamines and consequent (within one hour) physiological symptoms such as tachycardia, elevated blood pressure, nausea, perspiration or chills or pupillary dilation; 2) any two psychological symptoms such as psychomotor excitement, grandiosity, loquacity, hypervigilance, or elation; and 3) maladaptive behavioral effects such as problems in social or occupational functioning or impaired judgment.

Delirum is the term for the syndrome that used to be called acute brain syndrome. It involves a clouding of consciousness and memory disruption along with evidence of two of the following: speech difficulty, perceptual problems, sleep problems, or hypo- or hyperactivity. The duration of delirium is typically short, no more than a week. In the specific instance of amphetamines (Amphetamine Delirum, 292.81), delirium lasts only about five hours, starting about an hour after ingestion of the substance.

The Amphetamine Delusional Disorder (292.11) is the presence of paranoid or grandiose delusions directly related to amphetamine abuse. Amphetamine Withdrawal requires evidence of two of the following three symptoms: disrupted sleep, increased dreaming, or fatigue, as a result of prolonged heavy use of amphetamines. Suicidal ideation and depression are also common.

As with the other substance abuse and dependence patterns, Amphetamine Abuse (305.7x) requires evidence of continuous or episodic use of amphetamines for at least a month, along with either social or vocational complications from this abuse, or pathological use patterns, such as intoxication for an inordinate length of time. Amphetamine Dependence (304.4x) requires all of the conditions for the abuse pattern and, in addition, evidence of either tolerance, wherein one requires increasing dosages to achieve the same effects (or a loss of effect with the same dose), or withdrawal, wherein one shows severe psychological and physiological reactions on attempting to cease using the drug.

## MMPI

The elevation on scale 4 that is common to most drug abuse patterns is particularly evident in this syndrome. It is combined with an elevation on scale 9, reflecting the heightened activity and agitation associated with amphetamine use. There is also a significant elevation on scale 6, depending on the degree of abuse, and whether or not paranoid ideation has begun. Elevations on scales 8 and 3 are also relatively common. Since amphetamine abuse is often a coping mechanism to deal with depression, this will be manifest in a degree of suppression of scales 2 and 0.

## 16 PF

As with the other drug abuse patterns, low C and $Q_3$ scores are expected. The rejection of standard mores and the high activity level characteristic of amphetamine abuse are reflected in higher scores on M, F, E, and $Q_1$, and probably to a lesser degree on H. Prolonged abuse is likely to result in a higher L score, which reflects the development of a paranoid trend. Since these individuals, especially when they are still experiencing the effects of intoxication, are not likely to pay attention to a particular question for any length of time, scores on B should not be particularly high. A low score on G would be expected as well as a moderately low score on H, the latter reflecting the autonomic over-reactivity generated by this particular drug.

## Treatment Options

Since amphetamine abuse or the abuse of other similar stimulant drugs is often related to underlying anhedonia or depression, existential techniques to confront the apathy, and the cognitive behavior techniques described later for depression, are useful here. It is extremely important to teach persons that they can get involved with and control their world without the crutch of a stimulating drug (Cheek & Miller, 1981; Sobell et al., 1982).

Covert sensitization, a subcategory of the techniques known as Covert Conditioning, is useful for drug disorders (Cautela & Wall, 1980). This is an imagery procedure that asks the client to imagine a highly aversive contingency or event occurring immediately on the cessation (in imagination) of the behavior that one is attempting to eliminate (in this case, involving the specific components of the amphetamine abuse sequence). This is repeated over a number of sessions and is efficient to the degree that the client can develop adequate images, and to the degree that the imagery is experienced as vivid and real.

Since amphetamine abuse is often a logical extension of an abuse of other prescription or nonprescription pills for dieting, concomitant techniques to help with obesity are often useful to prevent the return to the use of amphetamines. Supportive group therapy, teaching of a relaxation response, in some cases hypnosis, and especially behavioral control therapies are useful here. For example, it is important that the person never associate eating with other activities, such as reading or watching television; the eating has to come with independent cues. Teaching the persons to be able to interrupt meals for brief periods of time is a useful exercise. Analogously, they should be admonished to take smaller portions into the mouth, chew the food much longer, keep desirable foods out of the house as much as possible, purposely slow the pace of eating at times, and eat in only one spot in the house. They should keep a diary of eating behaviors so that awareness increases and therefore contingency contracting can be carried out to lower the size of the food portions.

## Opioid Use Disorder

Even though the opium poppy has been used as a mind-altering substance for at least 6,000 years, two events in particular spurred the increased abuse patterns noted throughout the last century. Early in the nineteenth century, morphine (ten times stronger than opium) was isolated from the opium poppy, and approximately fifty years later Alexander Wood perfected a more effective drug delivery system—the hypodermic needle. Morphine was soon included in many patent medicines, although it was supplanted in use near the end of the nineteenth century when Wright discovered heroin, a semisynthetic opioid derived from morphine. Interestingly, heroin was at one time used to cure morphine addiction, just as another addicting drug, methadone, is now used to treat heroin addiction.

Heroin induces a warm, sensual euphoria, usually followed by sleepiness and lethargy. Unfortunately, tolerance develops rapidly, and eight to twelve hours after an injection the individual is likely to experience withdrawal symptoms, the severity depending on the amount ingested and the duration of time the person has been abusing. Even so, these symptoms are seldom as severe as the mad ravings portrayed in the media. In fact, most addicts describe withdrawal as quite similar to influenza symptoms.

Perhaps no one has expressed so clearly the reinforcement from heroin as French humanist and poet Jean Cocteau:

Everything we do in life, including love, is done in an express train traveling towards death. To smoke opium is to leave the train while in motion; it is to be interested in something other than life and death. (Jarvik, 1967, p. 52.)

## DSM-III

The DSM-III requires the same criteria for opioid abuse and dependence as it does for all the substances heretofore mentioned. In the section on organic mental disorders, the DSM-III lists Opioid Intoxication (305.50), which is the effects of a single dose toxic enough to produce pupillary contraction, psychomotor retardation, apathy, and the experience of either euphoria or dysphoria. Itching, flushing of the skin, nausea, and analgesia also typically occur. The diagnosis requires: 1) evidence of recent use; 2) pupillary contraction; 3) at least one psychological sign such as euphoria, dysphoria, apathy, or psychomotor retardation; 4) at least one neurological sign such as drowsiness, attention or memory problems, or slurred speech; and 5) maladaptive behavioral affects such as avoidance of responsibility or problems in social and vocational functioning.

Prolonged or heavy use often results in Opioid Withdrawal (292.00), in which restlessness, irritability, nausea, and muscle and joint pains are commonly experienced.

## MMPI

Elevations on scales 2, 4, and 8, which are generally characteristic of the drug abuse patterns, are found in opiate abuse (Penk et al., 1980). Elevations on scales 3 and 6 are also likely, which reflects the egocentricity and problems with authority characteristic of this pattern, though it is true that the elevation on scale 6 may not be as high as it is for a person who is dependent on amphetamines. In certain opiate abusers, there is a high scale 9, indicating a person who is easily bored, has a low frustration tolerance, and is in that sense narcissistic. In another subgroup, the more relaxed or Bohemian opiate abuser, a 4–5 code type is common. Scores on scales 2 and 9 will vary depending on whether the person is feeling euphoric or dysphoric. Since the person is not likely to be tested while in the midst of an episode, the rise on scale 2 is more likely. It is interesting that opiate abusers seldom show a profile as pathological as most of the other significant drug abusers do. As noted earlier, the MacAndrew Alcoholism Scale is useful here (MacAndrew, 1965).

## 16 PF

Opiate abusers are likely to be high on scales I and M. This reflects their paradoxical indulgence in fantasy while they maintain an apathetic view of events in their world, along with their avoidance of either stress or commitment whenever possible. They are also relatively high on O, though typically not as high as alcoholics. They are relatively high on A, which is different from a number of other drug abuse patterns; this reflects their lack of paranoid response toward the environment, at least in relation to the amount seen in the other drug abuse patterns. They tend to be slightly above average on L, although this will vary depending on the testing situation.

Opiate abusers tend to be average on scales $Q_3$, H, and $Q_1$, and lower on N, which again differentiates them from those with other drug abuse patterns. However, like all of these patterns, they are low on scales C and E. They are also low on B, reflecting their lower socioeconomic status and educational attainment, as well as the lack of initiative found in these persons.

## Other Test Response Patterns

Keiser and Lowy (1980) present evidence that heroin addicts tend to be significantly higher on digit span scores than on other WAIS-R subtests. This fits with the evidence that a digit span score well above the mean of the client's other WAIS-R subtest scores is correlated with an interpersonal detachment syndrome characterized by superficial and emotionally distant relationships.

## Treatment Options

The confrontive group experience first evolved with the opioid disorders, primarily through institutions like Synanon and Phoenix House. These groups are effective with a number of clients, though they have been burdened by problems resulting from their resistance to any reliance on professionally trained staff. As a result, there is a lack of objectivity in assessing techniques and outcome and a lack of awareness about the wide range of treatment techniques discussed in the professional literature, not to mention the techniques that are being developed. In any case, a method of providing a more therapeutic social network is critical in dealing with opioid addicts, as they easily return to their destructive peer group setting (Cheek & Miller, 1981; Sobell et al., 1982).

Just as heroin was once used to treat morphine addiction, methadone, also an addicting drug, is now used to treat heroin addiction. It appears to be effective in certain cases, though the clinician must be aware of possible secondary abuse of the drug used for treatment, particularly in addicts who are psychopathic. Methadone can be useful at least in the initial stages of treatment. Since it does not cause the distinct euphoria of heroin, it can be taken orally and less often than heroin; also, its lower cost may allow the addict to move out of the criminal system.

# 3

## The Schizophrenic and Paranoid Disorders

### Schizophrenia

Many clinicians would argue that schizophrenia is the most serious of all mental disorders. Although other disorders are more common or may involve more immediate distress, the pervasive effect of schizophrenia disorder throughout all areas of an individual's functioning and the complexity of problems it presents in etiology and diagnosis would support the assertion that it is the most serious mental disorder. About one out of every one hundred people in the United States will receive a diagnosis of schizophrenia at least once in his or her lifetime (Berger, 1978). The schizophrenic who has been released after a first hospitalization unfortunately still has about a 50 percent chance of returning to the hospital within two years. It has consistently been estimated that schizophrenics occupy approximately two-thirds of our mental hospital beds and almost one-fourth of all hospital beds. These statistics reflect the long period of time that schizophrenics traditionally spend in institutions.

There are a number of premorbid predictors of schizophrenia worth assessing in a client (Meyer & Salmon, in press):

1. A schizophrenic parent or parents, a less potent variable being the presence of other schizophrenic blood relatives. There is evidence that for daughters, the earlier that their mother became schizophrenic, the higher is the likelihood that they, too, will become schizophrenic. For sons, however, this is not as critical, with a more important issue being the time of separation from a disturbed mother. The earlier separation occurs, the more damaging it is for a son.
2. A history of prenatal disruption or birth problems.
3. Low birth weight and/or low IQ relative to siblings.

4. Hyperactivity; cognitive slippage; any signs of central nervous system dysfunction, particularly in the left hemisphere (Tucker, 1981), such as convulsions; evidence of enlarged cerebral ventricles; significant reaction time problems; or an abnormally rapid recovery rate of the autonomic nervous system.
5. An early role as the scapegoat or odd member of the family.
6. Parenting marked by emotional and/or discipline inconsistency, including double messages.
7. Rejection by peers in childhood or adolescence, and perception by either teachers or peers as being significantly more irritable or unstable than other children.
8. Rejection of peers, especially if accompanied by odd thinking processes, ambivalent emotional responses, and/or a lack of response to standard pleasure sources.

## DSM-III

To apply the diagnosis of schizophrenia, the DSM-III requires evidence of one of the following: 1) significant delusions or hallucinations (excluding auditory hallucinations of only one or two words); 2) loosening of associations; 3) reduced speech content if it is accompanied by delusions or hallucinations; 4) inappropriate or flat affect; 5) catatonic or disorganized behavior. There must be an active phase, and the disorder must continue for at least six months including a prodromal, active, and residual phase. For example, a prodromal phase of one month followed by an active phase of three months and a residual phase of two months would be enough for a diagnosis of schizophrenia, as would any other combination of periods of time in these three categories that adds up to six months. Typical delusions of schizophrenics include somatic delusions, delusions of being controlled, thought broadcasting, or grandiose delusions. This symptomatology must not be directly related to a depressive or manic disorder. Schizophrenic symptomatology must precede the affective disorder, or else the affective disorder must be a relatively minor component. During the active phase of the disorder there must be some significant impairment in areas of daily functioning, such as interpersonal relationships, school, or work.

The preschizophrenic personality of individuals who later become schizophrenic can often be described as eccentric and isolated, mildly confused and disorganized, suspicious, and/or withdrawn. As a result, such individuals are likely to require the additional diagnostic qualifier of such categories as schizotypal, borderline, introverted, or paranoid personality disorder.

A major innovation in the DSM-III classification system should be noted. The DSM-II category of simple schizophrenia is not included in the DSM-III. It was felt that simple schizophrenia was an inaccurate categorization since individuals so labeled did not really manifest hallucinations, delusions, or blatant thought disorder. Rather, they showed primarily a combination of inadequacy and social withdrawal. Although this is a significant level of disturbance, such persons are more accurately classified as having a borderline or schizotypal personality disorder.

Several studies have pointed to the problems of making accurate sub-classifications within the overall category of schizophrenia. Most clinicians find this classification meaningful, as these categories clarify commun-ications and facilitate discussions of treatment and prognosis. As regards the overall diagnostic category of schizophrenia, an important study by the World Health Organization (1979) has demonstrated the reliability of this concept in a variety of sociocultural settings.

## MMPI

As might be expected, most clinicians agree that scale 8 is typically elevated above the 70 T score in schizophrenics, since this directly reflects their tendency to escape reality through fantasy behavior and to process infor-mation inadequately. Most schizophrenics tend to score in the 75-90 T range, particularly as they move toward chronicity (Johnson et al., 1980). Extremely high scores are more likely to indicate severe patterns within other diagnostic categories, or to reflect an attempt to "fake bad."

A variety of scale patterns have been noted. Lachar (1974) points out that the 7-8/8-7 profile suggests possible chronic schizophrenia, whereas the 2-7-8 code type or a similar combination is more likely to be associated with an earlier stage of schizophrenia (Golden & Meehl, 1979). A pattern that appears especially predictive of schizophrenia is the F scale's (in T scores) being greater than 70 and less than 95, scale 8 greater than 75 and less than 100, and scale 7 less than scale 8.

When a profile is obtained where scale 8 is high, scale 1 is around 85 T and at the same time 10 to 20 T greater than scales 2 and 3, this suggests a schizophrenic with somatic delusions. The unusual 3-8/8-3 profile also indicates an individual with high somatic concerns but with a greater ten-dency to dissociate. A primary elevation on scale 6 is not consistently obtained in schizophrenic profiles, though it is likely in paranoid schizo-phrenics and occurs occasionally in some catatonic schizophrenics.

The 8-4/4-8 profile can also indicate schizophrenia, particularly when hostility and anger are major components. This individual has probably had a particularly bad childhood. When the clinician sees an 8-9/9-8 pro-file, it is commonly that of a schizophrenic who finds it extremely difficult to vocalize the issues at hand, is consistently problematic to work with therapeutically, and is often disruptive in functioning.

Schizophrenics are usually elevated on the F scale, and Gynther et al. (1973), note that a very high F scale obtained in a psychiatric population is likely to indicate a confused individual, rather than one who is "faking bad." Though it does occur in certain instances, a major elevation on scale 3 is not typical in schizophrenic profiles. A particularly high scale 5 in a woman who appears to fit within the traditional feminine role should alert the clinician to look for other indications of schizophrenia. In a somewhat similar vein, Holland and Watson (1980) find male schizophrenic VA inpatients to be high on L, F, 5, 6, and 8.

In this regard, Goldberg's formula (Graham, 1977) for determining psychosis, using T scores, should be noted. The L score must be added to the scores for scales 6 and 8, and then the scores on scales 3 and 7 must be subtracted. Using a lower cut-off point of 45, one is allegedly correct 70 percent of the time in using the label schizophrenia, though this seems to be a sign of paranoid schizophrenia more than schizophrenia in general. Newmark's formual (T on Sc > 80 < 100; total Sc raw score is no more than 35% of K items; T score on F > 75 < 95; on Pt > Sc) has proven to be effective, primarily with schizophrenics under 45 years of age (Newmark & Hutchins, 1980).

## 16 PF

On the 16 PF, schizophrenics tend to be high on O, $Q_4$, M and I. This reflects their propensity to engage in fantasy as a way to control intrapsychic conflict and their tendency to withdraw and not deal in a practical fashion with the world. This pattern at the same time reflects the high level of anxiety and insecurity experienced by most of these individuals. This fits well with the concept that they are stimulation avoidant, as opposed to the primary psychopath who is stimulation seeking.

Schizophrenics also tend to be low on scale C, though often surprisingly not as low as many of the other psychiatric disorder categories. They are consistently low on scales F and H, which reflects a stimulation-avoidant pattern, as well as the depression that is likely to accompany such a high level of disturbed functioning. Though numerous schizophrenic individuals may score in the average range, in general they tend to be somewhat lower on $Q_2$, G, and $Q_3$. Along with their significant inability to cope with the world, they also tend to be low on scale B. As schizophrenia becomes chronic, C, E, F, and H tend to be lower, and I and M become higher.

### Other Test Response Patterns

On the WAIS-R, several patterns are commonly found in schizophrenia (Lehmann, 1975; Blatt & Allison, 1968, 1981). First, subtest scatter is common and the verbal scaled score tends to be higher than the performance scaled score. Within the subtests themselves, there is a tendency to succeed on harder items while at the same time surprisingly to fail some of the easier items. Scores tend to be higher on block design and digit symbol, and occasionally on information and vocabulary, while they typically are lower on arithmetic, picture arrangement, and comprehension. A low similarities score often includes several overinclusion responses, and a low score on comprehension is usually accompanied by evidence of irrelevant associations. A high similarities score is a good prognostic sign for schizophrenia. There are often peculiar arrangements in the picture arrangement test, and in the picture completion test frequent reference is made to items not intended to be there. In addition, process schizophrenics do less well than reactive schizophrenics on the picture completion subtest, relative to their other scores.

Ogdon (1977) reviewed a wide range of studies that used the Rorschach and noted several response patterns found to be associated with psychosis in general and schizophrenia in particular: 1) poor quality and a low number of human movement responses (i.e., responses in which humans are perceived as involved in at least some minimal action); 2) animal movement responses in which the organization of the response is very poor; 3) an abnormally high or low number of pure form responses (i.e., responses in which the client made the response based simply on the form of the blot, without reference to any other aspect); 4) responses dictated only by the color of the blot (i.e., pure C responses); 5) an abnormally low number of responses in which all aspects of the blot are integrated into the response (i.e., whole or W responses); 6) a lower-than-average number of popular or P responses (i.e., responses perceived by most people); and/or 7) perseverating by continually seeing the same or analogous responses throughout several blots in sequence.

Exner (1978) has noted several differences between schizophrenics and normals on the Rorschach. Schizophrenics obtain more F- and M- responses than do either borderlines or normal persons, though there may be a high percentage of F responses. Borderline individuals average 6.4 popular responses, whereas schizophrenics average only 3.6. Not surprisingly, schizophrenics have almost twice as many odd or unusual responses than do even borderline cases, and certainly far more than do normal individuals. Schizophrenics also give three times fewer S responses and two times fewer T determinates than normal individuals.

Others have noted that schizophrenics are more inclined than other groups to show a massing of pure color responses, and they occasionally show very arbitrary FC responses (e.g., pink rats). Color shock or pleasantly verbalized comments about color in the cards are considered to be favorable prognostic signs in schizophrenia (Phillips & Smith, 1953). Along with the deviant verbalizations, such as fabulized responses (e.g., two rabbits with a baseball bat), contaminations (e.g., the head of a beetle-tiger), and other incongruous combinations (e.g., a woman with the head of a horse), schizophrenics tend to show overelaborate symbolism and absurd responses in their patterns and also show a number of mangled and distorted perceptions. Schizophrenics are more likely to show a perseveration of Dd responses, which reflects a high degree of overcontrol in their response patterns combined with underactivity in the actual perceptions. They also may show a massing of sex responses and particularly refer more often to the sexual act rather than to sexual organs. As in most of the tests, there is a tendency for the quality of responses to deteriorate toward the end of the test. Not only do schizophrenics show a higher percentage of F— responses, but they also show higher levels of articulation of the object as they perceive it within the F response (Ritzler et al., 1980). In essence, their ego resources are being channeled into fantasy behavior.

On the Thematic Apperception Test (TAT), schizophrenics are prone to tell rambling, confused stories or to have a very restricted response record. They are more likely to make comments of self-reference or show personal reactions such as disgust in response to the cards. In general, they make more bizarre comments and show less ability to concentrate on their responses (Karon, 1981).

Proverbs have also been used to distinguish schizophrenics from other groups. Johnson (1966) found that only those proverbs that are commonly understood, such as "it never rains, but it pours," are consistently useful in distinguishing schizophrenics from other groups, such as persons with organic brain damage. Schizophrenics are more likely to give peculiar yet abstract responses to these proverbs.

*Treatment Options*

There are several prognostic indicators that point to a positive chance of remission once schizophrenia does occur (Meyer & Salmon, in press): 1) sexual-marital status: being married, or at least having a previous history of stable, consistent sexual-social adjustments; 2) a family history of affective disorder rather than schizophrenic disorder; 3) presence of an affective pattern (either elation or depression) in the acute stage of the schizophrenic disorder; 4) abrupt onset of the disorder and onset later than early adulthood; 5) adequate premorbid vocational adjustment; 6) evidence of premorbid competence in interpersonal relationships, and higher socioeconomic status; 7) a short length of stay in the hospital, and an absence of electroconvulsive therapy (ECT) treatment; 8) a relatively high score on the WAIS-R similarities subscale score; and 9) evidence of clear precipitating factors at the onset of the disturbance.

More than almost any other disorder, schizophrenia warrants a multifaceted treatment plan because of its complexity. Chemotherapy, usually with the phenothiazines, the butyrophenones, or the thioxanthenes, is useful as one component in the treatment of many schizophrenics, particularly for those who are hospital-prone clients of low competence. Since there can be major problems with their ability to take the medication after they are released from the hospital, the long-acting agents, such as the phenothiazine Prolixin, can be useful, though they do have a restricted range of effectiveness and problems with side effects. With all the antipsychotic chemotherapy at least 35 percent of the clients show muscular problems and feelings of lethargy alternating with restlessness. Approximately 5 percent (up to 40 percent in the elderly) develop tardive dyskinesia, a typically irreversible syndrome that involves grimacing, lip-smacking, and involuntary neck and head movements. Also, particularly with the phenothiazines (the most commonly used drug) a significant number of deaths due to aspiration asphyxiation have been noted, since they tend to suppress the gag reflex. In addition to the side effects noted above, there is loss of creativity and spontaneity and a reinforcement of the patient role, since the client sees the treatment as totally external to one's self. Though chemotherapy can be useful, antipsychotic drugs are no doubt prescribed too often (Helman, 1981; Curran et al., 1982).

ECT has consistently been used with schizophrenics since its discovery, but it has not shown marked success (Scovern & Kilmann, 1980). Psychosurgery, dialysis (Diaz-Buxo et al., 1980) and megavitamin therapies have been tried with increasing frequency in recent years, and as yet there is little significant evidence for success with schizophrenia. There is increasing attention to nutrition therapies, with some modest promise of success. For example, Wurtman, Growden, and Barbeau (1979) found the administration of lecithin and choline increased the effectiveness of other interventions by chemotherapy.

Token economies have been used effectively in bringing the disrupted and institutionalized schizophrenic back to a semblance of normal functioning, and it is in this development of simple and basic behaviors that token economies are most applicable. Milieu therapy, occasionally only a euphemism for sitting around the ward, is optimally a total treatment approach that adds the values of patient-governance and input to the concepts of group process and the "moral therapy" of the nineteenth century. Milieu therapy should also include an available combination of new and effective treatment techniques directed toward the overall improvement of schizophrenia. In this regard, occupational, activity, and art therapies can be useful adjuncts. Developing adequate vocational skills is important, and these skills should not be for obsolescent vocations, as is often the case in prison and mental hospital programs. Cognitive retraining, and family and group therapy as the person moves back into the home system, are also important (Curran et al., 1982; Bagarrozzi et al., 1982).

Ellsworth et al. (1979) thoroughly examined the issues in milieu therapy and advised that the milieu is much more effective when there is a mixture of both chronic and acute patients. They noted a cluster of specific factors that facilitate the positive effects of milieu therapy, notably the availability of a separate television room, updated magazines and reading material, music at meals, stalls separating the toilets, and pleasant pictures on the walls. This may only be a reflection of the Hawthorne effect (wherein changes per se, rather than necessarily positive changes, act to produce a positive effect), as such changes at least implicitly communicate caring. Whatever the reason, these changes promote a positive effect.

## Undifferentiated Schizophrenia (295.9x)

This category is marked by prominent schizophrenic symptoms; however, there are symptoms from various subtypes, or for some reason the criteria for the other categories are not fulfilled. This category fits most clearly the above comments, testing indicators, and treatment suggestions for the overall category of schizophrenia.

## Disorganized Schizophrenia (295.1x)

Disorganized Schizophrenia was termed Hebephrenia in earlier DSM classification systems. The diagnosis of disorganized schizophrenic denotes an individual who shows incoherent or disoriented speech and remarkably inappropriate affect, often in the form of random giggling, flat affect, or incongruous affect. Delusions or hallucinations do not show the structure or pattern common to other schizophrenic disorders. Other elements commonly associated with disorganized schizophrenia include odd facial grimaces, extreme social withdrawal, and very peculiar mannerisms. As would be expected from the preceding description, social functioning is severely disrupted.

Overall, disorganized schizophrenia is characterized by very poor premorbid adjustment, slow onset (usually starting in adolescence or early adulthood), and chronicity of adjustment. These individuals are likely to develop more chronic and apathetic patterns with time, and the likelihood of significant long-term remission is quite low.

### DSM-III

To obtain a formal DSM-III diagnosis of disorganized schizophrenia, the individual must first meet the criteria noted for schizophrenia. In addition, they must specifically show some incoherence in speech, accompanied by flat, silly, or very inappropriate affect, and unaccompanied by systematic delusions.

*MMPI*

Gynther et al. (1973) note that the 8-9/9-8 profile is commonly associated
with the behaviors typical of disorganized schizophrenia. This is particularly true if the affect is silly or inappropriate. When it is flat, scale 9 tends
to be lower, and scales 7 and 2 are likely to be higher. In actual practice,
these individuals are often so severely disturbed in functioning that they
cannot adequately complete the MMPI, at least to the degree where it is
suitable for scoring. The reader is referred to the section on malingering,
since some of that material relates to the patterns to be expected.

*16 PF*

The same problems in adequately scoring the MMPI also hold true for the
16 PF. In those individuals who are able to perform the task adequately,
their 16 PF profile is likely to fit the overall schizophrenic pattern mentioned
earlier, with only a few minor changes. Scale C is likely to be lower in disorganized schizophrenics than in others, as are scales $Q_3$ and N. They also
tend to be higher on scale A and lower on scale L, which reflects their
willingness to interact interpersonally as expressed through fantasy, but
their inability to actuate this interaction in reality.

*Other Test Response Patterns*

While the overall schizophrenic pattern is most likely to be reflected on the
WAIS-R, this test emphasizes the very odd response patterns to an even
greater degree. Proverbs are especially peculiar, and the disorganized
schizophrenic is probably not able to provide even the distorted rationale
that paranoid schizophrenics may volunteer if they feel comfortable enough
with the tester. If the affect of the disorganized schizophrenic is silly or incongruous, there is usually an extreme scatter in the quality of responses,
and this will affect the subtest patterns and the within test scoring. They
tend to do more poorly on block design, digit symbol, and object assembly
than do other schizophrenic clients.

On the Rorschach, form level is very low, and although there are occasional M responses, these are likely to be of poor quality and reflective of
disrupted ideation.

*Treatment Options*

The particularly low level of functioning of the disorganized schizophrenic
warrants the use of most of the techniques noted previously in the treatment
option section of the category of schizophrenic disorders (Curran et al.,
1982). Chemotherapy is consistently required, and token economies are

particularly useful. Until disorganized schizophrenics can develop the basic appropriate behaviors of even the most minimally normal individual, many of the other therapy techniques, such as psychotherapy, group therapy, and occupational therapy, are virtually impossible. Since disorganized schizophrenics are likely to have a markedly poor premorbid adjustment, an emphasis on vocational training is important if they are to make any ultimate transition to normal living. Thus, rigorous training in basic social skills, first via the token economy and then later through a total milieu approach, is necessary.

In choosing a specific therapist for an extremely disturbed client, the clinician might recall the classic differentiation between A and B therapists, first studied by Whitehorn and Betz (Goldstein & Stein, 1976). They found that A therapists were significantly more successful with the extremely disturbed individual. These therapists are characterized as noncoercive problem solvers; they are able to persuade while at the same time communicating a sense of acceptance of and empathy with the schizophrenic's bizarre thoughts and fantasies.

### Catatonic Schizophrenia (295.2x)

Severe psychomotor disturbance is the essential feature of catatonic schizophrenia. The first of the two major subdivisions is that of Stuporous Catatonia, in which a movement is severely reduced, and catatonic stupor, rigidity, or posturing is evident. Some may even show "waxy flexibility," a condition in which the body is passively receptive to posture control. It is possible to manipulate such individuals physically just as one would move a store manikin, and they can remain in the manipulated position for extremely long periods of time.

The Agitated Catatonic, or Excited type, is marked by uncontrollable verbal and motor behavior. These are apparently purposeless motor behaviors and are not necessarily influenced by external stimuli. Individuals in this phase can be quite dangerous and may break into frenzied violence in which they hurt or kill themselves or others. This is not an outgrowth of personal hostility, but rather a response to other persons as objects in their way. Before the use of psychomotor control drugs, agitated catatonics would sometimes drive themselves to the point at which they would die from severe exhaustion and fatigue.

Two different courses typically are observed in catatonic schizophrenia. The chronic form of this disorder is primarily manifest in the stuporous types, and the progression in the disorder is slow and steady. The prognosis for remission is low, and the person may eventually develop into an undifferentiated schizophrenic pattern.

In the periodic type, an abrupt onset is usually followed by alternating periods of agitated and stuporous catatonia. Remission is more likely, though there may be recurrences. They are particularly dangerous at the point of the shift from stupor to agitation, primarily because ward personnel have few cues as to when the shift will occur.

## DSM-III

In addition to meeting the standard criteria for schizophrenia, a diagnosis of catatonic schizophrenia requires that at some time during the active phase of the illness the symptom picture is dominated by a catatonic pattern that includes catatonic negativity or excitement, catatonic rigidity or posturing, or catatonic stupor. Mutism is also common in this disorder. It is interesting that although the catatonic subtype was once considered to be one of the most common schizophrenic patterns, it is now relatively rare in Europe and North America, according to DSM-III.

## MMPI

The 2–7–8 pattern, with 2 most likely to predominate, is often reflective of the catatonic who is confused and yet oriented toward stuporous catatonia (Johnson et al., 1980). Agitated catatonics are more likely to show an 8–9 pattern. If this agitation has been transferred intellectually into hostility, an elevation on scale 4 is more likely, and concomitantly scale 6 is usually elevated. The 0 scale is high, reflecting significant discomfort with and withdrawal from interpersonal relationships.

## 16 PF

This pattern is similar to the prototypical pattern for schizophrenia, though it will differ on certain scales depending on whether the person tends toward stupor or agitation. This will be reflected particularly in scales F, $Q_4$, and, to a degree, $Q_3$ and E. Since this pattern may border on the hostility and social isolation of the paranoid, the L scale is likely to be affected more so than for other schizophrenics, and, to a degree, this is also evident in a higher $Q_2$ score.

## Treatment Options

Agitated catatonic schizophrenics may force a coercive control of their behavior, so chemotherapy, the "modern straitjacket," is often necessary to bring a semblance of order into their world. Token economies are also useful for ameliorating the extremes of either agitated or stuporous catatonia. The possibility of an associated manic component in the agitated catatonic must not be overlooked, and for that reason a trial period of lithium therapy can be employed.

The stuporous catatonic is not unlike the severe depressive on several continuums, so the reader might consult some of the techniques useful for moving a person out of a depressive episode (Lewinsohn & Hoberman, 1982; Beck, 1976). Direct Therapy, which can be seen as a psychoanalytic analogue to Implosive Therapy, is useful primarily with paranoid and catatonic schizophrenics (Karon, 1976; Rosen, 1953). Through a prolonged verbal assault on the person's inner fantasies and fears, the client is goaded into at least a retaliatory response. Once this occurs, the therapist can move into more supportive and interactive roles.

### Residual Schizophrenic Disorder (295.6x)

This diagnosis is applied to the individual who has already been labeled schizophrenic under the above criteria, but in whom the disorder has lessened to the point that there are no longer any prominent psychotic symptoms. It is similar to the conceptual label *in partial remission* that is applied in the same situation to the affective disorders.

DSM-III requirements for the diagnosis of Residual Schizophrenic Disorder are a previously diagnosed schizophrenic episode with symptomatology that no longer includes *prominent* psychotic symptoms. However, signs suggestive of schizophrenia remain, such as difficulties in social behavior or interpersonal communications, odd or peculiar mannerisms, or inappropriate or flat affect. Here, DSM-III has difficulty with the goal of making a diagnosis operational. A judgment as to whether symptoms are still prominent is subjective, especially in view of the potency of certain chemotherapeutic agents to mask or suppress a wide variety of behavioral responses. Nonetheless, the category is likely to be used often since it is potentially applicable to many individuals.

Whether or not this category will be too easily applied is a matter for concern. This is especially true in light of the results of Rosenhan (1973), who established how easily a similar diagnosis was applied without adequate scrutiny when people were released from a hospital with a prior psychiatric diagnosis.

### MMPI

Since the category is residual schizophrenia, it could be debated how much psychopathology is likely to be evident in the MMPI profile. It is reasonable for the clinician to expect that in most cases the general profile of schizophrenia will be evident, but without the extremes of response. For example, a significant elevation on scale 8 would still be likely, but it should be less than in a person with active schizophrenia. Similarly, an elevation on scale F is reasonable, though on occasion this may be an individual who is trying to avoid remembrance of the schizophrenic episode and who becomes very defensive in that regard. As a result, scale K would be high. When this happens, the person is also likely to be defensive about any kind of intrapsychic exploration.

It is typical to expect a relatively low 9 score in most residual schizophrenics, particularly since many of them are still on medication to suppress behavior. Other changes will be dependent on the specific type of schizophrenia, as well as on the premorbid personality, which is likely to come to the fore as the schizophrenic symptoms are suppressed.

## 16 PF

Much the same suppression of extreme scales would be expected on the 16 PF. $Q_4$, O, C, M, and H should still be on the negative side of the continuum, yet they will be somewhat muted from prior levels. Scale B should be somewhat higher and now more accurately reflective of the person's actual abilities. A higher score on $Q_3$ should reflect the fact that the individuals now have more control in their world. Other scores will be affected by the type of schizophrenia manifested, the premorbid personality, and the feelings of security about present adjustment.

## Treatment Options

Since by definition the symptom picture of residual schizophrenia excludes pervasive and permanent psychotic symptoms, it is questionable whether any values from chemotherapy are, or could be, offset by the physical and psychological risks. It would seem that trial periods without medication should be more common for such persons than they are.

The residual symptoms are usually in the area of social and interpersonal behavior and, as such, require systems that provide adequate feedback to the schizophrenic about these behaviors (Curran et al., 1982). Such groups as Recovery, composed of expatients, can be useful in helping previously hospitalized clients adjust, but there is the risk that mildly bizarre behaviors in the social and vocational world are reinforced, or at least too easily tolerated, without feedback. Hence, it is important to move quickly into group therapy situations in which the predominant ethic is normality and in which feedback without inappropriate behaviors is generated in a supportive and accurate fashion. Similarly, the family can be trained in providing this feedback in a positive manner through family therapy situations (Bagarrozzi et al., 1982).

If attentional problems persist into the residual phase, biofeedback of electroencephalographic (EEG) patterns can be employed to increase those patterns associated with attention, such as decreasing the percentage of alpha waves, the classic indicator of nonattention (Hendrix & Meyer, 1974). Biofeedback of muscle patterns is potentially useful to decrease the motoric side effects of tardive dyskinesia, or even to lower the excitability level of the agitated catatonic, though this latter task would indeed be challenging.

## Schizophreniform Disorder (295.40)

The major substantive difference between the Schizophreniform Disorder and Schizophrenia is duration. If the disorder lasts less than six months but the symptoms are that of schizophrenia, the term *schizophreniform disorder* is appropriate. The diagnosis of schizophrenia requires symptoms for six months or more. So, even though repeated incidents of the schizophreniform disorder may account for a cumulative duration of more than six months, the diagnosis remains the same. If the duration of disorder is less than two weeks, the appropriate diagnosis is Brief Reactive Psychosis.

The major reason for the differential diagnosis is that the schizophreniform disorder shows several characteristics that differ from schizophrenia. There is a better prognosis in the schizophreniform disorder, the individual is far more likely to recover to the premorbid level of functioning, and there is evidence of genetic predisposition in this disorder.

### Diagnostic Consideration

There is a high likelihood that the symptom picture is going to include much emotional upset and turmoil, reflecting the acute variable. This is opposed to some of the schizophrenic patterns, so scores on the MMPI, 16 PF, and other tests are likely to be slightly accentuated. For example, on the MMPI, one is more likely to see higher 8, 7, and F scales. This profile occurs in schizophrenia as well, although not so consistently. On the 16 PF, higher scores on scales O and $Q_4$ and lower scores on H and C are likely to be found more consistently than with schizophrenics.

### Treatment Options

Since the schizophreniform disorder is essentially a schizophrenic adjustment that has not yet lasted for six months, the techniques noted as appropriate for the treatment of schizophrenia are applicable here. This is particularly so for psychological techniques, as every effort should be made to help the client avoid the patient role, and even worse, extended institutionalization. Like Rosen (1953), Hogan (1980) advises the use of an implosive technique for any brief psychotic episodes. This is possible since anxiety is high and has not yet crystallized into bizarre avoidant mechanisms.

## Brief Reactive Psychosis (298.80)

The primary distinguishing feature of this psychotic reaction is its short duration, ranging from several hours up to two weeks. Once it exceeds two weeks, the diagnosis is changed to Schizophreniform Disorder.

This disorder is triggered rather suddenly by an event of extreme stress—the loss of a loved one, a traumatic war experience, or other such stress. Unable to deal with the stress, the individual withdraws into a state of mental confusion, typically characterized by extreme emotional lability, bizarre behaviors, and perceptual distortions, including hallucinations and delusions. Individuals with histrionic, schizotypal, and borderline personality disorders, as well as adolescents and young adults manifesting emotional instability of various sorts, are especially prone to this reaction.

Unlike the schizophreniform disorder and the organic mental disorders that display comparable symptoms, the Brief Psychotic Reaction is sudden in onset and of short duration. Unlike the factitious disorder, which in some respects may be considered a stress reaction, the person with the brief psychotic reaction appears to have little or no voluntary control over his or her symptoms.

### DSM-III

The DSM-III requires slightly different criteria for a diagnosis of brief psychotic reaction as opposed to schizophreniform and schizophrenic disorders. A major difference is the absence of emphasis on duration-related issues, such as work and school impairment. The diagnosis requires evidence of at least one of the following: 1) distorted or incoherent thinking; 2) delusions; 3) hallucinations; or 4) severely disorganized or catatonic behavior. It also requires evidence of some recognizable stressor, a duration of symptomatology of not more than two weeks, and no period of clear increase of psychopathology prior to the stressor.

### Test Response Patterns

The test response patterns are again similar to the schizophrenic disorders and even more so to the exaggerated patterns of the schizophreniform disorder, particularly since acute emotional distress is apparent here. Those accentuations noted in the section on test responses in schizophreniform disorder are applicable here, with some minor exceptions. Those exceptions relate to the probability of lower ego strength and indications of more permanent disorder that are found in those other patterns. Hence, scales 4 and 6 on the MMPI would be even less likely to be elevated, and scale 0 is not as likely to be very different from normal in these individuals as in schizophrenia. On the 16 PF, the C scale is not as likely to be as low, nor is the H scale, as these are reflective of more disturbed ongoing personality functioning.

## Treatment Options

Since this diagnosis is warranted when the person has shown psychotic behavior only for two weeks or less, the techniques appropriate for the treatment of schizophrenia or severe affective disorder (see relevant sections) can be supplemented by the techniques of crisis intervention. Most importantly, every effort should be made to keep clients from withdrawing from their social or vocational world and adopting a patient role. If at all possible, the family should be involved in the treatment, both as a mode of cutting off pathological behaviors and as a means of providing emotional support.

In addition, the brief psychotic disorder is effectively treated with Covert Modeling. In this technique, clients are asked to imagine a whole set of new behaviors and imagine themselves performing these behaviors. With practice, and with contracting for gradually moving aspects of the imagery patterns into their existing world, a positive effect can be generated.

## Atypical Psychosis (298.90)

This category is used to designate those individuals who for some reason do not fit into any of the previous categories. For example, atypical psychosis might refer to individuals with a monosymptomatic somatic delusional system, or a psychosis with such a confusing clinical picture that a specific diagnosis would be wrong.

## Paranoid Schizophrenia (295.3x)

This disorder is discussed here because it is a juxtaposition of concepts from both schizophrenia and the paranoid disorders, the focus of the next section. Paranoid schizophrenia shows the most fragmented thought processes of any of the paranoid disorders, and for that reason is included under schizophrenia. However, at the same time there is a delusional system that is the mark of a paranoid disorder. In order to warrant the DSM-III diagnosis of paranoid schizophrenia, the person has to fulfill the criteria for schizophrenia, and, in addition, present a symptom picture dominated by preoccupation with persecutory or grandiose delusions, delusions of jealousy, or hallucinations with a delusional content.

A number of researchers (Gillis & Blevins, 1978; Haier et al., 1979; Bernheim & Lewine, 1979; Johnson & Quinlan, 1980) have found evidence to establish that paranoid schizophrenia is a somewhat different disorder than other forms of schizophrenia. The paranoid schizophrenic is typically brighter and more socially competent than other schizophrenics, with the first episode typically occurring later in life. They also show less anxiety, relatively less judgment impairment, smaller deficits on most cognitive tests, and are more concerned with erecting boundaries in tasks and in their personal world than are other schizophrenics. There may even be differences in blood chemistry between these groups; however, these data have been contradictory to date.

Though paranoid schizophrenics are typically more adequate socially than other schizophrenics, their reactions are consistently more stilted or intense than are normal responses. This is particularly so if anger and suspicion rather than grandiosity are the focus of the symptom picture. Reasonably appropriate affective responses often exist in paranoid schizophrenia, in contrast to the other schizophrenias.

*MMPI*

Johnson et al. (1980) found that the 8–4 pattern, with high scores on 7, 2, and 6, is characteristic of paranoid schizophrenia. The 8–6/6–8 and the 6–9/9–6 profiles are also typical for paranoid schizophrenics (Gynther et al., 1973), and if the 6 is the predominant scale with 4 also raised, the person should be considered one of the more dangerous paranoid schizophrenics. If the 8 dominates in the profile, then prepsychotic schizoid traits are more likely.

A high F scale is typical, and an F minus K ratio greater than 11 is not necessarily an indication of an invalid profile in a situation with high 6, 8, 9 and 4 scales. If the 7 scale is low, auditory hallucinations are particularly likely to occur. When the individual is more inclined toward grandiose than toward persecutory delusions, an 8–9/9–8 profile is more likely, with the 2 scale being lower than usual. The 1 and 3 scales are often relatively low in the protocols of paranoid schizophrenics, though Gilberstadt and Duker (1965) suggest that the 1–6/6–1 pattern with a 4 scale less than 70 T should be considered a cue to look for further evidence of paranoid schizophrenia.

*16 PF*

The paranoid schizophrenic 16 PF profile is similar to the overall schizophrenic profile, with some significant differences. Paranoid schizophrenics, especially females, are more likely to be high on the L scale, reflecting the jealous paranoid component essential to the disorder. Paranoid Schizophrenics are also more likely to be high on $Q_3$, as anxiety is more controlled by projecting conflict and feelings onto other agents. As a result, the O score is less, the C scale higher, the E scale higher, and the $Q_4$ scale somewhat lower than is found in the usual schizophrenic protocol. Also, because paranoid schizophrenics on the average are more intelligent, scale B is higher.

*Other Test Response Patterns*

On the WAIS-R, paranoid schizophrenics are likely to be higher on the similarities and picture completion subtest, while relatively lower on the digit symbol and picture arrangement subtests. This reflects the unusual interpretations they tend to make, as well as their compulsive traits, which are usually more evident premorbidly. On the comprehension subtest, they are occasionally lower because they tend to make peculiar and overinclusive proverb interpretations. This trait is also found in the Benjamin Proverbs (Johnson, 1966).

This is one instance when the use of more exotic proverbs can be helpful. Paranoid schizophrenics, particularly if they are bright, often understand the common interpretation of common proverbs and will state what it is, even though they themselves may entertain other interpretations. The exotic proverbs can bring out the delusional material more clearly.

On all tests, including the WAIS-R, paranoid schizophrenics show overconcern about the correctness of their responses and will often question the examiner as to what is the correct response. They tend to make deviant replies in response to numerous stimuli and are happy to argue about the meaning of any question presented to them. On the Rorschach, paranoid schizophrenics are again very concerned about the meaning of the test, particularly since the ambiguous stimuli are not easily interpretable. They are more likely to look at the back of the card, and to make excessive Dd responses. They show a fairly high F+ percentage, but not with the quality seen in the other paranoid disorders. If they are more oriented toward the persecutory dimension, a low number of responses is likely unless they can be made at least minimally comfortable in the testing situation.

If responsive, paranoid schizophrenics are likely to show a higher number of M responses and to show a low number of C responses, particularly if there is a degree of integration in their adjustment. Responses are occasionally seen as "coming at" the person, and there are more "mask" responses than usual, as well as percepts of animals or humans being attacked or surrounded. There is an overemphasis on W responses, but often with poorer form than one would expect based on their intelligence level. Content often includes grandiose or cosmic concepts as well as responses that define boundaries, such as "edge" or "border" responses (Johnson & Quinlan, 1980).

On the TAT, grandiose and pretentious stories are likely, with the person often being too negativistic to cooperate in pinning down details of the story. They are likely to use a story as a forum for making philosophical comments or moralizing about situations. Alternatively, if they feel threatened, they may refuse even to tell a story, or will give very short and concrete descriptions of the pictures.

## Treatment Options

Several of the neuroleptic drugs have been used with the severe paranoid disorders. Although no single drug has been consistently effective, there is some evidence that chlorpromazine, haloperidol, and a trifluoperazine-amitriptyline combination may have some benefit when used as an adjunct to other treatment techniques in severe paranoid disturbance.

The significant level of disturbance and more bizarre quality of the paranoid schizophrenic, as contrasted to that of the other paranoid disorders, may warrant more intrusive methods. ECT has been used with some paranoid schizophrenics in an apparent attempt to disrupt the consistency of the belief system. However, ECT contains all the risks of any intrusive procedure, which is so important here since a fear of being intruded on in any number of dimensions is central to the paranoid disorders. In addition, there is the probability of short- and long-term memory loss, which could easily increase the sense of vulnerability so critical to many paranoids (Squire et al., 1981).

Chemotherapy can lessen the anxiety often generic to the paranoid delusional system. Again, in addition to side effects per se, there are the risks of apparent intrusiveness, plus increased delusions in response to any side effects, even those that have little long-term danger.

In the more bizarre paranoid disorders, the therapist may have to crash through the defenses erected by the paranoid system rather than waiting for trust to develop in a series of psychotherapy contacts. Direct Analysis (Karon, 1976; Rosen, 1953) has been useful in this regard. Interpretations are forced on the paranoid individual, made necessary by their massive avoidance procedures. These interpretations usually center on what are thought to be major inner conflicts, notably in the areas of aggression, sexuality, and inadequacy. Once the person is moved into a more normal mode of functioning through any technique, approaches should then emphasize the development of trust, along with empathy for the person's distorted beliefs. The reader is referred to the treatment techniques discussed in the next section on the paranoid disorders.

## The Paranoid Disorders

The paranoid disorders are psychotic conditions in which the symptom picture is dominated by persistent persecutory delusions or delusions of jealousy. There are no significant hallucinations, and the disorder lasts at least one week. The symptoms are not primarily attributable to a schizophrenic, affective, or organic mental disorder, or any combination of the three. Unlike paranoid schizophrenia, there is not much fragmentation of thoughts in the delusions. Also, there is seldom as severe an impairment in daily functioning as there is in paranoid schizophrenia. Paranoid schizophrenics typically have more than one delusional system, but it is not uncommon in the paranoid disorder that there is only a single focus in the delusions.

The paranoid disorders can be oriented on a continuum based on the degree of integration in the delusions, with paranoid schizophrenia being the most fragmented and paranoia the least. The paranoid personality disorder can be seen as an extension of this continuum in that there is no true delusional system at all. I will also discuss the relatively rare disorder of shared paranoid disorder, known traditionally as folie à deux. The traditional term, *paranoid state*, is no longer used.

The paranoid disorders seldom show disruption in occupational functioning or intellectual activities, but they do show disruption in marital and interpersonal functioning. These are relatively rare disorders, and since these individuals are usually coerced into treatment, they are not always cooperative in a diagnostic situation. For that reason, the reader should consult the section on malingering. Since anger is often a factor in the personality makeup and on occasion can be so extreme that there is danger to others, the reader is also advised to consult the subsection of this book on aggression potential.

### MMPI

While one would expect scale 6 to be elevated in this disorder, this is not always the case. Paranoids with good defenses may not want to reveal their delusions and as a result may score rather low on scale 6, with some instances being inordinately low, even relative to normal scores. It must also be remembered that blacks tend to score higher on scale 6 throughout the range of normal and paranoid patterns, and this has to be considered in any diagnostic judgment. Overall, paranoids are likely to skip a number of the questions and often express irritation at being forced to make a binary true-false decision.

Unlike persons with other psychiatric disorders, paranoids will show a high K score and a relatively low F score and, consistent with that, a lower score on scale 4 than would be expected. The more disturbed the individual is (the more toward the paranoid schizophrenic end of the continuum), the more likely the "paranoid trough" will occur, consisting of high scores on scales 6 and 8, with a relatively lower score on scale 7. Since denial and projection are common features of the paranoid disorders, reasonably high scores on scale 3 can be expected.

## 16 PF

It was originally thought that paranoids would score high on the L scale, but this is not always so, which again reflects the situation where the client is guarded in revealing the content of his or her concerns. Hence, the diagnostician should score for "faking bad" (Winder, O'Dell, & Karson, 1975; Krug, 1980) in order to check for the extremity of this response pattern. On the paranoia end of the continuum, as opposed to the paranoid schizophrenic end, scores on $Q_3$, N, and B are likely to be higher, while I is lower.

### Treatment Options

The concerns of the paranoid about intrusiveness make this set of disorders most difficult to treat. The therapist can crash through the defenses via techniques such as direct analysis, chemotherapy, or even psychosurgery. The consequently disrupted psychological functions then have to reintegrate—not always an easy task. In addition, the iatrogenic effect of coercively intruding on an individual who already has a low threshold for perceiving intrusiveness presents real difficulties in the later development of trust.

To the degree the paranoid individual is more integrated in functioning, intrusive techniques can be avoided and the therapist can focus on developing trust. In that manner, paranoids may gain recourse to another individual, a feeling often absent in them. Therapists must attempt to maintain their integrity and honesty while at the same time empathizing with the paranoid's delusional beliefs. As Barrett (1980) concludes, the critical feat is to gain the trust of an individual who is pervasively untrusting, and at the same time to accept and yet not participate in the paranoid's delusional system.

### Paranoia (297.10)

Paranoia is rarely observed in clinical practice, for several reasons. First, it apparently does not exist as commonly as many other disorders. Second, the higher level of personality integration allows paranoids to avoid seeing a clinician, even when their world is being disrupted. Since they are inclined to isolate themselves under stress, it is very hard even to coerce them into treatment.

It has occasionally been asserted that paranoia, sometimes referred to as a simple delusional disorder, is not a distinct diagnostic category from other possible categories such as schizophrenia or affective disorder. However, Kembler (1980) reviews research in this area and concludes that, indeed, paranoia is separate from either schizophrenia or affective disorder and deserves to be designated as such.

## DSM-III

Paranoia is marked by a highly structured and chronic delusional system, of at least six months duration. If it has occurred for a shorter time, it is usually diagnosed as Acute Paranoid Disorder (298.30). This system focuses on few issues (usually just one), and after the acceptance of the first premise, the logic is reasonable and orderly. To apply a diagnosis of paranoia, the clinician must find that the person meets the overall criteria for paranoid disorders and shows a chronic and highly systematized delusional system accompanied by clear thinking processes and emotional responses that are consistent with the delusional system.

## MMPI

There are less data in the literature on the MMPI responses of paranoids than there are for most other psychopathology groupings. On occasion, a paranoiac will show a spike on scale 6, with most of the other scales relatively low. This is not common, however, as the defenses usually do not allow that kind of disclosure. A moderate elevation on scale 6 along with an elevation on scale 4 is more common, reflecting the paranoid delusions and the hostility and social alienation that typically accompany them. At the same time, this suspiciousness and anger can result in a querulous and complaining attitude if the client has been forced into a diagnostic situation, and hence a higher K scale relative to other psychopathology groups, with a concomitant lower F scale, can be expected. In addition, scale 9 is usually moderately elevated.

## 16 PF

Just as on the MMPI, paranoid individuals may skip many items, and the clinician should examine this closely if someone else is doing the scoring. Scale L may be elevated, though paranoids are often well enough defended so that this is not the case. $Q_3$ is likely to be particularly high, and scales N and $Q_1$ are likely to be low. These scores all reflect the guardedness and the integration around the delusional system that mark a paranoid individual. Paranoids are likely to be lower on scale A than their behavior would suggest, which reflects the inner guardedness not always directly manifest in their initial interpersonal contacts.

Paranoids are likely to be relatively low on $Q_4$, indicating the denial of anxiety, and low on $Q_1$, again indicating a conservative and guarded approach toward the world. They are relatively high on B since paranoia is a coping mechanism more common in brighter individuals. The chronic and unshakeable aspects of the delusions are reflected in higher scores on scales G and E. Scale G points to the persistently moralistic nature of the paranoid's belief systems, and scale E points to the need for dominance that is embedded in the paranoid's coping strategies. The paranoid individual is likely to be relatively low on M, as inner fantasy is antithetical to the use of projection and denial.

*Other Test Response Patterns*

On the WAIS, paranoids are likely to attain high arithmetic and picture completion scores, reflecting their hyperalertness toward the environment. They also do well on similarities and comprehension, in large part because they take a meticulous approach to these tests and are thus likely to gain two-point answers. Their propensity toward abstraction also helps them in the similarities tests.

During the tests, they are likely to be argumentative, critical, and condescending about both the purpose of the test and the actual questions used. They may even object to the examiner's writing down responses, or they may want to examine what has been written. On the Rorschach, they are likely to attain a very high F and F+ percentage, reflecting their constriction, as well as many Dd and space responses. Unless they feel comfortable, they are likely to reject cards that the clinician is reasonably sure they could handle intellectually, and, in general, the record provided is sparse. Although they characteristically have few M and color responses, the more grandiose paranoids do show M responses. Phillips and Smith (1953) suggest that any "eye" or "ear" responses, as well as any looking at the back of the cards, are indicative of a paranoid orientation. There is a concern for the symmetry in the cards, and, as in other tests, there is criticism of the test itself, particularly if the ambiguity of the Rorschach stimuli becomes threatening (Beck, 1951)

*Treatment Options*

Paranoids will typically undergo treatment only when coerced by possible legal sanctions or the threat of the loss of a relationship. They are inclined to be condescending and only make a pretense of interest, at least at first.

Since paranoia is marked by a well-integrated system of personality functioning, albeit based on bizarre premises, intrusive techniques are likely to backfire and further alienate the client from the treatment process. It is hoped that consistent contact in psychotherapy will lead to a development of some minimal trust in the relationship. This trust gives paranoids a much needed feedback resource, a person with whom they might test out the adequacy of their delusional system.

As Barrett (1980) so lucidly points out, the therapist must accept and empathize with the paranoid and yet not lose integrity as a therapist by participating in the delusional system. For example, the therapist may note correlates between his or her own life and the client's, which gives the client a potential new frame of reference as well as a new model for coping with vulnerability and fear. Humor, notably absent in many paranoids, can be modeled, as can other cognitive coping systems.

As paranoids move away from their delusional systems, a variety of cognitive retraining procedures (Meichenbaum, 1977) can be brought into play. The clinician might also consider group therapy, though the transition from individual to group therapy is particularly tricky for the paranoid. If it can be accomplished, an even greater potential for consensual feedback, so lacking for most paranoids, is then available.

### Shared Paranoid Disorder (297.30)

The category Shared Paranoid Disorder has traditionally been termed *folie à deux*, which can be interpreted as "the madness of two." This double insanity involves one person who is originally paranoid in some form, and a receiver who passively incorporates the paranoid beliefs into his or her own system. These receivers are in a close and intimate relationship with the dominant individuals and have a history of being dependent psychologically on this controlling person. When they break away from the relationship, the paranoid belief system dissipates.

### *DSM-III*

The DSM-III states that the essential feature in a shared paranoid disorder is a delusional system that develops as a result of a close relationship with an already paranoid person. Thus, it is clear that the diagnosis is specifically reserved for the secondary individual, the receiver.

Since the paranoid ideation of the receiver is likely to dissipate if the relationship is broken, the paranoid elements are not the dominant focus of the personality. The need for affiliative dependency is a primary factor, usually in conjunction with passive aggressive hostility that is expressed through the channel of the shared paranoid belief system.

## MMPI

The receiver is typically very defensive about the paranoid beliefs, and in one sense wishes to manifest them to gain the approval of the dominant other. Thus, a raised score on scale 6 is likely. Several questions on L tap a willingness to trust others, and as a result the receiver's dependency keeps the L scale from being extremely high.

Interestingly, depression is common here, as are psychopathic components; hence, scales 2 and 4 are likely to be raised. Males who are receivers are higher on scale 5 than other paranoids, whereas females are lower on scale 5. Scale 7 is also likely to be moderately raised, as is scale 8.

## 16 PF

Since these individuals are fairly open about their paranoid beliefs, they score high on L, and the submissiveness is reflected in lower scale E and H scores. They are also, for the same reason, relatively higher on I and N. They are not likely to show as high a $Q_3$ score as other paranoid individuals, as their personality integration derives from the other person rather than from their own personality. They are also not likely to be as bright as other paranoids, hence B should be lower.

## Treatment Options

The sender, the dominant individual in the shared paranoid disorder, often manifests classical paranoia; the reader is referred to the previous section for the modes of treating this pattern. The first issue for the shared paranoid disorder system is to separate the parties, either by hospitalization or by some other means. At this point, the paranoid elements of the receiver are likely to dissipate since they are heavily based on the dependent relationship with the dominant personality. Cognitive retraining procedures and assertive therapy for the dependency are especially appropriate. A group therapy experience can give the person the much needed personality support and at the same time provide access for modeling new and more appropriate belief systems.

# 4

## Affective Disorders

The focus in DSM-III is on two major subcategories, Episode and Chronic Disorder, as in Manic Episode, and Chronic Hypomanic Disorder. The manic episode is marked by a circumscribed period of intense manic behavior, whereas the chronic hypomanic disorder requires evidence of consistent manic behavior for a period of at least two years, and the behavior in this category is not of psychotic proportions. A chronic hypomanic disorder, however, may include periods referred to as manic episodes.

It is important to note that DSM-III does not provide for a diagnosis where mania alone (without some evidence of depression) is found. The authors of DSM-III believe that such a pattern occurs very rarely, if at all. Thus, the diagnosis of whether or not there is a manic episode is useful to determine whether the affective disorder is a bipolar syndrome or depression alone.

Within the depression subcategory of the affective disorder, the same differentiation used with mania is applied, but the formal DSM-III terms are *Major Depression* and *Dysthymic Disorder*. Likewise, the same differentiation is used for the mixed affective disorders, substituting the terms *Bipolar Affective* and *Cyclothymic* to designate the severe and the chronic behavior problem patterns respectively.

### Treatment Options

Treatment of the affective disorders depends on which affect is predominately manifested, mania or depression. When it is mania, the primary treatment of choice has been lithium therapy (Lipton, 1978; NIMH Staff, 1977). If this is not successful, others have used some of the antipsychotic medications, which can at least suppress the behavior. ECT has also been used, but this is only reasonable as a last resort. When the quality of the manic episode shifts toward irritability and suspiciousness, appropriate techniques for the paranoid disorders, noted earlier, can be considered.

A wide variety of treatments have been useful for depression, although depression remains a pervasive problem for our society (Lewinsohn & Hoberman, 1982). Classical treatment wisdom advises the use of chemotherapy and/or ECT. The problems with chemotherapy are the significant side effects, the further disruption of any sense the depressives might have that they can control their own destiny, the fact that they do not work in all cases (although they do in the majority), and delay in action of often up to two weeks.

ECT has been recommended where immediate disruption of the depression response is required, especially when suicide is a possibility. ECT is appropriate for the severe psychotic depressions, though the treater must consider the cost-benefit issues of short- and long-term organic dysfunction as a result of the ECT, and the possible exaggeration of learned helplessness through the use of such a coercive treatment—many theories of depression emphasize learned helplessness as a generic factor.

Several studies, including that of Weeks, Freeman, and Kendell (1980), report no detrimental long-term effects from ECT. However, such studies consistently contain methodological approaches that do not deal with the actual issues involved. In the Weeks, Freeman, and Kendell (1980) study, for example, the number of ECTs received by clients was low compared to the number administered in traditional psychiatric practice, and there was no random assignment of clients to the ECT and non-ECT group. Breggin (1979) provides substantial data to indicate that ECT results in impaired judgment and insight, shallow emotional reactions, confusion, and global disruption of intellectual functioning, these effects being permanent and resulting from the electrical insult to the brain. He also notes that there is still very little informed consent asked for in telling patients about the possible results of ECT.

Existential therapies are useful where the central quality of the depression is apathy rather than psychomotor retardation. Also, the cognitive behavior therapies have been specifically helpful throughout the range of depressive disorders. The reader is referred to the individual sections in this syndrome grouping for further elaboration.

## Manic Episode

Mania has been described since ancient times. Hippocrates accurately noted many of the symptoms but attributed manic behavior to an excess of yellow bile. While depression is a common affective disorder, mania is not and accounts for only about four percent of psychiatric hospital admissions. Its incidence, however, appears to be increasing in the United States. A possible explanation for this increase is that there is now a reasonably effective and straightforward cure for mania, while in the past it was considered very difficult to treat. Clinicians may now be more amenable to putting borderline cases into what is now a category with a better prognosis.

Throughout the literature, three cardinal features of the manic phase have been described: 1) hyperactive motor behavior, 2) labile euphoria and/or irritability, and 3) flight of ideas.

Two important behavioral variables are useful in making a differential diagnosis between severe manic episodes, schizoaffective disorder, and a more emotionally labile form of schizophrenia. First, while all three categories are distractible, schizoaffectives and schizophrenics are primarily distracted by internal thoughts and ruminations, whereas manics are distracted by the external stimuli that often go unnoticed by others. Secondly, schizoaffectives and schizophrenics during an active phase tend to avoid any true relationships with others, whereas the manic is usually profoundly open to contact with other people (NIMH Staff, 1977).

Positron-emission tomography (PET) is a radiological technique that determines patterns of glucose metabolism in the brain. These patterns can be abnormal for both manics and schizophrenics and yet still differ from each other. Schizophrenics, especially schizophrenics of low competence, show decreased glucose metabolism in the frontal cortex; manics in the midst of an attack show increased glucose activity in the right temporal region. There are some drawbacks to this diagnostic technique. First, although a differentiation between a schizophrenic of low competence and an active manic is not usually hard to make, it can be difficult when the behavior patterns are more similar. There is little evidence that PET can make that differentiation with any consistency. PET is also expensive and requires the introduction of a catheter into a blood vessel, a small though clear risk. In addition, a radioactive substance is introduced to the brain, and the long-term risks of such a procedure are not yet known.

## DSM-III

To warrant a diagnosis of manic episode, the DSM-III requires the existence of one or more clear-cut periods of predominantly euphoric and/or irritable mood (not due to an organic cause); in addition the person's behavior must either be severe enough to be hospitalized or continue for at least one week. There must also be evidence that contraindicates schizophrenic symptoms, and at least three of the following symptoms must be present (four symptoms if the mood is irritable rather than euphoric): hyperactivity, pressed speech, flight of ideas, inflated self-esteem, need for less sleep, excessive distractibility, excessive impulsiveness, or indiscreet behavior.

It must again be noted that the DSM-III does not provide for a diagnosis of mania in the absence of depression. Thus, the diagnosis of manic episode is a primary diagnostic question in the eventual decision as to whether a bipolar diagnosis or a diagnosis of depression alone is warranted. The primary diagnosis of manic episode may be further delineated by the qualifiers "in remission" or "psychotic," the latter of which requires the presence of delusions or hallucinations, which may be either mood "congruent" or "incongruent." Severity per se does not warrant the label psychotic; there must be delusions or hallucinations. The auditory hallucination of simply hearing one's name called out is not enough to meet this requirement.

## MMPI

A high 9 scale, along with elevated scores on 8, 6, and usually 4, are predominant in the severe manic episode. Winters et al., (1981) found the 9–6 code type to discriminate manics from schizophrenics effectively. Scales 3 and 0 are usually elevated in manics, and scale 2 is low, except in the depressive phase of Bipolar Disorders (Silver et al., 1981). The 6 scale is particularly related to the irritability factor. Those individuals who are not irritable but are primarily euphoric usually do not score high on the 6 scale or even the 4 scale. Very irritable manics will occasionally have their highest elevations on scales 3 and 4, with lesser elevation on 9, 6, and 8. To the degree that there is an attempt to control tension and anxiety, scale 7 is higher. Severity is related to the F scale—the higher it is, the more likely the individual will manifest a psychotic level of disorder. In moderate level manics, the F scale may be lower with the K scale raised, reflecting a denial of psychopathology.

## 16 PF

Manics score high on scales F and H, and low on N. This results from their high activity levels, combined with a lack of insight about the reactions they engender in others. They also tend to be high on scale A and scale E.

To the degree they are euphoric, manics are a bit higher on A relative to E, and lower on L, whereas they tend to be opposite to the degree they are irritable. Their high level of tense and driven behavior is reflected in a low Q₃ scale, with a tendency to be moderately low on Q₂ and C, while moderately high on O.

## Other Test Response Patterns

The frenetic behavior patterns of the manic should result in higher WAIS-R scores when speed per se is an issue, such as in digit symbol. However, the lack of allowance for feedback through checking of one's own performance results in lower scores on block design, picture arrangement, and object assembly. They may often come quite close to the required response, but in their impatience offer an incomplete solution as the finished solution. If their manic behavior includes continuous talking, they may do well on subtests such as comprehension, vocabulary, and similarities, in which persistence can result in extra points. However, at the same time, if the mania takes the form of impatience, they would likely also score low on these tests. Throughout both the WAIS-R and the Rorschach, they are likely to manifest a desire to move on to a new item or task.

This frenetic behavior should result in a number of poor quality W responses on the Rorschach, with simultaneous notice of details that others may ignore. Response latencies are typically very short. Shafer (1954) asserts that a high number of confabulation responses and/or shading responses, in combination with a high percent of W, C, CF, S, and Dd responses, are indicative of mania, a result generally confirmed by Wagner and Heise (1981).

### Treatment Options

The single most recommended treatment for mania is lithium therapy; it is reported to reverse the manic factor in approximately 75 percent of the cases treated (Lipton, 1978; NIMH Staff, 1977). Hollon and Beck (1978) further demonstrated that combining psychotherapy with lithium therapy is superior to the use of lithium alone.

Lithium salts were originally used, but lithium carbonate is now used because it is less toxic in nature, is chemically convenient, and contains a high percentage of lithium relative to weight. Since lithium is rapidly absorbed by the kidneys, it has to be taken in divided doses to prevent any cyclical physiological response from overwhelming the client. As a result of the need for consistently administered, divided doses, education of the patient is critical. Doses must be taken on schedule, so when a patient indicates a lack of intelligence and/or discipline, mechanisms for controlled administration are necessary.

Since manics may have elaborated some negative behavioral habits in addition to the apparent physiological disorder, behavioral training is advised in addition to the lithium. It is helpful to teach the client to consider plans thoroughly before beginning to actuate them, to follow through with them once the decision is made, and to stay with interpersonal commitments.

### Major Depressive Episode

As with the manic disorders, depressive disorders are divided between Major Depression and the Dysthmic Disorder (or Depressive Neurosis), based again on chronicity and severity. It is estimated in DSM-III that approximately 3 percent of males and 6 percent of females have had a depressive episode sufficiently severe to require hospitalization. An important aspect of the explanation for the twofold incidence of depression in females compared to that in males is the accentuation of behavior prescribed by traditional sex role expectations (Meyer & Salmon, 1983).

Altman and Wittenborn (1980) found that several factors predict depression in women such as low self-esteem, a preoccupation with failure, a sense of helplessness, a pessimistic attitude toward the world, and narcissistic vulnerability. This research was added to by Cofer and Wittenborn (1980) who found, in addition to the factors just mentioned, that a critical mother and a dependency-fostering father were also important in the genesis of depression in females.

## DSM-III

If there is a single major depressive episode, the formal DSM-III diagnosis is Major Depression, single episode (296.2x), whereas the occurrence of more than one is diagnosed Major Depression, recurrent (296.3x). Both require an absence of any manic episodes.

The diagnosis of Major Depressive Episode requires evidence of dysphoric mood, or loss of interest or pleasure in most of one's usual activities for at least two weeks. This reaction cannot be the result of a schizophrenic or organic disorder or simple bereavement such as follows the loss of a loved one. At least four of the following consistently present depressive symptoms are required for the diagnosis: 1) sleep disturbance, 2) agitated or retarded psychomotor ability, 3) loss of weight or appetite, 4) loss of interest in usual activities, 5) loss of energy, 6) guilt or loss of self-esteem, 7) slowed or disrupted thinking, or 8) sleep or death ideation.

A major depressive episode is delineated by the same qualifiers as the manic episode. "In remission" simply requires evidence of a previous episode with the person's being essentially free of depressive symptoms. The psychotic designation requires evidence of either hallucinations or delusions, depressive stupor, or some evidence of significantly disturbed reality testing. The disorder can also be sublabeled as to mood-congruent or mood-incongruent psychotic features. Again, severity per se is not enough to warrant a psychotic diagnosis.

Another secondary label is "with melancholia." This requires evident loss of pleasure or even reactivity to stimuli that have previously been important in this regard, plus at least three symptoms.

## MMPI

Scale 2 is, of course, consistently elevated in chronic depressive disorders. The 2–7/7–2 combination is commonly noted across the depressive spectrum (Lachar, 1974). A concomitant high scale 4 suggests possible passive-aggressive accompaniments to the depression, and it has been noted by several observers that a high scale 4 in depressives correlates best with both hostility and depressive thoughts rather than with psychomotor retardation. The 3–2 and the 2–8 profiles are also indicative of possible depression (Lachar, 1974; Silver et al., 1981). As the 8 rises, the latter profile is more likely to be schizoaffective, and such persons are likely to be agitated and have a specific suicide plan. Johnson et al. (1980) found the 2–8–7 combination to be characteristic of severe depression. Overall, Winters et al. (1981) found these MMPI code types (2–7–8, 2–8, 4–8–2) to discriminate a group of depressives from schizophrenics effectively.

In all of these situations, as scores rise on both F and 8 and scores on scale 9 become lower, the depression is proportionately more severe, there is retarded motor behavior, and the depression is prone to move into the psychotic range. Scale 9 is also an indication of avoidance patterns and correlates with the depression. The clinician occasionally sees a 2–0 profile, which suggests a chronic depression. Also, the profile of a high 1 and relatively low 2 scale, along with verbalizations of depression, suggests a situationally generated depression, possibly even an extended bereavement.

*16 PF*

In the marked and moderate range of the depressive episode, individuals are likely to score relatively high on scales O, $Q_4$, L, M, and I, particularly where there is still a degree of agitation in the depressive response. They also score high on $Q_2$. As the disorder moves toward a psychotic dimension, scores are higher on O, L, M, and lower on C, $Q_3$, and H. They revert to average on $Q_2$ and are now lower on A. Because of their apathy toward the environment, they also score low on B.

*Other Test Response Patterns*

On the WAIS-R, the classic sign of depression has been an overall performance scale score significantly less than the verbal scale score. Depressed clients are likely to fail on WAIS-R items that they should typically be able to answer, simply because they give up on them. Within the performance scale scores, picture completion is usually the highest. Within the verbal scale scores, digit span is expected to be the lowest (Keiser & Lowy, 1980), with arithmetic also being very low, and vocabulary rather high. "I don't know" responses and a general lack of persistence are common.

On the Rorschach, long reaction times to the cards and the rejection of several cards are probable. Concomitant with that, the number of responses is usually less than twenty. The individual is often highly self-critical while responding to the Rorschach, and a high F percent and a high percentage of popular responses are common. FY or MY responses are seen as indicative of depression (Phillips & Smith, 1953) and something like a YF response would in particular suggest depression. There are typically few C and CF responses, a low number of M responses, and a low number of W responses (Wagner & Heise, 1981). Dysphoric content is common, and "cloud" and vista responses occasionally occur.

Stories on the Thematic Apperception Test (TAT) are short and stereotyped and are often only descriptions of the cards rather than an actual story. It is difficult to carry on an inquiry in either the TAT or the Rorschach since the person may give only monosyllabic portrayals of each card.

Severe endogenous depression, which is primarily denoted by motor retardation, depressed mood, lack of reactivity, depressive delusions, and self-reproach (Nelson & Charney, 1981), shows some promise of being reliably diagnosed by the overnight dexamethasone suppression test (DST) (Carroll, 1981).

## Treatment Options

Since the Major Depressive Episode often involves a severe level of depression, possibly including psychotic components, more intrusive techniques are likely to be used. However, the techniques discussed in the next subsection on the Dysthymic Disorder are useful as well.

ECT has often been used for severe depression; it is probably one of the few syndromes for which there is good evidence of its effectiveness (Scovern & Kilmann, 1980). However, that effectiveness must be balanced against the high psychological and physical costs of the technique. Similarly, psychosurgery has been used in which a destructive lesion is placed in areas that control emotional response, such as the limbic system. Mirsky and Orzack (Trotter, 1976) similarly found psychosurgery to be effective for depression, although they paradoxically observed that those clients who reported the greatest improvement also manifested the highest amount of cognitive loss following the psychosurgery.

Since ancient times, human beings have used drugs to alleviate depression, notably alcohol and other self-medications. The two major subcategories of antidepressants used in recent times are the tricyclics and the monoamine oxidase inhibitors (MAO); researchers now hypothesize that the therapeutic effect in both of these drug forms may emanate from a massive antihistamine effect (Kolata, 1979). Both require substantial trial and error adjustment on dosages (titration), and both require from several days to several weeks before any positive effects occur. Since the monoamine oxidase inhibitors have more significant side effects, the tricyclics have been favored in recent years. They are most effective with severe depressions that have a significant endogenous component, but the rate of effectiveness is seldom better than 70 percent (Fabry, 1980). When the tricyclics are administered to someone who actually has a bipolar disorder in a depressive phase, there is a very real danger of stimulating a manic episode.

There is some evidence that a certain small subgroup of major depressives may have a disturbance in rapid eye movement (REM) sleep patterns. This specific pattern is marked by an abnormal temporal distribution of REM sleep, in which there is an inadequate capacity to sustain REM sleep conditions. This same capacity tends to decrease with age in all individuals and may explain why sleep problems are much more common as we age. Vogel and his colleagues (1980) treated this subgroup of depressives by depriving them of REM sleep for short periods of time and found that this significantly decreased their depression. It is interesting that depressed patients who are responsive to this technique were unresponsive to the tricyclic antidepressives, though in a comparison among studies, REM sleep deprivation and drug treatments were equally effective. However, it takes about three weeks for the REM sleep deprivation technique to bring about improvement. When specific brain dysfunction has caused depression, the disease is more likely to be found in the nondominant hemisphere (Tucker, 1981).

Any of the intrusive techniques have a number of risks, which, of course, can be balanced by gains in controlling the depression, and secondarily, in preventing any suicide behaviors. Yet it is most important that they be implemented in an overall treatment that includes a variety of techniques designed to control the depression psychologically and to upgrade the skills needed to prevent future depression (Lewinsohn & Hoberman, 1982). The reader is referred to the next section on the Dysthymic Disorder.

## Dysthymic Disorder (Depressive Neurosis)
## (300.40)

Many of the symptoms characteristic of the depressive episode are noted here. However, although they are not as severe or as common, they are of greater duration. A duration of two years is required for the diagnosis (except for children and adolescents, where the requirement is one year), and periods of dysphoria cannot be separated by periods of normal mood of more than two months. Dysphoria and apathy are commonly noted, though neither severe impairment in social or vocational functioning nor significant suicidal preoccupation is consistently present. Along with the above characteristics, the DSM-III requires that at least three depressive symptoms occur that are new behaviors for that individual.

*MMPI*

Since this personality profile does not show the anxiety, agitation, and possible psychotic components of the major depression, a lower overall profile is expected. For example, scale 9 is not as likely to be low nor is scale 0 likely to be as high as in the depressive episode. Yet, scales F, 2, and 7 are high. If scale 4 is raised, there is reason to look for a passive-aggressive use of the depression (Silver et al., 1981; Fowler, 1981). If somatization is a major factor, scale 1 should be high.

*16 PF*

Similarly, the 16 PF profile is not as extreme as in the depressive episode, though the general outline is the same and is similar to the pattern for the more neurotic aspects of the depressive episode. With that stipulation, scale C is not as likely to be low nor is $Q_4$ likely to be quite as high.

*Other Test Response Patterns*

Several short scales (of approximately twenty questions) have been specifically designed to measure depression and can be helpful in screening procedures. Two of the most commonly used have been the Zung Self-Rating Depression Scale and the Beck Depression Inventory. Both have been found to have adequate validity, though some have commented that the Zung Scale is too age specific for certain groups, since normals under nineteen years of age and over sixty-five years of age unfortunately tend to score in the depressive range (Fabry, 1980).

Performance on other tests will be similar to that of the depressive episode, though again the clinician should temper the interpretation of these patterns with the awareness that this is less severe than major depression, with the symptoms more integrated into the ongoing personality.

*Treatment Options*

Monitoring is an important adjunct to any treatment of depression. Harmon, Nelson, and Hayes (1980) found that self-monitoring of both mood and activity produced decreases in depressed mood, as well as increases in self-reported participation in chosen activities, with slightly better results in this latter area. With regard to their future perspective, depressives should understand that occasional upsurges of anxiety and depression will occur throughout their life and that these should not be construed as indications of a return to pathology. This is an important admonition for all groups with psychopathology. In many cases, as these persons move toward a cure, they develop hope that they will never encounter any experiences similar to their past disorder. Hence, when these naturally emerge in at least a minor form, there is a tendency to drop their coping patterns. Adopting a cognitive set to counteract this phenomenon is most important (Lewinsohn & Hoberman, 1982).

Chemotherapy is often used with the dysthymic disorder, but it is not as appropriate as it is for the more severe depressive episode. Since learned helplessness is often a factor in this disorder, chemotherapy, ECT, or similar treatments can easily exacerbate this component by pointing out in a direct way that patients cannot play a major role in redirecting their life situation. As a result, a package derived from the following psychological treatment methods is recommended.

The clinician can employ contingency management techniques, as they aid the client especially in developing a new self-percept less confounded by helplessness and apathy. It is initially advisable for the therapist to avoid reinforcing any of the client's depressive verbalizations. The clinician can use audiotapes of the sessions to indicate to clients how thoroughly they are inclined toward these verbalizations. This approach can be augmented by a contractual agreement with the client to avoid such verbalizations, and instead to increase the number of positive verbalizations (Meichenbaum, 1977). Such behaviors can be consolidated by using the Premack Principle and, in addition, by training the family and friends of the client to reinforce positive behaviors and verbalizations.

Imagery techniques are also useful. For example, Lazarus (1971) recommends a variation of systematic desensitization that he terms "time projection with routine reinforcement." Clients are first hypnotized, deep relaxation is induced, and then they are asked to imagine that they are in the future and are engaged in what had been previously pleasant activities. The client is then asked to return to the present while still maintaining these positive feelings and images from the future. By continually shifting back and forth, this time-projection strategy aids the depressed person to develop more consistent present images of pleasurable activities; Lazarus indicates that this then generalizes into behavior.

Probably the most important psychological treatment methods of depression are the cognitive-behavioral techniques, derived primarily from Beck (1976). Through discussion and consciousness-raising techniques, clients are taught to view their thoughts more objectively (i.e., to distance themselves from these maladaptive thoughts). Such common depressive thoughts as "I am totally worthless" are suggested as hypotheses rather than facts, a phenomenon rather than a reality. In addition, the client is taught to "decenter." Through feedback, possibly in a group, depressives learn that they are not the focal point of all events, such as a disparaging glance on the street. Implicit in all this is the need for clients to learn to validate any self-made conclusions more objectively, a behavior notably absent in depressives. The belief systems that a person lives by are then examined, since impossible standards are commonly promoted within the self-system. This is not unlike the approaches of George Kelly's (1955) personal construct theory or Albert Ellis's Rational-Emotive Therapy (Ellis, 1973).

Another useful cognitive-behavioral treatment for the Dysthymic Disorder is covert negative reinforcement, since depressed individuals often find it difficult to envision positive behaviors at all and therefore are not particularly responsive to covert positive reinforcement techniques. In covert negative reinforcement with depression, a highly aversive image is developed and is then terminated by the imagination of the performance of the desired behaviors. It is critical that the switchover of images take place as quickly as possible.

Finally, a number of life style modification techniques can be used (Lewinsohn & Hoberman, 1982). Assertive training is appropriate (Sanchez & Lewinsohn, 1980) so that the person does not introject anger and frustration. Within the context of group therapy, the person can contract for a series of graded tasks, all of which are increasingly pleasurable and thus likely to change the overall negative set these individuals carry. Such experiences appear especially therapeutic to the degree that they also increase the client's sense of mastery over events in the world (Klee & Meyer, 1981).

## Bipolar Disorder

The diagnosis of Bipolar Disorder, Manic (296.4x) requires that the individual has in the past shown a depressive episode and is now manifesting or has recently manifested a manic episode (the reader is referred to the criteria in the sections on depressive episode and manic episode).

The converse is required for the diagnosis of Bipolar Disorder, Depressed (296.5x). The diagnosis of Bipolar Disorder, Mixed (296.6x) requires that depression and mania occur in rapid alternation or in combination and that the depressive symptoms that do occur are prominent, lasting for at least a full day. Bipolar Disorder, Mixed replaces the traditional term *Manic-Depressive Psychosis*, as it is usually understood.

The MMPI, 16 PF, and other test data patterns are generally similar to what is expected in single episodes. The reader is referred to the appropriate sections for the behavior pattern manifest at the time. However, it should be noted that depressives tend to be lower on scales K, 2, 6, 7, and 8 than do bipolars (Donnelly et al., 1976). Clients with bipolar affective disorder show larger average cortical evoked potentials than do normals, who in turn are higher than schizophrenics, with this particularly so at high stimulus intensities. It has also been found that the shift from mania to depression is physiologically marked by increases of blood levels of phosphorous and calcium. A similar phenomenon has been observed when certain withdrawn depressives move toward more agitated behavior.

## Treatment Options

The treatment of the bipolar disorder is directed in large measure toward the dominant affective mode at the time. Lithium therapy is used to alleviate severe mania and has occasionally been effective with the depressive component as well, though the standard chemotherapy for the depressive component is that noted in the previous section on the depressive episode. It should again be noted that administration of the tricyclic antidepressants to an individual with bipolar disorder who is in a depressive phase may induce a manic episode. As the person moves toward a better level of functioning, the psychological treatment techniques noted in the sections on manic episode and dysthymic disorder become the primary mode.

## Cyclothymic Disorder (301.13)

The Cyclothymic Disorder is the DSM-III term for the traditional term of *cyclothymic personality*. As with the dysthymic disorder, this diagnosis requires a disorder duration of two years, and the fulfillment of the symptom patterns for both the manic and depressive syndromes, alternately. The reader is referred to previous sections for those diagnoses as well as the concomitant patterns expected on the MMPI, 16 PF, and other tests. This disorder has traditionally been thought to be very rare, but recent evidence suggests that it is at least moderately common.

## Treatment Options

In most instances, the manic phase of the cyclothymic disorder is not severe enough to warrant significant intervention. Rather, it is more like a relief stage, and at worst requires the psychological techniques noted in treatment of the manic episode. The depressive components are appropriately treated by the techniques detailed in the section on the dysthymic disorder. The clinician should be careful to watch for the possible emergence of a classic bipolar disorder, and if the client shows any increasing pathology, lithium might be considered. Some clinicians have found the use of a diary helpful with the cyclothymic disorder. As clients keep a diary, they become more attuned to those factors in their world that are likely to set off the pattern.

## Atypical Affective Disorders

As usual, the DSM-III has provided categories labeled Atypical Bipolar Disorder and Atypical Depression. These are simply residual categories in which there is clear evidence of a general pattern, though it does not exactly fit the specific diagnostic requirements. For example, when periods of normal mood have lasted for more than two months in a significant dysthymic disorder, the diagnosis of atypical depression is appropriate even though the other criteria for dysthymic disorder are met.

## Schizoaffective Disorder (295.70)

The Schizoaffective Disorder has traditionally been included as a subgroup under schizophrenia. In the DSM-III, however, it is being listed as a separate disorder, probably because of the evidence that this type of disorder has several characteristics different from those disorders that remain under the schizophrenic rubric. Also, clinicians simply find this term to be useful. Schizoaffective disorder is more likely to have an acute onset and has a better prognosis for avoiding long hospitalization and recovering to a premorbid level of functioning. In addition, it has been noticed that blood relatives of persons with the schizoaffective disorder do not have a significantly higher proportion of the same disorder than do normals, a finding different from that of schizophrenia.

### DSM-III

The essential feature of this disorder is a combination of schizophrenic and affective symptoms. The affective component (either significant depression, mania, or an alternating mixture of the two) occurs before or concomitant with the onset of the schizophrenic symptomatology. Evidence for both clear schizophrenic and affective symptomatology must be present, and there is no requirement of a duration of six months to diagnose this disorder. This is essentially a residual category, as the clinician should have ruled out the major depressive disorders, schizophrenia, or the schizophreniform disorder.

### MMPI

Because of the confluence of two pathological trends, the profiles in schizoaffective disorders are likely to appear quite disturbed. Johnson et al. (1980)

find that a spike 8, with high scores on scales 2 and 7, is characteristic of the schizoaffective disorder, particularly when depression predominates. Another common pattern for the depressive schizoaffective is the 8-2 profile (Kelley & King, 1979). It is probable that these individuals have considered suicide and even have a specific suicide plan. The possibility of acting out this plan is often related to the 9 scale. As the score moves up, it indicates an increase in the amount of available energy and makes actualization of the plan more likely.

If the affective component is more in the manic direction, a common profile is an 8-9/9-8, with a higher score on scale 4 as compared to the schizoaffective, depressed type. In both types, scale 7 is elevated, as is the F scale (though both are more elevated in the depressed type).

### 16 PF

The 16 PF resembles the overall schizophrenic profile, but with the following qualifications. In the manic type of schizoaffective disorder, a higher A, F and H, and a lower N and $Q_4$ are more probable than in schizophrenia or schizoaffective, depressed type. Conversely, the schizoaffective, depressed type is inclined to show the reverse profile, having a fairly low F score, as well as lower scores on A, B (reflecting less attention to the task), E, H, and M. They also manifest a lower C and a higher O score, indicating more blatant distress and emotional upset.

On the other tests, the typical patterns obtained by the schizophrenic are likely, with the added content and style factors specific to either the manic or depressed syndrome.

### Treatment Options

As with the bipolar disorder, the treatment in large part depends on the affective flavor of the disorder. Since it is usually depression, the reader is referred to the sections on the depressive episode and the dysthymic disorder. In those rarer cases that have a manic component, the reader is referred to the section on the manic episode. The section on the schizophrenic disorders is also relevant here.

# 5

## Anxiety Disorders

This grouping of disorders is a subgroup of the disorders traditionally termed *neurosis*. This term is ambivalently used in DSM-III as a major category term since it is felt that it has some inappropriate connotations and that it stems from a narrow conception of the role of anxiety and conflict in disorder. The anxiety disorders in DSM-III do not encompass traditionally included categories such as conversion reactions or dissociative reactions, which are now dealt with in separate sections. The DSM-III category of anxiety disorders is meant to include only those in which anxiety is still present or at least operative. Some clinicians would argue that this is not necessarily so for the Obsessive-Compulsive Disorder, but it is included here nevertheless.

This section is first divided into the Phobic Disorders, which are further subdivided into Agoraphobia, Social Phobia, and Simple Phobia. The other primary categories are the Panic Disorder, Obsessive Compulsive Disorder, Generalized Anxiety Disorder, Atypical Anxiety Disorder, and Post-Traumatic Stress Disorder, which are referred to as the Anxiety States.

### MMPI

The classic general signs for neurosis on the MMPI are elevations on scales 1, 2, 3, and 7. In fact, scales 1, 2, and 3 are often referred to as the "neurotic triad." The neurotic disorders, of which the anxiety disorders are a traditional subclassification, have an MMPI that slopes from left to right, whereas the psychoses are expected to slope from right to left. The character disorders tend to peak more in the middle, though the word *tend* in this latter axiom is emphasized.

107

The F scale is high in the neurotic profile. If it is very high and scales L and K are 50 T or less, the clinician should look for 1) a blatant cry for help that could point to a variety of disorders; 2) faking bad; or 3) in a hospitalized psychiatric population, the diagnosis of confused psychotic (Gynther et al., 1973). As a result of the relative openness about anxiety, anxiety disorder profiles show some elevation on most of the scales, with the exception of 9, 5, and 6.

## 16 PF

The general profile for the anxiety disorders has higher scores on O, $Q_4$, L, M, and I, with a moderately high score on $Q_2$. In addition, one would expect scores to be lower on C, $Q_3$, F, H, E, and G.

Karson & O'Dell (1956, p. 83) list the individual scales in their order of importance in contributing to the second order anxiety scale derived from the 16 PF. They list these as $Q_4$, O, C, L, and $Q_3$. If very high, $Q_4$ can additionally be interpreted as a cry for help, as it shows an r of .75 with scale 7 of the MMPI. $Q_3$ is an index of emotional lability, that is, a reflection of the ability to bind up anxiety. Scales M and I pick up an ongoing vulnerability or sensitivity to stress.

The anxiety disorders, especially in males (Krug, 1980), are relatively higher on scale M than in those who suffer psychosomatic disorders. It is hypothesized that in neurotics with anxiety the greater inclination to fantasy makes them more prone to anxiety reactions, whereas psychosomatics have a more practical and concrete cognitive process, thus being more likely to use denial (Silverman, 1976) and less prone to use fantasy behavior to cope with distress.

## Other Test Response Patterns

Impaired concentration from high anxiety would likely result in lower scores on arithmetic and digit span on the WAIS-R. In addition, as a result of anxiety and its accompanying inefficiency, lowered performance scores in general could be expected. In particular, awkwardness and a lack of orderly checking could lead to mistakes on object assembly and block design that one would not otherwise be expected to make. This anxiety may also result in surprising misses or errors in the early part of the information subscale.

A classic sign on the Rorschach of high anxiety and the inability to cope with it is extreme (both ways) reaction time to the cards. Color shock, or the inability to integrate and respond appropriately to the color cards, is also commonly noted as a sign of anxiety or neurosis (Phillips & Smith, 1953; Beck, 1951). The novelist Joseph Heller has described the phenomenon of color shock well:

> Some look like Van Dykes, and these I'm tempted to tug. Others have sideburns and shock me a moment like card number eight on the Rorschach test again. I was struck speechless when that damned color shock card appeared. I was stupefied.
>
> J. Heller
> *Something Happened*, p. 435.

Poorly integrated W responses and a form level below the acceptable range of 65 percent to 80 percent are also a common result of the high anxiety. Shafer (1954) states that several P or C responses, along with a moderately low F percentage, and oral threat content responses, such as wolves, are indicative of potential for anxiety moving into panic.

## Treatment Options

A wide variety of techniques are used in the treatment of the anxiety disorders. One option is the development and maintenance of a relaxation response as an antidote. Other possible options are systematic desensitization, implosive therapy techniques, and covert conditioning techniques (Emmelkamp, 1982). They aid in the avoidance of anxiety-generating situations and facilitate the ultimately critical variable in the treatment of the anxiety disorders—helping clients eventually to confront the sources of their fear (Greist et al., 1980). To the degree that the client is highly labile and reactive physiologically, the anxiety-lessening techniques such as relaxation training are useful, whereas if that is not as strong a factor, an emphasis on skills training may be more productive (Ost et al., 1981). Treatment requirements for the obsessive-compulsive disorder differ markedly from those of the generalized anxiety disorder or even the phobias, and the reader is referred to the specific sections for treatment suggestions.

## Phobic Disorders

The phobic disorders are patterns in which chronic avoidance behavior is combined with an irrational fear of a particular object or situation. Many people experience nondisabling phobias of one sort or another. For example, many people avoid extreme heights or strongly fear touching snakes. Since either of these fears can easily be controlled by environmental avoidance patterns, they are not usually disabling. A classic phobia is disproportionate, disturbing, and disabling, and is marked by responses to a discrete stimulus. People with phobias may assert that their avoidance is reasonable because of the overpowering anxiety they feel, but they do not usually claim that this anxiety is rationally justified.

## Agoraphobia

Agoraphobia is conceptualized by the DSM-III authors as the most common phobic disorder. However, strong support could be mustered to assert that simple phobias are far more common, though possibly not of as great a significance in terms of personal cost.

Agoraphobia is a phobic fear of being alone, or being in the midst of people with no help available. Typically, the development of agoraphobia is preceded by a stage of panic attacks, and the diagnosis is qualified as either Agoraphobia "with panic attacks" (300.21) or "without panic attacks" (300.22). The diagnosis of agoraphobia takes precedence over that of panic disorder.

Agoraphobics develop a strong sense of helplessness and anticipate that panic will set in at any time, leaving them without any means of control or defense. Their ultimate fear seems to be that they will be left alone, with the possibility that panic will occur and overwhelm them. As Albert Ellis (1979) states, such individuals have a very low threshold for Discomfort Anxiety.

Even though agoraphobia is an important concept in DSM-III, it was not even listed in DSM-I or II. It could be hypothesized that the rapid rise in the occurrence of this disorder reflects the increasing interpersonal alienation and heightened requirements for competence in vocational and social functioning that mark our society. In addition, other factors such as the rising divorce rate and alleged breakdown of the family unit, along with our increased urbanization and high level of social and geographic mobility make it easier than ever to experience being alone in facing change and stress.

Often, such pressures first coalesce in adolescence, though they may have been preceded by attacks of separation anxiety and occurrences of school phobia in childhood. Social or vocational role changes make one particularly vulnerable to this disorder. Hence, women in a traditional housewife role who are going through menopause at the same time their children are leaving home are likely to be vulnerable to this pattern. Agoraphobics are prone to become housebound and attempt to break up their anxiety through manipulative behaviors toward significant others. Since these defenses are seldom effective, such individuals may with time become bothersome and tedious to those around them, and consequent depression will then complicate the agoraphobia. Alcohol and other drugs may be used to dilute the anxiety, leading to an overlay pattern of addiction. It has been asserted that approximately 5 percent of the population has at some time suffered from agoraphobia, and the disorder is common in both psychiatric and cardiac practices.

*DSM-III*

Agoraphobia is specifically defined as the avoidance of any situation, particularly being alone, where people fear they could not be helped or get in touch with help in the event of sudden incapacitation. These fears pervade their world and, as a result, they avoid being alone in open spaces, or avoid public places where help is possibly not available if there is an emergency. As a result, their normal behavior patterns and experiences are disrupted.

*MMPI*

Agoraphobics, whether or not they experience panic attacks, should score relatively close to the modal pattern for anxiety disorders presented in the previous subsection. Even when the diagnosis "with panic attacks" is warranted, it is not likely that the person would be experiencing the panic at the time of testing. It would, however, suggest that the individual is not adept at binding up anxiety, so there will be some scores on the MMPI and 16 PF that will differ. The 2–7/7–2 profile with scales 1 and 3 close to average is a likely one here, reflecting the high level of anxiety, the rather vague targets for the anxiety, and the absence in most cases of accompanying extensive somatic concerns or conversion reactions. Scales 4 and 9 would also be expected to be relatively low, and scale 8 would depend partially on how well the anxiety is integrated. The 0 scale is likely to be raised, even above the other neurotic disorders. The uncommon 7–0/0–7 profile, which reflects anxiety and inadequacy, might well suggest an agoraphobic orientation.

*16 PF*

Scales such as $Q_4$ and O will be high and somewhat dependent on whether or not this is with or without panic attacks, with the latter suggesting higher scores. Slightly higher scores on scales I and L might also occur, reflecting the isolation of the individual who has developed agoraphobia. Similarly, scale A would probably be low in this disorder, whereas it is not commonly as low in the anxiety disorders.

*Treatment Options*

Chambless and Goldstein (1980) point out that agoraphobia is particularly difficult to treat, with only about 20 percent of cases receiving significant and lasting relief. They state that the agoraphobic very much needs to feel accepted, and the initial fostering of dependency is encouraged here more than with most other types of clients. As clients are eventually weaned off the dependency, assertive training is useful to help them deal with their personality dependency and general lack of self-sufficient behaviors. The repressed feelings, often directed toward significant others, can be elicited by having the client write a diary with a focus on those feelings, and then catharsis techniques can be more systematically employed.

The tricyclic antidepressants, which appear to block the re-uptake of serotonin and norepinephrine by the presynaptic neurons and thus to increase their concentration at the synaptic cleft, can help eliminate the panic aspects of agoraphobia with panic attacks, but they do little for the agoraphobia.

The panic experience, so common in agoraphobia, is probably most effectively dealt with by Implosive Therapy, or flooding. Implosive therapy can be presented either in imagination or in vivo, depending on the particular case, and it is more successful if the implosion is carried out when anxiety is not muted by tranquilizing drugs. The stimuli can be presented either live or via audiotape, though therapist presence facilitates the effects in the latter condition (Sherry & Levine, 1980). The client's ability to develop vivid imagery is a positive factor.

Even clients who are able to approach and handle the feared object after implosive therapy may still retain a basic fear sensation (Mineka, 1979). This feeling typically dissipates with time, though it can initially be disconcerting to the client and even to the therapist. As the fears of the agoraphobic become more specific, usually as the panic recedes, techniques such as relaxation training, systematic desensitization (SDT), and other behavioral control methods offer the highest chance of a successful intervention (McPherson et al., 1980). In certain situations, use of neighborhood self-help groups to reduce agoraphobia may be considered (Sinnot et al., 1981). They have often proved to be of help.

## Overanxious and Separation Anxiety Disorder

If the person is under eighteen and is manifesting anxiety similar to agoraphobia, the appropriate diagnosis could be either the Overanxious Disorder (313.00) or the Separation Anxiety Disorder (309.21). These two disorders are typically seen in early adolescence or childhood rather than late adolescence. They predict later disorders such as agoraphobia, the phobic disorders in general, the generalized anxiety disorder, or other similar patterns.

The diagnosis of overanxious disorder requires symptomatology for at least six months and evidence of at least four of the following: unrealistic worry about the future or past, or about ability in such areas as academic subjects, athletics, and social interactions; tension and inability to relax; proclivity toward self-consciousness and embarrassment; an excessive need for reassurance; or somatic complaints without a physical basis.

A diagnosis of separation anxiety disorder requires evidence of disturbance for only two weeks and at least three of the following symptoms: worry that a major attachment figure such as a parent will be harmed or will not return; worries about being separated from attachment figures, such as being lost or kidnapped; nightmares about separation; resultant school phobia; resultant reluctance or refusal to sleep; apparent resultant physical symptomatology at points of potential separation; temper tantrums or evidence of psychological distress upon potential separation; resultant social withdrawal and/or depressive symptomatology; or reluctance to stay alone or at home without the major attachment figure.

## Social Phobia (300.23)

Social phobics are marked by anxiety about possible scrutiny of their behavior by others, usually accompanied by clear anticipatory anxiety of acting in a manner that will be considered shameful by others. As a result of the anticipatory anxiety, social phobics make strenuous efforts to avoid such situations. Social phobias can be centered around such behaviors as eating or riding in public, using public lavatories, or blushing. However, the most common social phobia is one in which the person is acutely fearful of making public presentations.

A common manifestation of this form of social phobia is severe anxiety concerning public speaking. This often leads to a classic vicious cycle. First, such persons experience anxiety about a public performance. If they then attempt to proceed in spite of the anxiety, the upset often detracts from the adequacy of the performance, possibly even causing them to twitch or shake visibly. Their prophecy that they will perform poorly and be embarrassed is then fulfilled, and future anticipatory anxiety is facilitated.

This disorder is relatively rare; it usually begins to evolve in late childhood or early adolescence, although spontaneous eruptions in adult life are not that uncommon. The disorder is rarely incapacitating, though it may stunt an individual's professional and economic advancement, particularly if the person's position requires making public presentations. Social withdrawal is not characteristic of this pattern, and if this is present in a substantial fashion, the diagnosis is not appropriate.

## DSM-III

Social phobics show consistent avoidance of specific social situations in which they could be scrutinized and/or possibly be embarrassed. Accompanying fear is disruptive and irrational, and there is marked anticipatory anxiety. However, they have insight into the inappropriateness of their behaviors, and the pattern is not accompanied by severe psychopathology in other areas.

## MMPI

Since these individuals are not markedly disturbed in any area other than their social phobia, their MMPI profiles are relatively normal. The F scale is at least mildly elevated, which reflects their concern about obtaining help. They are higher on the 0 scale, reflecting their problems in social functioning, though this latter elevation is not consistently high. They are a bit lower on the 9 scale, indicating their lowered interest in interacting with the environment, and scales 3 and 2 may be somewhat elevated.

## 16 PF

Again, there is an absence of the more extreme scale scores that are found in the anxiety disorders, even including the obsessive-compulsive personality. Yet, scores on scales E and H are usually low, and scores on I and $Q_4$ are reasonably high. Scores on scales C and L should be more toward the average than they are in the more blatantly disturbed anxiety neurotics.

## Treatment Options

The standard treatments for phobias—systematic desensitization and implosive therapy—are helpful with the social phobic (Emmelkamp, 1982). Foa, Steketee, and Ascher (1980) argue that SDT is the most effective treatment here. Analogously, the clinician can then train clients to overcome their fear in a graded-task approach, wherein they gradually develop their public presentation skills in front of increasingly larger groups. Role playing that develops specific skills, such as rescuing a mistake made in front of an audience (a technique refined and made famous by Johnny Carson) is helpful in giving such clients a sense of control that allows them to go on if the anticipated and feared mistake does occur.

Propranolol, as well as the standard minor tranquilizers, can at times be helpful with the anxious mood that often accompanies the social and simple phobias, though it does not cure the phobia, particularly for the subgroup of phobics who are found to have a hyperresponsive beta-adrenergic system. Propranolol, however, is contraindicated where there is indication of a tendency toward asthma or congestive heart failure.

## Simple Phobia (300.29)

The Simple Phobias are those that most people commonly associate with the term *phobia*—fears of bugs, snakes, or any other discrete objects or situations not included in Social Phobia or Agoraphobia. The simple phobias are usually relatively chronic disorders, typically arising in childhood, and tend to occur more frequently among women (or at least they are more commonly reported by women).

As noted earlier, most individuals have at least one mild, nondisabling phobia of one sort or another. Fears of heights or snakes are very common, though usually these can be easily controlled. As noted, a classic phobia is *disturbing*, *disproportionate*, and *disabling*, and is marked by responses to a *discrete stimulus*.

### DSM-III

The DSM-III criteria for simple phobia are similar to those for the other phobias except that the targets are simple and specific. The person must show avoidance behavior, which is distressing to the individual or interferes with functioning. This behavior must be in response to an irrationally feared situation or object. If there is an element of active danger in these objects or situations, such as in fear of heights, the reaction must be disproportionate. It is also required that phobics recognize the irrational aspect of their anxiety.

Fear of dirt or contaminated objects may at first appear to be a simple phobia. However, such a fear is more often a sign of the complex anxieties and conflicts that suggest an obsessive-compulsive disorder.

### MMPI

Simple phobics are more logical and rational in their thought processes, as well as less emotionally labile, than are people with more complex phobias such as agoraphobia. As a result, their MMPI profiles usually are not particularly remarkable. Both F and K may be at least mildly elevated, the F elevation reflecting the expression of concern and the K simultaneously reflecting an attempt to keep the disturbance compartmentalized as to type of phobia. Minor elevations on scales 2, 3, and 7 can be expected, reflecting the mild to moderate anxiety combined with the symptomatic depression that can be expected by the time they seek help. This also reflects the tendency toward denial and a lack of insight that is occasionally characteristic of such persons. If their controls appear to be breaking down and they are becoming concerned that panic will set in as a result of an expansion of the phobia, an elevation on scale 8, and possibly on scale 6, occurs.

## 16 PF

As with the MMPI, it would be extremely difficult to differentiate a simple phobic based on the 16 PF profile, since such phobias are so common and so close to normal functioning. However, following the theory that the individual has attempted to provide a focus for vague anxieties with the phobia, I would hypothesize at least some elevation on $Q_3$. Yet the fact that it has not been entirely successful should lead to a mild elevation on $Q_4$, as well as O. It has been hypothesized that the H scale is a measure of autonomic overreactivity, or what might be more broadly termed *emotional lability*, and as a result, a lower score on H would be expected.

## Treatment Options

The classic treatment for simple phobia is systematic desensitization, and it is effective throughout the range of phobias usually seen by clinicians (Emmelkamp, 1982). The clinician can actuate this approach either in imagination or in vivo.

The therapist can vary the desensitization procedure by including a modeling phase. In this approach, the therapist first models the desirable behavioral pattern and then physically guides the person through the performance of the desired behavior (e.g., actually helping the person pick up the feared object). This can be combined with verbal support as one goes through the procedure, as well as with covert conditioning techniques.

For those clients who are not responsive to SDT or implosive therapy, the technique of aversion relief, pioneered by L. Solyom, is often effective. Simple phobics who have obsessive or hysteric trends benefit more from this procedure. An application of aversion relief would be to ask the client to record on tape organized narratives of past and potential phobic experiences, in the first person, present tense. The tape is then played back to the client through earphones, and lapses of silence, approximately twenty seconds in duration, interrupt the narrative at the appropriate juncture and are followed by an electric shock. The tape then resumes immediately after the cessation of the electric shock (see Solyom, in Goldstein & Stein, 1976).

As noted in the prior section on social phobia, propranolol can reduce some of the accompanying anxious mood, though it does not cure the phobia. Propranolol is contraindicated where there is any evidence of asthma or congestive heart failure.

## Anxiety States
## Panic Disorder (300.01)

The Panic Disorder is primarily denoted by recurrent anxiety attacks and nervousness, which the individual recognizes as panic. The person experiences anticipatory anxiety, an initial period of often intense apprehension, and the thrust of anxiety that is accompanied by autonomic symptoms and discharge. On occasion, these attacks may last for a period of hours, though attacks are typically for a period of minutes during which the person literally experiences terror.

The disorder is recurrent and episodic, though in a few cases it may become chronic. The panic attacks are clearly separate incidents, and the anxiety experience is not a response to a phobic stimulus or to any event that is very dangerous in reality. Also, unlike the avoidance patterns noted in the phobias, panic disorder focuses more on the experience of terror and the temporary physiological discharge symptoms, such as cold sweats or hyperventilation. The terror experiences are not unlike "free-floating anxiety," an experience of anxiety with inability to specify any source or reason for the anxiety. The panic disorder is a good example of Albert Ellis's (1979) contention that "discomfort anxiety," the fear of being overwhelmed by the experience of anxiety, is central to the phobic and anxiety disorders.

### DSM-III

To diagnose a panic disorder, the DSM-III requires that there be at least three panic attacks that occur within a three-week period, and that these not be in response to a life-threatening situation, heavy physical exertion, or a phobic stimulus. It also requires the presence of at least four of the following symptoms during most of the attacks: dyspnea, palpitations, chest discomfort, choking or smothering sensations, dizziness, feelings of unreality, paresthesias, hot or cold flashes, sweating, faintness, trembling, or fears of going crazy, losing control, or dying.

To cope with these panic attacks, some individuals respond to this anticipatory fear of helplessness by becoming increasingly reluctant to leave the comforts and familiarity of home. If this fear increases, the diagnosis will likely change to Agoraphobia with panic attacks. It is also important in this disorder to rule out physical disorders such as hypoglycemia, hyperthyroidism, withdrawal from certain drugs, or any other disorders that could engender such psychopathology.

## MMPI

A common MMPI pattern for the anxiety neurosis, particularly where the emphasis is on anxiety such as in the panic disorder and the generalized anxiety disorder, is a 2–8 code, with high scores on 7, 3, 1, and 4 in that order (Johnson et al., 1980). As such individuals move toward chronicity, they show profiles similar to agoraphobics; the reader is referred to the preceding section. One fairly rare MMPI profile, the 3–9/9–3 pattern, has been characterized as typical of "free-floating anxiety" and as such, would predict this disorder, as well as a disorder to be discussed later, the generalized anxiety disorder.

The 1–3–7 profile has been characterized as showing high anxiety, passive dependency, and proneness to develop psychophysiological disturbance. Hence, it is possible for this profile to show up in a panic disorder. Scale 7 is likely to be consistently elevated in this profile, as well as scales 1 and 3, whether or not there is a primary elevation on other scales. In some individuals, an accompanying high scale 2 reflects a feeling of loss of control and a sense of hopelessness. As these feelings increase, 2–3/3–2 or 1–3/3–1 profiles are likely.

## 16 PF

The 16 PF profile of the panic disorder is similar to the standard profile for the anxiety disorders: high scores on O, $Q_4$, L, M, and I; a moderately high score on $Q_2$; and low scores on C, $Q_3$, F, H, E, and G. Since the $Q_4$ score is the measure par excellence of anxiety, it should be particularly elevated here, and in that regard $Q_4$ shows a consistently high correlation with scale 7 on the MMPI. Other differences from the standard anxiety disorder profile are: 1) scale L is not quite as high; 2) $Q_2$ may be moderately low rather than moderately high; and 3) scale G is not as low.

## Treatment Options

Since the hallmark of the panic disorder is episodic anxiety reactions accompanied by a high level of psychological tension, the development of a controlled relaxation response has first priority. Progressive Relaxation, Autogenic Training, or any other form of systematized relaxation training is helpful. This can be amplified by encouraging the client to take up ancillary interests such as meditation or yoga. In the initial treatment stage, it may be helpful to give the client a small prescription of tranquilizing medication to be used as needed. This helps avoid problematic side effects, only moderately intrudes on the person's sense of being able to handle it alone, and gives the person a sense that control is immediate and available.

Treatment can be amplified by having clients work on the relaxation training in a group setting. Not only does this give them the awareness that others share this problem, but it also easily sets up a discussion of problems in a quasi-group therapy setting. Later, they are more amenable to entering actual group therapy and thus may come into greater touch with the sources of their anxiety. As they do so, techniques more appropriate for the phobias, noted in prior subsections, can be brought into play so that they can confront and stay with the feared stimuli, a critical variable in obtaining significant cure (Greist et al., 1980).

## Generalized Anxiety Disorder (300.02)

Though the next consecutive listing in the DSM-III is the Obsessive-Compulsive Disorder, the Generalized Anxiety Disorder will be discussed first, as it is functionally a chronic and less cyclical version of the panic disorder. Again, as in the panic disorder, there is autonomic disturbance, although this is now evident in more chronic manifestations. Some "free-floating anxiety" may be present in the generalized anxiety disorder, but the essential feature is chronic autonomic hyperactivity, and thus is similar to the general physiological stress syndrome that Hans Selye (1956) describes.

Because it is a chronic disorder, persons have more apprehensive rumination than would be expected in a panic disorder, also muscular tension. Emerging patterns of hypervigilance and self-checking will crystallize into the variety of patterns that are subsumed under the diagnosis of Obsessive-Compulsive Disorder, which will be described next.

### DSM-III

The DSM-III requires evidence of persistent and generalized anxiety, as manifested in at least three of the following four categories: 1) motor tension (high fatigue, muscular aches, twitches, or easy startle responses); 2) autonomic hyperactivity (dry mouth, gastrointestinal distress, heart racing or pounding, or sweating disturbance); 3) apprehensive expectation (ruminations about injury or death to self or others or catastrophic expectations; 4) vigilance and scanning (hyperalertness, irritability, or related sleep difficulties). The DSM also requires that the anxiety be rather continuous for at least one month, that the disorder is not set off by a psychosocial stressor, and that the person is at least eighteen years of age.

## MMPI

The profile of this disorder parallels the general profile for the anxiety disorders. Similar to the panic disorder, the profile will show a high 2, as well as high 7 and 3 scale scores. The chronic autonomic hyperactivity is reflected in a relatively high 9 score, and if the person is beginning to fear loss of control about these behaviors, a rise on scale 8 is likely. A high F scale is also expected.

## 16 PF

As with the MMPI, the profile should resemble the modal anxiety disorder profile, with the extremes accentuated, as in the panic disorder. $Q_4$ should be very high, as should O, and H should be low.

## Other Test Response Patterns

The impairment and tension resulting from high anxiety should lower the digit span and arithmetic scores within the WAIS-R verbal scaled scores. In general, the performance scores should be lower than the verbal scores, particularly object assembly. The rest of the notations in this section about overall anxiety disorders are also applicable.

## Treatment Options

The focus in the generalized anxiety disorder is on chronic states of autonomic arousal, accompanied by apprehension (Emmelkamp, 1982). Biofeedback is particularly helpful in the treatment of autonomic tension, and the clinician is advised to use a variety of modalities sequentially, such as electromyography (EMG), EEG, or the various measures of skin change. Concomitantly, teaching the client a controlled relaxation response is helpful (see prior section on panic disorder). Some form of meditation training may be useful.

It may be necessary to administer tranquilizing medication as needed in the initial stages, then to move quickly toward treatments that emphasize the client's increasing ability to control the response. As a client begins to gain more control over the anxiety, a treatment technique such as Client-Centered Therapy, as originally advocated by Carl Rogers, may become the primary treatment mode. The focus on empathy and warmth, combined with the initial low demand for specific discussion material, proves helpful here.

## Obsessive-Compulsive Disorder (300.30)

Although the Obsessive-Compulsive Disorder is listed as one of the anxiety disorders in the DSM-III, the direct experience of the anxiety is not as evident as in the other anxiety disorders. Obsessive-compulsive patterns are seen by the person performing them as irrational and ego-alien, yet there are usually no panic experiences or sudden upsurges of anxiety on encountering the anxiety-arousing stimuli or mental images. At least initially, the person attempts to resist the obsession or compulsion.

The obsessive-compulsive disorder is an excellent transition category to the factitious and somatoform disorders. These disorders were traditionally included in the term *neurosis*, but anxiety is often not apparent in these disorders, just as it is also not so obvious in the obsessive-compulsive disorder. The ego-alien quality is what discriminates the obsessive-compulsive disorder from the compulsive personality disorder. In the personality disorder, the compulsions are ego-syntonic (i.e., they are not viewed by the person as in conflict with the essential qualities of the personality).

The usual age of onset for the obsessive-compulsive disorder is late adolescence or early adulthood. By the age of twenty-five, more than half of the treated obsessive-compulsives have already shown clear symptoms (Rachman, 1980). This syndrome occurs proportionately more often in middle- and upper-class individuals. This should not be surprising, especially in a society that so highly values achievement, since those with compulsive patterns are often quite efficient and productive. Obsessive-compulsives are brighter on the average than individuals with the other anxiety disorders—obsessions are intellectual coping strategies for anxiety (Rachman, 1980).

The obsessive-compulsive disorder has traditionally been thought to be relatively rare, at least as compared to the other anxiety disorders (Nemiah, 1975). This could be a function of the embarrassment that many of these individuals experience, which would result in a lower reported incidence. Many who might be willing to report phobic anxiety would be more distressed to disclose that they think and act in ways they cannot control.

The most common obsessions seen by clinicians are repetitive thoughts of contamination, violence, doubts about religion and one's duties, and self-doubts. The most common compulsions include checking behaviors, repetitive acts, and handwashing. The obsessive-compulsive disorder does not include compulsions to perform behaviors that are inherently pleasurable such as alcohol indulgence or overeating. A person may not be able to control these latter behavior patterns, but they are not ego-alien. While they do not want the detrimental effects of their behavior (e.g., alcoholism or overweight), they do not experience inherent discomfort about eating or drinking behaviors.

## DSM-III

The DSM-III requires evidence of obsessions (recurrent and persistent ego-alien impulses and ideas) and/or compulsions (behaviors viewed as not a product of one's own initiative, accompanied by a sense of subjective compulsion and a desire to withstand the compulsion). In addition, the person must be distressed and recognize the irrationality of the behaviors. Also, the clinician must rule out such syndromes as schizophrenia, organic mental disorder, or a major depressive disorder, since all of these may be accompanied by obsessions or compulsions. The obsessive-compulsive disorder is often chronic and accompanied by some disruption in personal functioning.

## MMPI

The two common profile combinations related to the obsessive-compulsive disorder are the 7–8/8–7 and 2–7/7–2 (Lachar, 1974). If a person obtains an 8–7 profile, the clinician is more likely to encounter a combination of deteriorating personality function and depression, whereas a 7–8 profile indicates some continuing struggle, and in that sense is more benign. In the 2–7/7–2 profile, depression about one's own functioning is a major component, and the person may have begun to show signs of social withdrawal.

It has been noted that the 2–7–8 high point combination is a common profile in patients, but rare in normals. It reflects people who are self-analytic and inclined toward catastrophic expectations and a sense of hopelessness. They require goal-directed therapy combined with emphasis on reinforcement for any achievements, with a concomitant de-emphasis of their tendency toward introspection and extensive self-analysis.

The spike 7 profile is rare but suggests an obsessive-compulsive diagnosis. Such individuals show a high number of phobias and obsessions and are close to breaking down and deteriorating into a psychotic condition. It should be noted that the scores on the 7 scale predict obsessiveness more than the compulsive aspects of the disorder.

## 16 PF

The modal 16 PF profile obtained by persons with an obsessive-compulsive disorder (IPAT, 1963) shows high scores on O, $Q_4$, and I, and moderately high scores on L and M. They obtain a moderately low score on C, and low scores on $Q_3$, F, H, and E. A comparison with the modal profile for the anxiety disorder shows that obsessive compulsives are only moderately low on

C and only moderately high on L and M, whereas persons with the anxiety disorders are high on C, L, and M. Also, persons with anxiety disorders show a low score on G, and a moderately high score on $Q_2$, whereas obsessive-compulsives perform in the average range on these variables. This is surprising; I would expect the obsessive-compulsive to score high on $Q_2$, relative to anxiety neurotics. Also, I would expect obsessive-compulsives to score high on scale B, since they tend to be brighter than most individuals with a diagnosis of psychopathology. It may well be that the IPAT sample did not tap these variables, and clinicians should be aware of this. It also is probable that obsessive-compulsives, particularly if they are still gaining a sense of control from the patterns and thus are not yet deteriorating, should score higher on $Q_3$ than should those with most other disorders, with the possible exception of the paranoid disorders. Also, one should consider the possibility that the G score will be higher than average in obsessive-compulsives.

## Other Test Response Patterns

On the WAIS-R, there is an overall higher IQ than in other disorders, reflecting the obsessive-compulsive's average to above average intelligence. Those who are primarily obsessive score higher on the overall IQ score, and in addition have a higher verbal than performance IQ score. Self-deprecation and questioning of one's performance, along with rather detailed verbalizations, are common. A meticulous approach to the block design and object assembly subtests is probable, occasionally leading to a loss of speed-bonus points but seldom resulting in inaccurate responses. Obsessive-compulsives usually do very well on vocabulary as well as similarities and comprehension because of their meticulousness. At the same time, however, their inability to change "set" can sometimes penalize them on similarities. They also do well on both arithmetic and digit span (Rapaport et al., 1968). The intellectualization characteristic of the obsessive-compulsive disorder can result in a decrease in picture arrangement performance. A rather precise approach can again be expected on the Bender Gestalt figures. The figures may be placed in a linear path, and a counting of the dots in appropriate cards is common.

On the Rorschach, expressions of doubt are expected, along with pedantic and esoteric verbalizations. Additionally, a high number of responses overall, a high number of W and/or Dd, a high F+ percent, edge details, and the likelihood of space responses are to be expected. There are generally few color responses, and if color responses of poor form occur, it is thought to indicate decompensation (Shafer, 1954).

Obsessive-compulsives like to criticize the blots as well their own responses and may express concern about the symmetry of the cards. Some surprising combinations or imagined responses (e.g., "two earthworms coming out of a rabbit's eyes" on card X) may occur. Similarly, pedantic wording and an emphasis on details rather than story content are common on the TAT, especially if the individual is oriented toward paranoia as well. Idealistic stories and esoteric, though nonemotional, fantasies may occur.

*Treatment Options*

Foa and Tillmanns (1980) recommend a combination of treatments for the Obsessive-Compulsive Disorder. The anxiety-discomfort component can be handled by SDT techniques and in vivo exposure supplemented by self-instructional training (Emmelkamp et al., 1980; Emmelkamp, 1982). This approach is effective to the degree that the individual becomes more adequate in focusing on the sources of anxiety. Thought-stopping techniques or paradoxical intention techniques work to eliminate the ritualistic behaviors. Although thought stopping is especially efficient in dealing with the obsessive component, Paradoxical Intention (discussed in the subsection on the compulsive personality disorder) is most efficient in controlling the compulsive aspects. As progress occurs on these fronts, standard group therapy and/or psychotherapy can be used and followed up by approaches more oriented to sensitivity (Perls et al., 1958). These help obsessive-compulsives get in touch with their high level of repression and suppression and at the same time be willing to self-disclose more easily.

The standard thought-stopping procedure for the obsessions asks clients to let the obsessions flow as in free association. Clients are then told that on a cue (e.g., a raised hand by the therapist), they should shout "Stop!" Generalization is introduced by having clients practice this at home, and to vary randomly the amount of time before vocalizing "Stop."

Thought stopping can be amplified by having clients visualize a pleasant scene immediately after saying "Stop," thus furthering the relaxation and the control of the interruption sequence. In addition, harmless though moderately painful shocks can be administered by the therapist as the word "Stop" is stated; this significantly reinforces the effect. The clinician can add biofeedback training to increase the percentage of alpha brain rhythms, since they are antagonistic to problem solving or ruminative thought sequences. At the same time, Hendrix and Meyer (1974) found that obsessives are so perfectionistic, particularly early in therapy, that they fight the process, which hinders progress and results in their viewing themselves as failing.

A clear and consistent program of *response prevention* (e.g., taking all soap and towels away from a handwasher, or turning off the water) combined with constant *exposure* to the eliciting stimuli to promote extinction provides the core of an effective treatment program for the compulsive aspects of the disorder.

## Post-Traumatic Stress Disorder
and Adjustment Disorder

The Post-Traumatic Stress Disorder was a late addition to DSM-III; the essence of the disorder is a delayed distress response pattern to an atypical and severe traumatic event, an event such that most people would have very negative and disturbed responses. These clients generally re-experience the stressor in intrusive thoughts and dreams, and depression and anxiety are common. Delayed disturbances in combat veterans, as from the Vietnam conflict, are often appropriately diagnosed here.

If the stressor is more within the normal range, with little in the way of a vivid re-experiencing of the trauma, the appropriate diagnosis is the traditional one of Adjustment Disorder. This diagnosis is appropriately qualified by the terms *with depressed mood, with anxious mood, with mixed emotional features, with disturbance of conduct, mixed disturbance of emotions and conduct, with work or academic inhibition,* or *with withdrawal.*

### DSM-III

To apply the diagnosis of Post-Traumatic Stress Disorder, there must be evidence of a substantial stressor that would seriously disturb most people, such as being raped, or being in an airplane crash, and re-experiencing of the stressful event is indicated by at least one of the following: 1) recurrent related dreams; 2) déjà vu about the event; or 3) persistent memories of the event. As a result, there is a distancing from the external world, as evidenced by at least one of the following: 1) lessened affect; 2) lowered interest in at least one usual interest or activity; or 3) detachment from others.

In addition, two of the following behaviors must be existent, not present before the stress: 1) sleep disruption; 2) hyperalertness; 3) guilt over survival; 4) memory or attention disruption; 5) intensified upset if re-exposed to stressor; or 6) avoidance of any stimuli for recall of stressor.

The post-traumatic stress disorder is sublabeled *acute* (308.30) if symptoms both occur within six months after the stressor and only last six months. Otherwise, it is labeled *delayed* and/or *chronic,* respectively (309.81). The Adjustment Disorder is a maladaptive reaction to a specific psychosocial trauma. It occurs within three months of the trauma and is evident in either excessive reactive symptoms or social or vocational disruption. The adjustment disorders are a separate category—they are not part of the anxiety disorders.

### Diagnostic Considerations

These disorders closely resemble the patterns seen in individuals with a panic disorder; the reader is referred to that section. The only major difference is that the person with a post-traumatic stress disorder or adjustment disorder may show fewer signs of disruption in overall personality functioning.

For example, MMPI scale 8 will probably be lower, as will the F scale. The 7–2 code type is particularly likely as it incorporates the emotional distancing and the distress that are characteristic of this disorder. On the 16 PF, scales C, G, and $Q_3$ should not be as low as in the panic disorder. Scores on $Q_4$ and O are especially likely to be high. Otherwise, the diagnostic comments on panic disorder, the generalized anxiety disorder, and the anxiety disorders generally apply.

### Treatment Options

In treating post-traumatic stress disorders and adjustment disorders, the clinician is advised to keep in mind the principles of crisis intervention: immediacy, proximity, and expectancy were developed in World War II to decrease the consequent problems of the severe distress of combat. Immediacy emphasizes early awareness and detection by others close to the person, treatment as quickly as possible, and an emphasis on returning clients to their typical life situation as quickly as possible. Proximity emphasizes the need to treat clients in their own world—not distancing them from their upset by hospitalization. Lastly, the clinician must communicate a clear expectancy that although fear and anxiety are normal processes here, they do not excuse clients from functioning adequately; the sick role is not reinforced, and there is an emphasis on experiences that demonstrate that they are regaining control of their world (Stern et al., 1980).

These principles can be specifically amplified by the treatment techniques used for the panic disorder and the generalized anxiety disorder, and the reader is referred to those sections. As the fears begin to focus more on specific concerns, SDT or implosive therapy is appropriate. Mild tranquilizers to be used as needed can also be a helpful adjunct treatment. Sessions with family and/or friends that help them implement the principles of crisis intervention in the client's immediate world also facilitate a return to adequate functioning (Bagarrozzi et al., 1982).

### Atypical Anxiety Disorder (300.00)

This category is a catch-all applied to apparent anxiety disorders that do not exactly fit the above categories. For example, where all the criteria for the generalized anxiety disorder are met, but the anxious mood has not lasted for up to six months, an Atypical Anxiety Disorder diagnosis would be appropriate. Any other such mixtures of symptomatology where anxiety and its control are still the primary features can be placed in this category.

# 6

## Factitious and Somatoform Disorders

### The Factitious Disorders

Factitious means not genuine and refers to symptoms that are under voluntary control of the individual, a syndrome first clearly defined by Asher in 1951. At first, this may sound like malingering. The difference is that in a factitious disorder the goal or reinforcement sought is not obvious or inherent in the apparent facts of the situation. Instead, the motivation is understandable only within the person's individual psychology. These patterns have been traditionally confused with the conversion disorders, but in both the somatoform and conversion disorders of DSM-III the symptoms are not under voluntary control. Also, in a conversion disorder, symptoms seldom follow a pattern that is true to the factitious disorders, and though the symptoms are not under voluntary control, they are usually associated with a degree of anxiety and occur frequently.

Factitious disorders are rare, and, according to Spitzer, Forman, and Nee (1979), the factitious disorder is the most difficult DSM-III category to diagnose, in part because the feigned symptoms are often accompanied by more subtle though actual physical disorder (Pankratz, 1981). When diagnosticians become aware of what they perceive as deception, they are inclined to make a diagnosis of an antisocial personality instead of a factitious disorder, and then give the person little attention (Pankratz, 1981).

The factitious disorders are subdivided into: 1) Factitious Disorder with Psychological Symptoms (300.16) and 2) Chronic Factitious Disorder with Physical Symptoms (301.51), the latter often referred to in the literature as Munchausen's syndrome. In the factitious psychological syndrome, the symptoms are mental rather than physical, and as a result they are often less well defined. These people usually talk around a point, or give approximate though evasive answers to direct questions, a pattern referred to as *Vorbereiten*). For example, if asked an arithmetic question such as "How much is 35 minus 12?" they may respond with 30 or 35. In that sense, they are not unlike persons with Ganser's syndrome, though that pattern usually lasts no more than a few weeks, even if treatment is no more sophisticated than supportive therapy. The factitious disorders, on the other hand, are chronic.

Munchausen's syndrome, termed Chronic Factitious Disorder with Physical Symptoms in DSM-III, was named after Baron Von Munchausen, an eighteenth century German equivalent of our own Paul Bunyan, both of whom are associated with tales of exaggeration.

The all-time champion victim of the Munchausen's syndrome has to be Stewart McIlroy, whose path through 68 different hospitals (with at least 207 separate admissions) in England, Scotland, Ireland, and Wales was retraced by Pallis and Bamji (1979). Though he used false names and different complaints, he was eventually identified by scar patterns and other permanent medical characteristics.

McIlroy is an excellent example of one who suffered mightily to satisfy his addiction. Pallis and Bamji (1979) estimate that over the years of his disorder he was subjected to thousands of blood tests and X-rays, his spine had been tapped at least forty-eight times, and his abdomen and body parts were crisscrossed with many scars from exploratory surgery. It is probable that he cost the British Health Services more than a million dollars.

The pattern is thought to be more common in males. This may only reflect a more ready acceptance of verbalizations of sickness from females, so that the diagnostician would be less inclined to recognize a factitious disorder in females.

## DSM-III

The DSM-III requires a documented history of multiple hospitalizations in order to diagnose chronic factitious disorder with physical symptoms. In addition, there has to be evidence that standard malingering is not a major factor, as well as evidence that the hospitalization was in response to the voluntary production of physical symptoms. The range of symptomatology is limited only by the imagination and the degree of sophistication about medical information. Some experience with hospitals or medical situations, either through prior hospitalizations or through knowledge from family members involved in the medical profession can contribute to this disorder (Pankratz, 1981). It is highly refractory to intervention, in part because the person can often find another cooperative physician; the disorder can take a high physical toll on the person, as seen in the case of Mr. McIlroy.

To diagnose a factitious disorder with psychological symptoms, the DSM-III requires evidence that: 1) the psychological symptoms have been voluntarily produced; 2) they reflect an individual psychology rather than commonly understood motivation (such as avoiding the draft); and 3) the person apparently is maneuvering to take on a patient role. This symptomatology is usually superimposed on other pathology, but it is important that the patterns not be primarily explained by the dynamics of another disorder.

## Test Response Patterns

The functional performance of individuals with these disorders is that of malingering, though the psychology that generates the behaviors is somewhat different. However, the patterns and symptom picture described in the section on malingering is appropriate, especially as regards malingering used to gain admission to a hospital. It is unfortunate that psychologists have not paid more attention to the issue of the detection of deception, as it is relevant to many disorders. The clinician is advised to depend on more than one test, such as the MMPI, for indications of malingering, since this gives more cues about malingering or a factitious disorder. Also, the careful gathering and evaluation of past records that is important in all disorders is critical here (Pankratz, 1981).

The factitious disorder with psychological symptoms generally parallels the classic signs of neurasthenia (Golden, 1979), in which the clinician can expect high 2, 7, 1, and 3 scales in that order of elevation. The deception and sophistication found here would also suggest a high 6 and 4 scale. A person with Munchausen's syndrome is more likely to show greater elevations on 1 and 3 than a person with psychological symptoms.

The Rorschach and other projective tests are helpful because they present a situation in which it is hard to decipher the situational demands and thus disrupt the sophistication and polish of such clients in their presentation of symptoms by the mere fact of requiring them to take the test. For that reason, it is advisable to use a projective test early in the battery, as disturbing their sense of surety about performance may cause a spilling into the tests that follow.

## Treatment Options

Biofeedback and other allied techniques are useful for any physiological disorder, regardless of the source, even including a physiological disorder that is a direct result of psychological conflicts. The factitious disorder is a different story, though, as the essential aspect is the deception. Not surprisingly, such persons are going to be openly hostile and avoidant of treatment, so unless they are coerced by a significant other they are not likely to become involved in treatment. If they are coerced, and if they are willing to participate at least initially, many of the principles that hold for the paranoid disorders are applicable here; the reader is referred to that section.

Reality Therapy (Glasser, 1980; Glasser & Zunin, 1973) is also an appropriate therapeutic focus here. It emphasizes that the person must accept responsibility for his or her behavior, and most importantly, for the consequences of that behavior. To the degree that reality therapy is effective, clients are more likely to come into contact with the conflicts central to their disorder, and at that point more traditional psychotherapeutic modes are appropriate.

## The Somatoform Disorders

Persons with somatoform disorders, like those with the factitious disorder, manifest complaints and symptoms of apparent physical illness for which there are no demonstrable organic findings to support a physical diagnosis. However, the symptoms of the somatoform disorders are not under voluntary control, as are those of the factitious disorders. Thus, the diagnosis of somatoform disorder is made when there is good reason to believe that the person has little or no control over the production of symptoms. Disorder and/or dominance problems in the nondominant hemisphere of the brain should be ruled out, because symptoms occur statistically more often on the left side (Tucker, 1981). While factitious disorders are more common in men, somatoform disorders occur more frequently in women.

There are four major subcategories of the somatoform disorders: Somatization Disorder, Conversion Disorder, Psychogenic Pain Disorder, and Hypochondriasis. There is also a catch-all category, Atypical Somatoform Disorder, in which individuals are placed if they fit the general criteria for somatoform disorder but not the specific criteria of the other four major categories. The Somatization Disorder is chronic with multiple symptoms and complaints, usually presented in a vague fashion. The Conversion Disorder focuses on one or two specific symptoms suggestive of a physical disorder, which on closer examination reflect primarily a psychological issue, either as a reflection of symbolic conflict or from the attainment of secondary gain. Psychogenic Pain Disorder is functionally a conversion disorder that refers specifically to psychologically induced pain states. Hypochondriasis is the consistent overresponse to and concern about normal and/or insignificant bodily changes, in spite of expert reassurance that there is no reason for concern.

### Treatment Options

Even though conscious deception is not a factor, Reality Therapy (Glasser, 1980; Glasser & Zunin, 1973) can be appropriate, particularly to the degree the person becomes aware of the unrealness of their physical symptoms. The therapist can facilitate that awareness through such methods as consciousness raising, hypnosis and amytal interviews, or other methods of getting in touch with the repressed facets of the personality. In this regard, though biofeedback may not be directly appropriate since there is no strictly physical damage, it can be helpful in modifying some of the symptomatology. Also, it may give the person some insight that the disorder is not primarily physiological (Budzynski, Stoyva, & Peffer, 1980; Hendrix & Meyer, 1974).

## Somatization Disorder (300.81)

The chronic though cyclic multiple somatic complaints that mark this subcategory of the somatoform disorders are not primarily due to any physical illness. Yet they may be mixed with other symptoms derived from an actual disease, so arriving at this diagnosis is initially difficult. It is not uncommon for this disorder to be an exaggeration of symptoms associated with a previous cured physical disease.

The diagnosis of Somatization Disorder is difficult because a self-report of symptoms combined with apparent prior history is convincing to most physicians. Family physicians or general practitioners are more often than not the target of these complaints and are not inclined to see the somatization disorder as real. Physicians often believe such people are only malingering or that, at the very least, there is a degree of faking involved. Hence, they are inclined to put them in the too commonly used categories of "crank" or "crock," and attempt in various ways to avoid spending any time with them.

Since it is the supportive atmosphere of the physician's manner and/or the hospital structure that is at least one of the needs of persons with a somatization disorder (and to a degree the conversion disorders), such evident rejections begin to lay bare the underlying inadequacy of these persons to cope effectively with their world. Depression then becomes an emergent and eventually paramount symptom, and the person may develop methods (e.g., alcohol) to deal with the depression. Alternately, the person with a somatization disorder may develop a new symptom picture and generate new systems of hospitals and physicians to work through. Restrictions of time and money, however, often bring the person full circle.

Symptoms are often presented in a vague though exaggerated fashion. Incidentally, this dramatic component was the linkage between the traditional diagnostic terms *hysterical neurosis* and the *hysterical personality*. Fortunately, the DSM-III terminology does away with some of the confusion inherent in these labels. Hysterical personalities are now referred to as having a histrionic personality disorder. Hysteria is typically subsumed under one of the somatoform disorders, usually as a conversion disorder that is still sublabeled the hysterical neurosis, conversion type.

One disorder occasionally misinterpreted as a somatization disorder, hypochondriasis, a conversion disorder, or even depression is myasthenia gravis, an immune-mediated polyclonal antibody disorder of receptors in the postsynaptic membrane. Referral to a neurologist for further considera- tion is advisable when the client shows the following symptoms: 1) signifi- cant somatic weakness, occasionally resulting in collapse after use of any particular muscle group; 2) visual disturbances, including the dropping of one or both eyelids (more likely to occur in the evening); and 3) difficulty in speaking and swallowing (Sneddon, 1980).

## DSM-III

The DSM-III requires evidence of a vague though dramatic and complicated medical history, with evidence that the physical symptoms began before the age of thirty. A person's own report of personal physical history is consid- ered enough to substantiate the diagnosis. In addition, there must be evi- dence of at least twelve reported symptoms (fourteen for women) out of the thirty-seven different symptoms that are listed in DSM-III under the fol- lowing seven subgroups: gastrointestinal, cardiopulmonary, pain, conver- sion symptoms, female reproductive system, psychosexual symptoms, or a belief that one is sickly.

Confirmation that the symptom has physically occurred is not required, but there should be indications of symptoms severe enough to require the individual to seek medical help or to alter the life situation in some way in response to the belief that it occurred.

Depression may accompany this pattern, but it is not diagnosed unless it is severe enough to warrant the diagnosis of depressive episode. In a schizophrenic with somatic delusions, the schizophrenic diagnosis takes precedence. The somatization disorder is thought to be diagnosed rarely in males, but approximately 1 percent of females are alleged to have this dis- order at some point in their lives.

Systems of health care based on the group practice model make restric- tion and detection of this disorder easier, since this model facilitates higher levels of interspecialist communication. Also, these practices are more likely to include psychological services and be more sophisticated in implemen- tation than an individual physician. Inclusion of psychological services turns out actually to reduce the cost of health care in most physical dis- orders, mainly by a reduction of repeated visits and unnecessary surgery (Olbrisch, 1977).

## MMPI

Scales 1, 2, 3, and 7 are elevated in most of the somatization patterns. As has been noted, some depression naturally accompanies this syndrome and is reflected in the moderate elevation on scale 2. If scale 2 is high, it is possible that the person is beginning to feel that he or she is losing control. Scale 1 is elevated in most of these profiles, and the 1-2/2-1 profile is best thought of as somatization disorder with underlying depression. In this instance, one might also consider alcohol abuse as a compounding variable.

Elevations on scale 7 point to the degree of passivity and complaining that can be expected. The 1-7/7-1 profile client demands physical care and responsiveness from physicians but is resistant to following orders and is difficult to change. A 3-8/8-3 profile has also been associated with this disorder, though the chronic worry, dependency, and schizoid tendencies of these individuals should warrant consideration of a psychotic diagnosis.

The 1-4/4-1 profile reflects a high level of physical complaints, as well as excessive narcissism and egocentricity. If 6 is elevated, anger or rage in the face of rejection by the physician is to be expected. The 3-6/6-3 profile is similar—there is anger as well as rigidity and lack of cooperation. This anger is more often directed toward family members; they are not quite as manipulative toward physicians.

When actual physical disorder is an accumulation of chronic psychological stress and accompanied by an equally high level of psychological repression, the 3-7/7-3 profile is common. A circumscribed physical disorder to which the person has responded with a reactive depression is more likely to produce a spike scale 2 profile.

The 3-9/9-3 profile is on the border between actual physical disorder and somatization disorder. A common complaint is acute upset accompanied by chest pain and anxiety. These individuals in particular respond well to superficial assurance and to continuing therapist contact.

A small subgroup of clients with a somatization disorder show virtually psychotic profiles. They are remarkably elevated on scale 4, sometimes above the 100 T level, and are also high on scales 6, 8, 2, 3, and 1, in that order. In fact, all scales except 0 and 5 may be well above the 70 T level (Propkop et al., 1980).

## 16 PF

Characteristics on the 16 PF commonly noted throughout all somatoform disorders, but particularly in the somatization disorder, are at least moderately high scores on N, I, and $Q_4$, moderately low scores on H and $Q_1$, and a low score on F. Karson (1959) suggests that individuals who are lower on A and M are also inclined toward this disorder. The M score, as well as the scale B score, reflects the client's degree of sophistication and in that sense correlates with different somatization patterns. The less sophisticated symbolic conversion patterns, which were seen more commonly in Freud's era, are more typical of naïve and less well-educated individuals.

Men who have both a high I and E score have conflicts between needs to be sensitive in interpersonal relationships and yet to dominate the relationship. Ambivalence about assertion and aggression is common and may surface in a somatization pattern. It has been hypothesized that women will encounter this same conflict as they move away from traditional female roles.

Clinicians have noted that persons with a somatization disorder also tend to be more average on C and $Q_4$ than do those with the anxiety disorders. They vary markedly on scales I and $Q_3$, depending on the degree of depression. Though a pattern with a combination of a low E and a high $Q_1$ score is relatively rare, it predisposes that person to the somatization disorders.

### Other Test Response Patterns

Performance scale scores on the WAIS-R are usually higher than verbal scale scores. In particular, the performance subtests that depend on motor coordination and speed are relatively high, with an occasionally surprising exception in object assembly. Within the verbal scale scores, lower information and digit span scores are expected, relative to higher comprehension scores. In females, where the somatization disorder incorporates histrionic components, the arithmetic score is low.

Persons with a somatization disorder typically do not provide a high number of responses on the Rorschach, and percent of W or complex M responses is usually low. They are more likely to give simple, popular responses, using only the easily discerned details. A high number of M responses is rare, and when they are provided, they often have a more static quality than do normal M responses. Responses involving color as a determinant are uncommon. Responses focusing on bony anatomy content and occasional pure C responses such as "blood" do occur.

### Treatment Options

The comments in the section on Somatoform Disorders are also applicable to the Somatization Disorders. The symptomatology here is more similar to actual physiological disorder than it is in several of the other somatoform disorders. Hence, biofeedback can be useful in turning around some of the surface physiological symptomatology and at the same time can give clients concrete feedback that may convince them, along with supportive therapy, to look at psychological vulnerability as the source of their disorder. Most persons with this disorder are defensive about it, and as a result, the comments about the Paranoid Disorders are applicable. At some point, a shift into an existential orientation may be necessary to confront clients fully with their escape mechanisms.

## Conversion Disorder (300.11)

The Conversion Disorder is similar in many respects to the somatization disorder. The difference is that in the conversion disorder there is a specific symptom or a related set of symptoms, and these symptoms are either used for the attainment of some secondary gain, or they express a psychological conflict. Conversion symptoms are not under voluntary control. Psychogenic Pain Disorder, discussed below, can be considered a subcategory of conversion disorder where the specific symptom is simply pain.

With some of the psychosexual dysfunctions (discussed later), it may be difficult to decide whether the problem directly expresses a psychological issue and is thus technically a conversion disorder or whether it is a physiological response to anxiety. In actuality, it may be a mixture of both. For these reasons, as well as for convenience, all of these cases are included in the psychosexual disorders. Some clinicians also might consider anorexia nervosa to be a conversion disorder; most would consider these syndromes different enough to warrant separate discussions, but there are parallels.

A conversion disorder is still referred to as a "hysterical neurosis, conversion type," and such individuals are said to manifest "la belle indifference," an attitude in which there is little concern about the apparent serious implications of the disorder. Persons with a conversion disorder appear to be aware at some level that their complaints do not predict the further dire consequences that others might infer from them. Although indifferent to their presenting symptoms, emotional lability in response to other stimuli is commonly noted (Slavney et al., 1977).

The attitude of "la belle indifference" is not found in all conversion disorders. Some people develop their symptoms under extreme stress and manifest that stress quite directly. Yet, even in these individuals, anxiety seems to dissipate over the duration of the disorder in favor of a focus on physical symptoms.

A dependent or histrionic personality predisposes individuals to the development of conversion symptoms. Another important predisposing factor is a history of actual physical disorder during which excessive caretaking behaviors or other secondary gains occurred.

### DSM-III

The DSM-III requires evidence of a disturbance that implies a physical disorder, with symptoms that are not under voluntary control and in which psychological factors are a primary cause. This is supported by evidence of avoidance or secondary gain patterns, often associated with evidence of symbolic representation of a psychological conflict. It is not limited to pain or sexual problems.

*MMPI*

Most of the comments made about diagnostic observations on somatization disorders are relevant here. It has been traditional to expect that in most cases of conversion disorder there is a classic Conversion V, wherein scales 3 and 1 are both high and 2 is relatively low. This is especially indicative of a conversion reaction in which the individual takes a naïve and Pollyanna-ish attitude and manifests "la belle indifference." However, Johnson et al. (1980) found that the 2–1–7 pattern, with a high score on 3, is more common in this disorder. If scale 3 is very high, scale 4 is low, and scale 1 is around the 60 to 70 T score range, histrionic characteristics are emphasized. In persons where "la belle indifference" is lacking, a higher scale 4 is likely.

Another profile seen occasionally in conversion disorders is the 3–9/9–3. These people experience conversion reactions in acute form, accompanied by at least moderately high anxiety levels. Over time, they are likely to show more histrionic characteristics, and the 9 scale should be somewhat lower.

*16 PF*

The observations on the 16 PF relevant to somatization disorders are applicable here as well. However, if there is "la belle indifference," N and $Q_3$ are higher and there is a relatively lower score on L. A high F score is also probable. Since these individuals are usually not as sophisticated as others in the overall group of somatoform disorders, a lower B scale is noted. Also, the concrete quality of their thinking predicts a lower M score.

*Other Test Response Patterns*

Although the overall group of conversion disorders is similar to the somatization disorders, those with "la belle indifference" in particular show higher scores on digit symbol and digit span on the WAIS-R. In addition, they seldom show bright normal or superior intelligence and do poorly on tests that measure more subtle intellectual discriminations, such as comprehension, similarities, and picture arrangement. Emotional distancing from the Rorschach cards, through such comments as "they are weird," "they are ugly," is common. They are prone to deny depressive or aggressive feelings in the content of the Rorschach and the TAT.

*Treatment Options*

Since the time of Freud, hypnosis as a means of directly suggesting a cure or as a means of exploring unconscious conflicts has been effective in the treatment of conversion disorders. Also, it is worthwhile to try a variety of placebo techniques with a client with conversion disorder, particularly one who focuses on the dramatic.

Hendrix, Thompson, and Rau (1978) successfully used behavioral techniques to cure the conversion disorder symptom of a clenched fist. In general, aversion relief and variations of the "time-out technique" (removing the person from the situation and not responding to his or her disturbed behaviors) can be useful here. In the cognitive behavioral technique of Covert Extension, the conversion disorder client would be asked to imagine the general conversion pattern while at the same time immediately imagining that the reinforcing events that usually occur with this behavior in the real world do not occur in imagination. The effectiveness of the technique depends on already having attained some awareness as to the source of the conversion disorder. Thus, it is best used as a subsequent procedure to such techniques as hypnosis, psychotherapy, or free association, which are used to first explore these unconscious ties.

### Psychogenic Pain Disorder (307.80)

Psychogenic Pain Disorder is a conversion disorder that specifically involves pain not due to a physical cause. Yet, as with the other somatoform disorders, a history of physical disorder involving the actual symptom is common. The emergence of a psychogenic pain disorder is facilitated by developmental stage transitions and by specific stressful events. Psychogenic pain disorder differs from the other conversion disorders in that the commonly associated histrionic features of sexual ambivalence, "la belle indifference," and dependency are not usually observed.

As with the other conversion disorders, psychogenic pain disorder may reflect a psychological conflict and/or exert a controlling influence on this person's interactions with other people, resulting in some secondary gain and/or allowance for avoidance. The pain seldom follows known anatomical or neurological patterns, and extensive diagnostic work reveals no evidence of organic pathology. In the more sophisticated patient, it may mimic well-known diseases such as angina or arthritis.

### DSM-III

The DSM-III requires evidence of nonorganic severe pain in which psychological factors are a primary cause, as shown by a clear stimulus-response relationship, maintenance of the pain by reinforcement of avoidance patterns, or by secondary gain. Again, the symptoms are of significant duration and are not under voluntary control.

## MMPI

Though psychogenic pain disorder can be considered a conversion disorder, the classic Conversion V is not always found (Strassberg et al., 1981; Fordyce, 1979). Depression is evident in many cases, hence the 2 scale may be elevated. Elevations (in order of degree) in the 1–2–3 scales are common. Interestingly enough, clients with a single pain complaint tend to score higher on these scales than do clients with multiple pain complaints (Strassberg et al., 1981). Clients who are using their illness to obtain compensation are more likely to score higher on scale 4, and scale 9 to a lesser degree, and other cues for malingering (see the chapter on malingering) should be considered.

As symptoms become more chronic and patients are rejected more often by diagnosticians and treaters, a rise in scale 7 is probable. When pain is focused in the extremities or is manifested in headaches or back problems (a pattern in which repression and denial are common), a 1–3/3–1 profile is likely.

One group of patients with multiple pain complaints shows high scores on 1, 3, 7, and 8, in that order. This group is characterized by somatic preoccupation, obsessive thinking, isolation, and denial of psychological problems. Another subgroup is denoted by high scores on scale K and scale 1, and a low score on scale 6. This group is particularly inclined to deny their psychological difficulties, almost in a naïve fashion, and is interpersonally insensitive (Propkop et al., 1980).

Clients with actual chronic pain do not often show much elevation immediately after the injury. However, if they are tested several months after it occurs, elevations on scales 1 and 3 are likely. Patients with chronic pain also are likely to become increasingly depressed, so an elevation on 2 is even more common. Many patients with chronic pain become addicted to toxic levels of pain-killing drugs and as a result begin to show cognitive slippage and other indications of brain damage. A 2–9, with an 8 that is high and greater than 7, or other indicators of disinhibition such as a high 4, accompanied by indications of distress, are potential indicators of this addiction and toxicity (Fordyce, 1979).

Certain patients with chronic pain appear to reflect a one-trial learning process associated with the originating trauma. As a result, they emit indications of phobic-like behavior on the MMPI. They are often suggestible and thus manifest a high L and K score, with a high scale 3 and a relatively high scale 1, often accompanied by a 7 scale that is elevated at least 10 points over scale 8 (Fordyce, 1979).

## 16 PF

The comments regarding conversion disorders are appropriate here, except those that focus on the symptom of "la belle indifference," since this is not typical for psychogenic pain.

*Other Diagnostic Considerations*

Beyond the standard means (psychological tests, hypnosis, "truth serums") for differentiating a conversion disorder from an organic condition, there are other methods specifically helpful in discriminating psychogenic from organic pain. Cortical evoked potentials have shown promise as a diagnostic instrument in this area, as well as in many other diagnostic situations. Also, certain EEG patterns appear more consistently in organic than in psychogenic pain, and assessment of blood plasma cortisol can be a helpful discriminator. Unfortunately, most people with somatoform disorders, and particularly conversion disorders, are seldom seen by a psychologist or psychiatrist, and such specific and more sophisticated assessments are never made.

*Treatment Options*

Since psychogenic pain disorder is a specific form of the conversion disorder, the comments in that section are appropriate. As noted, hypnosis is appropriate in conversion disorders, and David Cheek (1965) has pioneered in the use of hypnosis for the reduction of chronic psychogenic pain. He uses hypnosis to find the subconscious causes for the pain. In addition, while such clients are under hypnosis, Cheek asks them gradually to release this symptom, often having them point to a date on the calendar designating when they might be willing to give up the symptom. He then makes an appointment for that day, and gradually ties the insights under hypnosis into conscious awareness. With chronic pain, the musculature has often conformed over time to a bodily posture that continues the pain. Hence, even psychogenic pain may have an overlay of real pain. Biofeedback to release this tense muscle posture can be helpful. Other clinicians would argue that techniques derived from chiropractic, such as Rolfing, are useful here as well.

Secondary gain is particularly important in the conversion disorders. Therefore, the clinician should look at family and marital situations for possible reinforcement patterns, as well as for possible sites for intervention.

### Hypochondriasis (300.70)

Hypochondriacs unreasonably interpret normal or relatively unimportant bodily and physical changes as indicative of serious physical disorder. They are constantly alert to an upsurge of new symptomatology, and since the body is constantly in physiological flux, they are bound to find signs that they can interpret as suggestive of disorder.

In one sense, hypochondriacs do not fear being sick; they are certain they already are. Hypochondriasis is a relatively common pattern from adolescence to old age. It is seen most frequently in the thirty- to forty-year age range for men, and the forty- to fifty-year range for women (Meister, 1980). Meister also believes that there are many "closet hypochondriacs "— those who do not constantly go to physicians, yet are heavily involved in health fads, checking of body behaviors, and discussion of their concerns with close friends (who may relish this quasi-therapist role). These "closet hypochondriacs" would not earn a formal DSM-III diagnosis, as they do not fit some of the specific requirements, such as seeking out medical reassurance and going through physical examinations. Nonetheless, they manifest the disorder.

A number of common factors have been observed in the development of hypochondriasis:

1. In most hypochondriacs, there has been a background marked by substantial experience in an atmosphere of illness (Meister, 1980). This could include identification with a significant other who was hypochondriacal or early exposure to a family member who was an invalid.
2. Hypochondriacs often have had a strong dependency relationship with a family member who could express love and affection in a normal or intense fashion during periods when the hypochondriac had been ill, yet was distant or nonexpressive at other times (Meister, 1980).
3. Hypochondriacs often channel their psychological conflicts and their needs for existential reassurance into this pattern. As a result, the hypochondriac pattern of behavior may mask a mid-life crisis, or some other challenge that is not being met effectively.
4. A certain subgroup of hypochondriacs are postulated as having a predispositional sensitivity to pain and body sensation (Hanback & Revelle, 1978). This could be stimulated by prior physical disorder in systems in which the hypochondriacal pattern is now manifest.

All of these factors are naturally facilitated by reinforcement of the hypochondriasis in the client's world. Avoidance of tasks or demands because of being sick is often noted here.

This commonly used term *hypochondriasis* was not employed in the original drafts of DSM-III, as it was considered to be so similar to the somatization disorder. Yet the usually greater specificity of symptom complaints as well as the traditional acceptance of the term led to its incorporation into the final draft of DSM-III.

## DSM-III

There is not so much of a focus on actual physical symptoms in hypochondriasis as in the somatization disorder. Rather, such people interpret physical sensations and natural changes in their body as indicative of significant physical disorder, in spite of expert assurance that there is little danger. As a result, some area of social or vocational functioning is disrupted. Persons with a cardiac neurosis or cancer phobia may be placed in this category.

## Diagnostic Considerations

Hypochondriacs function similarly to individuals with the somatization disorder, except that hypochondriasis is more focused and intellectualized. As a result, the MMPI profile will be somewhat tempered, being lower on scales 1, 7, and 8 in particular. However, scale 1 still remains at least moderately elevated, and a common code type here is the 3–1/1–3 profile, as is the 1–2/2–1 when there is evident distress. Since there is at least a moderate amount of defensiveness associated with this disorder, the K scale and scale 6 are usually moderately high. If the person is relatively naïve in response to personal conflicts, the L scale is also somewhat elevated. Hypochondriacs who are inclined to discuss their problems with others should score lower on scale 0, indicating the extroverted aspect of their pattern.

As with the MMPI, the 16 PF is tempered from the profile usually noted with the somatization disorder. Specifically, C is usually not as low, nor is $Q_4$ as high. However, E, I, and $Q_3$ are usually higher, reflecting the even more controlled psychological world of hypochondriacs in comparison to that of persons with a somatization disorder.

Due to the mild obsessive component usually found in this disorder, hypochondriacs overelaborate their responses on the WAIS-R and thus tend to do better on comprehension, similarities, and vocabulary. These are people who cope with words; as a result, the verbal scale is often higher than the performance scale. Blatt, Baker, and Weiss (1970) found that a low score on object assembly was predictive of high bodily concern, including hypochondriacal patterns.

This same mild obsessive factor should result in longer latencies to the Rorschach cards, as well as a number of the other response patterns manifest in the obsessive-compulsive disorder; the reader is referred to that section, as well as to the section on somatization disorder. Anatomical responses to the cards are naturally expected, and there is some indication that this anatomy content increases as they proceed through the cards. CF is probably usually greater than FC, and there is a relatively low production of M responses.

## Treatment Options

Direct reassurance on medical symptoms is usually not a curative factor, though it is usually important that some reassurance is given so that the therapy can then focus on a consideration of psychological concerns. The development of trust is critical in this disorder; in that regard, the reader is referred to the discussion of trust development in the section on the paranoid disorders.

An analogous approach can be helpful with specific hypochondriacs. Therapists can suddenly state that they feel a hypochondriac client is dead right about his or her concerns. The shock from this expected agreement, with the apparent verification of their dreaded suspicions, can often elicit the underlying psychological concerns. This technique must be carried out with care, as it can backfire and solidify the hypochondriacal concerns.

Family therapy is often helpful with certain hypochondriacs. Many of them have evolved a response system in which significant others consistently reinforce their pattern; with the supervision of the therapist, this pattern can be broken. Family members can be taught to give the person psychological reassurance and caring responses, while at the same time ignoring or otherwise avoiding the reinforcement of the concerns about physical disorder (Bagarrozzi et al., 1982).

Physicians who take the overall disorder as a serious problem and who do not write these patients off as "crocks," can go a long way toward breaking the hypochondriac pattern. Once such patients begin to trust the physician, they can open up more about their total problems and then, under the umbrella of trust, possibly accept referral for psychological treatment.

In that regard, Barrett (1981) has noted the importance of underlying existential issues in the treatment of subcategories of hypochondriases, such as cancer phobia and cardiac neurosis. Several clients appear to use specific concerns in these areas as a distraction from more anxiety-arousing issues such as a basic realization of mortality or facing the potential to fail. Existential confrontation (Bugental, 1980), in a context of supportive psychotherapy, allows the hypochondriacal concerns to cease so that clients may confront these deeper problems. Many of the techniques specific to the obsessive-compulsive disorder are applicable here.


### Atypical Somatoform Disorder


This catch-all category includes any pattern that generally fits the requirements for somatoform disorder but does not fit the specifics of the individual patterns just covered. In actual practice, many individuals do not fit a specific somatoform disorder—not fulfilling the requirement of evidence in four or five symptom groups—and hence are included here.

# 7

## Dissociative Disorders

The Dissociative Disorders, traditionally referred to as the Hysterical Neuroses, Dissociative Type, are characterized by a sudden disruption or alteration of the normally integrated functions of consciousness. This disturbance is almost always temporary, though it may wax and wane, particularly in Amnesia and Fugue.

The various subcategories are: Psychogenic Amnesia, an acute disturbance of memory function; Psychogenic Fugue, a sudden disruption of one's sense of identity, usually accompanied by travel away from home; Multiple Personality, the domination of the person's consciousness by two or more separate personalities; and Depersonalization Disorder, a disturbance in the experience of the self in which the sense of reality is temporarily distorted.

There is also a category referred to as Other Dissociative Disorders, simply a residual category. The patterns most commonly included in this diagnosis are those of persons who experience a sense of unrealness that is not accompanied by depersonalization and who also show some trance-like states.

It can be argued that the depersonalization disorder, also referred to as the depersonalization neurosis, is not appropriately included in this general category, as there is no substantial memory disturbance. Yet there is a significant disturbance, albeit temporary, of the sense of reality, and thus the identity is certainly affected.

### Diagnostic Considerations

With the exception of the depersonalization disorder, the dissociative disorders occur rarely. As a result, there is not much significant literature on discrimination of these states by psychological tests. This is not as unfortunate as it might seem. In the dissociative disorders, the symptoms are usually reasonably clear indications of the particular subcategory, even though other disorders have to be screened out.

For example, many of these disorders have to be initially differentiated from schizophrenia. However, people with a dissociative disorder do not show the confusion and deteriorated functioning in most personality areas that are indicative of schizophrenia. These disorders may also need to be distinguished from those disorders in which the behavior mimics an organic condition, such as a tumor or epilepsy. Indeed, when the clinician is confronted with the symptomatology noted here, a medical consultation is usually warranted.

## Psychogenic Amnesia (300.12)

This is an instance when the commonly understood use of the term *amnesia* almost directly reflects the diagnostic implications. Psychogenic Amnesia is a temporary loss of ability to recall personal information. It can be information about a specific topic, or it can be memories of the immediate or distant past. Though media portrayals lead people to believe that the memory for all past events is lost in amnesia, this is rare. Recovery of memory is usually rapid, whereas the recovery is gradual in organic conditions, if it takes place at all. The alcohol amnestic disorder differs from psychogenic amnesia—in the former, the person is able to recall information for only a few minutes after it is obtained, since the ability to transfer information from short-term memory into long-term memory has been lost. This condition is also observed in some individuals who have had significant ECT treatments.

### DSM-III

The DSM-III requires evidence of sudden memory failure for important personal information that has been previously stored in memory. The memory failure is too significant to be explained by ordinary forgetfulness, and it is not explained by the alcohol amnestic disorder, by other organic conditions, or by such disorders as catatonia and stupor. It also needs to be discriminated from malingering, and such discrimination is often quite difficult. The findings of faking scales on psychological tests are helpful here; the reader is referred to the later section on malingering. Interviews with the use of amytal or hypnosis can also be helpful.

This disorder is typically observed in adult and adolescent females who are undergoing significant stress and also in young males experiencing the distress of wartime. A subjectively intolerable life experience, such as an unexpected loss, is a common catalyst for amnesia, as well as for the related following category, psychogenic fugue.

There are four common subgroupings of psychogenic amnesia. The first and most common type, localized, refers to the loss of memory for events during a circumscribed period of time (following a severe stressor such as an accident). Selective amnesia is a loss of memory for only certain types of events during that circumscribed period of time. Generalized amnesia is a failure to recall all events in one's life; this condition is rare. Continuous amnesia is a loss of memory from one time to another, and is also rare.

## MMPI

A high 3-4/4-3 pattern on the MMPI, particularly the 3-4 profile, means fertile ground for the development of dissociative experiences. This pattern is marked by immaturity and significant difficulty in coping directly and maturely with disturbances in one's psychological world. It implies the use of denial, either psychologically as in amnesia, or even physically and psychologically as in the fugue state. While scale 4 usually means sociopathy, it is also a measure of lack of social poise, naïveté, and immaturity, and so may be high here.

Scale 1 is occasionally raised in this profile, as is scale 8, depending on whether the person is gravitating toward somatic concerns as an expression of disorder or into a general loss of integrated decision making. The F scale is low compared to other groups of pathology. If anger and hostility are being denied and avoided, an elevation on scale K is likely. The naïveté of the amnesiac is also reflected in a higher L score than would usually be obtained in an individual of similar social and intellectual level.

## 16 PF

A modal profile for this type of disorder has not been determined. However, most clinicians agree that low scores on H and N are to be expected. Suppressed anxiety should result in at least a moderate elevation on $Q_4$, and the increasing loss of integration of self-concept should predict a lower $Q_3$ score. Higher scores on O and I, reflecting oversensitivity and apprehension, can be expected, particularly in the young adult and adolescent females who are manifesting this pattern. The suggestibility and sense of inadequacy often found in such individuals also reflect the contrast between their rigid problem-solving skills and their high degree of suggestibility and desire to place trust in an authority figure.

*Treatment Options*

Hypnotic techniques to gain access to subconscious material have been a traditional treatment for amnesia, and they are generally effective. Psychotherapy, with an emphasis on interpretation of possible conflicts before adequate realization of them, is also useful, particularly if a supportive atmosphere both in and out of the therapy hour can be generated. This gives clients the sense of safety and potential for reintegration that they so desperately look for. Since this disorder is so often a response to a significant stressor, the techniques discussed in the treatment of the post-traumatic stress disorder are also applicable here.

## Psychogenic Fugue (300.13)

Psychogenic Fugue is a specific form of amnesia in which people are unable to recall the essentials of their previous personality. In addition, they are likely to wander away from their home environment and assume an entirely new identity. Although they are seldom able to recall the behaviors that they carried out while in the fugue state, the recovery is usually complete.

This syndrome often occurs as a reaction to a severe psychosocial stressor, such as the unexpected breakup of a marriage or loss of a job without warning. It is facilitated by previous heavy alcohol or drug use, which points to the dissociative quality inherent in states of consciousness engendered by drug abuse.

Somnambulism, traditionally considered a dissociative reaction, is now listed in DSM-III as a sleep disorder. This is reasonable since it is usually not associated with any significant pathology. When it is clearly not associated with organic disorder, as it is in most cases, it is best considered a simple learned behavior that was not suppressed in the early stages of development (Meyer, 1975).

*DSM-III*

To diagnose psychogenic fugue, the DSM-III requires evidence that the individual suddenly assumed at least some elements of a new identity, left the home or place of work, and could not recall one's previous life.

This disorder is relatively rare. It bears some similarity to the multiple personality, since the new identity is often in sharp contrast to the previous identity. As noted above, the pattern usually occurs in response to a significant loss of some sort and is catalyzed in some individuals by the shock of a natural disaster or a war.

*Testing Considerations*

These individuals are seldom tested when they are still in the midst of the fugue state. As they are brought back into their natural environment, the recovery of memory begins to occur. When they are tested, they show patterns similar to psychogenic amnesia.

*Treatment Options*

Since psychogenic fugue is analogous to psychogenic amnesia, the techniques described for the treatment of the post-traumatic stress disorder are also applicable; a subjectively disturbing stressor is almost always a critical catalyst here. As a follow-up, it would be useful to deal with the subjective reasons for the severity of this trauma through humanistic and existential techniques, for example, through Gestalt Therapy, since its emphasis is on reintegration of the person's wholeness.

Janov's Primal Therapy (1980) is a technique that could be useful as one part of the treatment for the dissociative disorders, particularly with psychogenic fugue, as such clients have abruptly denied underlying conflicts and feelings. However, this is a good example of how a specific technique can unfortunately be elevated into the status of a school of psychotherapy

## Multiple Personality (300.14)

The Multiple Personality receives a great deal of attention in the media, in part because it is often confused with schizophrenia. From this attention, it could be concluded that it is a common disorder. However, Winer (1978) notes that there have been only about 200 reasonably well documented cases. The multiple personality should be considered extremely rare, and many clinicians never see a true multiple personality in their entire career.

Multiple personalities come into treatment because they note some peculiarities in their world—forgetting of certain interactions with people, general confusion, and loss of memories. A different personality is then discovered through psychotherapy, which is often supplemented by hypnosis. In some cases, personalities continue to be produced, first by the indirect suggestion of the therapist's interest and reinforcement, and then by the reinforcement of the therapist's reinvigorated concern for the person's problems (Gruenewald, 1978).

Amnesia is a pathognomonic sign of a future multiple personality, and stress is an important precipitating factor in the genesis of this disorder. Stressors in a person's psychological world often trigger the sudden transitions in personality noted here.

## DSM-III

According to DSM-III, the multiple personality is a person who is consecutively dominated by separate and distinct personalities that determine separate behavior patterns. The personalities are complex and reasonably well integrated, and the transition from one to another is sudden. The disorder is most commonly observed in young adult and adolescent females, and the separate personalities are often in stark contrast to each other. The next and later personalities are usually a crystallization into a personality of opposite facets from the original one.

## Testing Considerations

Since the personalities in a multiple personality will vary markedly, depending on what facets of that individual they are expressing, no particular patterns could be expected, though a 3–8/8–3 MMPI pattern is commonly noted in dissociative reactions. Fowler (1981) suggests that a 1–3/3–1 code type is also probable here. Histrionic and dependent personality components are often found in the separate personalities, and there is a greater likelihood of an acting out of aggressive and sexual impulse. The sections on the histrionic and the dependent personality disorder deal with this.

Osgood et al. (1976) demonstrated an ingenious application of the semantic differential to the assessment of the contrasting features of a multiple personality. Clinicians who happen to see this rare disorder could apply this method to monitor changes in the individual as he or she goes through various personalities and then begins to integrate again into one single personality. The section on malingering is useful since in this disorder people are inclined to malinger, in large part because of the disproportionate media attention.

## Treatment Options

The classic treatment for the multiple personality has been hypnosis, which is used to get in touch with the dissociated subpersonalities. In the few cases that have been available to clinicians for study, this has generally been reasonably successful, though the cost in time has been high. Also, it is arguable that since hypnosis itself may involve a dissociative experience, it may iatrogenically increase the tendency to produce multiple personalities, particularly in the short run.

One could argue that Transactional Analysis (Berne, 1964) would also further the dissociative process, since it so clearly emphasizes separate ego states. However, it could be useful in getting the person in touch with the message that all of us play different roles, and when these roles become crystallized, the potential for dissociative experience is heightened. This would at least place this experience closer to a normal experience and thus foster reintegration. Psychoanalysis has been used effectively with the multiple personality (Osgood et al., 1976), though the therapist may have to deal with the rather unique problem of multiple transferences.

## Depersonalization Disorder (300.60)

As noted earlier, the Depersonalization Disorder is dissimilar to other dissociative reactions, since consciousness is never truly segmented and significant memory loss is not a factor. Since there is no better place for it in the DSM-III, it is listed here because it includes a dissociation from the usual sense of reality.

In the depersonalization disorder, individuals experience a sense of separation from normal consciousness and may report feeling as if they are a separate observer of the self. The typical reality of the usual world seems as if it has been altered. This is an experience that many people have on occasion; the issue is whether or not it is a consistent pattern. It is interesting to note that if one follows a modern guru, such as Krishnamurti, the ability constantly to perceive one's functioning as a separate observer is the mark of progress toward enlightenment.

Since depersonalization is an experience many people undergo at times, the definition of disorder is appropriate on the basis of either frequency or a feeling of lack of control. Many people are not really bothered by such experiences, whereas others feel as if they are going crazy. In this latter situation, the sense of depersonalization can be conditioned to anticipatory anxiety, leading to a vicious cycle reinforcing the belief that they might indeed be going crazy.

Since this disorder focuses on an experience of a changing identity, it is not surprising that it occurs most frequently during adolescence. There is little impairment from the experience itself but when accentuated by a conditioned anxiety response, it becomes troublesome. In that sense, it is similar to the conditioned anxiety response that many argue is the cause in the flashbacks from certain drug experiences. Abuse of alcohol and drugs facilitates the development of this disorder.

### DSM-III

This disorder is still appropriately referred to as the Depersonalization Neurosis, and the present category retains some of the DSM-II characteristics. There is usually more anxiety here than in the other dissociative disorders, though the dissociative aspect is the essential feature.

The DSM-III requires substantive indication that an episode of depersonalization occurred potent enough to cause significant vocational or social disruption. The possibilities of minor organic dysfunction, anxiety disorders, or even a developing depressive episode must be ruled out.

## MMPI

This disorder was included in the DSM-II as the depersonalization neurosis, and the modal profile reflects this. Elevations on scales 3, 7 and F are likely, as these tap both the anxiety and hysteric components. The anxiety and identity confusion also lead to an elevated 8 scale, and since identity is threatened, changes in scale 5 away from stereotypical sexual role scores are expected. Since these individuals are usually young, active in their response to their distress, but inclined to denial accompanied by somatic concerns, elevations on scales 9 and 1 may also occur. The possible scale 4 elevation reflects the degree of hostility and anger and the lack of social sophistication that varies within this disorder. In rare cases, a spike 0 profile may be noted early in its development (Kelley & King, 1979).

## 16 PF

Instability and loss of a sense of reality are reflected on moderately low C and $Q_3$ scores. O and M are likely to be high, while the low scores on N reflect the naïveté and relative lack of sophistication. Individuals who manifest a depersonalization disorder are usually of higher intelligence, so scale B should be average or above.

## Treatment Options

Since in some respects the Depersonalization Disorder is as much an identity development disorder as it is a dissociative experience, any techniques useful for getting in touch with the less integrated aspects of the personality could be useful here. This could range from Roger's (1951) Client-Centered Therapy through Gestalt Therapy (Perls et al., 1958) and could be supplemented by an emphasis on the problems of self-labeling, as detailed by Meichenbaum (1977). In this approach, clients would be trained to label experiences viewed as alien as actually an integral part of their personality and something to be dealt with in a confrontive and honest manner.

Psychodrama could also be useful here.

In psychodrama a person is encountering his conflicts and psychic pain in a setting that will more closely approximate his real life situation than in most other therapeutic approaches. A young man in conflict with a parent talks directly to a person as an auxiliary ego playing his parent. His fantasy (or reality) of his hostility or love can be acted out on the spot. (Yablonsky, 1976, p. 4).

The acting out of such fantasies about one's own reality, or the experiencing of that reality, can ultimately lead to a positive, integrative experience.

# 8

---

# Psychosexual Disorders

This category in the DSM-III is used for those disorders in which a psychological variable is a significant factor in a sexual disturbance or disorder. If the disorder is caused by a physical factor, such as impotence from severe arteriosclerosis, it would be coded as an organic mental disorder. However, within this overall category, such conditions are rare.

In DSM-III, there are three main subdivisions: The Gender Identity Disorders, the Paraphilias (the DSM-III term for the traditionally termed *sexual deviations*), and the Psychosexual Dysfunctions. There is also a separate category labeled Ego-dystonic Homosexuality and a residual category entitled Psychosexual Disorder Not Elsewhere Classified.

## Transsexualism (302.5x)

The DSM-III category of Gender Identity Disorders, of which Transsexualism is the major subcategory, is hardly a category, as it comprises only Transsexualism, the parallel category for children called Gender Identity Disorder of Childhood (302.60), and a residual category called Atypical Gender Identity Disorder (302.85). In the early drafts of DSM-III, Transvestism was also included. Since it soon became clear that this was inappropriate, transvestism was placed in the paraphilia category.

Transsexuals are persons who strongly identify with the opposite sex, as manifested in cross dressing and a persistent desire for a physical change to the opposite sex. This strong desire to change gender and the feeling of having an underlying opposite-sex identity are what primarily differentiate the transsexual from the transvestite (Masters et al., 1982). Transsexualism is a chronic disorder and is almost always preceded by gender identity problems in childhood. A disturbed parent-child relationship, particularly the absence of a model of the same sex, predisposes a child to this disorder.

Also, any other characteristics, either physical or psychological, that cause identification of a child by others as one of the opposite sex (such as long hair and soft features in males) also facilitate transsexualism.

The first sex-change operation occurred in Europe in 1930. Most change is made from male to female, in large part because there is a greater initial demand for this type of change, but also, just as importantly, because the surgery for the reverse procedure, female to male, is much more difficult and has a higher likelihood of failure. Money and Wiedeking (1980) argue that this tendency is because maleness genetically is "femaleness repressed" (an extra Y chromosome that modified the basic genetic structure), and thus males become more vulnerable to gender confusion.

Clinicians have an important role not only in diagnosing transsexualism in standard clinical settings, but also in the psychological screening of such persons as appropriate for sex-change surgery. It is controversial whether or not this surgery is necessary. However, because such surgery is likely to continue, it is most important that people be thoroughly screened. Most reputable surgeons who deal with these problems mandate a team assessment by a psychologist, psychiatrist, and an endocrinologist. The traditional success rate of this surgery, about 12 to 1 in male or female sex reassignments (Pauly, 1968), undoubtedly reflects the thorough psychological screening techniques that have been done. As this procedure becomes more commonplace, screening will probably be more lax, and individuals who are inappropriate will have an increasing chance of being operated on. For example, certain schizophrenics have a delusional belief that they are of the opposite sex, and some disturbed homosexuals and transvestites who cannot deal with the demands of their perceived role conflicts may unconsciously view a sex change as an escape from these conflicts. The clinician involved in such procedures should especially consider indicators for schizophrenia, paranoia, transvestism, and homosexuality when dealing with potential transsexual candidates.

## DSM-III

There should be evidence of continuous (at least two years) and pervasive feelings that one is the wrong sex, with a consequent desire to change genital structure to the other sex, and then to live in the lifestyle of the opposite sex. There should be no evidence of directly related genetic abnormality, such as hermaphroditism. To warrant a diagnosis of transsexualism, the clinician may first have to screen for individuals who are primarily schizophrenic, as well as to consider if there should be a primary or ancillary diagnosis of either ego-dystonic homosexuality or transvestism.

The disorder is subcoded as "heterosexual," "homosexual," or "asexual," with this label determined solely by the dominant sexual preference in the history of the individual.

## MMPI

Tsushima and Wedding (1979), in a study that looked at the MMPI profiles of transsexuals, found them to be surprisingly within normal limits. Of course, scale 5 is high in males due to nonidentification with the traditional male role, along with the conflicts about sexual identity. While presurgical males-to-females were found by Fleming et al. (1981) to be high on 5, 6, and 8, presurgical females were high on 5, and relatively high on 8, 6, and 7. Postsurgical females (i.e., those who had been male) were high on 5, and relatively high on 6 and K. Postsurgical males were high on 5 and relatively high on 6. Fleming et al. (1981) note that the tendency to peak on 5 and 6 is consistent with the early research literature about MMPI profiles of transsexuals.

On occasion, scale 1 and, to a lesser degree, 3 may be slightly elevated, reflecting preoccupation with body structure. In accordance with the preceding, scale F may be elevated. On the other hand, if transsexuals perceive the need to present themselves as healthy to pass the screening, scale K would be quite high, and signs of pathology would be suppressed. If they are anxious and ambivalent about the identity issue, scales 4 and 8 may be slightly elevated; and if this has generated depression, scale 2 is raised.

## 16 PF

As with the MMPI, the pattern is generally within reasonably normal limits. However, the mode of sexual adjustment results in slightly higher I scores and slightly lower H, E, and N scores in most males, with the converse being true in most females. Scale B should reflect the average or above average intelligence in most transsexuals, and since they endorse attitudes that differ from the average, they are likely to be higher on $Q_1$ and M, and moderately low on G.

## Treatment Options

A classic option for the transsexual has been surgery to change the genitalia to that of the opposite sex. There is good evidence (Pauly, 1968) that in certain individuals this is an effective procedure, although ancillary psychotherapy for the social adjustment to the new sex is also an important adjunct. Also, covert modeling to retrain more masculine mannerisms and behaviors has proven helpful (May et al., 1981). In general, the surgical success is higher when the change is from male to female, rather than vice versa. This in large part reflects the much more complex surgery required when the change is from female to male, as well as the accompanying higher probability of problematic side effects and outright failure.

In some cases, surgery is an unnecessary intervention, as psychotherapy and the passage of time can deal effectively with these identity concerns. This is particularly true when therapy is combined with aversive sexual re-orientation training and other techniques of psychosocial conditioning (Barlow, Abel, & Blanchard, 1979; Meyer & Freeman, 1977). The clinician might also take note that the well-known attorney Melvin Belli (1979) argues persuasively that therapists can come under tort liability for taking a person through transsexual surgery, and it can possibly be considered under "criminal mayhem" statutes if there is any lack of clarity about the person's consent or ability to consent. Belli argues that adequate consent is problematical in most cases because the "compulsive" quality of the need to change sex is contradictory to the law's requirement that consent be "an affirmative act of an unconstrained and undeceived will" (p. 498). However, could not this concept of being compelled into treatment be applied to almost any disorder?

## Paraphilias

*Paraphilia* is the new DSM-III term for the sexual deviations, and both terms will be used interchangeably. The authors of the DSM-III assert, not altogether convincingly, that the term *paraphilia* is superior to that of *sexual deviation* or *variation*, since in paraphilia it is correctly indicated that the deviation (para) is in that to which the individual is attracted (philia).

Paraphilias consist of sexually arousing fantasy behavior associated with nonhuman sexual targets or nonconsenting humans, and/or sexual activity with humans that involves either simulated or actual pain or humiliation. The essential disorder is in the lack of capacity for mature and participating affectionate sexual behavior with adult partners. Traditionally, these disorders have been far more common in males, but this discrepancy has decreased in recent years. Occasionally engaging in such fantasy or behavior does not usually qualify one as a paraphiliac. Exclusivity, persistency, and pervasiveness are the hallmarks of the disorder.

The specific paraphilia categories included in DSM-III are: 1) Fetishism, 2) Transvestism, 3) Zoophilia, 4) Pedophilia, 5) Exhibitionism, 6) Voyeurism, 7) Sexual Masochism, and 8) Sexual Sadism. There is also a residual category termed Other Paraphilias that could be used often when making a diagnosis, since the range of potential sexual deviations is restricted only by the limits of the imagination. The variations included in the DSM-III are those that have traditionally been labeled as deviant that have involved a sociolegal issue. Thus, *variation* is an even more appropriate term than *deviance*, since the word *variation* more clearly implies this wide range of potential behaviors, plus the facts that many of these patterns may in certain circumstances be acceptable and adaptive and that the "deviance" of the disorder is many times only in the eye of the beholder.

### Diagnostic Considerations

In general, the paraphilias, unless they are confounded by the presence of other psychopathology, do not present modal abnormal patterns on either the MMPI or the 16 PF. Since they are obtained in a clinical setting, some pathology is suggested, or else society, through a legal or social agent (e.g., a marital therapist) is concerned about the pattern. Certain scales may then be markedly elevated.

Measuring sexual responses to suggested imagery or to actual pictures of various stimuli is helpful in specifying the focus of the sexually deviant fantasies that are a key to behavior (Meyer & Freeman, 1977). Direct measures of penile tumescence (via changes in a rubber tube encircling the penis, as in a pneumograph) are the most precise, though thermography has distinct advantages of ease of access and less embarrassment (Abramson et al., 1981).

### Treatment Options

Since the paraphilias range from disorders that involve passivity (sexual masochism) to those that involve coercive aggression and legal sanctions (pedophilia), treatments will differ as well (McConaghy, 1982). In general, aversive conditioning techniques have been useful, much as they are throughout the habit disorders (Fischer & Gochros, 1977). Since fears of heterosexuality are often involved, psychotherapy is a useful adjunct; and if fears become specifically focused and take on a phobic quality, systematic desensitization and the implosive therapies can be used. Cognitive behavioral approaches, such as covert sensitization, as well as the existential therapies, are useful adjuncts to deal with the issues of sociolegal guilt and lack of responsibility.

### Fetishism (300.81)

The DSM-III defines Fetishism as a condition wherein nonliving objects are used as the primary and consistently preferred method of stimulating sexual arousal. Though the traditional use of this term included an attraction to isolated though still attached body parts, this does not fit with the DSM-III definition. If the fetish is simply an article of clothing used in cross-dressing, the diagnosis would be transvestism. Also, if the arousal value is inherent in the object, such as a vibrator, the diagnosis of fetishism would be inappropriate.

Sexual stimulation from fetishes is typically obtained by tasting, fondling, kissing, or smelling the objects. Bras, panties, and shoes are the most common objects. The objects may be used while masturbating alone, and in some cases are a necessary preliminary to intercourse. A degree of fetishism is associated with any sexual experience. Normal foreplay includes attention to sexually arousing objects or parts of the body, with consequent sexual arousal and progression toward coitus. In fetishism, however, the fetish takes primacy as a necessary means for developing arousal and allows avoidance of intimacy (La Torre, 1980).

A confounding variable in fetishism, as well as in a number of other paraphilias, is the potential legal issue. Acts of breaking and entering are occasionally committed by the fetishist who is seeking a supply of women's used bras or panties. New articles of clothing are seldom arousing, in part because they are not identified with any individual person, and also because they do not have the odors that are often arousing to the fetishist. In many cases, the illegal behavior itself increases the excitation and consequently increases the sexual arousal.

Although fetishism tends to crystallize as a behavior pattern in adolescence, it often has precursors in childhood. It is chronic, and most fetishists are men.

## DSM-III

To diagnose a person as a fetishist, it is required that the fetish, a nonliving object, be a preferred mode of arousal while the client is alone, or is a necessary factor when used with a partner. It may occur in either actual behavior or fantasy. Transvestism, or objects that are inherently sexually stimulating as the only evidence of fetishistic behavior, would not warrant this diagnosis.

## MMPI

Fetishists seldom show a markedly elevated MMPI profile. If the fetishism reflects some insecurity with the male sex role or some disguised homoerotic trends, an elevation on scale 5 is expected (Graham, 1977). In fetishists who indulge alone, a fear of the opposite sex may exist, which would elevate scales 4 and 7 to a degree. When the fetishism is embedded in heterosexual relationships, such elevations are less probable. When there is a legal problem involving fetishism, the reader should consult the section on malingering.

*16 PF*

The fetishist who indulges while alone is more likely to be low on factor A. If the persons accept their fetishistic behavior, $Q_1$ should be reasonably high, whereas if they do not accept it, $Q_1$ may be at an average level or even lower. These clients are also likely to be relatively low on scale G and moderately high on M. If distressed by their pattern, high scores on $Q_4$ and O are likely. If they are being legally or socially coerced because of their pattern, defensive patterns such as malingering may be expected, and a higher score on L occurs.

*Treatment Options*

The aversive conditioning therapies are especially appropriate with fetishism, since specific behavior patterns are the central focus. Both mild electric shock and nausea-inducing drugs have been successfully used in aversive conditioning procedures in which the object of the fetish, or fantasy of it, is paired with the aversive stimulus (Barlow, Abel, & Blanchard, 1979; Meyer & Freeman, 1977). The aversion therapy procedures of both fear conditioning and aversion relief have been used. Once the person has decreased the arousal value contingent on the fetishistic object, training in more normal sexual patterns can be necessary (Masters & Johnson, 1970; Masters et al., 1982; Hendrix & Meyer, 1974; Meyer & Freeman, 1977).

In general, mild electric shock is preferable to such nausea-producing drugs as apomorphine since the contiguity between the avoidance stimulus and the deviant response is more easily controlled when shock is used.

## Transvestism (302.30)

Transvestism is the dressing in clothes of the opposite sex; it also includes any other voluntary manifestations of those behaviors traditionally thought of as specific to the opposite sex. DSM-III limits this concept even more by asserting that it is only diagnosed in males, a chauvinistic position for which it provides little in the way of supporting rationale. In the early drafts of DSM-III, transvestism was included under the Gender Identity problems. However, even though there are similarities to those disorders, transvestism is closer to the paraphilias and is more appropriately classified therein.

Beyond simple cross-dressing, the behavior must be sexually arousing. In most transvestites the cross-dressing behavior was initiated in childhood and in some was significantly reinforced by parents. It typically becomes paired with masturbation and eventuates in the classic transvestite pattern.

Transvestism is considered to be a rare disorder; an even smaller subgroup eventually goes from transvestism to transsexualism, where the diagnosis of transsexualism takes precedence.

Transvestism can be considered a specific form of fetishism. Just as in fetishism, an inanimate object is the stimulating variable, and there is often little or no dependence on human relationships for sexual gratification. When the transvestite has a partner, there may be masochistic fantasies that progress into behavior. This then adds a secondary diagnosis of sexual masochism.

## DSM-III

To warrant the diagnosis of transvestism, it must first be evident that the person, a heterosexual male, is not transsexual. Also, the cross-dressing must occur for a significant period of time and with reasonable frequency. At least initially it is carried out to derive sexual arousal, with consequent sexual frustration if the dressing is inhibited.

### Diagnostic Considerations

Transvestites do not show particularly pathological MMPI or 16 PF profiles. The clinician can expect a high scale 5 whether this is a male or female transvestite (however, DSM-III limits this disorder to males dressing as females). There is also a moderate rise in scale 3, which indicates some histrionic components, and possibly mild elevations in scales 4 and 6, reflecting concern about being discovered in a secret life style as well as hostility toward standard social mores.

On the 16 PF, moderately elevated L and $Q_1$ scales as well as moderately low scores on $Q_3$ and G occur. A higher score on N is also probable; and if anxiety is a reason for this clinical situation, elevation on $Q_4$ in particular, and possibly on O, could be expected.

### Treatment Options

Since transvestism is easily considered a subcategory of fetishism, the procedures noted in that subsection are equally applicable here. In addition to the aversive procedures, the therapist could use thought stopping to control the initial impulse to cross-dress (Fischer & Gochros, 1977). Since transvestism may have certain compulsive features, the reader is also referred to the section on the obsessive-compulsive disorder. Both the aversion therapy and the thought stopping can be amplified by the use of a portable self-administered shock unit. The person can wear this unit discreetly under clothing and, when the impulse arises, a shock can be administered in conjunction with the aversion or thought-stopping procedure.

Covert Sensitization (Cautela & Wall, 1980) is particularly helpful in the habit disorders and can easily be dovetailed with the aversive conditioning procedures in the therapist's office. In the Covert Sensitization procedure, some highly aversive contingency is imagined immediately on the occurrence of the fantasy of the undesired behavior. In this case, it is the transvestite pattern. As a result, the undesired impulse toward transvestism is weakened.

## Zoophilia (302.10)

The essential variable in Zoophilia is the use of animals as the means of producing sexual arousal. A DSM-III diagnosis is appropriate when such behavior or fantasy is consistently preferred even though there are other outlets reasonably available. Zoophilia occurs primarily in males and is very rare. It may occasionally be a sign of schizophrenia, in which case a diagnosis of schizophrenia would take precedence.

The traditional term *bestiality* referred primarily to having sexual intercourse with animals, whereas zoophilia refers to any type of sexual contact with animals. The preferred animal is usually one with which the person had contact during childhood, such as a pet or farm animal. Zoophilia is a moderately common theme in pornography and usually involves a female having a sexual experience with a pony or a dog. This theme is common because the usual consumer of pornography is male, and this appears to be an exciting theme for males. In actuality, Kinsey's data (1948, 1953) suggest that such patterns are extremely rare in females and only a bit more common in males, at least where the pattern has clinical significance.

### Diagnostic Considerations

In the typical person who shows clinical zoophilia, the major features are significant depression, problems in interpersonal skills, and anxiety. Hence, I would expect elevations on scales 2, 7 and 0 respectively. Also, the disordered sexual life could cause at least a mild elevation on scale 5.

In the 16 PF, the shame, anxiety, lack of interpersonal skills, and social isolation mean to this author that there should be high O and $Q_4$ scores, and relatively low A, C, and F scores. Scale B is low in these individuals, and similarly, N is expected to be low, and $Q_2$ moderately low.

### Treatment Options

There are few reports in the literature concerning the treatment of zoophilia. Aversive conditioning procedures would be helpful regarding any fetishistic components (McConaghy, 1982), and there have been some reports of success in curing cases of zoophilia with hypnosis. Since immaturity and inability to make adequate heterosexual contacts are often a factor, social retraining and the techniques of Rational-Emotive Therapy (Ellis, 1980) might also be applied.

## Pedophilia (302.20)

Pedophilia literally and ironically means "love of children," and a pedophiliac is one who consistently seeks out a sexual experience with children.

Pedophilia is extremely rare in females and, although it is not a particularly common behavior in any demographic group, it is seen most commonly in middle-aged males. There are significant differences between pedophiliac men who are inclined toward sexual experiences with male children and those who seek out females. Heterosexual pedophiles are more likely to be married and prefer a younger target—females age eight to ten, as opposed to the homosexual pedophile's preference for boys in the twelve to fourteen age range. Homosexual pedophiles show a poor prognosis for change, are less likely to know their victim already, and are more interested in proceeding to orgasm rather than focusing on the touching and looking behavior often preferred by heterosexual pedophiles. Many heterosexual male pedophiles have problems with potency and are likely to prefer ejaculation achieved through voyeuristic-exhibitionistic masturbation. When they do attempt intercourse with a child, they are more likely to generate trauma and pain and in that way raise their chances of being reported and eventually apprehended.

Pedophiles, whether homosexual or heterosexual, often feel inadequate about their sexuality, and the contact and/or comparison with the sexually immature target may alleviate this anxiety and allow a nonthreatening release for sexual tension.

Alcohol abuse is a common catalyst for this behavior, as are marital problems in pedophiles who are married. Another catalyst (which does not detract in any way from the pedophile's responsibility for the act) is victim behavior. Finkelhor (1979) collected interesting data that showed that an unusually high percentage of sexually victimized children had lived without their mothers for a significant period previous to the age of sixteen. It is possible that they may have missed a subtle training in behaviors conducive to fending off this type of sexual coercion. When the pedophiliac is mentally retarded or schizophrenic, evidence shows that in a number of cases the victim initiated the contact (Virkunen, 1975).

A subcategory of pedophilia is incest. While incest occurs in any potential family structure relationship, father-daughter incest is by far the most common target of societal concern. Three psychological subpatterns occur in this specific form of incest (Blair & Justice, 1979; Meiselman, 1978). The first pattern is the inadequate and psychosexually immature father who is functionally a pedophile and who often has sexual contact with his daughters, sons, and other children. Such individuals show a combination of pedophiliac and psychopathic diagnostic indications. The second is a true "primary psychopath." This person relates to virtually all people as objects, is promiscuous in all directions, and shows little remorse over any behavior patterns.

Family-generated incest is the third pattern, and it is marked by a passive and inadequate father and an emotionally disturbed mother. Persons engaging in this type of incest show characteristics of the pedophile, plus aspects of the passive-aggressive and dependent personality disorders.

## DSM-III

To warrant a diagnosis of pedophilia, the person must consistently search out and prefer sexual contact with prepubertal children. The DSM-III arbitrarily defines the required difference between the ages of the persons as ten years; it drops this requirement when the diagnostician has to consider a diagnosis in a late adolescent. In that case, the judgment is based on the age difference and the child's sexual maturity.

## MMPI

As might be expected from society's repugnance for this type of behavior, pedophiliacs are far more defensive than persons with most other paraphilias. As a result, elevated L and K scales are common. Denial, along with an avoidance of intrapsychic concern, is reflected in an elevated 3 scale and, in conjunction with the lack of significant guilt, the 4 scale is also raised. A number of two-point codes have been associated with this pattern, and most of them include the elevations on scales 3, 4, L, and K.

The particularly inadequate pedophile who has significant difficulties in dealing interpersonally with the opposite sex often presents a 1-8/8-1 profile. Those who show a consistent immaturity throughout many of their behavior patterns and who have problems in controlling impulse behavior may show a 3-8/8-3 code. Where the pedophiliac behavior is a classic counterphobic mechanism to deny feelings of inadequacy about masculinity, the 4-8/8-4, with a surprisingly low scale 5 score (considering the person's general behavior patterns), is obtained. Where the person is more aware of the disturbance in sexual identity, an elevation on scale 5 is seen.

## 16 PF

On the 16 PF, the emotional disturbance, impulsivity, and deviant mores are reflected in low scores on C, G, and $Q_3$. Anxiety and insecurity, possibly induced by the potential for being apprehended, elevate scores on O and Q$_4$. The deviant fantasy and the isolation from society because of the repulsiveness of the acts result in high scores on L and M. Homosexual pedophiles are moderately high on E and H and moderately low on I; the reverse is true for heterosexual pedophiles. Scores on scale B vary markedly, though on the average they are moderately low.

*Treatment Options*

Because of the disgust with which most people respond to this disorder, it is not surprising that the typical treatment approaches are somewhat coercive. Also, pedophiles rarely bring themselves into treatment and are typically coerced by sociolegal pressure (McConaghy, 1982). Castration is still a favored response in some cultures, and in our society, chemocastration is still considered to be a reasonable option. Antiandrogens such as cyproterone acetate (in Europe) or medroxyprogesterone acetate (in the United States) suppress the sexual libidos of male pedophiles; these drugs have also been used with rapists and exhibitionists (Walker, 1978; Walker & Meyer, 1981). They function by reducing serum testosterone levels to a level at which sexual arousal is diminished or is absent, and they have moderate success when combined with psychotherapy. The aversion therapies have also been used here, with moderate success.

Covert Sensitization has been successfully used to treat pedophilia. Aversive mental images are immediately associated with images and impulses for initiating and continuing pedophilic behaviors. Forgione (1976) presented an interesting variation on this approach. He filmed pedophiliacs while they re-enacted their pedophiliac behaviors in response to a child-like mannequin; simply watching the playback proved aversive and reduced the pedophiliac behavior. The clinician could vary this procedure additionally by taking selected slides from the tape and pairing electric shock with them to further the aversive response.

Since inadequacy in social interactions is a major factor in most pedophiles, assertiveness training, particularly directed toward adults of the opposite sex, is helpful here. It can be complemented by general social retraining toward an ability to attain mature heterosexual partners (Meyer & Freeman, 1977).

### Exhibitionism (302.40)

The term *Exhibitionism* was first introduced into psychopathology by Lasegue in 1877, though the act itself was described as early as 4 B.C. (Cox, 1980). It is the act of exposing the genitals to a stranger in order to obtain sexual arousal. Certain rare individuals do expose themselves without ever having been aroused, but they usually turn out to be psychotic, senile, or at least moderately mentally retarded.

The DSM-III argues that the condition is found only in males. Certainly there are few reports to police of females who exhibit themselves; yet, to assert that the behavior never occurs in females is unsubstantiated. Along with Voyeurism, exhibitionism has had the highest recidivism rate of all the sexual disorders (Cox, 1980).

## DSM-III

The DSM-III requires that there be repeated acts of exhibitionism toward unsuspecting strangers, in which arousal occurs fairly immediately upon the act of exposing, and in which the act of exposing and the consequent arousal are the means of final sexual gratification.

## Diagnostic Considerations

From the legal perspective, exhibitionism is probably the most commonly reported paraphilia, but the cost to victims and society is lower than that in some of the other disorders, such as pedophilia. It is estimated to account for about one-third of all sexual offenses reported to authorities, and only a small percentage of exposure acts are ever reported to the police (Cox, 1980; Hendrix & Meyer, 1976). Indications are that there is a bimodal distribution of the mean age of onset of first exposure, with peaks in the eleven to fifteen and twenty-one to twenty-five age ranges. The mean age of first arrest is approximately twenty-five years of age. Exhibitionists seldom gravitate toward more serious sexual offenses (Cox, 1980).

The high recidivism rate is partially explained by a markedly increasing recidivism for those who are convicted more than once. Even though there is a conviction rate of only 10 percent for first offenders, the rate is almost 60 percent for those with more than one previous sexual offense and 70 percent for those with previous sexual and nonsexual offenses. If intervention can keep the exhibitionist from exposing himself for eighteen months or more after treatment, there is a low likelihood of future exposing (Cox, 1980).

There is a high incidence of disrupted father-son relationships in the background of exhibitionists (this is true to a degree for most of the paraphilias). Exhibitionists show poor interpersonal relationships during adolescence, and masturbation is always of unusual importance to them as a sexual outlet, even when other partners are available (Cox, 1980).

Of the personality types that eventuate in exhibitionism (Smith & Meyer, 1980; Hendrix & Meyer, 1976), the Characterological type, a small group, is the only one that shows any significant danger to the victim. They have profiles similar to rapists, with the same elements of anger and hostility; the reader is referred to that section. The shock response of the victim is a major reinforcement, and there is little guilt or remorse.

A second subtype is the Unaware group, where the act is an outgrowth of extreme alcohol intoxication, organic brain disorder, or severe mental retardation. A third type is the Inadequate group. These individuals are similar to those with the avoidant personality disorder, though they have a few more obsessional features and more anger. The reader is referred to the section on the avoidant personality disorder, with the notation that scales 4 and 6 on the MMPI should be a bit more elevated here, as well as the correlated scales on the 16 PF.

The fourth group, the Impulsive type, is obsessional, tense, anxious, and sexually confused. Their behavior is an impulsive response to intrapsychic conflict and distress. It is this last group, the largest group of exhibitionists, which we will focus on in the following discussion of diagnostic parameters.

*MMPI*

A summary of MMPI data collected on exhibitionists shows them to be moderately nonconforming individuals who have a history of mild violations of social norms, but with no extensive allied psychopathology (Cox, 1980). The standard elevations throughout most studies are on scales 4, 8 and 5, though these are often below the 70 T mark. The elevations on scales 4 and 8 reflect the mild antisocial nature of the behavior, the lack of impulse control, and a degree of hostility toward the general environment. The elevation on 5 naturally reflects the sexual confusion. Exhibitionists are usually very low on scale 0 and moderately low on scales 1 and 9. To the degree scale 8 is elevated in relation to other scales, these persons are likely to be self-defeating and their exposure patterns are more likely to be discovered. For example, the exhibitionist seen by Hendrix and Meyer (1976) had exhibited himself about 800 times without ever being apprehended. Similar cases have shown a low 8 scale, but a high 4 scale and a moderately high 5 and K scale.

*16 PF*

Exhibitionists score moderately high on O and $Q_4$, though their scales may revert to average if they are not under some kind of legal scrutiny. Similar to obsessives, they are only moderately low on C and moderately high on scales L and M. To the degree they have been self-defeating in their exposure patterns, they are likely to show a low score on $Q_3$ and N, and a high score on H. Other scales are usually not remarkable.

*Treatment Options*

Exhibitionism shows a high rate of recidivism, as does pedophilia; for that reason, some therapists eventually resort to chemocastration through the use of such antiandrogen drugs as medroxyprogesterone acetate. However, the major treatment for exhibitionism is some form of aversion therapy. Some retraining in social skills and in orgasmic reconditioning also is usually necessary (McConaghy, 1982). Covert Sensitization can be used and is amplified by adding noxious odors and shocks at the time the exhibitionist is presenting the aversive images to himself (Maletzky, 1980).

Hendrix and Meyer (1976) demonstrated that exhibitionism can be controlled through a multifaceted treatment approach of one exhibitionist that included no aversive techniques. They used progressive relaxation to lower his tension-anger pattern, and cassette tapes along with autogenic training to further the relaxation response. Psychotherapy uncovered the suppressed anger and fear of interacting with females, and assertive training was used to control these situations. This was combined with increased self-verbalizations designed to heighten self-esteem and confidence. At that point, sexual counseling by the methods of Masters and Johnson (1970) helped in the attainment of adequate heterosexual relationships. Also included was systematic desensitization, which was used to dissipate a phobic fear of being rebuffed by females. In addition, Dr. Hendrix accompanied this exhibitionist to in vivo situations, such as the campus snack shop, and was introduced as his friend if necessary. Dr. Hendrix monitored and then later counseled the client on his socialization patterns.

## Voyeurism (302.82)

Voyeurs consistently search for situations in which they may view individuals or groups of individuals in the nude or in some form of sexual activity in order to obtain sexual arousal. Like homosexuals, pedophiles, and exhibitionists, voyeurs show a high recidivism rate. Virtually all cases of voyeurism reported to the authorities are males, though there is no evidence that this behavior never occurs in females. Our society is organized to respond differently to exhibitionistic and voyeuristic behavior of females.

Approximately one-third of voyeurs are married. Even though the age for the first time for a voyeuristic act is the middle to late twenties, there has usually been a significant history of sexual and other offenses throughout adolescence. As with exhibitionists, there is a large history of broken homes and marital distress. Voyeurs seldom maintained close relationships with sisters or other girls when they were young.

Most voyeurs are not markedly disturbed, and the simple act of obtaining arousal from looking is of course a normal part of many sexual experiences. Triolism, or the sharing of a sexual partner while one observes or is observed, is a major reinforcement in group sex experiences and is not classified as voyeurism.

Only a small proportion of voyeurs pose a danger to their victim. They are psychopathic in personality and show the following specific behavior patterns: 1) they are more likely to enter a building in order to carry out their voyeuristic behaviors; 2) in some way they draw attention to themselves while they are in the act (Smith, 1976).

## DSM-III

To make the DSM-III diagnosis of voyeurism, the clinician must establish that the behavior occurs with consistency, that the goal is sexual arousal, and that this is the extent of the sexual experience between the voyeur and his victim. The DSM-III further specifies that the target be people who are nude or undressing, or who are engaging in some sexual activity, and that the pattern be preferred as a means of sexual arousal. DSM-III apparently assumed that no woman ever engaged in such behavior.

## Diagnostic Considerations

Like exhibitionists the voyeur does not show extensive psychopathology on psychological tests and is similar to the exhibitionist in personality test patterns. Thus, the reader is referred to the prior subsection. Lachar (1974) suggests that the prototypal pattern for a voyeur shows elevated scores on 3, 4, and 5, with the elevation on 3 or 4 being the highest, and with T scores seldom being above 70. On the average, scores on scale 9 tend to be lower for the voyeur than for the exhibitionist. That very small subgroup of voyeurs who pose a danger to others has diagnostic patterns parallel to those of primary psychopaths, although they show more elevation on scale 5.

On the 16 PF, voyeurs are relatively close to the pattern of exhibitionist, but voyeurs average a bit higher on scales $Q_3$ and L. This reflects their more circumspect pattern of pathology, which is usually accompanied by a feeling that they would like to retain control of events in their world.

## Treatment Options

All of the techniques noted for the treatment of exhibitionists are equally appropriate to the treatment of the voyeur; the reader is referred to that section. In particular, the aversion therapies have often been used.

The treatment of one voyeur by a colleague of the author brought home the point that it is critical to be accurate regarding which stimuli are to be eliminated by the shock. This client had been administered shock upon presentation of the hypothesized arousal stimuli—a clear view of the nude bodies of a couple through a window. This treatment was ineffective until the shock was eventually paired with slides of open windows as they would appear from a distance of about thirty feet. This unique scene had become the initial discriminative stimulus for the arousal pattern, and the voyeurism decreased markedly when these slides were paired with shock in an aversive therapy procedure.

## Sexual Masochism (302.83)

Sexual Masochism has traditionally been considered as a need to engage in fantasy or actual behavior in which the experience of having pain inflicted on oneself is necessary to gain sexual arousal. The DSM-III emphasizes that this be actual behavior rather than simply fantasy alone.

The term *masochism* was coined in 1896 by Kraft-Ebbing and was taken from the works of Leopold Von Sacher-Masoch (1836–1895), whose novels focused on the theme of men being dominated by women. Sacher-Masoch actually experienced more fantasy masochism, as he primarily obtained excitement from the fantasy that his wife might be unfaithful to him and flaunt him with this fact.

Sexual masochism predominantly occurs in males and has beginnings in childhood experience where the infliction of pain in some way becomes tied to sexual arousal. Crystallized behavior patterns are usually evident by late adolescence (McConaghy, 1982). In some cases, there is an increased need for pain over a period of time. In extreme cases, a bizarre form of sexual masochism referred to as "terminal sex" occurs. A male (typically) hangs himself by the neck with a noose while masturbating, in order to increase sexual pleasure. Releasing the noose just before the loss of consciousness theoretically increases the pleasure. This practice has increased in recent years and occurs most commonly in the fourteen- to twenty-five-year-old range. Miscalculation is thought to cause as many as 200 deaths in the United States every year.

### DSM-III

A diagnosis of sexual masochism may be applied under either of the following conditions. First, the person intentionally participates in at least one episode where sexual excitement is produced by suffering pain or the threat of loss of life. Secondly, the person consistently prefers the experience of being humiliated, bound, or having pain inflicted in order to obtain sexual arousal.

*Diagnostic Considerations*

Masochists seldom come to the attention of legal authorities, or even therapists, unless they have been a victim of extreme sadism that requires medical treatment, and this is uncommon. In many respects, they closely fit with the personality characteristics of the dependent personality disorder; the reader is referred to that section. However, here would be more emphasis on the disordered sexual identification, as well as a higher level of intrapsychic distress. Hence, higher elevations on scales 5 and 7 occur. Scores on scales 9 and 6 are substantially lower than would occur in sadism, which reflects the masochist's passivity and apathy, as well as the subtle defensive quality that may be hidden from others.

Again, the 16 PF profiles should be similar to that of a person with the dependent personality disorder, with some specific exceptions. I would hypothesize that scale N should be significantly higher, as should scores on $Q_1$, and to a lesser degree $Q_2$. L is not usually as low as one might expect, since the submissiveness and adaptation to another is balanced by a subtle paranoid element, usually resulting in scores that are not extreme on this variable. A lower G score also reflects the unconventionality of this behavior, and in those individuals with guilt and a punitive conscience, a high O score is obtained. Scale B is relatively low. The masochist may well give Rorschach responses that clearly indicate a submissive control behavior pattern, such as being "yoked" or "chained." Small or passive animal responses may also be noted.

*Treatment Options*

Sexual masochism, to the degree that it is motivated by a need for sexual arousal, can be treated with the aversion therapies; the reader is referred to the section on exhibitionism. In most cases, this deviant arousal pattern involves interpersonal inadequacy, and pathological dependency pervades the relationship. In that instance, the reader is referred to the next chapter on treatment options for the dependent personality disorder.

The therapist could help the masochist focus on the quality of the relationship by a neo-analytic technique used by Kirman (1980), in which he has the client write letters to the significant other. This helps to focus the feelings and bring to consciousness the many aspects of the relationship which often remain out of awareness. One might also use the "empty chair" technique made famous by Fritz Perls. Rather than writing out his feelings, the client addresses the fantasized other in an oral dialogue; this is aided by its being done in a group. In either case, these feelings are used as a stimulus for new behavior patterns.

Covert Extension may also be employed. Here, the client is asked to imagine the masochistic behavior pattern, and then immediately imagine that the reinforcement that is expected to follow does not occur. Assertiveness training or psychotherapy with an Adlerian focus (Belkin, 1980) (since Adlerian therapy so directly focuses on inferiority issues) could complement and aid the development of a repertoire of more positive behaviors.

## Sexual Sadism (302.84)

Sexual Sadism is a condition wherein a person obtains sexual excitement from inflicting pain, injury, or humiliation on another. The term *sadism* is taken from the writings of the Marquis de Sade, whose works focused on sexual pleasure gained from inflicting pain and even death on others.

Most sadists show evidence of this pattern by early adolescence. The condition is chronic and is seen far more frequently in males than females. Sadism overlaps the concept of rape, though not all rapists are sadists, nor is the contrary true. However, the reader is referred to the section on rape since there are parallel diagnostic considerations.

### DSM-III

A DSM-III diagnosis of sexual sadism is appropriate under any three of the following conditions. First, the person consistently indulges in the infliction of physical or psychological pain in order to obtain sexual arousal, and the partner does not consent. Second, humiliation or mild pain is inflicted on a consenting partner to obtain sexual arousal, or third, the pain and/or injury to the consenting partner is extensive.

### MMPI

Unlike the sexual masochist, the sadist shows significantly disturbed patterns on the MMPI, with one or more scores above the 70 T level. Usually this is a score indicating a lack of impulse control, specifically scales 4, 8, and 9. The high score on 8 shows the unusual attitudes and thought patterns, as well as the hostility and aggression inherent in this disorder.

Most male sadists present a macho image, with stereotypic male behaviors. Physical prowess and aggressive thrill-seeking behaviors are often evident. This can result in a low score on scale 5, except that the confused sexual identification may counterbalance this, particularly if the person is oriented toward homosexual sadism. Females involved in sadistic behaviors tend to score high on scale 5.

*16 PF*

Sadists are likely to show high scores on scales E and H, emphasizing the dominant and aggressive components. In addition, their distance from standard moral systems results in a low score on G and a high score on $Q_1$ and M. $Q_3$ and L are also likely to be moderately high. A is usually low, reflecting the lack of any true interest in interpersonal relationships.

*Other Test Response Patterns*

In addition to Rorschach content responses that directly portray a sadistic element, such as hammers, explosions, and needles, figures that symbolize controlling authority, such as eagles, are occasionally noted. Mutilation content is also thought to be indicative of sadistic fantasy and possible sadistic behavior (Schafer, 1954).

*Treatment Options*

Since sexual sadism more often focuses on deviant sexual arousal than does sexual masochism, the aversive therapy techniques are appropriate; the reader is referred in particular to the section on exhibitionism. This approach could be aided by some of the cognitive approaches, such as Covert Sensitization. The person should also somehow be made aware of the psychological effect on the "victim," and "couple" therapy with the victim could be instituted. Other techniques for teaching more appropriate interpersonal behaviors, such as are noted in the section on exhibitionism, would also be helpful, as the sadism is often a reaction to inadequacy and/or modeling from early training where physical abuse was common.

## Ego-Dystonic Homosexuality (302.00)

Homosexuality has long been a topic of controversy, both with lay persons and within professional groups; this has been especially so in recent years. The DSM-I listed homosexuality as a sociopathic personality disturbance, and in the DSM-II it was shifted into the personality disorder category. However, in 1974 the American Psychiatric Association decided by a vote of 5,854 to 3,810 to exclude homosexuality per se as a mental disorder. Yet, they immediately derived the term *sexual-orientation disorder* to apply to individuals who experience distress as a result of their homosexual behavior.

In the original draft of DSM-III, the label *dyshomophilia* was coined to designate individuals whose sexual arousal is stimulated by the act and/or fantasy of homosexuality and who at the same time are distressed because homosexual behavior is incompatible with their intentions. The term *Ego-Dystonic Homosexuality* was substituted in the final draft.

The DSM-III offers no discriminating statements regarding male and female homosexuality, but there is evidence in the research literature that they differ. Male homosexuals are more likely to have engaged in homosexual experience earlier than females, to have masturbated more frequently and earlier, and to have engaged in more instances of oral-genital sex. Also, even though many male homosexuals form stable, satisfying, and monogamous relationships, male homosexuals tend to be more promiscuous and seek out more "one-night stands" (Tripp, 1976; Masters et al., 1982).

## DSM-III

To be labeled as an ego-dystonic homosexual, a person must show a persistent, unwanted, and distressing pattern of homosexual arousal, concomitant with a disruption of, or absence of, heterosexual arousal. Ego-dystonic homosexuality is listed as an Other Psychosexual Disorder in the DSM-III. It is not appropriate where it is a situation that has been traditionally labeled *latent homosexuality*, that is, where there is no direct evidence for the arousal by homosexual stimuli.

## MMPI

Scales 5, 3, and 4 are elevated in ego-dystonic homosexuality, though they are seldom above the 70 T mark. Lachar (1974) asserts that to the degree there is a fear and anxiety about the homosexual impulses, scale 5 is high and scale 3 is greater than 4. If scale 4 is greater than scale 3, they are more frank about their adjustment pattern. If both 4 and 5 are quite high (a relatively rare profile), an aggressive and flamboyant homosexuality, often combined with substance abuse problems, is a probability (Fowler, 1981). Graham (1977) suggests that any single discrete area of concern often pushes the F scale into the 50 to 64 T range, and this would be appropriate here. When scale 4 is very low in ego-dystonic homosexuality, it typically reflects fear of persons of the opposite sex (Graham, 1977). To the degree that preoccupation with one's sex role is a major factor in the conflict, scale 8 may also be elevated.

## 16 PF

Ego-dystonic homosexuals show higher scores on O, $Q_4$, L, and M. They are moderately low on C and $Q_3$ and moderately high on $Q_1$ and A. Male homosexuals vary widely on H, but female homosexuals tend to be above average. Females score average or below on I, whereas males tend to be above average, reflecting the conflicts with traditional role expectations that are often associated with ego-dystonic homosexuality.

## Other Test Response Patterns

Ego-dystonic homosexuals are likely to show sexual confusion in human responses on the Rorschach and give more responses with opposite sex figures and opposite sex clothing. Some ego-dystonic homosexuals deprecate characteristics of the perceived cross-sex figures. They also tend to perceive double-sex figures and more delicately delineated same-sex torsos. In that regard, they are statistically more likely to draw a figure of the opposite sex in their initial drawing in the various drawing tests.

## Treatment Options

The first issue in the treatment of ego-dystonic homosexuality is to make sure that the client truly wishes to reject the homosexual orientation; hence psychotherapy should precede any direct attempt to change the sexual orientation. Some have argued (Davison, 1976, 1978) that the therapist should refuse to participate in changing the sexual orientation. This runs counter to the tradition of the field, if not the culture, that persons who have made an aware choice ought to be aided in actualizing their "self" as they see fit, particularly since it does no harm to others.

Once the decision is made, the aversive conditioning techniques are used to suppress the homosexual arousal pattern. Masturbatory reconditioning builds up the heterosexual arousal pattern. Orgasm, and then increasingly greater amounts of time before orgasm, are filled with the newly desired images, and hence are reinforced by the orgasm. Supportive therapy and socialization training are also necessary at this time (Meyer & Freeman, 1977). Such efforts can be aided by systematic desensitization to reduce any phobic fears of females that may be hindering attainment of a heterosexual arousal pattern.

## Male Psychosexual Dysfunction

There are three major subcategories in the category of Male Psychosexual Dysfunction. First, Inhibited Sexual Desire (302.71) refers to a condition, psychologically generated, where a person consistently experiences little interest in proceeding into a sexual act. This occurs rarely as a separate disorder, and organic dysfunction should always be ruled out. It is most often a reflection of disorder in a marital relationship rather than individual pathology.

The second category is Premature Ejaculation (302.75). This disorder is an inability to exert voluntary control over ejaculation; it occurs in the absence of other significant pathology and is not an organic condition. It is difficult to define exactly what an absence of voluntary control means, and the DSM-III does not directly deal with this. Masters and Johnson define premature ejaculation as a clinical problem if the orgasm occurs involuntarily more than half the time before the partner's orgasm.

This disorder can be further subdivided into primary premature ejaculation (which is related to inexperience in the sexual area), a chronic, high state of arousal, and possible fears of dealing with intimacy. As might be expected, it is most often a disorder of the young and does not correlate with any significant pathology. In secondary premature ejaculation, a disturbance in the relationship with the partner results in conflict expressed through the premature ejaculation. The trouble is in the relationship, though individual personality factors of the partners may contribute (Masters et al., 1982).

The major DSM-III category in this area is Inhibited Male Orgasm (302.74), which is simply a persistent inhibition of orgasm—even if there is significant prior stimulation—that is not caused by other organic factors or major psychopathology. The major organic factors to be ruled out are spinal cord disorders, nondominant hemisphere parietal lobe dysfunction (Tucker, 1981), significant circulatory problems (often found in severe diabetics), and heavy alcohol or drug use.

The research literature refers to this condition as "erectile dysfunction," and most people simply term it *impotence*. The latter term is undesirable for several reasons, primarily since it connotes general personality inadequacy and weakness of character. It is interesting to note that weakness in the male and coldness in the female, as connoted by the terms impotence and frigidity respectively, are opposites of the characteristics most thoroughly prescribed by sexual roles in our society—power and competence for males and sensitivity and warmth for females.

The DSM-III has avoided defining "regular occurrence." Masters and Johnson (1970) define it as a clinical problem if the person experiences a failure in one-fourth of his attempts in intercourse. Most erectile dysfunction is partial; that is, he can attain erection but either cannot reach orgasm or does not maintain the erection for very long. Total erectile dysfunction over a significant period of time is relatively rare and suggests a biological cause.

### Diagnostic Considerations

Most researchers agree that persons with psychosexual dysfunction do not show markedly deviant profiles on standard psychological tests. There are some trends and differences, depending on whether the dysfunction is psychologically or biologically generated. Beutler et al. (1975) report a 90 percent success rate in using the MMPI to differentiate psychogenic versus biogenic erectile dysfunction, by two rules: 1) In psychogenic erectile dysfunction, scale 5 is typically above 60 T, whereas there is none if it is biogenic. 2) There is no consistency in the scores that are above 70; but when scales are above 70, they are usually scales that reflect the sexual role problems (i.e., scale 5, a histrionic denial of problems, as in scale 3, or in depression on scale 2). Munjack et al. (1981) also noted relatively high scores on 8.

Another particularly effective factor in clearly differentiating psychologically generated dysfunction from biogenic cases is the occurrence of nocturnal penile tumescence (NPT), or erections that occur during sleep. Just as most females show clitoral arousal while sleeping, most males experience a number of NPTs every night during sleep. Those individuals with biogenic erectile dysfunction have few if any NPTs while sleeping, whereas those whose dysfunction is psychogenic show a normal amount (Fischer et al., 1979). The one problem with this diagnostic tool is having someone stay awake all night to watch. In actuality, a postage-stamp-like piece of paper can be kept around the penis during sleep. If it is consistently broken, it indicates NPTs are occurring.

On the 16 PF, persons with erectile dysfunction are likely to show higher than average scores on $Q_4$ and O, reflecting their anxiety and insecurity. Their scores on E and $Q_3$ will vary depending on whether or not they have coped with the dysfunction by resorting to even more stereotyped masculine behaviors, resulting in high E and $Q_3$ scores, or whether they have become more submissive in relationships and see themselves as unable to control their world, which results in low E and $Q_3$ scores. If they experience guilt over failing in their relationship, scores on O are likely to be raised. A high level of performance anxiety is likely to correlate with at least an average or moderately elevated M score. They show more reproductive anatomy responses on the Rorschach, as well as more emphasis on pelvic anatomy and more use of the internal white space.

## Treatment Options

A number of physical, chemical, and psychological techniques have been developed to treat erectile dysfunctions (Masters et al., 1982). Certain prosthetic devices are used for organically based cases and occasionally for severe psychogenic cases as well. The Smith-Carion penile prosthesis is a silicone sponge that is surgically implanted in the corpora cavernosa, the parts of the penis that engorge with blood in an erection. The consequent permanent erection can be an embarrassment, and it interferes with urological diagnostic procedures. The alternative, the Scott prosthesis, is a hydraulic system. Erection is attained when a rubber bulb implanted in the abdomen or scrotum is pressed. It has the disadvantages of any implanted mechanical device and is also expensive. Penile artery bypass surgery can be used where a specific circulatory problem is the issue.

Testosterone derivatives have been helpful in some cases, but a hormone deficiency is seldom the critical issue. Most effective treatments are the psychological techniques developed by Masters and Johnson (1970), in which "sensate focusing" is used to help the client stop "spectatoring," or becoming too distanced from the act. This is particularly effective if it is carried out with a stable partner from the client's natural world. It can be aided by systematic desensitization for specific phobias that might hinder erection, such as vaginal odor. In many cases, problems in the interpersonal situation are major contributors to the erectile dysfunction, so marital (or couple) therapy, including an emphasis on improving communication skills in the distressed couple, is necessary to eliminate these precursors to the dysfunction sequence (Tullman et al., 1981).

The other major problem in males, premature ejaculation, is usually treated by the "squeeze technique." The couple is admonished to engage in sensate focusing without attempting intercourse. As ejaculation appears imminent, the partner squeezes hard just below the rim of the head of the penis, interrupting the cycle of pre-ejaculatory muscle spasms, and then the couple continues in the sensate focusing until control is gained (Masters et al., 1982). In many cases of premature ejaculation, a very high sexual drive level is operating, so counseling about increased frequency of masturbation can help alleviate it.

## Female Psychosexual Dysfunction

Some of the same issues, as well as most of the diagnostic considerations, noted about male psychosexual dysfunction apply equally well to the problems of female psychosexual dysfunction; the reader should consult that section. A category here entitled Inhibited Sexual Desire (302.71) means exactly the same as it does for men. There is no category similar to premature ejaculation, since that could not cause a problem in women. Other categories include Functional Dyspareunia (302.76) or Functional Vaginismus (306.51). Dyspareunia refers to significant pain during intercourse, and Vaginismus refers to the correlated muscular spasm that prevents intercourse, or at least makes it extremely painful. There is no significant personality pathology correlated with these patterns, though scales reflecting depression and immediate anxiety are likely to be raised, just as they are in premature ejaculation and in erectile dysfunction.

The category of Inhibited Female Orgasm (302.73) is also similar to that for males. Inhibited Sexual Excitement (302.72) in a female specifically

refers to the woman's inability to attain or maintain the swelling and lubri-
cation responses of sexual excitement for a period of time long enough to
allow the completion of sexual intercourse, even though the person engages
in sexual activity of sufficient preparation and duration.

## Diagnostic Considerations

It is generally agreed that female sexual dysfunctions are less likely to reflect
allied pathology, either generic or situational, than male sexual problems
(Masters et al., 1982). In part, this is because the female can perform adequately in spite of inhibited responses in different phases or activities of sexual arousal.

The 2–3/3–2 MMPI code is often found in these cases, though the elevations are not usually above the 70 T mark. This reflects an overcontrolled
individual who is denying responsibility for problems and at the same time
is experiencing depression from these problems. An anxious and introverted
woman with psychosexual dysfunction is more likely to have a 1–2/2–1 profile, again without the scales being markedly elevated.

To the degree that anxiety and guilt are a result of the psychosexual
problems, a high I and $Q_4$ are likely on the 16 PF. The other scales do not
vary in any consistent manner. In that small subgroup of females with
psychosexual dysfunction who have been traditionally labeled as hostile
and castrating, high scores on E, L, $Q_1$, and $Q_2$, and to a moderate degree
on H and $Q_3$, are found.

## Treatment Options

Just as with the male, the techniques of Masters and Johnson (1970) are particularly effective and can be similarly aided by systematic desensitization
of specific fears and phobias. Masturbatory training is emphasized more in
the treatment of female dysfunction than in male dysfunction. The woman
is advised to masturbate regularly with fantasies of intercourse, with the
male gradually taking his place in the masturbatory experience, and then literally in the vagina while masturbation still takes place to facilitate the
orgasm.

Nonorgasmic women, or those who are weakly orgasmic, have improved their ability to experience orgasm through exercise of the pubococcygeal muscle. To perform these exercises, referred to as the Kegal exercises,
the woman contracts the pubococcygeal muscle as though she were trying
to keep from urinating. This is performed in sets of ten, several times a day.
Various companies market electronic devices that act to stimulate the
muscles of this area through electrotherapy. These devices are purported to
tone and condition, involuntarily and quickly, the pelvic muscles and thus
to facilitate orgasm.

The other major female psychosexual dysfunctions, vaginismus and dyspareunia, are usually the result of involuntary spasms of the vaginal musculature. Vaginismus has been most effectively treated by the insertion of graduated catheters into the vagina (Tollison & Adams, 1979). The first one used may be as thin as a pen, and only when it can be tolerated comfortably for a period of time is one of somewhat larger dimension inserted. Eventually, a catheter the size of an erect penis is used. The technique is most efficient when the partner participates in the insertion of the catheters. It is also advised (Masters & Johnson, 1970) that the partner witness a pelvic examination, since this helps to dispel any irrational fears or mystique that may have developed. Possibly more important, it reassures the partner that the physical responses are not specific to his overtures for intercourse. Cox and Meyer (1978), as well as others, have found that various forms of relaxation training and general sexual counseling have also been helpful with dyspareunia.

# 9

## The Personality Disorders

The Personality Disorders are chronic and pervasive patterns of perceiving and responding to the environment, and they are sufficiently maladaptive to cause disruption in functioning, and consequently in environmentally generated subjective distress. In DSM-III, the personality disorders are listed on Axis II. Even if a prominent personality pattern does not warrant a formal personality disorder diagnosis, it can still be listed on Axis II, but without the relevant code number that formally designates it as a disorder.

Most individuals in need of a personality disorder diagnosis do not originally see much reason for changing themselves (Millon, 1981). This realization only comes when they move into situations that require higher levels of intimacy or more flexible behavioral adaptations. The fact that they cannot meet these requirements results in coercion from the environment, or at least feedback that they cannot ignore, resulting in referral for therapy.

The clinician needs to decide whether or not the personality disorder pattern is an outgrowth of another disorder, such as a major depressive disorder. For that reason the clinician needs to assess carefully the issues of chronicity and pervasiveness of behavior. The DSM-III does not list a specific time or duration necessary to warrant a personality disorder diagnosis, except when a personality disorder is diagnosed in children. In that instance, duration of at least one year is required, and even with that duration, the DSM-III still forbids the application of the term *antisocial personality disorder* before the age of eighteen.

The DSM-III Personality Disorders can be grouped in three clusters (the conceptualization of the author, not of DSM-III). The first includes the Paranoid, Schizoid, and Schizotypal Personality Disorders, as these are denoted by peculiar or eccentric behavior. The second cluster focuses on dramatic and emotionally labile behavior, and includes the Histrionic, Narcissistic, Antisocial, and Borderline Personality Disorders. The last cluster

179

emphasizes chronic fearfulness and/or avoidance behaviors, and includes the Avoidant, Dependent, Compulsive, and Passive-Aggressive Personality Disorders. There is of course a catch-all category termed Atypical, Other, or Mixed Personality Disorders, used for individuals who do not fit any of the criteria for a specific category, yet clearly fall within the overall patterns of the personality disorders.

*Treatment Options*

By definition, individuals with the personality disorders are not likely to seek therapy out of a perception of intrapsychic deficit or conflict (Millon, 1981). Their presence in therapy has usually been stimulated by some social or legal coercion. For the clinician in private practice, this is most likely in the form of distress generated among the client's intimate others. As a result, some form of marital therapy or family therapy is often required. In addition, some modification of long-standing habit patterns is also necessary, and for that, the assertive therapies, aversion therapies, and milieu-control therapies are often necessary.

A variety of family therapy options are available. The most frequent approach, in which the nuclear family members are seen by one or two therapists during the sessions, is termed *conjoint family therapy*. It is the type most often used with the personality disorders, as it provides the duration and intensified focus that are important here. Multiple impact therapy has a therapist team see family members both individually and in most of the possible combinations of relationships in the family. The emphasis is on an intensive therapeutic period lasting for days rather than weeks. It is particularly helpful where the family is reacting to stress or catastrophe.

The last type, kin network therapy, brings close friends, neighbors, and more distant family members into the therapy attempt. It is particularly useful in the schizophrenic disorders, or other allied disorders where the person has deteriorated socially. It could also be useful in personality disorders such as the schizoid, avoidant, and dependent personality disorders. Of course, any of these techniques can be worked into a multiple family group treatment model. In addition to its lower cost, it increases the breadth of feedback, and possibly breadth of impact.

### Paranoid Personality Disorder (301.00)

The Paranoid Personality Disorder can be thought of as anchoring the other end of the continuum of paranoid disorders from the most disturbed and fragmented pattern, paranoid schizophrenia. However, since there is neither thought disorder nor even a well-formed minor delusional system in the paranoid personality disorder, it is not listed under the paranoid disorders and is not a psychotic condition. Like the other personality disorders, it is a chronic, pervasive, and inflexible pattern of behavior that typically has been in evolution since childhood and is already recognizable in adolescence (Millon, 1981). Modeling of parental or other significant others is possibly even more important in this disorder than in the psychotic paranoid conditions.

Paranoid personalities manifest hyperalertness toward the environment and have a chronic mistrust of most people. As a result, their information base is consistently distorted and their affect is constricted. Consequently, they find it difficult to adapt adequately to new situations or relationships, paradoxical because of their hyperalertness to their environment. As Merriam (1976) has argued, they may often be right in assuming that other people are against them. Yet the paranoia is usually a disabling overreaction to a low initial level of scrutiny by the others.

Unless these individuals have almost absolute trust in another, they cannot develop intimacy and are continually seeking various ways to be self-sufficient. They avoid the emotional complexities of working out a meaningful relationship and tend to be litigious. For example, they may write negative letters to public figures, or bring lawsuits on minimal grounds. It is rare for them to come into therapy without significant coercion from others. The disorder is more common in men.

## DSM-III

The DSM-III desire for an operational definition for paranoid personality disorders results in clumsy criteria. The DSM-III requires evidence of chronic, pervasive, and unreasonable mistrust of others as indicated by at least four of the following behaviors: 1) expectation of harm or deception; 2) hypervigilance; 3) guardedness; 4) avoidance of responsibility for problems; 5) suspecting the loyalty of others; 6) selective and restricted information searching in order to support suspicions; 7) overconcern with hidden meanings and motives; and 8) pathological jealousy.

It requires evidence of hypersensitivity as supported by at least two of the following: 1) being easily offended; 2) excitability; 3) readiness to respond to any perceived threat; and 4) consequent inability to relax.

It is also necessary that they show restricted affect, as supported by at least two of the following: 1) a view by others as cold and unemotional; 2) pride about being rational and objective; 3) a restricted sense of humor, if any; 4) little or no expression of passive, warm, or tender feelings. Finally, this individual must not fit the requirements of either the paranoid disorders or schizophrenia.

## MMPI

As with the paranoid disorders, it might be expected that the paranoid personality will be high on scale 6. However, again this is not always the case, as such individuals are hyperalert about being perceived as paranoid and may guard against this. Hence, the range of scores from the paranoid personality disorders on scale 6 is extreme, though on the average they are well above the mean. Blacks score higher on scale 6 throughout the range of both normal and paranoid patterns; this fact has to be considered in a diagnostic judgment concerning a black person.

The paranoid personality will occasionally use some kind of random or devious answering scheme with the MMPI; the reader is referred to the section on malingering. They are easily irritated at the forced choice format, especially since they are only allowed a binary decision. They also become irritated at the significant self-disclosure required in many of the MMPI items.

The scales that tend to be highest in the paranoid personality disorders are scales 3, 6, 1, and K. This reflects the use of denial and projection, the inclination to focus on physiological concerns when in treatment, and the need to present a facade of adequacy. Since the clinician is not likely to see paranoid personality disorders unless persons have somehow been coerced into treatment (as in marital therapy), there may also be a mild elevation on scale 8, reflecting immediate distress, and the dawning awareness that the personality system is maladaptive. A moderately elevated scale 4 is also expected, though it is typically not as high as in many other disorders.

## 16 PF

Just as on the MMPI scale 6, a person with the paranoid personality disorder does not always score as high as might be expected on the L scale. This is another disorder where it is particularly worthwhile to score for faking bad on the 16 PF (Winder, O'Dell, & Karson, 1975; Krug, 1981) to assess the extremity of the response patterns.

The suspiciousness, guardedness, and lack of a disintegrating delusional system suggest that $Q_3$ will be high, and scales $Q_1$ and N will be low. $Q_4$ can be expected to be low, though if persons are seen for testing in a mental health situation that score is raised.

The moralistic nature of the paranoid personality attitude system predicts a higher G score. The need for dominance combined with a fear of vulnerability suggests a high E, low I, high N, and high H score. Scale A is likely to be lower than might be expected from overt behavior, reflecting an inner reluctance to be self-disclosing and to exchange intimacy. These people are usually higher on scale B than are most other psychopathology groups.

*Other Test Response Patterns*

The paranoid personality responds to the WAIS-R with the same argumentativeness and even condescension that is consistently seen in the other tests. Their meticulous approach results in many details, which aids their score in such tests as comprehension and similarities. At the same time their rigidity, suspiciousness, and peculiar information systems can detract slightly from the comprehension score, and thus the highest score in the profile is on similarities. These factors can result in good scores on both arithmetic and picture completion, and at the same time some peculiar picture arrangement sequences. If they become too meticulous and detailed, they do poorly on digit symbol.

On the Rorschach, they are prone to resent the ambiguous stimuli and hence respond with condescending criticism, occasional rejection, flipping of the cards, and a focus on detail responses. F% and F+ % are high, and there are relatively few M responses (particularly in light of their intellectual level), and few color responses. The more grandiose they are, the more likely they are to have W responses. Animal responses and popular responses are common, and the record is generally constricted.

*Treatment Options*

The reader is referred to the earlier section on the paranoid disorders, since most of the comments there relate to this disorder as well. As with other disorders in which there is a paranoid issue, it is essential to gain the trust of the client through empathy but not participation in the disorder patterns. It is especially necessary to empathize with and articulate the consequences of the client's behavior, such as the sense of being isolated and not understood or the interpersonal rejection that appears unfair to the client. If there is any positive change because of these approaches, catharsis techniques may be helpful to get at the conflicts that are causing these avoidance patterns, and then the therapist can begin to build in more appropriate socialization patterns.

## Schizoid Personality Disorder (301.20)

The essential feature of this disorder is impairment in the ability to form adequate social relationships. As a result, schizoid personalities are shy and socially withdrawn, or as Joan Didion states in *The White Album,* "only marginally engaged in the dailiness of life" (p. 121). They have difficulty expressing hostility and have withdrawn from most social contacts. But, unlike that of agoraphobia, the behavior is ego-syntonic.

If, in addition to the inadequate interpersonal skills, the person also shows peculiarities and difficulties in communication, the appropriate diagnosis is the next disorder to be considered, the schizotypal personality disorder. Schizotypals are more likely to have a family history of schizophrenia. Thus, that category predicts more consistently the eventual emergence of a schizophrenic disorder than does the schizoid personality disorder.

Schizoid personalities gravitate into jobs that require solitude, such as work as a night watchman (Millon, 1981). As they age or become vocationally dysfunctional, they are likely to move into a skid row situation, particularly if they are males. Even though they excessively fantasize and also communicate in peculiar ways, they show no loss of contact with reality.

## DSM-III

According to the DSM-III, though schizoids have few if any friends, they show no communication disturbance. The disorder, which is marked by social relationship deficiencies, introverted behavior, and constricted affect, causes vocational or social disruption. It specifically is noted in 1) emotional coldness, 2) lack of response to social reinforcement, and 3) few if any friendships. Before the age of eighteen, the appropriate diagnosis would be Schizoid Disorder of Childhood or Adolescence (313.22), which would be coded on Axis I. If the person is under the age of eighteen and only avoids relationships with strangers, not family or close friends, the diagnosis of Avoidant Disorder of Childhood or Adolescence (313.21) would be appropriate.

## MMPI

When the schizoid is reasonably well integrated and is not disturbed by pressures from the environment to change, a predominantly normal MMPI profile is attained. As Lachar (1974) points out, a high 0 scale score is obtained, and the others are not usually consistently elevated. If schizoids become more disturbed by the environment and begin to question the appropriateness of their functioning, a raised scale 2 occurs. As upset increases, a rise on scales F and 8 is likely, and a lesser one on scale 9.

The 1–8 profile has been labeled as that of a nomadic individual in whom there is little clear evidence of emotional lability. Attempts at interpersonal interaction are sporadic, and significant problems occur in dealing with persons of the opposite sex.

*16 PF*

The social isolation of schizoids is evident in low scores on scale A, as well as in low scores on E, F, and H. They are high on $Q_2$, and to a lesser degree on $Q_3$. To the degree that they fit the characteristics of the classic schizoid personality, they are lower on M, O, and I, and higher on C, whereas these scores move in the opposite direction as the criteria fit the schizotypal personality disorder more closely.

*Other Test Response Patterns*

The schizoid personality, as is true of most of the character disorders, shows somewhat higher WAIS-R performance scale scores than verbal scale scores. The interpersonal problems of both the schizoid and the schizotypal affect the verbal scales more directly. Within the verbal subtests, higher arithmetic and digit-span are characteristic of this and other groups that tend toward an interpersonal detachment syndrome (Keiser & Lowy, 1980). Within the performance subtests, lower picture arrangement and picture completion scores occur. Golden (1979) states that such individuals demonstrate a constricted use of space on the Bender-Gestalt Test.

Both the schizoid and the schizotypal, particularly the former, provide a constricted response record on the Rorschach, as well as some rejections. A high percentage of animal content responses and few color-based responses are expected. Occasionally, there is a vague response that cannot be pinned down, or even an occasional oddly supported FC response. Exner (1978) states that similar individuals are likely to have a higher Experience Potential than Experience Actual, and that their M production is usually high relative to the overall quality of the protocol. They are also likely to show slow reaction times to many of the cards. A constricted response record along with a blandness of theme and character portrayal is a common performance on the TAT.

*Treatment Options*

Like the person with an avoidant personality disorder, soon to be discussed, the schizoid has inadequate interpersonal relations. Unlike one with an avoidant personality disorder, the schizoid does not care. Hence, therapy is quite difficult, as there is little motivation to change the essential feature. Also, these clients are not likely to enter into therapy since such a relationship is the magnification of what is usually avoided. If for some reason they do become involved in therapy, the therapist must help them develop trust in that relationship and yet not overwhelm them with initial confrontations.

Thus, the process is analagous to gaining the trust of the paranoid personality. If that trust is gained, the source of avoidance can possibly be located and dealt with via systematic desensitization, client-centered therapy, or some other means to dissipate the withdrawal patterns.

Covert extension may even be useful here. Schizoids would be asked to imagine their distancing patterns vividly, and then immediately complete that image by envisioning that the usually occurring reinforcing events do not come to completion in imagination. Since in many ways the schizoid is trying to develop a completely new response pattern, covert modeling may also be used. In this, the client repetitively imagines the desired behavior, probably an interpersonal pattern, and possibly reinforces it by imagined positive outcomes.

### Schizotypal Personality Disorder (301.22)

The reader is referred to the previous category, the schizoid personality disorder, since many of the features of that disorder are found here. The essential difference is that in addition to the disturbances in social functioning, the Schizotypal Personality manifests peculiarities in the communication process. Schizotypal individuals are much more likely than the schizoid to show dysphoria and anxiety, and because of the odd thinking patterns, they are more likely to have developed eccentric belief systems and become involved in fringe religious groups. The schizotypal personality is also more likely to be emotionally labile, overtly suspicious, and hostile of others than is the schizoid. Many schizotypal individuals also meet the criteria for the borderline personality disorder, to be discussed in a subsequent section. In that case, both diagnoses should be given.

### DSM-III

A diagnosis of schizotypal personality disorder can be supported by establishing at least four of the following: 1) evidence of magical thinking; 2) ideas of reference; 3) social withdrawal; 4) presence of occasional illusions (rather than delusions), or depersonalization experiences; 5) peculiar communications (metaphorical, vague, digressive); 6) poor rapport or constricted affect; 7) suspiciousness; or 8) overreactivity to real or imagined social criticism.

It is not rare to find some evidence of schizophrenia in family members. If blatant schizophrenic symptoms begin to occur here, the schizophrenic diagnosis takes precedence and the schizotypal label is not used.

## MMPI

Golden and Meehl (1979) find the 2–7–8 code type to be especially consistent in preschizophrenics, which makes it likely to be manifest in the schizotypal personality disorder as well. As with the schizoid, scale 0 is typically raised. Because of the more pervasive disorder reflected in communication problems and labile emotionality, scales F and 4 are also relatively high in addition to 2, 7, and 8. If depression is not a major factor, 2 and 7 will be lower. If the person is more inclined to be nomadic and to have flat affect and somatization in addition to the communication problems, a pattern with a moderately elevated F and higher scores (in order) on 8, 1, 2, and 3 can be expected.

## 16 PF

To the degree the schizotypal shows aspects similar to the schizoid, the profile will resemble that discussed in the prior subsection. However, as is more likely, emotional lability, confusion, and suspiciousness are present, so scores on B, C, and $Q_3$ would be lower, and scores on $Q_4$, E, A, and L will be somewhat higher. Also, scores on O are typically higher than in the classic schizoid personality disorder.

## Other Test Response Patterns

As is evident, there are some similarities to the test patterns of schizoids. However, in many respects the schizotypals are closer to the schizophrenic, particularly in their performance on tests such as the WAIS-R and Rorschach. The section on schizophrenia is useful in this instance. The patterns noted there for the acute or less disturbed schizophrenic are most applicable here.

## Treatment Options

The comments noted in the subsection on the schizoid apply to a degree to the schizotypal personality disorder. The section on schizophrenic disorders is also useful because the schizotypal individual is seen as predictive of later schizophrenic functioning. Hence, the therapist's attention must be directed not only toward the interpersonal withdrawal processes, but also to the emergent disturbances in affect and thinking that are common. Family therapy may be useful in preventing the emergence of a full-blown schizophrenic disorder.

## Histrionic Personality Disorder (301.50)

The Histrionic Personality Disorder is commonly encountered in clinical practice (Gardner, 1965). The disorder is marked by dramatic and intense behavior, problematic interpersonal relationships that others perceive as superficial and shallow, and problematic sexual adjustment. These persons are seeking of attention and overreactive, with the response being expressed more dramatically and intensely than is appropriate, hence the term *histrionic*. This category has traditionally been labeled the hysterical personality. However, as noted earlier, hysteric wrongly suggests a disorder that parallels the causes and symptoms of what has been previously labeled the hysterical neurosis.

Histrionic personalities may elicit new relationships with relative ease, as they appear to be empathic and socially able. However, they turn out to be emotionally insensitive and have little depth of insight into their own responsibilities in a relationship (Barrett, 1980). They quickly avoid blame for any difficulties of interpersonal relationship, and in that sense, show a degree of the projection that is characteristic of the paranoid disorders. Even though they may be flirtatious and seductive sexually, there is little mature response or true sensuality. If one accepts the apparent sexual overture in the behavior, the histrionic individual may act as if insulted or even attacked (Millon, 1981).

There has been a consistent controversy as to whether this disorder occurs with any frequency in males. This is not surprising, since the meaning of the Greek root term *hystera* is uterus. Ancient explanations for this disorder blamed an unfruitful womb, which became distraught and wandered about the body. Hippocrates thought marriage would cure hysteria by anchoring the womb. Even Freud suggested marriage as a cure. Since conflict over expressive sexual needs may be a factor, such medicine might even work at times. Sometimes, though, this medicine brings on "iatrogenic" problems that are worse than the "disease."

It is clear that this disorder is found in males, but because the symptoms are a caricature of the traditional role expectations for women, it is more common in women (Barrett, 1980). The DSM-III suggests that it is uncommon in males, and that when it does occur, it is likely to be associated with homosexuality, an assertion that is best regarded as a theoretical speculation. There is evidence that the same developmental patterns in females that eventuate in histrionic behavior lead to more antisocial behavior patterns in males, and this would fit with the role expectation theory.

### DSM-III

In general, histrionic personalities show attention seeking and overly dramatic behaviors and are seen by others as shallow and insincere. Specifically, the DSM-III requires, first, dramatic and intensely manifested behavior as evidenced by at least three of the following: 1) exaggerated emotionality; 2) tantrum behavior; 3) hyperemotionality to minor or even innocuous stimuli; 4) attention seeking; and 5) stimulation seeking.

Secondly, disturbance in interpersonal relationships is shown by at least two of the following: 1) passivity and dependency designed to gain reassurance; 2) being seen by others as shallow and insincere; 3) egocentrism; 4) vanity and demanding behavior; 5) manipulative suicide threats or behaviors.

## MMPI

The 2-3/3-2 profile is the code most commonly encountered in the histrionic personality disorder. When the histrionic personality is seen in the clinical situation, there are usually distress and upset, possibly accompanied by manipulative suicide gestures. Thus, an elevation on scale 2 above 70 T can be expected (Slavney et al., 1977). When distress is not so marked, the expected elevation on scale 3 takes precedence. The rare 3-9/9-3 profile is also indicative of histrionic functioning (Kelley & King, 1979).

Scales 4, 7, and 8 are also likely to be moderately elevated. Scale 4 reflects the histrionic's tendency toward egocentricity, overdramatization, and shallow interpersonal relationships. The underlying self-doubt and anxiety raise the 7 score, and the tendency toward impulsive emotionality and self-dramatization elevates scale 8.

Scales L, F, and K usually fall within normal limits. If the individual has begun a defense by focusing on somatic complaints, scale 1 may be elevated. Scale 5 is likely to be elevated in males, reflecting the association of hysteria with traditional feminine role behaviors. It is usually quite low in females. Scale O is not usually markedly elevated; any elevation, however, is surprising—these people make a first impression on the unsophisticated that they are highly sociable. If controls are breaking down, and the histrionics feel as if they are losing control, a higher score on scale 9 is expected, though it is usually within normal limits.

## Other Test Response Patterns

A classic sign of the histrionic on the WAIS-R is that the verbal scale score is typically less than the performance scale score. Within the verbal scales, the information subscale is usually low, as is the arithmetic subscale (particularly in females). Histrionic females are prone to make complaints about the arithmetic test or to make comments to the effect that "I've just never been able to do math at all." Digit span is expected to be moderately high, and comprehension is often the highest subscale. The histrionic is occasionally inclined to moralize in response to some of the items, particularly in the comprehension subtest.

Within the performance subtests, those that tap speed ana visual motor coordination (such as digit symbol) are high, as is picture completion. Block design is sometimes surprisingly low compared to the other tests of similar skill requirements.

On the Rorschach, histrionics often provide a surprisingly low number of responses considering their apparent intensity and involvement. They may portray some of the cards as scary or ugly or use another similar term. They may see monstrous or frightening animals and give responses involving sexual innuendo. At the same time they deny dysphoric content in the cards. There are a relatively low number of W and M responses relative to intelligence. There are blocked responses to color or shading, and one could expect a reasonably high number of M responses. Occasionally, the histrionic will make "blood" responses to the color cards.

## Treatment Options

Histrionics being prone to dramatic and exaggerated patterns, they are most responsive, at least initially, to a dramatic therapy approach. Hypnosis, some of the consciousness-raising techniques, and even dramatic placebos can be useful here. Low-key or nonintense therapy approaches may be seen as invalid by such clients simply because of the lack of intensity.

Once there is some engagement in the therapy process, a shift has to be made to an approach that deals with the disturbed interpersonal relationships and avoidance of responsibility. Group therapy can eventually be helpful as it provides the consensual data so important to convince the histrionic of their disorder. However, unless there have been some trust and dependency generated in the group and/or the therapist, denial and flight from therapy will be quick, and the critically necessary confrontation with the fear and anxiety that have been kept out of consciousness is avoided (Greist et al., 1980).

## Narcissistic Personality Disorder (301.81)

This new DSM-III category centers on individuals who are somewhat a product of our modern social value systems. They manifest an unrealistic sense of self-importance, exhibitionistic attention seeking, inability to take criticism, interpersonal manipulation, and lack of empathy, with consequently substantial problems in interpersonal relationships.

No doubt such people have always existed, but it appears as if this pattern has become more common recently. It is not a surprising development when there are advertisements about "The Arrogance of Excellence," and self-help seminars urging people unequivocably to live out the axiom "I'm Number One" (with little evidence that there is much room for a number two or three close behind). As the cultural historian Christopher Lasch (1978) so lucidly describes, a Narcissistic Personality Disorder is a logical development from such societal values.

The pattern is usually evident in adolescence, and the disorder is chronic. As with the other personality disorders, narcissistic personalities only come to the attention of a clinician when coerced by circumstances (Adams, 1978). The prognosis for major change is moderate at best. Narcissistic personalities are similar to antisocial personalities, except that they are not so aggressive or hostile, and their value systems are more asocial and hedonic than antisocial.

*DSM-III*

According to DSM-III, the essential features of the narcissistic personality disorder are: 1) grandiose self-evaluation with related fantasies; 2) exhibitionistic attention seeking; 3) emotional lability after criticism or defeat. In addition, they manifest at least two of the following indications of interpersonal problems: 1) no ability to empathize; 2) an assumption that they will receive special treatment from others without any need for reciprocal behavior; 3) exploitative interpersonal behaviors; 4) vacillating relationships that are either excessively idealized or defensively devalued.

Such people naturally have a rather fragile personality integration and may on occasion manifest brief psychotic episodes. As a character in Peter de Vries's novel *Consenting Adults* (1980, p. 183) so aptly puts it, "I have this crush on myself—but the feeling is not returned." They also may show characteristics of the histrionic and/or antisocial personality disorder, and if so, an additional diagnosis can be used.

*MMPI*

Lachar (1974) finds that individuals who can develop only superficial relationships score low on scale 0. Since the narcissistic personality disorder is so interpersonally exploitative, an elevation on scale 4 is also expected. They often fit a stereotypical sexual role, so males are low on scale 5 (though certain male homosexuals manifest a high level of narcissism and scale 5 would then be high).

If their patterns are ineffective in coping with the environment, they show situation-generated depression, so a rise on scales 2 and 9 can be expected. If instead they become suspicious and irritable, a rise on scale 6 occurs. If they begin to descend emotionally into a brief psychotic disorder, scale 8 should reflect this.

*16 PF*

Their inflated sense of worth and extroverted assertiveness are expressed in high scores on A, E, and H, while the asocial value system and exploitativeness are evident in low scores on G and $Q_3$. They also score moderately high on $Q_3$. They are variable on scales C, O, and L, depending on the degree of personality integration, and whether or not they are moving toward a brief psychotic episode, suspiciousness, or depression.

*Other Test Response Patterns*

Throughout the testing situation, narcissistic personalities are prone to avoid tasks that demand introspection and/or persistent problem solving, particularly if they can use wit or charm to distract the clinician. If the charm does not work effectively, they occasionally feign inadequacy to avoid a task. They are also likely to produce some pedantic, almost condescending, responses. They occasionally will assert that they only guessed when they sense that they have missed an arithmetic solution, even when the evidence shows that they did not guess.

As a result of these tendencies, they do more poorly on WAIS-R tasks that demand persistence and detailed responses, such as object assembly, vocabulary, comprehension, and block design. The picture arrangement subtest occasionally elicits personalized comments that reflect the narcissism. Overall, they do a bit better on the performance scales than on the verbal scales.

On the Rorschach, such personalities are inclined to give "to me" responses. If they feel the clinician is positively attending to them, they provide more responses than do histrionic individuals, yet seldom in accurate detail, particularly in the M and W responses. As a result, these responses show poor quality. In a related fashion, the F+ % is not high. If they are at all distressed, they produce constricted records that focus on popular and animal responses.

They have a higher number of C responses than individuals with the obsessive-compulsive disorder, and those that occur in the obsessive record are better integrated into the overall response pattern. The narcissistic personality seldom responds directly to shading, but often makes texture responses that are apparently suggested by form or outline. If the narcissism is channeled into direct body expression, responses such as people exercising may be noted. Responses that have an ornate or flashy quality are found, as are responses that focus on fancy clothes or food. Responses focusing on clothing, particularly exotic forms of clothing, or else gem or perfume responses, are also thought to be indicative of the narcissistic personality disorder (Schafer, 1954). Also, an emphasis on both CF and pure C responses is indicative of narcissism.

TAT stories are often void of meaningful content, and the narcissist will detract from the essence of the story by a cute ending or a related joke. Cards that demand a response to potentially anxiety-inducing fantasy, such as 13 MF, may result in either a superficially avoidant story or one with blatantly lewd or shocking content, again reflecting an avoidance of the essential features of the cards.

## Treatment Options

The narcissistic personality may be even more difficult to engage in therapy than is the antisocial personality, in large part because the therapist seldom has as much coercive control. Almost the only time narcissistic personalities enter therapy is when they fear the loss of a dependency role, as in a marital situation. Transactional Analysis within marital therapy (Berne, 1964) may be of help, as it can give both spouse and client a way of more positively conceptualizing the narcissism, that is, as the "child" in the personality.

Feedback to the extent the pattern can be more easily accepted should be followed by some modeling of new behaviors either in role-playing with the therapist, in a multiple marital group setting, or in imagination. Role playing and quid pro quo behavioral contracting are useful adjuncts in attempting to change these behaviors, though they require helping the narcissistic personalities to articulate their needs, a difficult step.

## Antisocial Personality Disorder (301.70)

The essential characteristic of the Antisocial Personality Disorder is the chronic manifestation of antisocial behavior patterns in persons who are amoral and impulsive. They are in general unable to delay gratification or to deal effectively with authority, and they show narcissism in interpersonal relationships. The pattern is apparent by the age of fifteen (usually earlier) and continues into adult life with consistency across a wide performance spectrum, including school, vocational, and interpersonal behaviors.

Although the DSM-III discusses only the overall category of antisocial personality, there is good evidence that it can be further subdivided into categories of primary psychopath and secondary psychopath (Lykken, 1957; Schmauk, 1970; Zuckerman et al., 1980). The primary psychopath is distinguished by the following characteristics: 1) they have a very low level of anxiety and little avoidance learning; 2) they are significantly refractory to standard social control procedures; 3) they are high in stimulation-seeking behaviors, particularly the "disinhibition" factor that refers to extroverted, hedonistic pleasure seeking. The reader is referred to a detailed discussion of personality, diagnostic, and treatment considerations dealing with this subdivision in Meyer (1980). It is advisable to delineate the consequent ramifications of the differences in a primary and secondary psychopath in a clinical report, since such discriminations are glossed over by the use of the overall term *antisocial personality disorder*.

## DSM-III

The DSM-III term *antisocial personality disorder* has resulted from evolution through a variety of terms and now supersedes the terms *psychopathic* and *sociopathic*, at least in formal diagnostic labeling. Pritchard's (1835) term *moral insanity* is considered by many to be the first clear forerunner to the present antisocial personality disorder label. The term *psychopath* first emerged in the label *psychopathic inferiority*, introduced by Koch late in the nineteenth century (Cleckley, 1964).

Terms incorporating the phrase *psychopath* were common until the DSM-I, published in 1952, used *sociopathic personality*. The DSM-II, in 1968, introduced the term *antisocial personality*, which is used in the DSM-III.

In spite of this evolution (or possibly because of it), there have been significant data indicating that this diagnostic grouping is a meaningful concept to clinicians (Gray & Hutchinson, 1964). In a study on the diagnostic reliability of the standard categories, Spitzer et al. (1967) found the highest level of agreement ($r = .88$) when clinicians assigned persons to the antisocial personality category. It is interesting that the lowest index of agreement ($r = .42$) was found with psychoneurotic reactions. Since Spitzer is the chief architect of DSM-III, it is not surprising that the term *neurotic* has been so ambivalently treated in DSM-III.

To apply the diagnosis of antisocial personality disorder the DSM-III requires that the individual be eighteen years of age. Also, there should be evidence that the behavior has been relatively persistent. Incidentally, if the individual is younger than eighteen, the appropriate diagnosis is Conduct Disorder.

Onset before the age of fifteen is supported by evidence of two or more separate types of acting-out behavior. At least four of the following must have occurred since the age of eighteen: problematic occupational performance; a felony conviction or three or more arrests (not for a traffic violation); two or more separations or divorces; repetitive fighting; repetitive avoidance of financial responsibility; transient traveling without a goal; recklessness; failure to accept social norms; repetitive deception of others.

## MMPI

The 4–9/9–4 profile has been considered the classic profile of the antisocial personality. As Megargee and Bohn (1979) show, distinct bimodality indicates an amoral psychopath who fits most of the classic descriptors of the antisocial personality, yet is not particularly hostile. The following section details the MMPI subclassification system on the criminal personality as researched by Megargee and Bohn (1979) and researched and reviewed by Gearing (1979).

When the profile contains a definite spike 4 profile with only a secondary moderate elevation on scale 2, it is more likely to be a primary psychopath who in addition is easily provoked to violence. The primary psychopath who is prone to violent behavior commonly scores high on scales 8, 6, and 4. Such individuals appear to be especially dangerous if they have a high scale 9 score in addition to the high scores on scales 8, 6, and 4. Within a psychopathic population, the level of scale 6 is an indicator of whether hostility is overt or suppressed.

The bimodal 4-9/9-4 profile, noted earlier, is more indicative of secondary psychopathy, as is another common code, the 2-4/4-2 profile with moderate elevations on the other scales. In the 4-9/9-4 group, to the degree 9 is greater than 4, one is more likely to observe a high level of tension and possible somatic concerns. The rare spike 9 profile (when not under treatment because of a spouse's complaint of marital difficulties) is indicative of a primary psychopath who has also abused drugs heavily.

A high F scale is more characteristic of the secondary psychopath than the primary psychopath. When one obtains a 4-8/8-4 profile and most other scales are low, a hostile, cold, and punitive psychopath who borders on schizophrenia should be considered (Lachar, 1974). The expression of aggression in the psychopath appears to be inhibited to the degree that scales 2 and 3 (and 5 for males) are high. Aggression is much more likely, as noted earlier, when scales 6, 8, and 9 are high. When psychopathic individuals are seen in a hospital setting rather than as outpatients, they are more likely to score higher on scales F, 1, 2, 3, and 7, reflecting their greater situational distress.

## 16 PF

The modal 16 PF profile for primary psychopaths finds high scores on scales O, L, and M, with average high scores on $Q_4$ and A. They obtain low scores on $Q_3$ and G, with a moderately low score on C and B and a moderately high score on A. They generally score high on E, though this fluctuates rather wildly, and some primary psychopaths may obtain very low scores.

Golden (1979) also suggests that a high N score is typical of the psychopath, and this appears to be logical, since shrewdness and manipulation of others are characteristic of this pattern. Those psychopaths who are particularly high on the stimulation seeking variable should score low on G and $Q_3$, and high on $Q_2$ and L. Within all subgroups of the antisocial personality disorder category, a high M score is thought to predict recidivism.

The modal profile for secondary psychopaths shows high scores on scales $Q_4$, O, and A, with low scores on C, $Q_3$, and H. They are also moderately low on G and $Q_1$, and tend to be average or below on N (in contrast to the primary psychopath), though again they also vary widely on N. On the average, they are not as low on scale B as the primary psychopath.

*Other Test Response Patterns*

On the WAIS-R, antisocial personalities, especially those more inclined toward primary psychopathy, generally have a performance IQ higher than the verbal IQ, possibly by ten points or more. If they have had school-related problems, as is almost always the case, their low scores in the verbal subtests are on information, arithmetic, and vocabulary, reflecting their lack of adequate achievement in academic subjects. On the comprehension subtest, the "marriage," "bad company," and "laws" items can bring out relevant content. Also, some explanations of the picture arrangement subtest elicit similar material. Picture completion and block design usually give two of the higher scores, and these persons usually do reasonably well on object assembly. Digit symbol is also often quite high (Keiser & Lowy, 1980).

In certain older individuals (with a mean age of forty-four) probably best considered as secondary psychopaths, Heinrich and Amolsch (1978) found an unusual WAIS-R pattern consistently associated with persons who have a poor work and marital history, show drinking problems, are assaultive while drinking, and are inclined toward somatic concerns and situational depression. They show a verbal IQ greater than a performance IQ by 6 to 21 points; high vocabulary and comprehension scores; low digit symbol, block design, and object assembly scores; and an average picture completion score.

On the Rorschach, antisocial personalities usually present a casual though alert facade, which is then in contrast to their at least moderately constricted and shallow protocol. If they are defensive, the record will be quite constricted, and they may reject cards that they can clearly handle cognitively. Otherwise, an average number of responses is provided. Vague percepts may be seen at first, and then developed in a flashy and flamboyant manner, possibly accompanied by cute though hostile comments. There may be guarded rejections of cards, and there is usually a delayed response to the color cards. They do respond to color (particularly the primary psychopath) though often in a fairly primitive and impulsive manner.

While there are a low number of M and W responses, an absence of shading, and a low F+ % (Schafer, 1954), there are a high number of popular responses. There are a high number of animal responses, rather than human responses, and weapons are occasionally noted.

The TAT stories are often somewhat juvenile in theme, and though the protagonist may be caught in a negative act, there is little mention of punishment. If, on the other hand, they perceive the social demand of the situation as requiring some commentary on punishment, they will so comment, yet with a superficial shallowness (Karon, 1981).

*Treatment Options*

The treatment problem with all the personality disorders—getting the client into therapy and meaningfully involved—is acute in the antisocial personality disorder. Confrontive therapies can be effective (Yochelson & Samenow, 1976; Meyer, 1980), but they require some form of coercion such as institutionalization to keep the person in therapy. In such a setting, behavioral techniques, notably the aversion therapies, have been used to reduce some of the disordered habit patterns. Aside from institutional settings, the chief time a therapist is likely to see an antisocial personality disorder is in a disturbed family situation. Marital and family therapies that work on a quid pro quo rather than on a good faith contracting approach are of most help.

Attention should also be paid to the stimulation-seeking nature of these clients. This need can be interpreted to one with an antisocial personality disorder as similar to that of the alcoholic, in that the person needs somehow to fulfill this drive or be inclined to go off into deviant patterns. The paradoxical effect of stimulant drugs, as used for hyperactives, can be helpful with a small subgroup of the more manic psychopaths, but much care must be taken in management.

Therapists can work with psychopaths to develop means of gaining stimulation in less self-destructive ways. A consistent pattern of engagement in sports and other strenuous and/or exciting activities and jobs that provide for a high level of activity and stimulation are helpful.

## Conduct Disorder

According to the DSM-III, the Conduct Disorder is the precursor to the antisocial personality, though paradoxically it is coded on Axis 1 while the antisocial personality is coded on Axis 2. Unlike the antisocial personality, it is broken down into four subcategories and thus may actually predict some other disorders as well.

These four separate diagnostic subtypes each have a separate code number. The breakdown is on two different continuums, first, undersocialized-socialized and second, aggressive-nonaggressive. To earn the label *aggressive*, the person has to have engaged in a repetitive pattern that involves physical violence against persons or property, or confrontive type theft, such as armed robbery. The label *nonaggressive* is earned if there have been acts that violate either the rights of others or major appropriate societal norms, as shown in persistent runaway behavior, lying in or out of the home, nonconfrontive stealing, or rule violations such as substance abuse or truancy.

The label *undersocialized* is earned if there is no more than one of the following social attachment indicators: 1) has at least one peer group friendship that lasts more than six months; 2) shows significant consideration for someone else, even without an apparent advantage being gained; 3) refuses to blame or inform on comrades; 4) shows some guilt or remorse that is not situationally generated (by being caught); 5) manifests concern for the well-being of comrades or friends. If the person shows more than one of those indicators, then the label *socialized* is appropriate.

The diagnosis of Conduct Disorder requires evidence of the pattern for at least six months. If the person is eighteen years of age or older, there should be evidence that they do not meet the criteria for the antisocial personality disorder. A full evaluation of the family is essential to adequate diagnosis of the conduct-disordered child (Rogers et al., 1981).

The breakdown of the conduct disorder categories in many ways reflects a refinement of the primary versus secondary psychopath concept discussed in the previous section. The undersocialized aggressive (312.00) comes closest to the violent acting-out of the primary psychopath, and the socialized nonaggressive conduct disorder (312.21) is closer to the secondary (or neurotic) psychopath who is engaged in passive acting-out behaviors. The categories also reflect some of the differences noted in Megargee's research on the criminal personality (Megargee & Bohn, 1979) and the reader is referred to chapter 10. The undersocialized, nonaggressive disorder receives the code number 312.10, while the socialized, aggressive disorder receives the code number 312.23.

### MMPI

A moderately elevated 4–9 code, with most of the other scales not particularly high, is typical of most of the socialized nonaggressive conduct disorders. A combination of the 4–8–9 scales with generally elevated scales throughout would be more consistently found in the undersocialized aggressive conduct disorder. A caret-shaped profile on the validity scales (low L, high F, and low K) typifies the most severely emotionally disturbed behavioral disorder.

The 8–4 profile, with an elevation on 6 as well, is likely to be found in the undersocialized aggressive who also has a paranoid component, but the 8–4 profile without a high 6 would be more likely with the individual who is acting out aggressively, but who is somewhat more socialized. The 2–4/4–2 profile, with a distinctive slope to the right of the profile and possibly a mild elevation on scale 6, is characteristic of those who are more likely to be undersocialized and nonaggressive.

## 16 PF

On the 16 PF, the socialized individual should score somewhat higher than
the undersocialized on scales A, B, G, and to a moderate degree on N and
$Q_3$. They are likely to be lower on L, $Q_1$, and to a moderate degree on E.
The aggressive continuum is reflected in several scores. The aggressive individual is likely to be higher on E, H, and L, and lower on B, C, G, I, and M,
and moderately lower on N and $Q_3$. $Q_4$ particularly reflects the examination
situation, as well as other environmental conditions. The socialized individual may experience more situational anxiety and thus have a higher score.

## Other Test Response Patterns

To the degree that the client is socialized, WAIS scores will be more even
between and within the verbal and performance tests. To the degree that the
client is undersocialized, performance scores are likely to be higher than
verbal scores. To the degree that avoidance of school is a factor, scores
should be lower on information, arithmetic, and vocabulary, relative to
other subtests. The ability to abstract has been hypothesized as important in
curbing physical aggression; hence, aggressive individuals may be lower on
similarities, all other variables being equal.

The undersocialized individual is more likely to be resistant to the
testing process itself and to show negativism throughout this test as well as
the Rorschach. The undersocialized individual should do somewhat more
poorly on comprehension and picture arrangement than clients who are
more aware and attuned to social norms. From a general perspective, individuals with conduct disorders who are more involved with passive or
status offenses are more likely to have higher intelligence overall than those
who are involved in more aggressive acting-out behaviors (Hays, Solway, &
Schreiner, 1978).

On the Rorschach, undersocialized and aggressive individuals are likely
to reject cards, to avoid the task in a variety of ways, and to show more
direct manifestations of violent and bizarre content than are more socialized
and/or nonaggressive clients. Those tending to be undersocialized and
aggressive are also likely to show the following characteristics: lower F percent, higher F− percent, lower W percent, lower M percent, more pure C,
CF greater than FC, more animal responses, more emphasis on D and popular responses in an overall protocol with a low number of responses.

## Treatment Options

If the individual is more undersocialized and aggressive, there is a need for a
highly controlled living system which includes all aspects of functioning.

Token economy programs, combined with an emphasis on basic academic and vocational skills, will likely be necessary, along with a focus on the control of behavior (Philips & Ray, 1980). The more subtle strategies designed for the primary psychopath and the paranoid may also be appropriate. In response to the more socialized and nonaggressive individual, the requirement of a highly structured and supervised residential program is lessened. An emphasis on a group living model comes to the fore, and in some cases, outpatient treatment with such approaches as Reality Therapy and the more traditional psychotherapies can be useful. A focus on parent training and classroom control using time-out procedures, contracting, and reinforcement structuring would also then be appropriate. Family therapy is usually of help (Bagarrozzi et al., 1982).

## Borderline Personality Disorder (301.83)

This disorder was a confusing entity in the original DSM-III drafts, but now seems to have been more clearly defined. At first glance, it may seem to overlap with the schizotypal personality disorder, as both imply an easy transition into a schizophrenic adjustment. However, individuals in the Borderline Personality Disorder category are neither as withdrawn socially nor nearly as bizarre in symptomatology as are schizophrenics. Though the DSM-III does not specifically mention it, this category seems to be a resurrection of an old term at one time much favored by clinicians, *the emotionally unstable personality.* Persons in the borderline personality disorder category show significant emotional instability, are impulsive and unpredictable in behavior, are irritable and anxious, and avoid being alone or experiencing the boredom to which they are prone. There is some evidence that as these individuals improve they show more predictable behavior patterns, yet this is combined with increasingly evident narcissism (Adler, 1981).

### DSM-III

To diagnose borderline personality disorder, at least five of the following are required: 1) unpredictable impulsivity in two areas such as sex, drug, or alcohol use; 2) physically self-damaging behaviors; 3) uncontrolled anger responses; 4) unstable interpersonal relationships; 5) unstable mood; 6) unstable identity; 7) persistent boredom experiences; and/or 8) avoidance of being alone.

This disorder is thought to be relatively common, yet may be a confusing diagnostic category for clinicians. This category would probably be more commonly used if the older term *emotionally unstable personality disorder* were reinstituted. A multiple diagnosis with schizotypal and histrionic components is not improbable. If the person is under the age of eighteen, the diagnosis of Identity Disorder takes precedence.

## MMPI

In many respects, the syndrome of borderline personality disorder parallels that of schizophrenia, not with the distinct emphasis on delusions or hallucinations but at the same time with a higher level of responsiveness toward other persons. Elevations on scales 3, 4, and 7 should be expected, and on 8 to the degree to which the person is deteriorating. While the F scale should be lower, scale O should be higher than in schizophrenia, as should scale K. Scale 6 should show elevation if problems in management of anger are involved, and the rare 2-6/6-2 code type is likely to receive a diagnosis of borderline personality disorder or a similar one (Kelley & King, 1979). If mood instability is involved, and the person is in a manic phase, a rise in scale 9 and a drop on scale 2 are likely, with the opposite expected in the converse mood situation.

## 16 PF

If these persons avoid being alone, even though there is instability in interpersonal relationships, A should be high, and $Q_2$ should be low. Overall, scales C, H, and $Q_3$ should be low, with high scores on $Q_4$ and O. Mood at the time of the testing will determine the score on F, and the degree of suspiciousness will be reflected in the height of the L scale. On the average, moderately low scores on M and N can be expected, though these can fluctuate markedly.

The variable self-assertion and avoidance exhibited in borderline personality disorders emerge on scale E, although such individuals can be docile and passive in order to fulfill their dependency needs. At other times, they are aggressive, paranoid, and manipulative, particularly when they are rejected. Also, since their social instability and irritability disrupts their social functioning, probable rejection results in their occasionally appearing at the more assertive end of the E continuum.

## Treatment Options

This category is truly a polyglot syndrome and will therefore require equally variable treatment responses. The impulsivity demonstrated in this disorder suggests that the reader should refer to comments regarding the antisocial personality disorder, as well as those regarding substance abuse or possibly one of the sexual deviations. The comments on the antisocial personality regarding stimulation seeking are particularly relevant, since boredom is common in the antisocial personality. Schizotypal and histrionic components are also typical and require the treatment responses noted in those categories. Since there is usually some disordered autonomic functioning, biofeedback and relaxation training may be appropriate. Group therapy can be helpful if the person will allow the development of trust in the group, but such clients are difficult to work with and can exert a cost on the progress of the group, which makes it unwise to include them.

## Identity Disorder (313.82)

The DSM-III connects the Identity Disorder with the borderline personality disorder, although they are not too similar. To diagnose an identity disorder the DSM-III requires evidence of disturbance for at least three months, impairment in social or occupational functioning, and uncertainty about identity in three of the following areas: career choice, sexual patterns, friendship choices and behavior, moral values, religious identification, peer group loyalties, and long-term goals. This disorder naturally occurs most commonly in late adolescence, when people are forced by society to make choices and face changes in these areas. Most people who face these choices experience some distress; a clinical diagnosis is indicated when this distress persists and is so severe that it results in significant disruption of life.

*Diagnostic Considerations*

The depression and anxiety consistently found in this syndrome predict elevations on MMPI scales 2 and 7, and there is some elevation on scale 8, reflecting a sense of alienation and isolation from others with a consequent feeling of self-doubt. Scores on scale 5 are usually at either extreme, depending on which way the person's identification is swinging. People of higher intelligence and socioeconomic status tend to move to the upper extreme of scale 5, particularly males. Where this disorder has resulted in impulsive behaviors and/or feelings of alienation from others, elevations on scales 4 and 6 are probable.

As a reflection of high anxiety, $Q_4$ is typically elevated on the 16 PF, and the concern about values is manifested in a high O and F, as well as a low $Q_2$. There is a degree of guilt, which differentiates this pattern from that of a psychopathic personality, and this is seen in the elevations on G and O.

Performance on the WAIS-R is similar to that of disorders such as the depersonalization disorder and the anxiety and depressive disorders. The thrust of the person's identity disorder will determine the patterns here. The most probable marker of an identity disorder on the WAIS-R is the comparison of obtained IQ scores to academic or work achievements, as it is likely that the IQ score will be above the level of achievement.

The depression and anxiety usually evident in an identity disorder are reflected in the standard Rorschach patterns for this disorder. The responses are usually filled with figures that are more passive and inadequate than normal, and occasionally there is an allusion to infants or young humans or animals, which suggests an attempt to hold on to an earlier period of a more integrated identity. If the identity disorder is focused on the sexual area, responses similar to those noted in ego-dystonic homosexuality can be expected.

### Treatment Options

Therapies that are effective here are similar to those usually applied to the depersonalization disorder as well as to some of the more neurotic disorders. The Client Centered therapy of Carl Rogers is especially appropriate, since Rogers initially developed this while working with young ministerial and graduate psychology students who were going through various identity conflicts.

If the client has moved too far in avoidance of choices, the Reality Therapy of William Glasser may be more appropriate. An existential perspective is important in whatever therapy takes place. Clients need to face the choices that they are avoiding and also to envision and accept the consequences. An adolescent therapy group is often useful here, as it gives such clients awareness that others are moving through the same choices, and it provides feedback about new choices and initiatives.

### Avoidant Personality Disorder (301.82)

These individuals are shy and inhibited interpersonally, yet at the same time desire to have interpersonal relationships, which distinguishes them from those with the schizotypal or schizoid personality disorders. They also do not show the degree of irritability and emotional instability seen in the borderline personality disorder.

A major feature of this chronic disorder is an unwillingness to tolerate risks in deepening interpersonal relationships (Millon, 1981). These persons are extremely sensitive to rejection and seem to need a guarantee ahead of time that a relationship will work out. Naturally, such guarantees are seldom available in healthy relationships. Thus, the friends they manage to make often show a degree of instability, or are quite passive.

In many ways, this disorder is close to the anxiety disorders, since there is a degree of anxiety and distress, and low self-esteem is common. However, the behaviors that produce the distress are relatively ego-syntonic. Their depression and anxiety are more related to the perceived rejection and criticism of others.

This disorder is seen more often in women and is relatively common. Any disorder in childhood that focuses on shyness predisposes one to the avoidant personality disorder.

## DSM-III

To diagnose an avoidant personality disorder, the clinician must observe the following as consistent and chronic behaviors: 1) avoidance of relationships without guarantees of acceptance; 2) strong fear and sensitivity to rejection; 3) consequent social withdrawal; 4) in spite of any withdrawal, a continued interest in the affection inherent in a relationship; and 5) consequent diminished self-esteem. If they are under eighteen years of age, the appropriate diagnosis would be Avoidant Disorder of Childhood or Adolescence (313.21).

## MMPI

A 2–7/7–2 profile is common, reflecting depression about assumed rejection, as well as apprehension and self-doubt about the ability to deal with others. To the degree that this has resulted in social withdrawal, a high score on scale 0 is expected, as well as a moderate decrease on scale 9. Since this disorder often appears in females who are strongly identified with the traditional feminine role, a low score on scale 5 occurs. If the individual still has energy available and it is being channeled into anger, a 3–4 profile, with allied mild elevations on 2, 7, and 6 can be expected. If functioning is beginning to go to pieces as a result of the rejection and social withdrawal, an elevation on scale 8 occurs.

## 16 PF

Low scores on scales E, C, and H are consistent in this syndrome, reflecting shyness, threat sensitivity, passivity, and emotional upset. High scores on $Q_4$ and O are evidence of the expected tension and insecurity, and a moderately high score on I reflects fear of rejection and sensitivity. Social clumsiness is balanced by a hyperalertness in social situations, hence particularly deviant scores on N are not too common. The self-perception by avoidant personalities that they should automatically be accepted interpersonally results in a higher than average A score. However, actual experience, of which they are somewhat aware, keeps this from being extremely high and may even temper it to average or below in some profiles. These people tend to be moderately low on $Q_3$ and M, though this is highly variable. The L score, usually low, will depend on whether or not they have begun to channel their rejection into anger and suspiciousness of others.

*Other Test Response Patterns*

To the degree they feel accepted by the examiner, they do better on the verbal subscales of the WAIS-R than on the performance subscales. Since avoidant personalities are often females with strong traditional role identities, low scores on arithmetic are common. Dependency may be reflected in some of the content of the comprehension items, as well as in the picture arrangement subtest, which is low in introverted clients. Blocked or relatively inactive M responses on the Rorschach are common. A high number of popular responses occur, and content may focus on more passive animals such as rabbits and deer (occasionally being hurt or killed), or on passive interactions in the M responses.

*Treatment Options*

The need for assertiveness training is often as great in this disorder as it is in the dependent personality; the reader is referred to that subsection below for suggestions equally applicable here. In addition, the avoidant personality is more concerned with the risk in relationships—hence, existential and confrontive therapy approaches are useful adjuncts. The Rational-Emotive Therapy of Albert Ellis (1973, 1980) is especially useful, as it was worked out on a population that had these kinds of concerns. Since the Adlerian therapies (Belkin, 1980) focus on issues of inferiority, there may be special applicability here. Also, since there is a neurotic-like component to this pattern, Paradoxical Intention approaches may be useful.

Another helpful treatment for dependent and avoidant personality disorders is covert negative reinforcement; this technique is most useful when the client cannot easily envision the desired behavior and would not be highly responsive to covert positive reinforcement. In covert negative reinforcement, the client imagines a highly aversive event, and then imagines this event is terminated by the performance of a new set of desired behaviors. It is critical that there be as little time lapse as possible during the switchover in images.

### Dependent Personality Disorder (301.60)

The Dependent Personality Disorder directly reflects its name. These people have a pervasive need to cling to stronger personalities who are allowed to make a wide range of decisions for them. They are naïve and show little initiative. There is some suspiciousness of possible rejection, but not to the degree found in the avoidant personality disorder.

In one way, dependent personality disorders can be seen as successful avoidant personality disorders. They have achieved a style that elicits the desired relationships, though at the cost of any consistent self-expression of their personality. They show elements of agoraphobia, not crystallized, and they lack any real self-confidence.

Since this is an exaggeration of the traditional feminine role, it is not surprising that it is far more common in women. If the individual is not presently in a dependent relationship, anxiety and upset are common. Even if enmeshed in a dependent relationship, there is still residual anxiety over the possibility of being abandoned.

### DSM-III

To make a diagnosis of dependent personality disorder, the following should be noted with some consistency over a significant period of time: 1) they subordinate themselves to another to the point of abrogating their own essential needs; for example, they may even tolerate physical abuse by a spouse; 2) they have low self-confidence and allow others to assume responsibility for decisions, so anxiety is experienced if they are left alone for any significant period of time.

### MMPI

The 2–7/7–2 profile is characteristic of an individual who is experiencing anxiety and depression, who is passive-dependent and docile, and who presents a picture of severe dependency. A high 3 scale is also common here and the K scale is mildly elevated. Naïveté and passivity are reflected in a surprisingly elevated L scale, and the F scale is usually in the average range.

The acceptance of the stereotypal feminine role shows up on a low scale 5 score, and the lack of resistance to coercion from authority is reflected in a low 4 scale. Scale 9 is also low, reflecting passivity and lack of initiative. Scale 0 tends to be elevated, although this is variable depending on emerging concern about their own behavior, as well as their sense of comfort about the permanence of their dependency relationships. If anger is beginning to develop as a result of any consistent rejection of the dependency, some elevation on scale 6 occurs. Otherwise, this is rare.

In young men, an interesting and rather rare profile, the 1–9/9–1 code type, with both T scores greater than 70, has been found to indicate passivity and dependency. However, there is a hostile component directed toward females that is associated with this profile, so the dependency relationship would probably be directed toward males. Thus one would look to the 5 scale for elaboration on the issue of sexual identity and possible preference.

*16 PF*

The dependent personality disorder should result in scores quite low on the classic 16 PF dependency factors—scales E, L, M, $Q_1$, and $Q_2$ (Karson & O'Dell, 1976, p. 90). In addition, the I score should be high in females. In males, moderately low scores on O and $Q_4$ may be noted, and A is high.

There is probably a low score on $Q_3$ and N, and a high score on O. Surprisingly, there is not a particularly low H score, and it may even be above average.

It is also noteworthy that a low score on L is not consistently found in this disorder. This may reflect not only a high threshold for jealousy, but also the unconscious anger alleged to be a result of the submergence of one's personality to another.

*Other Test Response Patterns*

On the WAIS-R, the performance scale score may be higher, although this is not as consistent as in some of the other personality disorders. Arithmetic and information seem to be consistently low, relative to other scores, reflecting a withdrawal from a problem-solving approach to the world. Within the performance subtests, lower scores on object assembly occur, and occasionally odd responses indicating a need for support are found in the picture completion subtest.

A constricted use of space is a common feature in the drawing of the Bender-Gestalt figures.

The Rorschach record is highly reflective of the attitude of the examiner. If the dependent personalities feel that the examiner desires a high number of responses and feel accepted in the testing situation, they will produce an extensive record. Otherwise, a record with a less than average number of responses can be expected. As with the avoidant personality, responses indicating passive animals and passive M responses are found, as well as a high number of popular responses. There is also a tendency toward use of color rather than form in determining responses, relative to other personality disorders, and there is a likelihood of perceiving small detail responses.

*Treatment Options*

Assertive training is a standard feature in the treatment of the dependent personality disorder. It may need to be preceded by methods that help the clients gain a greater awareness and articulation of their dependency, via consensual feedback from a group, from catharsis, or from other consciousness-raising techniques.

In the response—acquisition stage of the assertive training, modeling is carried out with audio- or videotaped demonstrations by the same status, age, and sex models. Covert modeling is particularly helpful where persons are trying to develop a whole new behavior style. Clients imagine another person performing the assertive behaviors that they wish to have in their repertoire. After response acquisition, there is response reproduction, in which behavioral rehearsal, role playing, and even directed practice are useful. After this, response consolidation is effected through clear feedback, again possibly using audio- or videotape. Changes are crystallized into the ongoing personality through cognitive self-reinforcement and by requests and contracting for increasingly widening the range and the targets of the assertive behavioral responses. Since this disorder often occurs in the context of family or marital difficulties, attention will have to be paid to the partner who may view any changes as threatening.

### Compulsive Personality Disorder (301.40)

This disorder is occasionally confused with the obsessive-compulsive disorder, but there are significant differences between the two syndromes. First, the compulsive personality seldom becomes obsessed about issues. Second, the term *compulsive* here refers to a lifestyle in which compulsive features are pervasive and chronic and does not refer to a specific behavior. Third, the compulsive lifestyle is ego-syntonic, and for the most part, persons only come to treatment when coerced in some fashion.

Compulsive personalities are preoccupied with rules and duties, are unable to express warmth and caring except in limited situations, are highly oriented toward a lifestyle marked by productivity and efficiency, and are generally distant from other individuals (Barrett, 1980). They can be described as workaholics without warmth.

It is true that a degree of compulsivity is effective, particularly in our society. It becomes a problem when it overwhelms the rest of the personality. Paradoxically, compulsives are often indecisive and poor planners of their time, a result of their narrow focus and concern with precision, even though the precision may be irrelevant. They are inclined to be excessively moralistic, litigious, and hyperalert to criticism and perceived slights from others.

### DSM-III

To diagnose a compulsive personality disorder, the DSM-III requires consistent evidence of: 1) overemphasis on details to the exclusion of an overall perspective (they see the trees rather than the forest, and not even all of the trees); 2) constricted emotionality; 3) excessive devotion to vocation and productivity; 4) need for dominance in personal relationships; and 5) indecisiveness.

## MMPI

Compulsives attain a moderately high K scale and seldom have highly elevated MMPI profiles, as they are not inclined toward self-disclosure. They attain elevations on scales 3 and 1, the latter particularly so if physical complaints have become a focus for their distress. They find it more comfortable to see themselves as having a physical rather than a psychological disturbance. The 9 scale is also elevated; in large part this elevation reflects how autocratic and dominant the individual is in personal relationships. Litigiousness and developing paranoid concerns are reflected on scale 6. A moderately high 7 score may occur if there is a querulous and complaining attitude, though scale 7 usually reflects obsessionalism rather than compulsive factors.

## 16 PF

Compulsives also present a reasonably normal profile here. It is recommended that if there is a suspicion of compulsivity, the protocol should be scored for faking good. Since there is denial of anxiety, $Q_4$ is low, and the need for control of intrapsychic processes leads to a high $Q_3$ score. Isolation from other people results in a high $Q_2$ score, and the rigidity and possibly developing paranoia lead to a high L score. Scale A is also lowered for the same reasons. Scores are not particularly low on C or high on O. They tend to be high on E, the degree depending on the orientation toward dominance in interpersonal relationships. They are moderately high on G or N, and moderately low on I and F. Since the coping system of compulsives results in better academic performance and intellectual achievements, they attain one of the higher scale B scores.

## Other Test Response Patterns

As a result of an emphasis on achievement and productivity, persons with compulsive personality disorder score at least in the average range and usually above on the WAIS-R. They will give overly precise and detailed answers, which helps on comprehension and similarities. But in tests based on speed, such as digit symbol, block design, object assembly, and picture arrangement, the same traits can lower the scores. Their interpersonal and problem-solving rigidity causes difficulties with the more complex puzzles in picture arrangement. Generally, they attain a higher verbal IQ than performance IQ.

On the Bender-Gestalt Test, they are inclined to count the dots or small circles in the cards, and also may orient all the figures in a precise arrangement.

On the Rorschach, there is an emphasis on Dd and D responses, with a high F+ % and fewer W and color-based responses. Some responses are described in detail. Relative to those with the other personality disorders, they provide a high number of responses overall.

## Treatment Options

Cautela and Wall (1980) suggest the use of Covert Conditioning procedures to counteract the compulsivity, and in particular recommend the use of the Covert Sensitization technique. This technique involves the imgination of a highly aversive event or contingency immediately on developing the imagery of the undesired behavior—in this case, the compulsive pattern to be eliminated. It is effective for this pattern, as well as for a number of the habit disorders.

In Paradoxical Intention, clients are simply instructed to do the very act they have been resisting. As this proceeds, clients are told, by a number of apparently absurd instructions, to vary the circumstances and quantity of the behavior produced. As this occurs over time, they develop a greater sense of control over the behavior and may then choose to give it up. Group therapy is a helpful follow-up, because these clients are likely to regress into their cold and distancing compulsive behaviors if the changes are not thoroughly incorporated into their lifestyle for some length of time.

## Passive-Aggressive Personality Disorder
### (301.84)

The essential behavior pattern in the Passive-Aggressive Personality Disorder is indirectly expressed resistance to social and occupational performance expectations, which results in chronic ineffectiveness. The core disorder is hostility that is not directly expressed, so "double messages" to others result. The underlying hostility affects significant others, yet the passive-aggressive denies, often as if insulted, any aggressive or hostile motivation. The actual behavior expressed may be either passive or aggressive, but physical aggression seldom occurs.

Most parents have had the experience of a child pushing them to the limits of their control and then backing off. Like that child, the passive-aggressive becomes acutely sensitive to such limits and is consistently able to go that far but not farther. When this pattern becomes an integral part of a social and vocational lifestyle, a passive-aggressive personality disorder exists. Although these patterns are commonly modeled and learned in childhood, such a family usually reaches a state of mutual detente. The pattern then causes severe problems when it is transferred into any new intimate, consistent contact relationship, such as marriage.

The passive-aggressive personality disorder takes the standards and the belief system of significant others and turns them around to immobilize the others effectively. The strategy (which is not thought to be a conscious behavior) is to present the "enemy" (often a person depended on) with a choice that forces one either to capitulate or to violate individual belief systems. That person is thus immobilized, yet has no adequate reason to justify retaliation (Barrett, 1980).

## DSM-III

Since the authors of DSM-III were initially concerned about the rationale for continuing this diagnostic category, surprising in light of the consistent use it receives, they emphasize that it is only used when behavior does not first meet the criteria for the other personality disorders. To warrant the diagnosis, there has to be evidence in social or vocational areas that there has been indirect resistance to performance demands, resulting in chronic problems in these areas. At least two of the following behaviors are required to substantiate this indirect resistance: 1) dawdling, 2) stubbornness, 3) procrastination, 4) purposeful inefficiency, 5) convenient forgetfulness. If the client is under the age of eighteen, the appropriate diagnosis would be Oppositional Disorder.

## MMPI

The 3-4/4-3 combination is commonly seen in the passive-aggressive personality disorder. Where scale 3 is greater than 4, and both scales are relatively high, the individual is oriented toward the passive mode. When scale 4 is higher than 3, and accompanied by a moderate to high elevation on scale 6, the aggressive mode is predominant. If both scales 3 and 4 are high together, there is a tendency toward dissociative responses (Lachar, 1974).

Elevation on scale K is also probable since passive aggressives will downplay their faults and show a lack of insight about intrapsychic dynamics. An avoidance of responsibility, possibly through somatic complaints, produces mild to moderate elevations on scales 1 and 7. Scale 9 is average to low in this pattern, except when hostility is a counterphobic defense against dependency. Then, the rare 3-9 profile may be given. Also, when a man is being seen as a result of his wife's complaint of marital problems, a spike 9 profile has been found to be indicative of passive-aggressive functioning (King & Kelley, 1977).

The passive-aggressive personality who is closest to actual loss of control of the aggression shows a 4–6/6–4 profile, with high F and 8 scales, as well as a low scale 2 score. Persons with this profile have much cross-sex hostility. If the scores here are very high, consider an emerging paranoid schizophrenic adjustment.

## 16 PF

The 16 PF profile of the passive-aggressive personality disorder is generally not remarkable. The E score fluctuates, depending on whether the passive (low E score) or aggressive mode is operative. The apparent dependency of many passive-aggressives would suggest a low $Q_2$ score. However, this is balanced by underlying hostility and resistance, which raises the score into the average range and occasionally to an above average score. Passive-aggressives are usually moderately low on G, though not markedly low on C. The interpersonal manipulation inherent in this pattern results in a high N score and at least an average L score. The L and H scores are higher in the aggressive mode, with the I score being lower.

## Other Test Response Patterns

Golden (1979) found passive-aggressive individuals to be high on the comprehension scale of the WAIS, but in general the performance scale score is slightly higher than the verbal scale score. They do well on visual-motor tasks, such as digit symbol, block design, and object assembly. They also do well on digit span but are only average on arithmetic. Elaboration of responses on picture arrangement and comprehension may cue the passive-aggressive orientation.

On the Rorschach, a high percentage of FC and space responses are noted, as well as a relatively high number of texture and popular responses. Occasional odd combinations of aggressive and passive content may occur such as children and guns. Passive-aggressive personalities may produce responses that directly suggest their pattern of relating, such as people arguing or animals sneaking, or in other ways passively manipulating others.

Many authors have asserted that the use of white space suggests the negativistic tendencies that are characteristic of a passive-aggressive personality. An aggressive content item response, such as bombs, fire, scissors, or volcanoes, is more likely to be evident in the passive-aggressive personality who is inclined actually to threaten aggression on occasion. Phillips and Smith (1953) assert that a rough texture response is also characteristic of this pattern.

## Treatment Options

The critical task for the clinician treating a passive-aggressive personality disorder is to set up feedback situations so that the persons can no longer effect their interpersonally controlling patterns, and yet also cannot effectively deny their existence. Some form of family or marital therapy is often indicated.

Also, any form of effective data presentation about personality patterns is helpful, especially if it can be stored for future use. For that reason, audio- or videotapes of different sessions are useful in confronting passive-aggressives with their patterns. Consensual feedback from a group is also useful in overcoming their avoidance mechanisms. Since inadequacies are often at the core of this pattern, assertive training may be appropriate. If anger is the focus, assertive training is still helpful, but it may need to be embellished with methods that focus on catharsis.

## Oppositional Disorder (313.81)

The Oppositional Disorder is commonly considered as a precursor to the passive-aggressive disorder. Many of the same behaviors are noted. However, there is a more direct expression of hostility and negativism in the oppositional disorder. The DSM-III requires that the pattern last for at least six months and that the person be older than three and younger than eighteen years. There has to be evidence of at least two symptoms, specifically 1) stubbornness, 2) minor rule variations, 3) temper outbursts, 4) persistent argumentativeness, or 5) provocative behavior in general, as well as no evidence that the behavior goes so far as to violate or aggress against the rights of another, such as is found in the conduct disorder. This behavior is typically carried out toward significant others, such as teachers and parents, and it may persist into various self-destructive social interactions. These persons show a degree of conformity and usually resist any interpretation that they are oppositional, just as passive-aggressives do.

### Diagnostic Considerations

In general, the diagnostic considerations here are analogous to those in a passive-aggressive personality. However, there are some differences since aggression may be more overtly expressed, rebelliousness is more commonly a factor, and the client is younger. As a result, scales 4 and 6 on the MMPI are more likely to be high. On the 16 PF, scale E would typically be somewhat higher, reflecting the stubborn aggressiveness, and G would be quite low, reflecting the rebelliousness. Since the oppositional individual is likely to be more naïve socially, N would be lower than in the passive-aggressive personality, and $Q_1$ and $Q_2$ would probably be a bit higher. A more overt antiestablishment attitude is probable, so persons would be more resistant to taking the tests. On the Rorschach, they express more avoidance and negativism. More pure C and fewer popular responses can be expected than in the passive-aggressive personality disorder.

## Treatment Options

Treatment is similar in many respects to that for the passive-aggressive personality disorder. Considerations expressed in the section on the paranoid disorders regarding the development of trust are also relevant here. Since the oppositional disorder is often the manifest evidence of a family disorder, family therapy should be considered (Bagarrozzi et al., 1982).

# 10

## The Criminal Personality

Although the DSM-III discusses the overall category of antisocial personality, it does little to distinguish the various types of individuals who are easily subsumed under the label of criminal personality (Monroe, 1981; Meyer & Salmon, in press). By far the most exhaustive and elegant research on the psychological test discrimination of the criminal personality has been carried out by Edwin Megargee and his colleagues (Megargee & Bohn, 1979). Their typology, based on empirically derived and validated MMPI research, has been exhaustively studied by Megargee and his colleagues and students in a variety of settings and has also received strong and independent verification from other researchers (Edinger, 1979; Gearing, 1979).

Megargee established ten reasonably discrete subcategories of the criminal personality, using incarcerated prisoners. These ten typologies and their associated MMPI patterns are presented here; readers are strongly cautioned, however, to use Megargee's computer tapes if they are going to do any extensive diagnostic work in this area, as these tapes would provide a much more accurate assessment of those individuals who fall on the borderline of two or more patterns. Any reader who is consistently involved in diagnostic work with prisoners should be familiar with both Megargee and Bohn (1979) and Gearing (1979). The system is not generally applicable to short-form MMPIs. Even if one is not doing computer assessments, Megargee and Bohn (1979) provide more extensive decision rules for the categories than are available here. Megargee will provide computer tapes for his system at cost or will score, profile, and classify MMPIs if a special answer sheet is used; he also encourages people to send him research information concerning his classification system. He can be reached at the Department of Psychology, Florida State University, Tallahassee, Florida 32306.

Megargee's ten subtypes were given alphabetized names (e.g., Able, Baker) and in the early publication were listed in alphabetical order. In the later and more comprehensive publication (Megargee & Bohn, 1979), the

subtypes were listed in order from the least pathological to the most pathological, and that system will be followed here. The ten types are thus described below.

### Megargee's Ten Criminal Subtypes[1]

*Item*

Individuals in the Item subclassification show little or no psychopathology,
and this is fortunate since this is the largest group of the ten, comprising 19
percent of his prison sample. They are generally nonaggressive, friendly,
and extroverted, and are likely to have been incarcerated for a victimless
crime. They come from stable and warm family backgrounds and have had
the fewest problems when growing up. They seem able to make committed
and lasting friendships.

They present an essentially normal MMPI profile, with the major characteristic being an overall absence of elevation, though about 50 percent of
this group manifest one T score greater than 70. That high point is usually
on the 5 or 9 scale. There is no consistent two-point code associated with
this group. Any elevation tends to be on scales 9, 4, or 5.

Though Items are inclined to pilfer things while on prison work assignment, they are at the same time rated as the most dependable workers by
their supervisors. They show a low recidivism rate, and it would probably
be just as useful to them, and certainly far less expensive, if they were to be
immediately placed on probation.

*Easy*

The Easy subgroup, like the Item group, has relatively benign psychopathology. They comprise 7 percent of Megargee's sample. They are brighter
and appear to have had more natural advantages than the other subgroups.
Yet they are ironically well characterized by their randomly assigned label.
Not only has life been easy, they have also taken it easy—they are classic
underachievers. Interestingly enough, they have had a high number of siblings who were behavior problems, though all indications are that the
parental situation was good for Easy inmates themselves.

On the average, they show a "benign profile" on the MMPI, with all
scores under the 70 T mark. A 4–3 profile is most common, and scale 2 is

---

1. This material adapted from *Classifying Criminal Offenders* (SAGE LIBRARY OF SOCIAL
RESEARCH, Vol. 82) by E. Megargee and M. Bohn, copyright 1979, pp. 118–135 and 177–233
is reprinted by permission of the Publisher, Sage Publications (Bevery Hills/London).

often relatively elevated. This group is occasionally confused with sub-sequent groups Baker and George, although these latter groups are more likely to show a spike on 2 than is the Easy subgroup.

The Easy subgroup shows little upset or discomfort at being in prison. They have the lowest recidivism rate of all subgroups, probably because they have the most in the way of natural assets on which to draw. Probation into academic and vocational training would appear to be a much more efficient option for this group than incarceration.

### Baker

Bakers are a relatively small subgroup, only 4 percent of the sample, and they are best labeled as neurotic delinquent. They are passive, anxious, and socially isolated individuals who are inclined to depend on alcohol to deal with everyday problems and upsets.

The most common MMPI profile obtained is the 4–2, and the second most common is the 4–9. On the average, Bakers are moderately high on scale 4, with a secondary elevation of scale 2 and an interesting and consistent spike on 6 (though this is not a high spike). They can be confused with Georges, but Georges show a higher elevation on the neurotic triad, scales 1, 2, and 3. Also, a mild elevation of 6 is more characteristic of Bakers than Georges.

Oddly, Bakers are surprisingly disruptive in the institution, but in a passive-aggressive fashion. The combination of supportive psychotherapy, vocational counseling, and an Alcoholics Anonymous program is the optimal treatment.

### Able

Ables are the second most common group in Megargee's population, comprising 17 percent of the overall group. Ables are sociopathic, opportunistic, self-assured, and immature. Rather than being hostile or antisocial, they are amoral and hedonistic.

The essential feature of the Able MMPI profile is bimodality, with distinctive peaks on scales 4 and 9. The 4–9/9–4 two-point combination covers 83 percent of this sample. They are unlike the Delta subgroup, where scale 4 is much greater than scale 9. Ables typically show little or no elevation on scales other than 4 and 9.

Though Ables moved into subcultural delinquency at an early age, all indications are that they had a good family background. This background may explain why they perform well in the prison, at least when supervised. A controlled community living situation is thought to be the best disposition for this group.

*George*

The George group, 7 percent of the sample, closely resembles the Able group, except that Georges are brighter and come from a more deviant family background. Georges "do their own time" and are characterized as quiet though not passive loners.

The 2–4/4–2 profile, with a distinctive slope to the right, is characteristic of this group. They are close to the Baker profile in some respects, but show higher elevations overall, and the profile has more slope to the right. Also, there is no secondary spike on scale 6 in Georges. They can be confused with the Easy subgroup, but the scale 3 score is less prominent in the profile of Georges.

*Delta*

Unlike previous groups, Deltas, who comprise 10 percent of the population, are a definite pathological subgroup. These bright psychopaths are sociable, yet they are easily provoked to violence. Reflecting the classic descriptors of the primary psychopath, Deltas are impulsive, unable to delay gratification, amoral, do not profit from experience, prone to violence, and they seldom experience guilt or anxiety.

Deltas are likely to show a spike on scale 4, with an occasional secondary spike on scale 2. They are relatively low on scales 6, 8, and 9, so on occasion they can be confused with the Able subgroup, a group that is very different behaviorally. The best method of discrimination is to look for the distinct bimodality on scales 4 and 9 that marks the Able subgroup.

*Jupiter*

This rare subgroup, 3 percent of the population, shows indication of making efforts toward a positive adjustment, but they are badly handicapped by very deprived family backgrounds. Unfortunately for this group, modeling is an enduring influence in teaching a person to deviate from the rules of society. As a result, Jupiters do not always make a good adjustment in spite of their apparent motivation.

The Jupiter MMPI profile is singularly marked by a climb to the right on the scales. Scale 8 is the most common peak scale, with scale 9 close behind, and then a high elevation of scale 7 further behind. This group is defined by exclusion. If an MMPI profile fits the concept of a climb to the right, and is excluded from other categories, it is labeled Jupiter.

Just the opposite of Easys, Jupiters do not have the good family background, skill preparation, or even the ability, but do have the motivation. As a result, a heavy emphasis on developing basic academic skills, vocational training, and a supportive group experience at a half-way house are necessary ingredients for the rehabilitation of Jupiters.

### Foxtrot

Foxtrots, 8 percent of the sample, have all the bad characteristics listed. They experienced poor family backgrounds, are poorly educated and not very intelligent, are antisocial, and are disturbed emotionally. They are evasive and easily provoke anger in others.

They are classically high on the 9, 4, and 8 scales, and the elevation on the 8 scale is helpful in discriminating this group from the Able subgroup, as Ables appear more average on 8 and lower in general on the other scales.

Foxtrots do make friends with a few similarly deviant individuals, though by and large they provoke hostility. They are easily aggressive toward staff personnel if there is much contact with staff. Foxtrots can use help of any sort, and not surprisingly, they are quite unresponsive to any efforts to provide it. As a result, they have a very high recidivism rate.

### Charlie

Charlies, comprising 9 percent of Megargee's population, are bitter and hostile antisocial personalities, with a definite paranoid element. In addition, they are usually intellectually, academically, and socially deficient. They are alienated and hostile loners who easily become violent.

Charlies show characteristic MMPI elevations on 8, 6, and 4. The 8–6 and 8–4 profiles are the most common. Charlies can be confused with Foxtrots, but they have a high 6 score relative to Foxtrots. Charlies may also be confused with the How subgroup, although Hows tend to be high on scales 1, 2, and 3.

From the perspective of violence in the prison, violence in the community, and the high probability of recidivism, Charlie is one of the most disturbed criminal subgroups. Treatments useful for paranoid individuals are especially applicable here.

### How

The How subgroup is large, comprising 13 percent of the sample. They are similar to Jupiters in that they are significantly handicapped by a deprived early environment, but Hows are much more psychologically disturbed and less willing to change than are Jupiters. They are highly anxious individuals, who also show some depression. Part of this depression stems from their role as "reluctant loner," since they consistently face rejection by others, rather than withdrawing themselves from social contact.

Like the Item subgroup, their MMPI profile is defined more by elevation than by specific subscale scores. Whereas Items are defined by low elevations across the scales, Hows show high elevations on most scales, and particular elevations in a jagged pattern on scales 8, 2, 4, and 1. The profile is distinctive in its jagged elevation throughout the right and left sides of the profile. Scale 8 is the highest scale in more than 50 percent of the profiles obtained.

Like Foxtrots, Hows are prone to be aggressive toward staff if there is a high amount of staff-inmate contact. Psychotherapy and chemotherapy, as well as any vocational and social engineering program available, are needed in rehabilitating them. Unfortunately, rehabilitation is seldom successful, and the recidivism rate is high.

## Summary

Megargee and Bohn (1979) have collected data from a number of researchers indicating that their system is relevant throughout most state and federal penal institutions. Also, they have supporting data to show that the system is applicable to women with almost the same accuracy and efficiency as it is for men, the sample from which it was derived. Race was considered throughout Megargee's research, so this does not seem to be a disqualifying factor in applying this MMPI system. There are minor age differences among the subgroups, to be expected, and an offender's subgroup type may change with age. Overall, Charlies and Jupiters tend to be younger, and Easys tend to be older.

# 11

## Disorders of Impulse Control

This section in DSM-III is primarily a catch-all grouping for those patterns that are not efficiently classified elsewhere. The essential features of a Disorder of Impulse Control are a buildup of tension prior to the act, failure to resist the impulse, an experience of pleasure or release on carrying out the act, and consequent harm to others and/or oneself. Even though there may be some guilt after the act, it is essentially ego-syntonic, and there may be little in the way of conscious resistance to the impulse.

The subcategories in this section of DSM-III are Pathological Gambling, Kleptomania, Pyromania, and Explosive Disorder. There is a residual category, Other Impulse Disorder. Rape will be discussed in this section because it fits well here, even though it is not specifically mentioned as a category heading in DSM-III.

### Overall Test Response Patterns

On the MMPI, a lack of impulse control is generally reflected in elevations on scales 4, 6, 8, and 9. On the 16 PF, high scores are usually obtained on F and $Q_1$, whereas low scores on $Q_3$ and G are typical. Performance scale scores are higher than verbal scale scores on the WAIS-R. Within the verbal scale, arithmetic and information are usually two of the lower scores. Response times to the Rorschach are short, and the record may often have a lower than average number of responses. F and F+% are lower than normal, and there is a greater use of color than in most disorders.

### Pathological Gambling (312.31)

This is a new DSM-III category, and its characteristics are progressive and chronic preoccupation with the need to gamble, with consequent disruption in some area of the individual's world. Estimates of the number of gamblers in the middle 1970s in the United States varied between one and ten million. Since more states have moved toward legalized gambling, thus making it increasingly accessible to people, it is expected that the rate will continue to rise. Compulsive gamblers, like antisocial personalities, are stimulation seeking, and both specifically show "disinhibition" or the inability to control impulses (Zuckerman et al., 1980). The initial streak of compulsive gambling is usually set off by a first big win.

Many compulsive gamblers report that they only feel alive when they are gambling and may refer to the rest of their life experience as boring. They are generally nonconformists and are narcissistic and aggressive (Dell et al., 1981). A number of compulsive gamblers work only to make enough money to gamble heavily when they get to a spot like Las Vegas. Others have a more normal outward appearance, especially those who gamble in more legitimate outlets such as commodities and stock markets.

Most gamblers are extroverted and competitive individuals who are brighter than average; they surprisingly often experienced learning difficulties as they grew up. Most had placed their first bet by the age of fifteen. Other factors that predispose to Pathological Gambling are an overemphasis in early family life on material symbols, with little value placed on financial planning and savings; an absent parent before the age of sixteen; and availability of a gambler in the family as a model.

## DSM-III

To diagnose pathological gambling, the DSM-III requires first that persons not meet the criteria for the antisocial personality disorder, and second, that they show progressive preoccupation with gambling, which consequently disrupts their world in at least three of the following ways: 1) breaking the law in order to obtain money for gambling as by fraud; 2) defaulting on debts; 3) borrowing money illegally; 4) having family or marital problems; 5) losing track of losses or gains; 6) being absent at work due to gambling; 7) having poor judgment in financial issues, perhaps including desperate borrowing from friends.

## MMPI

There are few data on the modal test patterns for this group, although the variables noted above correlate with the personality descriptors associated with the bimodal, moderately elevated 4-9 profile. However, when they are seen by a clinician, pathological gamblers have already begun to experience substantial distress and hence are likely to score higher on scale 2. The stimulation-seeking quality is reflected on scale 9, and the extroversion characteristic of this pattern is seen in a low scale 0. At the point of referral, they would also probably be agitated and distressed, which in combination with their impulsiveness should result in an elevation on scale 7. A moderate elevation on scale 3 can also be expected since the tendency to reject responsibility for changes and forces in their world is reflected here. F or K scale elevations will depend on the situation in which persons are being tested. If for some reason they are defensive about gambling, the K scale would be elevated. On the other hand, there are situations in which being labeled "disturbed" would help them avoid some of the consequences of their behavior. As a result, a high F scale would occur, which in turn would also elevate a number of the other scales.

## 16 PF

On the 16 PF, the extroversion, stimulation seeking, and lack of self-control that characterize this pattern are reflected in high A and H scores and a low $Q_3$ score. $Q_1$, and to a slightly lesser degree C and O, will be dependent on the characteristics of the testing situation, that is, on whether the subjects have reasons to be defensive or open about the pathological gambling.

They are also likely to be higher on E in particular, and also on B, F, N, and L. A lower score is obtained on I.

## Treatment Options

Since the disorder in pathological gambling is very likely to surface first in family problems, family therapy is often necessary (Bagarrozzi et al., 1982). In addition, Gamblers Anonymous, modeled on Alcoholics Anonymous, is useful for many pathological gamblers who have made at least a moderately strong commitment toward changing their behavior.

Since stimulation-seeking is often a critical variable in the reinforcement pattern for pathological gambling, the comments regarding fulfilling the need for stimulation seeking, detailed in the section on the antisocial personality disorder, are relevant here.

## Kleptomania (312.32)

Most authorities agree that thievery in various forms has been on the rise in our society. For example, statistics annually compiled by the United States Department of Commerce suggest that about 140 million instances of shoplifting occur every year, and that almost 25 percent of business losses are accounted for in this fashion. They suggest that about one in every twelve shoppers is a shoplifter, although no more than one in thirty-five shoplifters is ever apprehended.

Certainly many people steal simply because it seems so easy to get something free, for a lark, or to be one of their crowd. However, a small proportion of these individuals show Kleptomania. They are distinguished from typical thieves in that kleptomaniacs seldom have any real need or use for an object and may even throw it away. They usually prefer to steal while alone, and there is an "irresistible impulse" quality to their behavior.

Kleptomania often begins in childhood, primarily through stealing small items or sums of money from parents or friends. Stealing behavior as a means of being accepted into an adolescent peer group is another common feature in the background of kleptomaniacs. There is usually evidence of depressive features, reflecting inability to control the behavior, as well as some problems in interpersonal relationships. For example, many older women who show a kleptomaniac pattern are widowed or emotionally neglected by their husbands; the behavior gives them a thrill, sometimes sexually tinged, though they often pay for it with remorse. In fact, many show a clear sense of relief when apprehended. Kleptomaniacs are usually not significantly disturbed psychologically in areas other than this lack of specific behavioral control. Yet, the condition is often chronic.

## DSM-III

The DSM-III offers the following diagnostic criteria for this pattern: an irresistible impulse accompanied by rising tension before the act; the actual stealing behavior then accompanied by a sense of release or even pleasure, sexual arousal, or euphoria; no apparent need for the item or important monetary profit. There is a lack of planning and little involvement with others in the pattern.

## Diagnostic Considerations

Consistent with the comment that kleptomaniacs are not often significantly disturbed psychologically, their MMPI and 16 PF protocols are also usually unremarkable. If persons are being seen in the criminal justice system rather than the mental health system, they are likely to show a higher K score on the MMPI, and to the degree they are unsophisticated, a higher L score. If they are being seen in the mental health system, or if they are viewing psychopathology as a means to avoid criminal sanctions, F will be higher. Scale 2 is moderately raised, reflecting the situationally generated depression, as well as the sense of inability to control their impulses. In that regard, scale 3 is also likely to be mildly raised. Scale 9 is average or low, and scale 0 is usually a bit elevated, reflecting their propensity for being alone with their conflicts.

Similarly, on the 16 PF they tend to show some elevation on scales $Q_4$ and O, and are usually not high on scale A. Scale $Q_3$ will vary depending on whether it directly reflects their inability to control impulses, which would result in a low score, or whether they are counterphobically trying to control their impulses, which would raise $Q_3$.

### Treatment Options

Since schizoid behaviors and/or depression are common precursors to kleptomaniac behavior, treatment approaches for those patterns are often important here. For the specific behaviors of kleptomania, the aversive therapies are often used. Kellam (1969) employed a particularly ingenious aversive procedure to control shoplifting in a chronic kleptomaniac. Kellam required this person to simulate his entire shoplifting sequence, which was filmed. As the film was played back, the client was asked to participate with internal imagery in what was going on, and a painful shock was administered at crucial points. Such a technique could be amplified by having a person take a portable shock unit and self-administer shock whenever the impulse arose. If the shock unit is clumsy, the persons could be instructed to hold their breath until discomfort ensues, since this acts as an aversive cue.

An alternative aversive technique is to have such clients go into a store, and if the impulse becomes so severe that they feel they will not be able to resist, they are to take an expensive and fragile object and drop it on the floor. Embarrassment, the need for a coping response with store employees, and the need for restitution all act to create a very aversive moment.

Other clinicians have treated kleptomania by systematic desensitization, hypothesizing that the behavior will subside if one can decrease the tension in the sequence of anxiety arousal-completion-release. As anxiety then lessens, more adequate coping behaviors for dealing with anxiety are developed. Cognitive-behavioral techniques and/or existential approaches that deal with the loss of interests and meaning evident in some kleptomaniacs, particularly older females, may also be necessary.

### Pyromania (312.33)

As with thievery, deliberate fire-setting behavior appears to have increased substantially in modern society. Of course, most cases of arson are not really indicative of pyromania. It is now estimated that as many as eighty percent of business property fires are caused by arson. In these cases, the perpetrator is far more likely to be an antisocial personality who is doing it for pay—a "paid torch." Cases of arson in which there is no clear reward for the individual who started the fire could indicate pyromania, but mental retardation should also be considered (Foust, 1979).

Pyromaniacs, like kleptomaniacs, experience a buildup of tension prior to the behavior, as well as a release on performing the fire-setting. The behavior is often first seen in childhood and adolescence and is seldom the only antisocial behavior displayed. Hyperactivity, problems in school, poor peer relationships, and stealing are commonly associated behaviors. It has been found that fire-setting in childhood, when combined with either enuresis and/or cruelty to animals, is predictive of assaultive crimes in adulthood, but these crimes may or may not include fire-setting.

Pyromania is much more common in males than in females and is often found in an individual who has had trouble in making transitions through developmental stages. Analogously, there are data showing that peaks in the incidence rate in arson occur around the ages of seventeen, twenty-six, forty, and sixty in males. If there is a problem with alcohol, pyromaniacs show patterns of alcohol abuse rather than addiction, and they often show an inordinate interest in fire-fighting paraphernalia. They are either indifferent to destruction or stimulated by it.

## DSM-III

As with kleptomania, the DSM-III requires evidence of the build-up of an irresistible impulse before the setting of the fire, continuing inability to resist the impulse, and a release of this tension on setting the fire. There should also be an indication that either profit or some sociopolitical belief system is not the basic motive for the fire-setting.

## Diagnostic Considerations

As with kleptomania, there is not much consensual clinical literature nor are there hard data to indicate the patterns one can expect here. However, on the average, pyromaniacs are more disturbed than kleptomaniacs. They are likely to score high on scales 4 and 8 of the MMPI, though not usually at a psychotic level. They will probably also score higher on scales 6 and 9, and to the degree the impulses are denied, scale 3 is elevated. The F score, as well as the 4 score, is elevated to the degree there is an anti-authority component. Moodiness, a sense of alienation from others, and inability to control impulses are also reflected in any elevations on scales 8, 0 and 6.

On the 16 PF, pyromaniacs show more evidence of disorder than kleptomaniacs. Pyromaniacs will likely be low on scales C, G, and $Q_3$, as well as higher on scales L and $Q_4$. They are also likely to show some elevation on scales E and H, reflecting their destructive and controlling orientation toward the environment. Analogously, this component as well as the distancing from others may raise scale $Q_1$ and lower scale A. Scale B on the average is low, reflecting the usual less-than-average intelligence.

Pyromaniacs may show labile and impulsive affect responses, as indicated by a number of uncontrolled reactions to the color cards of the Rorschach. In fact, it is suggested that when children with borderline psychosis provide "blood," "fire," or other similarly destructive associations to the Rorschach color areas, potential dangerousness in general, and possible fire-setting behavior in particular, should be suspected (Foust, 1979).

## Treatment Options

The significant disturbance that usually accompanies pyromania suggests that a wide variety of treatment options may have to be considered, depending on the trend of the overall pathology. Since these individuals are often adolescents or young adults, family therapy is especially warranted, and since schizoid patterns are typical, the reader is referred to that section.

Two specific behavioral techniques are appropriate for the fire-setting behaviors. Overcorrection requires the individual to make a new and positive response in the area of specific disorder. For example, public confession and a restitution of damages through working for the individual who is offended would be one type of application for pyromania. Negative Practice has also been used. The pyromaniac is required to perform a behavior ad nauseam until it takes on aversive qualities. For example, the client is required to strike thousands of matches in sequence, over several sessions. These techniques would be embedded in an overall treatment program.

## Explosive Disorder

The distinguishing feature of the explosive disorder is a sudden eruption of aggressive impulses and the loss of control of these impulses in an individual who normally inhibits or does not experience them. Regret and guilt are common, and the behavior is disproportionate to any environmental stressors. Because prodromal physiological or mood symptoms are occasionally reported, and because there is occasional consequent partial amnesia for the behavior, the pattern was traditionally referred to as "epileptoid." A concomitant clear diagnosis of organic epilepsy is not common. However, in a number of these cases, there are some nonspecific EEG abnormalities or minor neurological signs. The presence of such signs is not so rare, even in a sample of apparently normal individuals, but clear evidence for a physiological contribution should be thoroughly considered (Monroe, 1981).

## DSM-III

The DSM-III divides this disorder into two separate categories. The term *Explosive Disorder* is qualified by the prior terms *Isolated* (312.35) or *Inter-*

*mittent* (312.34), depending on whether there has been a single or more than one episode. In either case, there is no prior evidence of impulsivity or aggression, and the behavior during the episode or episodes is disproportionate to any apparent stressors. The disorder appears most commonly in late adolescence or early adulthood.

### MMPI

As noted in the section on aggression potential, persons who are consistently assaultive and without guilt tend to score high on scales, F, 4, and 9, with secondary elevations on 8 and 6. However, though this does not fit with the descriptors of this disorder, even the intermittent explosive disorder, Fowler (1981) notes that high 4 and 6 scores can be expected here.

The 4-3 profile, as described by Davis and Sines (1971), would be more likely to call for the explosive disorder diagnosis. In this profile, there is a peak on 4, a secondary peak on 3, and little significant elevation elsewhere. This profile, mainly seen in males, is particularly characteristic of individuals who maintain a quiet ongoing adjustment but are likely to demonstrate occasional hostile-aggressive outbursts. Such behavior may or may not warrant the diagnosis of intermittent explosive disorder, depending on the characteristics as described above. Gearing (1979) indicates that this profile is applicable to females, and does occur quite generally, though there is some evidence that it is less applicable to adolescents.

To the degree that both 4 and 3 are highly elevated, the likelihood of aggressive episodes increases. In general, when scale 3 is greater than 4, the potential for control and inhibition of the aggression is increased, whereas to the degree that 4 is greater than 3, control dissipates.

Lachar (1974) suggests that the rare 3-9 two-point code is indicative of persons who are emotionally labile and who show recurrent and consistent hostility and irritability. Since they naturally suppress the hostility in clinical assessment, they could be diagnosed as an explosive disorder. However, it is more likely that they are either a passive-aggressive personality disorder or a histrionic personality disorder, or both.

There is a derived scale on the MMPI, termed the Over-Controlled Hostility scale (Megargee, Cook, & Mendelsohn, 1967), composed of 31 MMPI items. Though a few studies have not been positive, most have supported the validity of this scale in predicting persons who show outbursts of aggression. Hence, they could easily fit with the DSM-III diagnosis of explosive personality. The scale has been an accurate predictor in incarcerated adult populations, but has been weak at times in the normal population. Nevertheless, it is one of the most well-researched scales and is worthy of consideration.

*16 PF*

Since these individuals generally show regret over their behavior and see it as ego-alien to a degree, a low score on G is not likely, whereas it would be in most cases of aggressive behavior. Also, C is not usually low, nor are $Q_4$ or N high, as would be common in the psychopath. $Q_3$ is usually high, reflecting the attempts at control that are characteristic of this person, and $Q_1$ is usually moderately low. In spite of their passivity, they do not score markedly low on E or H; neither are they very high. They are average or lower on M and N, reflecting the general denial of the aggression and the lack of introspection about motives and conflicts.

*Other Test Response Patterns*

There is some evidence that quiet but potentially explosive persons attain lower picture arrangement scores on the WAIS-R than do more extroverted and consistently aggressive types. Comprehension and similarities subtests are usually relatively lower here. Rorschach patterns are quite constricted, and there is less abstraction content. M responses are not that uncommon, and when they do occur, they tend to be more passive. Responses with content such as "blood" or "explosions," or responses indicating inner tension and turmoil occur in a number of explosive disorders. Responses with a color component tend to have poorer form than otherwise expected. Minor neuropsychological signs on a variety of tests are often associated with this disorder, and it is a reasonable axiom that there is some impaired brain functioning, though seldom any gross brain damage.

*Treatment Options*

It is critical in treating this disorder to get the clients in touch with their on-going anger responses, usually suppressed, and at the same time to teach them more effective ways either to abort the anger or to deal with it productively. Awareness techniques, such as those found in Gestalt Therapy (Perls et al., 1958), can put them in touch with the anger that is typically not evident in their usual functioning. Group therapy can provide the feedback essential to breaking down their defenses against seeing themselves as having chronic anger. The keeping of a diary or the writing of letters (not delivered to the target) to significant others who may be a factor in generating the anger (Kirman, 1980) also aids clients to get in better touch with their anger.

Once this is accomplished, the therapist could attempt to use the development of a controlled relaxation response to abort the anger. Similarly, biofeedback training to develop an overall relaxation response could be useful, as it could abort the anger in the way it has been used to abort epileptic seizures (Hendrix & Meyer, 1974). Assertiveness training or other analogous procedures could then be used to structure more effective ways to cope with the ongoing frustration and anger. Lithium treatment has been found effective with that subgroup of persons with intermittent explosive disorders who show evidence of a latent or cyclical manic component. Clients in this category also occasionally respond well to ethosuximide, and those with a CNS lesion causing the rage have been helped by propranolol (Yodofsky et al., 1981).

## Rape

Rape does not appear as a diagnostic entity per se in DSM-III. However, it is a most important syndrome, is often an impulsive behavior, and shows certain diagnostic correlates. A discussion is in order here.

There are a number of classification systems for rape, one of the most consistently influential being that of Cohen, Seghorn, and Calmas (1969). The following reflects their concepts.

Aside from the rapes that occur as an incidental result of such disorders as severe organic brain dysfunction or schizophrenia, and rapes that are an impulsive and ritualistic gesture (the plunder of war), there is reasonable agreement that there are three major rape patterns. The first occurs where aggression is the major component and sexual satisfaction is somewhat irrelevant in the motivational system. These rapists are hostile toward females and in general carry a high level of aggression potential. The upcoming section on aggression potential deals with the diagnostic considerations relevant to such persons.

The second type of rapist needs to administer pain to another person to obtain sexual satisfaction. It is a requisite, and so this type of rapist is classified under the psychosexual disorder of sexual sadism; the reader is referred to that section.

A third major category of rapists is that where the aggression is an avenue toward sexual contact and satisfaction, yet also in some ways to interpersonal contact. This is the individual whose diagnostic correlates are presented here. This sexually motivated rapist fits with the results of Barbaree et al. (1979), who found that in most cases, forced sex simply fails to inhibit arousal in rapists, though it does so in most normal individuals. Incidentally, Abel et al. (1981) did find that some rapists (i.e. the aggression subtype) are especially aroused by stimuli that connote a woman who is aggressive or manipulative, or sexual images that include aggression.

### Characteristics of Rape

Rape has traditionally been defined as the unlawful penetration of a female's vagina by a man's penis, reinforced by some form of coercion, and without the consent of the victim. However, it is increasingly recognized that it is absurd to require penile penetration to define rape. Homosexual rape occurs, as does rape of men by women (though very rarely). Statutes are being rewritten in states to reflect this.

Rape is a common crime and is said to account for approximately 5 percent of all crimes of violence. About one in every 2,000 women is a reported rape victim every year. However, it is estimated that only about ten percent of actual rape victims ever report to police. Also, only about two in twenty rapists are ever arrested, one in thirty prosecuted, and one in fifty convicted. More than fifty percent of reported rapes take place in the victim's home, and in about forty percent of the cases the rapist is known to the victim.

### The Rapist

Most rapists are married, and a great percentage of married rapists have regular sexual relations with their wives. However, their sexual performance is often impaired during the rape (Groth & Birnbaum, 1979). Like most other antisocial personalities and criminals, rapists are generally lower than average in intelligence.

Rada, Laws, and Kellner (1976) and other researchers have found elevated levels of plasma testosterone in some samples of the most violent rapists. However, in general, there is not much correlation between rape and physiological measures. An impossible problem is obtaining such measures at the critical predictive point, the time just before the rape, as many of these physiological variables differ markedly for any one individual depending on when they are assessed. However, measurements of penile response to sexual imagery (Abel et al., 1981; Abramson et al., 1981) may be useful here, as well as in making at least some tentative predictions about future behavior when that is important in disposition.

### MMPI

It has been generally found that rapists are more disturbed across the board on such tests as the MMPI than are assaultists per se or exhibitionists. In many ways, rapists correlate with the dimensions of the antisocial personality; the reader is referred to that section. Common profiles in rapists are the 8-4/4-8, 4-3, and 4-9. The 8-4 is characteristic of rapists of adults, and the 4-8 is more characteristic of a rapist of children (Armentrout & Hauer, 1978).

Rapists may obtain a high K scale score, reflecting the fact that they are typically under scrutiny for a criminal offense; the reader is referred to the section on malingering. Scale 5 is usually low in these individuals, especially if there is a strong identification with the stereotypical male role. Scale 0 is mildly elevated if there is general ineptitude in interpersonal skills. This type of behavior, along with an inclination to deny responsibility for behaviors, is seen in an elevation of scale 3. Scale 4 naturally reflects the hostility and aggression, as well as the lack of standard moral controls on behavior.

Rader (1977) has suggested that the 4–3 profile characterizes the more repressed rapist who is inclined toward significant violence. In this case, scale 6 is also likely to be elevated, though this depends on the degree of hostility allowed into awareness. Scales F and 8 are elevated to the degree the individual is losing control of impulses and is degenerating into more fragmented pathology, though faking bad must also be considered.

## 16 PF

Rapists, if they are at all self-disclosing, score away from the average on a number of dimensions. The primarily sexually motivated rapist is more likely to score toward the average profile than is the aggression-motivated rapist. However, both types are likely to have low scores on C, reflecting their emotional instability; a low score on Q and G from their inability to control impulses and urges; and a high score on O from their insecurity. The sexual rapist who is more naïve, suspicious, interpersonally open, and less aggressive is likely to score low on N, moderately low on H, and moderately high on $Q_4$ and I. Aggressively motivated rapists will score low on A and moderately low on I, but high on E, H, and $Q_2$. Both types are less than average on scale B.

## Treatment Options

Castration has been a time-honored approach for dealing with the rapist, yet runs afoul of legal considerations and the whims of some liberals. Nonetheless, chemocastration, via drugs that lower the serum testosterone level, is still used (Walker, 1978; Walker & Meyer, 1981). These drugs lower the likelihood of sexual arousal, but side effects are substantial and, in addition, the drugs are not consistently effective. New suggestions for the legal disposition of the rapist even include some irony analagous to the above suggestions. Fersch (1980) states that in rape "the criminal act ought to be brought under assault and battery with a dangerous weapon. Then the attention could be focused on whether or not the accused possessed a dangerous weapon" (p. 14).

The aversive therapies have been commonly used here and have shown moderate success. More effective ways of coping with anger are also necessary, possibly introduced by modeling or role-playing. Marital therapy may be specifically indicated (Bagarrozzi et al., 1982), since for many rapists the initiation of the rape sequence immediately follows a marital battle.

## Anorexia Nervosa (307.10) and Bulimia
## (307.51)

Anorexia nervosa is not a classic impulse disorder wherein the impulse overcomes the individual. Rather, there is an overcontrol of the impulse to eat. There is also occasional accompanying binge eating (bulimia), so it is included in the impulse disorder section.

The essential features of anorexia nervosa, according to DSM-III, are an intense concern about becoming overweight and a persistent feeling of being fat, even when weight loss has begun or has even been substantial. This is combined with a refusal to continue body weight at the minimally appropriate level, considering age and height, and evidence of a weight loss of at least 25 percent from the original weight. If the individual is less than eighteen years of age, a projected and extrapolated weight at eighteen may be used as the criterion.

This apparently voluntary self-starvation is seen primarily in middle and upper socioeconomic classes of women. It typically occurs first during puberty as a young woman becomes more conscious of her self-image. Sexuality may be channeled into the eating area, as these women usually avoid sexual acting-out. After the "sin" of eating, they may resort to self-induced vomiting and laxatives to "cleanse" the body of food (Bruch, 1978). Some anorectics also show episodes of bulimia (binge-eating), and in general, they are more disturbed than anorectics who do not show bulimia (Garfinkel et al., 1980). Approximately one in every 250 females between the ages of twelve and eighteen develops this disorder, and follow-up studies variously estimate mortality rates at between 5 and 15 percent.

The parents of the anorectic are typically very controlling though caring individuals. As a result, the anorectic appears to use the disorder to control the family as a statement of independence in the narrow area that they can paradoxically control. The salient personality characteristics are excessive dependency and sensitivity, introversion, perfectionism, and a subtle but persistent selfishness and stubbornness (Bruch, 1978).

The converse pattern from anorexia nervosa is bulimia, a chronic pattern of binge eating. Bulimia is known as the gorge-purge syndrome, and the word itself comes from the Greek words for ox and hunger (Casper et al., 1980). The essential features according to DSM-III are recurrent binge eating combined with depression and remorse following the binges, with awareness that the pattern is disordered and cannot be stopped. It is associated with attempts to control weight by diets or vomiting, and also by eating in an inconspicuous manner using high calorie foods.

Although anorectics are typically shy, they are passively controlling and stubborn. Those bulimorectics who are also anorectic are more likely to be extroverted perfectionists who attempt to control their peers in direct ways. Some bulimorectics are obese, though many weigh in at normal levels, whereas anorectics are usually almost cadaverously thin (Casper et al., 1980). Both disorder groups come from families in which food is a focus, as in socialization or recognition. Anorectics will often cook exotic meals for others, although they may eat only a small portion themselves. Bulimorectics do not usually like to cook because they are afraid they will eat all the food before the guests show up.

### Diagnostic Considerations

The combined dependency and perfectionism of the anorectic are likely to elevate scale 7 of the MMPI, while the general psychopathology here should elevate 6 and 8 (Small et al., 1981). The subtle selfishness, self-centeredness, and stubbornness should elevate scales 1 and 3 somewhat. The interpersonal avoidance and sensitivity would tend to elevate scale 0. At the same time, all of the patterns are influenced by the denial of pathology, so scales L and K tend to be elevated while F is depressed. The anorectic who also shows episodes of bulimia is more likely to score higher on scales 2, 3, 4, 6, and 7 than the anorectic who does not also manifest bulimia (Garfinkel et al., 1980).

Bulimorectics are more likely to be extroverted, and should therefore show a low 0 scale, as well as a higher scale 8, reflecting the sense of loss of control. Since they are more overtly self-disclosing, all scales should be more highly elevated on the average, particularly scale 2 and scale 4.

On the 16 PF, the anorectic tends to score low on scales A, F, H, and $Q_1$, and moderately low on M, while the bulimorectic tends to score high on these scales, particularly A, H, M, and $Q_1$. The anorectic is higher on $Q_3$ and $Q_2$; the bulimorectic tends to be in the middle on these scales. The anorectic also scores quite high on G, whereas the bulimorectic scores toward the middle. The anorectic is surprisingly toward the middle on scales I and L, reflecting the subtle stubbornness and selfishness that are not apparent in initial interactions. Both usually score quite high on scale B, reflecting their tendency to be in the upper range in intelligence and socioeconomic status. Both also tend to be reasonably high on O.

These same factors, higher intelligence and socioeconomic status, predict overall high scores on the WAIS, with verbal scores usually being a bit higher than performance scores. The perfectionism and compulsivity evident in anorectics, combined with their conservative and production orientation to school situations, usually results in elevations of information and vocabulary. Their stubborn perfectionism usually slows them down somewhat on the digit symbol test as well as on block design and object assembly, yet they seldom make the errors of impulse that are more often noted in the bulimorectic.

There has been little in the way of research on Rorschach patterning in anorexia nervosa (Wagner & Wagner, 1978), though there are some detected commonalities. Reflecting the perfectionism and denial of pathology, the total number of responses is low, and response latencies are slow. The D:M ratio is out of balance, as there are a low number of movement responses, a response pattern often noted in persons who are striving beyond their resources—the perfectionism characteristic of the anorectic. There is a high F and F+%, though occasional closely integrated color responses and subtle sexual and anatomical responses are included. Not surprisingly, responses that focus on food are common. Wagner and Wagner (1978) conclude that in most other respects they resemble the conversion disorder.

The bulimorectic is believed by this author to have a higher number of responses and a more adequate W:M ratio, although content that focuses on food is similarly present. There is much greater use of integrated color, though the F+% is lower, and overall there is less use of form.

*Treatment Options*

Since anorexia nervosa may often result in very severe weight loss that threatens life, hospitalization combined with forced and/or intravenous feeding may be necessary. At this stage, a behavior modification program to develop feeding behaviors may be helpful, though the critical issue is in deriving the reinforcements that can build up the feeding behavior.

A more psychodynamic approach has been found to be useful as the person moves into more normal functioning (Bruch, 1978; Palazzoli, 1978), with a focus on the ambivalence over dependency, the high need for perfectionism, and, as trust develops, the subtle selfishness and narcissism that emerge. Family therapy is also likely to be necessary as so much of this pattern is related to the interactions over dependency and control in the family.

The bulimorectic can respond to many of the same therapy techniques noted for the anorectic. In addition, an adolescent group therapy experience is also helpful. This provides a sense of control as well as a source of feedback. The adolescent group can be useful for anorectics as well, but only after they have made substantial improvements through other techniques. The bulimorectic may also need counseling toward simple control of eating behaviors, such as is used with the more standard problem of obesity and persistent eating disorders.

# 12

## Malingering (V65.20)

The DSM-III designates malingering as a condition attributable to mental disorder. The issues of malingering and response sets are especially important in considering the categories of factitious disorder, antisocial personality disorder, substance dependence, schizophrenia, and the dissociative disorders.

The specific DSM-III criteria for malingering include the voluntary presentation of physical or psychological symptoms. Malingering is understandable by the circumstances of the situation, rather than from the person's individual psychology, as is true of a factitious disorder.

Malingering is likely to occur in job screening, military and criminal justice situations, or wherever a psychological or physical disability has a payoff. It occurs more commonly in the early to middle adult years, is more common in males than in females, and often follows an actual injury or illness. Problematic employment history, lower socioeconomic status, or an associated antisocial personality disorder are also common predictors of this disorder. The reader is advised to consult the MMPI portion of the section on the psychogenic pain disorder regarding the issue of chronic (actual) pain versus malingering.

### MMPI

It is appropriate here to broaden the concept of malingering to any type of response that distorts the production of an accurate record; this is the context in which the following discussion is placed. On the MMPI, interest is naturally centered on the validity scales as predictors of distorted response sets. The traditional rule of thumb has been that if the F-K ratio is +11, such people are trying to fake bad; that is, to present a distorted picture of themselves that emphasizes pathology. If the score is −12 or more, the emphasis is on trying to look good and denying pathology. However, it is generally agreed that these axioms only hold if F and K are relatively low. For example, psychotic and other severely disturbed individuals, particularly with the anxiety disorders, are likely to score in a T range of 65 to 80 on the F scale, hence at first may appear to be malingering.

Gynther et al. (1973) have shown that profiles with F scores that are in the T range above 95 are commonly associated with extremely disturbed individuals who manifest hallucinations, delusions, and general confusion. This is particularly so when one is dealing with an inpatient population. Also, individuals who have a T score of greater than 100 on the F scale have probably either responded to the MMPI in a random fashion or have answered all the items "true." If all or the great majority of items are answered "false," the T scores are typically in the 80 to 99 range.

The overall profile for a random response set is an L scale of approximately 60 T, an F scale of approximately 115, and K around 55, with an elevation on scale 8 being close to 100 T for females and at approximately 115 for males. Scale 6 is usually the lowest score. If there are all "true" responses, the F scale is practically off the top, the L scale is about 35, and K scale is at 30 T. The profile peaks are on scale 8 at 130 for males and almost 110 for females, with a secondary peak on scale 6 at 100 T for both. It is worthwhile for the clinician at least to scan quickly the response sheet before turning it over for scoring. In cases where careless or random responding has occurred, it is often immediately evident, and the problem can be dealt with at that time.

By alternating true and false responses, one obtains a T score of about 55 on L, a T of 110 on F, and 65 for K, with a particularly strong peak on scale 8 (up to 120 T). Scores throughout the rest of the profile are high (Graham, 1977).

A common profile for a malingerer has an inverted V with an F scale at approximately 80, the rest of the profile is a jagged sawtooth pattern, with scales 4, 6, and 8 at approximately 80 T, scale 2 slightly above 70 T, scale 7 slightly below 70 T, and the other scales in the normal range. A person who is deliberately faking good obtains a "V" on the validity scales, with L sometimes as high as 70, F around a T score of 50, and K again close to 70 T. Most of the scales on this profile are at or below the 50 T scale line, and the highest scores are usually on scales 1, 5, and 4, with low scores on 6 and 0 (Fowler, 1981).

In general, when F and K are both high, look for deliberate faking, and if L is high, but F and K are within acceptable limits, consider an individual who is either naïve or very unsophisticated, or both, and who at the same time is trying to look good. If K is high, and L and F are within a normal range, a more sophisticated defense system is probable, and the profile can be considered as an indication of subclinical trends.

Another relatively common pattern that results from a form of malingering is the 1-3/3-1 pattern, with a high K scale and very low scores on 2, 7, and 8. Such an individual is quite defensive, and unwilling to admit any faults at all. These people will not tolerate the patient role and have a poor prognosis.

## 16 PF

There are scales for faking good or faking bad on the 16 PF, derived by Winder, O'Dell and Karson (1975). The faking good scale, which they refer to as a "motivational distortion" scale, is calculated by taking the sum of the responses that the individual gives to the following specific responses: 7-c, 24-c, 61-c, 62-a, 81-a, 97-a, 111-a, 114-c, 123-c, 130-a, 133-c, 149-c, 173-a, 174-c, ,and 184-a.

The faking bad scale is calculated in the same manner, by totaling how many of the specific marker questions that an individual scores on the raw data sheet. The responses that are used to calculate this score are 14-a, 38-a, 42-c, 51-b, 52-c, 55-c, 68-c, 80-a, 89-c, 117-a, 119-a, 123-a, 143-a, 176-c, and 182-c.

Winder et al. assert that a cutoff score of 6 is useful for determining both faking good and bad. However, Krug (1978) obtained data on a much broader and more representative sample, and he finds one major difference in the cutoff scores.

Krug's sample included 2,579 men and 2,215 women. On the faking-good scale, scores ranged from 0 to 15, with a mean of 6.36 and a standard deviation of 2.87 for men, while women's scores ranged from 0 to 14, with a mean of 5.71 and a standard deviation of 2.72.

Krug's data suggest that the cutoff score of 6 for the faking-good scales, as suggested by Winder et al., is much too liberal, since in using this cutoff score almost 55 percent of those people who are routinely screened would be labeled as faking good, instead of the approximately 7 percent that Winder et al. report. Krug's data would suggest that a raw score of 10 on the faking-good scale would be a much more appropriate cutoff point. Only about 15 percent of people taking the test would attain a score this high.

On the faking-bad scale, men ranged from 0 to 12, with a mean of 2.45 and a standard deviation of 2.27, while women scored from 0 to 11, with a mean of 2.24 and a standard deviation of 2.04. Winder's suggestion of a cutoff score of 6 for the faking-bad scale is supported by Krug, since both report that fewer than 10 percent of those taking the test will score above 6 on this scale.

It should be noted that in general college students show lower average scores than the adult population on both of the faking scores, and high school students score even lower than the college students; hence an age factor may be operating.

Those who are attempting to fake good and deny anxiety score very low on O and $Q_4$, and, in general, those who are faking good score in the following directions: C+, H+, L−, O−, $Q_3$+, $Q_4$−, and G+. Those who are faking bad tend to present a mirror image of these data.

Krug offers the following rules to be used when scores range from 6 and above:[1]

*For Faking Good:*
1. For a score of 7, subtract 1 from C and add 1 sten score point to $Q_4$.
2. If the score is 8, subtract 1 sten score point from A, C, G, and $Q_3$, and add one point to L, O, and $Q_4$.
3. If the score is 9, subtract 1 from A, C, G, and $Q_3$, while adding 1 to F, L, O, and $Q_4$.
4. If the score is 10, add 1 to F, L, and O, and add 2 to $Q_4$, while subtracting 1 from A, G, H, and $Q_3$, and subtracting 2 from C.

*For Faking Bad:*
1. If the score is 7, add 1 to C.
2. If the score is 8, subtract 1 from O and $Q_4$, while adding 1 to C.
3. If the score is 9, subtract 1 from L, O, and $Q_4$, while adding 1 to C, H, I, and $Q_3$.
4. If the score is 10, subtract 1 from L and $Q_4$, while adding 1 to A, H, I, and $Q_3$, and adding 2 to C.

Individuals who randomly mark the 16 PF answer sheet show a very flat profile, with a low score on scale B.

## Rorschach Test

A major problem with the use of the Rorschach, as well as other projective techniques, in the detection of deception is the apparent susceptibility to faking psychosis on the test as is evident in the study by Albert et al., 1980. Albert and his colleagues studied four different groups of Rorschach protocols. The first group, the Psychotic protocols, were obtained from actual mental hospital inpatients who were administered the Rorschach with standard instructions. The second group, labeled Uninformed Fakers, were obtained from college students who were given the instructions to malinger

---

1. From S. Krug, Further evidence on the 16 PF Distortion Scales. *Journal of Personality Assessment*, 1978, 42, 513–518. Printed with permission of the Society for Personality Assessment and the author.

paranoid schizophrenia; that is, "you want the test result to show that you are a paranoid schizophrenic and not show that you are faking," with no other allied instructions. The third group, the Informed Fakers, were given the same instructions as the Uninformed Fakers, and additionally heard a twenty-five-minute audiotape describing paranoid schizophrenia, which included actual examples of paranoid delusional thinking and thought processes. However, at no point did it mention the Rorschach test or provide any specific suggestions as to how to fake psychosis on it. The fourth group, the Control group, consisted of college students on whom the protocols were obtained under standard instructions.

The protocols were sent for judging to clinicians experienced in the use of the Rorschach. Each judge was sent a random set of four Rorschach protocols and asked to provide a psychiatric diagnosis, to indicate certainty of the diagnosis, and to rate protocols on dimensions of psychopathology and malingering. Results suggested that these experts were unable to discriminate the fakers from the actual psychotic individuals, although they did discriminate all psychotic groups from the normal group. The group most often seen by these experts as psychotic was the "informed faker" group. This study suggests that the Rorschach is effective in pointing to psychotic psychopathology, though as yet, effective cues for distinguishing malingering from other psychopathology have not been found. The small N in the above study is noted, and there is a need for more research.

With the above in mind, it is generally agreed that clients (especially if unsophisticated) who are malingering will respond to the Rorschach with a reduced number of responses and will additionally show slow reaction times, even when they do not produce particularly well-integrated or complex responses. They take a cautious attitude, and as a result produce few responses primarily determined by color. There is a high percentage of pure F responses, and also a high number of popular responses. They easily feel distressed by the ambiguity of the stimuli and will subtly try to obtain feedback from the examiner as to the adequacy and accuracy of their performance. Also, Seamons et al. (1981) note that if the F%, L, and X+% variables are in a normal range, and there are a high number of texture, shading, blood, dramatic, nonhuman movement, vista, or inappropriate combination responses, malingering to cause a false appearance of a mentally disordered state should be considered.

It is ironic that psychologists have not carried out much research on the detection of deception, since it is a critical issue in many diagnostic decisions. In addition, psychologists have not been sophisticated in methods other than psychological test measures of deception, and even here, tests have been largely restricted to the MMPI. Many people who use the 16 PF have been unaware of the deception scales that have been derived from it.

Only recently have psychologists shown an interest in adding physiological methods of deception assessment to their armamentarium. At the same time, most states are passing laws that allow the title of "polygrapher" and "lie detection examiner" only for individuals who have training that is restricted to certain physiological tests. Also, as Balloun and Holmes (1979) demonstrate, less efficient or confusing assessment modalities are used in the standard examination format and may even be mandated by state law.

Psychologists also do not make much use of systematized interview observat ns or techniques that change the set of the person taking the test in order to gain a more truthful response. Several consistent behavioral cues have been noted in individuals who present a dishonest portrayal of themselves (Mehrabian, 1971). For example, on the average, such individuals nod and gesture more than the honest interviewees do, and they have less frequent foot and leg movements. They also talk less, speak more slowly, and at the same time have more speech errors and smile more often. In addition, the dishonest interviewees tend to take positions that are physically farther from the interviewer. High voice pitch and many hand movements, relative to the individual's standard performance, are also indicative of deception.

There is no real support for the idea that people who are deceiving will necessarily avoid eye contact. There is some evidence that females will look longer into the eyes of male examiners while lying, but perhaps not into a female examiner's eyes. These same cross-sex results hold for males as well, but not as markedly (Burns & Kintz, 1976).

With reference to the set in which the test is taken, Macciocchi and Meyer (1981) told people that the test that they were going to take had built-in scales to detect deception. These subjects provided more honest and less socially desirable response patterns than those who were told nothing but merely encouraged to be honest in their responses. Of even more importance, a group of subjects were told that if there was any hint in the psychological tests that they might have been deceptive, they would be given a lie detection examination. They were then even more honest and self-disclosing in their response patterns, compared to when the threat of detection was only by psychological test scales. More research in this area is needed to set test conditions more effectively so as to gain more honest responses.

Clinicians also need to look more to specific tests if there is any question of dishonesty. For example, scales that tap a social desirability response set, such as the Marlowe-Crowne Social Desirability Scale (Marlowe & Crowne, 1964), give an idea of the direction of a client's response set. They are also helpful in conjunction with the other more standard detection scales built into such tests as the MMPI and 16 PF.

It would be useful if graduate training programs in psychology emphasized more the use of physiological measures in detecting deception. The psychologist's extensive background in the study of human behavior and expertise in interviewing and psychological testing could easily be supplemented by this specific training. This would not only facilitate the accuracy of general psychological testing—it would also provide our court systems with a much more expert and effective effort toward the detection of deception.

# 13

## Suicide and Aggression Potential

### Aggression Potential

A major issue in many psychological referral situations is the potential for acting out, either toward others or oneself. Given the low base rates of such behaviors, making a highly accurate prediction to actual behavior is virtually impossible (Monohan, 1981). However, there are test data that can aid the clinician in making predictions at a higher level than that allowed by impressionistic data or chance. There are several indicators of potential for aggression against others in the MMPI. As in all areas of psychopathology, certain specific scales have been developed to assess aggression potential. Ironically, in the general testing situation, the examiner would have to know the "answer" already, at least to a degree, to employ such scales. They are of help when there are prior cues, and it is worthwhile for the clinician to keep a range of specific tests available for such situations. An example in this area is the overcontrolled hostility scale (0–H), devised and refined by Megargee and his colleagues (Megargee & Cook, 1975). This scale is a subset of MMPI items and effectively identifies a subgroup of assaultive criminals who are generally overcontrolled in their response to hostility but who sporadically are extremely assaultive.

The type of individual discovered in this scale is similar to the one with the 4–3 profile type described by Davis and Sines (1971). The profile peak is on scale 4, the second highest elevation is on scale 3, and there is little significant elevation elsewhere. This profile is characteristic of men who maintain an ongoing quiet adjustment, yet who are prone toward hostile aggressive outbursts. They may or may not fit the aforementioned criteria for the intermittent explosive disorder. Davis and Sines hypothesize that those with the 4–3 profile type are consitutionally predisposed to this behavior by some kind of a cyclical internal mechanism that occasionally causes these acute emotional outbursts. Later research confirmed the validity of this profile as suggestive of aggression potential across a number of settings, included among females (Gearing, 1979).

To the degree that both 4 and 3 are highly elevated in a typically non-aggressive person, the likelihood of an occasional aggressive outburst increases. In general, when scale 4 is greater than scale 3, control decreases. Conversely, as scale 3 increases over scale 4, potential for more ability to control and inhibit aggressive impulses increases. In females, the 4–3 pattern has also been commonly associated with promiscuity. This is probably true with males, but because of traditional sex role expectations, such behavior in males is not as commonly a focus in assessment.

Consistently assaultive individuals, whose overt interpersonal patterns are more consistent with this behavior, have high scores on scales F, 4, and 9, with secondary elevations on 6 and 8. All five of these scales have been classically regarded as scales that suggest a lack of impulse control. Persons with high scores on these scales combine social resentment and hostility, a lack of moral inhibitions, suspiciousness and resentment toward authority and the world in general, and a lack of impulse control. Such a combination easily engenders hostility, even with minimal environmental stimulation. General problems in social adjustment also occur and combine with social resentment and envy of others to elevate the 0 scale. A high scale 5 score is generally indicative of ability to suppress aggression.

A specific criminal subgroup, Charlie, with elevations on these scores, is described by Megargee and Bohn (1979); the reader is referred to that section. Charlies who are hostile, paranoid, and dangerous individuals showed characteristic elevations on scales 8, 6, and 4, in that order, with distinctly low scales on 1, 2, and 3. From an overall perspective, Jones et al. (1981) found high scores on F, 6, 7, and 8 to predict violent incidents in a prison setting.

The subgroup How, also studied by Megargee and Bohn (1979), seeks interpersonal contact but is consistently rejected and builds up much anger and hostility, as well as anxiety. In that subgroup, scale 8 is usually highest, followed by scales 2, 4, and 1. The overall profile is distinctly elevated, with higher elevations on the above scales in a noteworthy jagged pattern.

The "double M" profile, with distinct elevations on 2, 4, 6, and 8, refers to individuals who are very unstable and also dangerous to self or, more likely, to others. It is hard to bring them into a therapy situation, and if they appear, they are difficult to change.

## 16 PF

There has not been as much research on the prediction of aggression with the 16 PF as there has been with the MMPI. However, several scales considered together do modestly predict aggression. Scales that tap aggression potential per se are E, L, and Q₁, and in each a high scale is predictive. General impulsiveness is reflected in high scores on F and H. Low scores on G, O, and Q₃, along with a high score on F, are thought to be predictors of low ego control and thus to contribute to a prediction of acting out.

## Other Test Response Patterns

Persons who are inclined toward easy aggression seem less able to deal with their concerns by articulating them verbally; this may be reflected in the WAIS-R, since they usually obtain a verbal scale score that is lower than the performance scale score. Kunce et al. (1976) found a specific instance of this effect. Individuals prone to aggression were low on the similarities score relative to all other scales. Kunce and his colleagues suggest that a low ability to discuss abstract issues verbally is related to problems in impulse control. While this very specific prediction of the overall conceptual scheme has not been replicated, clients who act out aggressively tend to score lower on the similarities, vocabulary, and block design subtests.

Problems in aggression control are usually correlated with present or previous difficulties in adjusting to school. Hence, within the verbal section of the WAIS-R, scores tend to be lower on information, arithmetic, and vocabulary relative to the other three scales taken as a whole. Quiet but hostile and explosive individuals attain low picture arrangement scores, relative to the more extroverted and consistently aggressive type.

On the Rorschach, individuals who are prone to aggressive behavior typically show short reaction times, do not provide extensive response records, and may give quick responses to Card I and the color cards (Beck, 1952). They tend to be low in the number of FC responses, and high in C and CF responses and in the number of popular responses (Phillips & Smith, 1953). They also allegedly give responses associated with recreation. Content such as swords or guns, explosions, blood, or aggressive animals such as crabs is expected in those individuals who consistently act out aggressively—assaultive psychopaths. The explosion-oriented response is more characteristic of the person who is making an attempt to control aggression—the explosive personality. Conversely, the potential for assault is contraindicated by a high number of F+, D, and FC responses, a high amount of abstraction content, and/or a higher number of popular and original responses.

The reader is referred to the previous sections on the antisocial personality disorder and the passive-aggressive personality disorder, since these disorders in particular contain the potential for ongoing aggression, and the criteria described there are applicable here as well. With a person who shows periodic aggression, the reader is referred to the sections on the explosive personality and on the paranoid disorders.

## Suicide Potential

As with aggression, the clinician is often called on to make predictions about suicide potential, and it is an equally difficult task (Monohan, 1981). Though suicide is still an issue of concern in legal arenas, it is not still considered a crime. Only in recent times has our legal predecessor, England, stopped employing a practical response to a suicide attempt, hanging. Hanging had superseded an even more flamboyant approach, driving a stake through the heart of one who attempted suicide.

Most authorities believe that the suicide rate has been rising, but it is still not clear whether this is because of a greater willingness on the part of the coroners and police officers to use the term, or whether there is a true increase in suicide. The research of Murphy and Wetzel (1980) suggests that the suicide rate significantly increased throughout the years 1949 to 1974; there is good reason to believe that this has not since abated. However, they point out that before these findings are used to authorize an expansion of traditional efforts to increase the number of suicide prevention centers, one should note that the rise in the suicide rate has coincided with a rise in the distribution and visibility of these centers in the United States. Interestingly, the opposite effect has been noted in England.

Suicide appears to be increasing among young adults; at present it is the second highest cause of death for white males, aged fifteen to nineteen (approximately 88 per 100,000). For many years, the reported rate of suicide in the United States has been approximately ten to twelve per 100,000 population. In several European countries, notably Sweden and Switzerland, rates of approximately 25 per 100,000 population have been reported. However, it is not clear whether this reflects true differential rates.

More men than women actually kill themselves (at approximately a rate of three to one), although more women than men attempt suicide, again at approximately a 3 to 1 rate (Schneidman, 1979). The majority of suicides, approximately 90 percent, are committed by whites, and most of the data about suicide concern whites.

Suicidal individuals tend to give clues to those around them. Seriously suicidal individuals tend to perceive life in a negative manner and associate many attractive concepts with death; the reverse is true for those who are not so intent on self-destruction. Such measures as the semantic differential could be helpful in this regard. Approximately 80 percent of those who have made a suicide attempt discussed their intent to do so with persons around them and they are usually open to discussing their suicidal concerns with clinicians. Suicidal persons are more likely to 1) have had a parent or other important identity figure who attempted or committed suicide, 2) have a history of family instability and/or parental rejection, and 3) be involved (if married or similarly occupied) with a loved mate who is competitive and/or self-absorbed. The initiation of the suicidal event is especially likely to be triggered by the loss of an important social support, such as a confidant (Slater & Depue, 1981).

The clinician should also consider the person's access to lethal instruments, since the highest suicide rates occur among police officers and physicians. While it could be argued that the high level of frustration in the work of both of these groups may be an important variable, most suicide experts believe the critical variable is their high access to lethal means, guns and poisonous drugs respectively.

In general most people who are severely depressed and suicidal are more dangerous to themselves when they begin an upswing out of the depths of depression. If successive testings by an MMPI or specific depression scale reveals an initial upswing in a depressive who has discussed the possibility of suicide, precautions should be emphasized at that time. A dimension useful to most clinicians is the concept of manipulative versus genuine suicide (Neuringer, 1979). Both types will be discussed below.

*MMPI*

The prototypical pattern for a suicidal individual is the 2–7/7–2 code combination. The 2–7/7–2 code particularly reflects suicidal ideation, and anytime 2 is elevated above 80 T the clinician should pursue the question of possible suicidal ideation. Reflecting the dictum that "If you want to know something specific about clients, you should ask them about it," the critical items concerning suicide should always be checked. The likelihood of this ideation's being actualized increases as scores on scales 4, 8, and 9 rise. Such a rise reflects an increasing loss of control over impulses, a rise in the energy available for behavior, and an increasing sense of isolation and resentment toward other people. A rise in scale 8 also reflects poor judgment; hence, suicidals who are not totally genuine in their suicide motivation may actually kill themselves whether they want to succeed or not, as the judgment may bring inadvertent "success."

Some people are suicidal for only a short period of time, usually when there is a severe loss in their psychological world that has not yet been integrated. Such people are temporarily suicidal, and if they can be restricted during this period of time, and treated, they are likely to reintegrate and move away from the suicidal ideation. A high spike on scale 2 is characteristic here.

The 2–4/4–2 code type is more likely to reflect a manipulative suicide. Where both scales 4 and 6 are elevated, in addition to at least a moderate elevation on scales 2 and 7, repressed anger and interpersonal hostility are basic to the suicide attempt as manipulation. It is an attempt to inflict punitive guilt and consequent behavior control on another.

Several observers have noted that an additional pattern, at least in women, has been associated with suicide attempts. The major features are a low K scale and a high 5 scale (both suggesting a strong, almost counter-phobic rejection of femininity), a paradoxically high score on scale 3 in-dicating a histrionic component, and a high score on scale 0 reflecting a sense of social isolation and rejection. These women feel alienated and disturbed in their self-identity, yet have no sense of a possible option to deal with this distress. Since they are impulsive as well, the potential for an acting-out behavior is heightened.

### Other Test Response Patterns

Exner (1978) has provided the most elegant and effective research on the use of Rorschach in the prediction of suicide. He offers eleven variables which together form a prediction for suicide potential. Some of the variables are scored within Exner's system, and the reader is referred to page 204 in Volume 2 of his text. The eleven variables he cites as important are as follows:[1]

1. FV + VF + V + FD is greater than 2
2. An occurrence of a color-shading blend response
3. Zd is greater than ±3.5
4. 3r + (2)/R is less than .30
5. Experience Potential is greater than Experience Actual
6. CF + C is greater than FC
7. S is greater than 3
8. $X^+\%$ is less than .70
9. Pure H is less than 2
10. P is greater than 8 or less than 3
11. R is less than 17

Exner's data indicate that if 8 or more of these signs occur, the clinician will correctly identify such individuals as actual suicides 75 percent of the time and will also successfully predict attempters at a 45 percent rate. Mean-while, only 20 percent of depressed controls, approximately 12 percent of schizophrenic controls, and no nonpatients will be identified in a false-positive manner.

Other authors have supported Exner's concepts that the number of responses is low in suicidals, that less integrated color responses are more common, and that the number of popular responses are either very high or low. Also, there is some indication that transparency responses (such as

1. J. Exner, *The Rorschach: A Comprehensive System.* Vol. 2: *Current Research and Ad-vanced Interpretation.* New York: Wiley, 1978, p. 204. Used with permission of the publisher.

light bulbs) or cross-sectional responses (such as X-rays) are found more commonly in potential suicides than in other persons.

Phillips and Smith (1953) state that content suggesting decay or geographic depression (e.g., canyons) is indicative of suicidal ideation. Others have argued that landscape or serenity associations are indicative of suicides who have not yet communicated their intent. Responses that suggest hanging or drowning or other direct means of suicide should obviously alert the examiner to further consideration.

Extra data may be available if an individual has already attempted suicide but has been prevented from completing it—the suicide note. The work of Edwin Schneidman and Norman Farberow (Schneidman, 1979) over many years has found that people who attempt suicide and genuinely mean to kill themselves write notes that are matter-of-fact and practical in their content. They may ask the target of the note to pay back small debts, return small items, or otherwise show seemingly trivial concerns, and they do not show much emotional content. It is as if they have already integrated the idea that they will be dead, so emotion is no longer directly tied to living relationships. Those individuals who attempted suicide yet apparently had no real intent to kill themselves left romantic, emotion-laden notes, thus attempting to institute guilt in the others and pressure them to change their behavior. Obviously, they believed they would be around to reap the fruits of that change.

# 14

## Central Nervous System
## Impairment and Retardation

### Central Nervous System Impairment

A common referral question is whether or not there may be Central Nervous System Impairment, referred to throughout this section as CNSI, though traditionally called Organic Dysfunction or Organic Brain Damage. Earlier in this book, I have used these less accurate terms, since they are so commonly used by clinicians. The intricacies of specific CNSI evaluation will not be discussed here; this would require more material than is appropriate for this book. If there is reason to think there is CNSI, and if there is a request for a specific and localized diagnosis, it is important to have a full evaluation carried out by a clinical neuropsychologist and/or a neurologist.

An example of the range of information needed for a full neuro-pyschological assessment is seen in Appendix C, as provided by Paul Salmon of the University of Louisville. It is evident from Appendix C that a good history is always critical. Sudden onset of symptoms, whatever their nature, should alert the clinician to possible CNSI. Changes in functioning of any sort are important data, so information from family and friends can be helpful.

Close observation of speech quality and problems, dress, grooming, gait and coordination while walking to and from the office, and affect can all provide clinical signs to help the clinician. Any signs of asymmetry should particularly be noted. For example, one person with visual field deficits neatly shaved one side of his face, but only roughly and sloppily shaved the other side. Obtaining some subject-as-own-control data is also useful, such as finger-tapping tasks or touching body parts with either hand with eyes open and closed. There are also normative or test data, the focus of this section.

If the clinician is to carry out a substantial neuropsychological assessment, more extensive methods of obtaining normative data, such as the Halstead-Reitan battery, or some of those detailed by Lezak (1976), are appropriate here. It is worth noting for many years the Halstead-Reitan battery, which includes a WAIS-R or WISC-R and requires about four to five hours test time was seen as the "benchmark" battery by clinicians. In the last several years, however, much more diversity has emerged, and this diversity extends into application as well. Such batteries are prognostic as well as diagnostic and can be extremely useful in other applications, such as evaluating the effects of drug trials. A good intermediate level screening battery for CNSI might include a WAIS-R, MMPI, specific tests for lateralization such as the Purdue Pegboard and/or tapping tests, tests for sensory response, and other tests that help cover the required variety of modalities and functions (Benton Visual Retention Test, Rey Auditory Verbal Learning Test, Symbol Digit Modalities Test, Sklar Aphasia Scale) (Salmon, 1982; Schwartz, 1981).

However, any diagnostician must be aware of the common signs of CNSI in the standard tests and in behavior, particularly in the event that no one has yet asserted the possibility of organic dysfunction. For example, the interaction of type of symptoms with rapid versus gradual onset can distinguish between cerebral impairment and such psychopathology as the affective disorders. When a syndrome with a gradual onset of a wide range of affective symptomatology is accompanied by neurological and cognitive deficits, along with aphasia or agnosia and/or a loss of sphincter control, irreversible CNSI is probable. If the affective symptomatology is unaccompanied by the latter symptomatology, and the depression and/or mania are severe and possibly accompanied by persistent delusions, an affective or bipolar disorder is more probable.

If instead, there is a rapid onset of symptoms focusing on confusion, agitation, attentional problems, and disrupted sleep patterns, along with problems in self-care (including impaired sphincter control), and a focus primarily on visual hallucinations, there is a high probability of acute CNSI. If death does not occur, recovery is often reasonably rapid. But if symptoms do not include such evident self-care problems and instead include delusions or auditory hallucinations, then an affective or schizoaffective disorder is probable.

The discrimination between right and left cerebral hemisphere impairment has fascinated clinicians for a long time. As an overall rule, specific deficits in spatial orientation and perceptual and/or organizational functions point to right hemisphere disorder, whereas specific problems in language, motor, and executive functions suggest left hemisphere impairment. Right hemisphere impairment is more likely to be manifest in a disruption of emotion-laden knowledge and a disruption of the nuances of speech (Tucker, 1981).

Difficulties in right-left spatial orientation problems have traditionally been seen as suggestive of disorder in the right hemisphere. But language is a critical factor in such discriminations, and hence attention to the quality of a client's difficulty may lead to a hypothesis that there is left hemisphere disorder instead.

Benton (1980) has commented on the ability to make facial recognitions as a diagnostic sign. His data, as well as those of others, suggest that specific facial agnosia, that is, the loss of ability to recognize familiar friends and family, is a good indicator of bilateral lesion. On the other hand, consistent problems in facial discrimination, such as in identifying new acquaintances, point to right hemisphere impairment, and if the lesion turns out to be even more localized, it is probably posterior rather than anterior.

A clinician might consider including a test like the Reitan Aphasia Screening Test, a shortened version of Halstead and Wepman's Aphasia Screening Test (Lezak, 1976), in his or her routine test battery. It takes only about ten minutes to administer and is a rough assessment of spatial and verbal factors, as well as aphasia. It is a good gross screening measure for significant cerebral impairment, as normals seldom make errors and perform effortlessly. If a client makes even two or three errors, it is worthwhile to take a deeper look for more signs of cerebral impairment.

One excellent item on this test is the request for the client to produce a Maltese cross. Clinicians could add some version of the Maltese cross, in conjunction with a few other figures such as those like to cards A and 7 of the Bender-Gestalt, to the routine self-administered battery in Appendix B. The clinician can also include a finger-tapping test, using a simple event counter. The general assumption is that performance will be about 10 percent better with the dominant hand (thus the opposite hemisphere), so any substantial deviation from this pattern can be suggestive of disorder in one or the other hemisphere.

## MMPI

There is no modal MMPI profile for organic dysfunction, and for good reason—there is no modal CNSI pattern. In this area, a dominant axiom should be individual differences. Yet there are a number of patterns that should alert the clinician to consider possible CNSI. An obvious first sign is not a code type, but an examination of how the person completed the form. For example, persons with visual field deficits may neglect portions of the answer form, thus invalidating the profile. Extremely erratic profiles will show up in the validity scale elevations; the reader should consult the section on malingering for information.

In general, persons with a left hemisphere dysfunction (especially to the degree that this is the dominant hemisphere) will show a "catastrophic response" pattern on the MMPI; those with right hemisphere dysfunction are more likely to appear "indifferent" (Tucker, 1981). Lachar (1974) notes that the relatively rare 1-9/9-1 two-point code, with a low scale 2, is found in a number of persons with acute CNSI. This most commonly occurs where there is a dawning awareness in clients that they have suffered a loss of function, and where they are dealing with it in a counterphobic manner. As they lose the will to fight in response to the loss and depression emerges, the two-point code of 2-9/9-2 is more common. When their personality functions begin to fall apart and are accompanied by activity levels raised against their phobia, the 9-8/8-9 profile may occur (Gynther et al., 1973). While scale 8 is often the highest scale in epileptic patients, scales 1, 2, and 3 are more likely to be elevated in clients with multiple sclerosis. Scale 8 is also often elevated as aphasic clients begin to withdraw.

Persons with CNSI from a toxic substance are likely to show a generally elevated MMPI profile with a particularly high score on scale 8, and scores on most other scales at about 70 T, except for the 5 scale. Scales that tend to be higher in this profile are 1 and 2. When CNSI occurs as a result of senility or a neurological degenerative process, elevations are more likely on scales 2 and 8, both around the 70 T mark. The senile group tends to have a slightly higher elevation overall in the other scores, with scale 1 being particularly higher than in the neurological degenerative group (Pennington, Peterson & Barker, 1979).

According to Lachar (1974), the classic signs of chronic CNSI are scores elevated above 70 T on scales 8, 6, 4, and 2. Scales 1 and 3 are usually low, except with those who have multiple sclerosis and similar clients. Watson, Plemel, and Jacobs (1978) find that the scale 1-scale 7 ratio is especially higher for CNSI clients than other groups with psychopathology. Also, the F scale is high, particularly if damage is severe. In chronic CNSI, the 9 scale is often a barometer of the person's reaction to it; a lower 9 scale score indicates either acceptance or a lack of reaction to it, while a high 9 scale suggests an attempt to cope, poorly at times. When scales 8 and 6 are very high and there are other solid indications of CNSI, the CNS disorder is probably accompanied by schizophrenia.

When dealing with possible CNSI cases, particularly in the aged, the MMPI may have to be administered over several sessions, because of fatigue and/or attention problems, or it may only be possible to use a short form (Schwartz, 1981).

## 16 PF

Because of the variety of reactions subsumed under the term *central nervous system impairment* (CNSI), a modal profile for CNSI is not available. However, persons with CNSI are generally high on scales O and $Q_4$, reflecting their sense of insecurity and anxiety. Those individuals who have moved into depression would probably not score so high. $Q_3$ is low, reflecting the degree of personality disintegration, and scale B is lowered, indicating the correlated loss of intellectual functioning. Moderately low scores on $Q_2$, F, and H are also standard. The scores on scale E vary markedly, depending on the reaction to the awareness of loss. If persons have become depressed and submissive to a hospital environment, E is low, whereas if they are attempting counterphobic mechanisms, it is elevated. G tends to vary markedly as well, but usually is at least moderately high.

## Other Test Response Patterns

Before looking at possible cues from specific WAIS-R subtests several overall perspectives that can aid the clinician in this type of assessment must be stated.

A. On the WAIS-R, the general rule has been that low verbal scales relative to performance scales indicate left hemisphere lesions. To a lesser degree, the converse is true—low performance scores relative to verbal scores indicate a right hemisphere lesion. Unfortunately, these discrepancies are not always clear-cut or perfectly correlated, but it is a good first rule. Russell (1979) asserts that left hemisphere damage may produce a very low profile, and it is difficult to differentiate this damage from mental retardation. Persons with right hemisphere damage do better on comprehension, similarities, and vocabulary than on other tests, and on picture completion within the performance tests. Those clients with diffuse CNSI do better on verbal tests than performance tests, particularly on vocabulary and information, but also do well on picture completion in the performance tests. They do particularly poorly on digit span, as do all groups, as well as on block design and arithmetic.

   Overall, it is reasonable to assert that a low performance-high verbal pattern is more suggestive of overall CNSI than is the high performance-low verbal pattern.

B. In general, marked verbal performance splits are likely to indicate intracerebral tumors or cerebrovascular accidents. Clients with cerebrovascular accidents are then more likely to show disrupted differential performance on grip strength and tapping tests than do clients with tumors.

C. In verbal subtests that require a high level of verbal precision and identification (the vocabulary scale), expressive speech problems are suggested by hesitating and circuitous speech—the patient cannot find the precise word.

D. The picture completion subtest can also be helpful in assessing the difficulties in expressive speech. It is important that the clinician create very specific demands. If the clinician's style is to accept approximate answers easily, or pointing rather than naming, for example, the client is not adequately pressed to make the precise designation.

E. General performance areas where the ability for abstract thinking is required, such in the similarities subtests and the proverbs on the comprehension subtest, test intellectual abstraction ability, and thus identify more diffuse cerebral impairment, or at least cerebral trauma that leads to a wide range of impairment.

F. The overall range between lowest and highest WAIS-R subscales is a good indicator of general impairment. When the range between scale scores is greater than five in persons without another handicap such as lack of education, the clinician should consider the possibility of CNSI.

G. The highest WAIS-R subscale scores provide a reasonably good index of premorbid intellectual functioning in cases of cerebral impairment, but only when they are scales that correlate reasonably well with the full scale WAIS-R, as in the vocabulary subtest. When digit span is the highest postmorbid scale, it would not be an especially efficient predictor.

H. Within-subtest scatter, or consistently missing easy items while answering hard ones accurately, is an important indicator of the ability to maintain set. Clients with certain cerebral impairments find it hard to keep the program in mind and to process the data at the same time. For example, they may keep the general problem in mind on the arithmetic subtest and forget the exact numbers in the process, or the reverse.

Digit symbol is commonly low in all brain-injured persons. Arithmetic is almost as consistently low, especially in those with left hemisphere injuries. In combination with digit span, arithmetic is an excellent measure of the degree of transient anxiety as well. Information may be low in persons who are suffering early CNSI in the left hemisphere, but it remains reasonably high in most CNSI cases, as do comprehension and similarities. Picture arrangement most often reflects right hemisphere disorder, as do object assembly and block design (Russell, 1979). The diagnostician may see unusual placements in block design and object assembly, placements that the client finds difficult to explain. Picture completion and similarities are rarely affected, except in chronic CNSI. Most schizophrenics do better on information than on similarities; this can be one cue to distinguish between them.

Block design also helps in the discrimination between CNSI and schizophrenia. It usually remains relatively high in schizophrenia, whereas it is virtually always affected to some degree in CNSI. It is particularly low in diffuse brain injuries and in injuries involving the parietal lobe. In another important discrimination, object assembly is often one of the higher scores in mentally retarded persons, whereas both CNSI and schizophrenics, as well as depressives, are prone to do poorly (Golden, 1979).

On The Wide Range Achievement Test (WRAT), disorders in reading ability should cue the clinician toward the possibility of temporal-occipital left hemisphere disturbance. A significant loss of spelling ability should suggest the possibility of parietal and/or occipital dysfunction.

The classic signs of CNSI on the Bender-Gestalt are perplexity, impotency, distortions, significant rotation of designs, and peculiar sequencing. Impotency, or statements indicating dissatisfaction with one's performance, are common throughout all the tests when such a client runs into difficulty. Also common is the element of perplexity, wherein a person overtly indicates confusion and uncertainty about handling the task given.

On the Benton Visual Retention Test, signs similar to that on the Bender-Gestalt are evidence of CNSI. More specifically, Golden (1979) states that persons with CNSI are most likely to make three types of errors here: first, the omission of a peripheral figure; second, rotations; and third, size errors (a loss of the size relationship between the major and peripheral figures). It is important to note that even though rotations do occur in normals, they are more likely to be stabilizing errors; when a figure that is drawn to sit on an angle, it is then rotated so that it sits flat. Alexias or aphasias may be involved if the client has difficulty recognizing previously learned configurations, such as the circle or square (Bender, 1938).

Much like the other drawing tests, distortions, perplexity, impotency, and perseveration in response to the Draw-A-Person Test are classic signs of cerebral impairment. The clinician might find it useful to have clients routinely write their name as well as a novel sentence (e.g., "the shed is next to the house") on the same page with the person they have drawn. In general, clients with left hemisphere impairment can often do the over-learned task reasonably well, that is, write their name, while at the same time they have marked difficulties with the novel sentence. Also, as a general rule, if the drawing is adequate but the writing is bad, the left hemisphere may be impaired, whereas if the drawing is poor and the writing is acceptable, the localization, if any, may be in the right hemisphere.

One of the best analyses of the differences in the style of drawings between those with right hemisphere CNSI and left hemisphere CNSI was carried out by Elizabeth Warrington (Warrington, 1969). The following contrasts generally reflect her insights:

| Right Hemisphere CNSI | Left Hemisphere CNSI |
| --- | --- |
| scattered and fragmented | simple and coherent |
| loss of adequate spatial relationships | spatial relationships are adequately retained |
| corrective lines are added | gross lack of detail |
| drawings are made energetically, almost driven | drawings are made slowly and laboriously, haltingly at times |
| orientation to the general task is faulty or lost | orientation to the general task structure is reasonably accurate |

It is important to look for perseveration in the drawing tests, as well as in a wide range of performance areas. One cerebrally impaired client kept doing an infinite division problem almost to a point of exhaustion, at which time he simply said, "There's too much of this."

On the Rorschach, perplexity, repetition, and impotency are also common, not surprising in light of the ambiguity of the stimuli. There is often a delayed reaction time to the cards, and persons may turn the cards in a confused manner, indicating an attempt to cope with a task in which they lack confidence.

Overall, there are a low number of responses, with the average time per response quite high, and a deterioration of the response quality as clients proceed through the cards. Constriction, being bound to stimuli (e.g., "This is where some ink has been splashed"), fragmented responses, and a high need for more structure are common. Positional responses are more common than normal. Occasional perseveration of content occurs, even in some cases to the point where there is a repetition of automatic phrases. In particular, there may be a perseveration of CF responses in the last three cards. "Color naming" as well as crude CF and C responses are given, in contrast to a low number of M responses and a low F+%. Vague W responses, with good form Dd responses, may be found. Responses about anatomy content and those in which humans or animals are mutilated reflect the client's own concerns about deterioration.

Before moving on to the next section, several "uniformity myths" are presented, as collected by Salmon (1982), that have unfortunately been pervasive in the traditions of CNSI assessment.

*Uniformity Myths*

The term *brain damage* is an accurate description of the effects of central nervous system impairment.

Individual differences do not significantly affect the manifestation, course, or outcome of CNS impairments.

Lesions of CNS tissues constitute a homogeneous class of phenomena.

Brain injuries are relatively static events, and are comparatively insensitive to the effects of time.

The clinician's role in neuropsychological investigations is confined primarily to diagnostic activities.

## Mental Retardation

Mental Retardation is another common referral problem for the clinician; it is generally agreed that about 1 percent of the population falls into this category. The DSM-III requires indication of subaverage intellectual functioning in an individually administered test, correlated problems in adaptive coping behaviors, and onset before the age of eighteen. If onset is later than the age of eighteen, the term *dementia*, subcoded as an organic mental disorder, is appropriate. The criteria for severity are noted in the following four subcategorizations.

Mild mental retardation (317.0x) is designated by IQ scores of 50 to 70. This is the largest group of retarded individuals, comprising about 75 percent to 80 percent of the overall retarded population; such persons are commonly referred to as educable. Many of these individuals develop sixth or seventh grade academic skills by the time they are in their middle adolescence.

Moderate mental retardation (318.0x), approximately twelve percent of the retarded population, is classified by an IQ score of 35 to 49. This group usually requires at least moderate supervision, particularly in financial matters and/or when under stress. They seldom progress beyond the third-grade achievement level, but can often communicate adequately.

Severe mental retardation (318.1x) is classified by an IQ score of 21 to 34, and comprises about 7 percent of the retarded population. This group is not likely to profit from any vocational training, though they can usually learn elementary self-care skills.

Profound mental retardation (318.2x), 1 percent of the retarded population, is designated by IQ scores of 20 or below.

If there is good reason to believe that significant intellectual retardation is present with functioning at least below an approximate IQ of 70, and for some reason the individual is untestable, the term *unspecified mental retardation* (319.0x) is used. The diagnosis of Borderline Intellectual Functioning (162.89) requires evidence of problems in adaptive coping, and an IQ score of 71 to 84.

Since the MMPI requires approximately a sixth-grade reading level, it is seldom administered to most mentally retarded persons. The Improved Readability Form (IRF), derived by Ward and Selby (1980), can occasionally be used effectively here; the reader is referred to the initial portion of the chapter on the Clinical Correlates of the MMPI and 16 PF. Regardless of which method of administration is used, such clients sometimes respond with a random response pattern; the reader is referred to the section on malingering.

Aside from the overall scores obtained on the WAIS-R, there are certain trends in the subtest patterns of mentally retarded individuals. First, they score relatively high on object assembly, whereas persons with CNSI score low. Performance subtests may exceed the verbal subtests, but this is not always the case. Academically oriented tests, such as information and arithmetic, are usually low. Also, the similarities test is relatively low while comprehension and picture completion are higher.

On the Rorschach, a low number of overall responses are usually obtained which contain a low F+ %, a high F%, few or poor M responses, and a high percentage of animal responses. When W responses are made, they are of poor quality. Repetitive and perseverative content occurs, and apparently impulsive inferences to content from the stimuli of the blots are common. On the Bender-Gestalt, changes in angulation, closure difficulty, irregular use of space and sequence, a probability of rotations, and collision tendencies are noted. Simplistic drawings, such as attachment of the appendages to the head, are seen on the Draw-A-Person Test in more severely retarded persons.

# 15

## Insanity, Civil Commitment, and Competency

### Insanity

Since insanity, as well as civil commitment and competency, are receiving increasing concern and attention from clinicians, they will be discussed here in relation to some of the concepts noted earlier in this book.

The tests and standards used to assess insanity, or more broadly, criminal responsibility, vary considerably. The traditional formulation, referred to as the M'Naghten Rule, is still influential in many states, but has typically been modified in some form or another. In its purest form, the criterion is whether or not a person committed an unlawful act as a result of "defect of reason" arising out of "a disease of the mind" which results in not "knowing the nature of the act," or, if the individual was aware of it, he or she was not aware that it was wrong. This is often referred to more cryptically as the "knowing right from wrong" standard.

In 1954, the Durham Rule, whose primary author was Judge David Bazelon, focused chiefly on the issue of whether or not the unlawful behavior was "the product of mental disease or mental defect" (Durham v. United States, 214 F.2d 862 D.C. Cir., 1954). However, though this rule received initial acclaim, it has seldom been followed since.

Today, the most influential legal definition of insanity is that formulated by the American Law Institute (ALI), and it is included in the Model Penal Code. It is comprised of two major sections:

1. Persons are not responsible for criminal conduct if, at the time of such conduct, as a result of mental disease or defect they lack substantial capacity either to appreciate the criminality (wrongfulness) of their conduct or to conform their conduct to the requirements of law.

2. The terms (*mental disease* or *defect*) do not include an abnormality manifested only by repeated criminal or otherwise antisocial conduct.

The rationale for the adoption of the American Law Institute Rule, known as the ALI Rule, is best exemplified in the case of People v. Drew (Sub., 149 Cal. Rptr 275, 1978).

> First, the ALI test adds a volitional element, the ability to conform to legal requirements, which is missing from the *M'Naghten* Test. Second, it avoids the all-or-nothing language of *M'Naghten* and permits a verdict based on lack of substantial capacity. . . . Third, the ALI Test is broad enough to permit a psychiatrist to set before the trier of facts a full picture of the defendant's mental impairments and flexible enough to adapt to future changes in psychiatric theory and diagnosis. Fourth, by referring to the defendant's capacity to "appreciate" the wrongfulness of his conduct the test confirms our holding . . . that mere verbal knowledge of right and wrong does not prove sanity. Finally, by establishing a broad text of nonresponsibility, including elements of volition as well as cognition, the test provides the foundation on which we can order and rationalize the convoluted and occasionally inconsistent law of diminished capacity (p. 282).

Before proceeding, it should be remembered that the expert witness, the clinician who offers an opinion in this area, does not make the ultimate decision, as stated in *United States v. Freeman* (357 F.2d 619):

> At bottom, the determination whether a man is or is not held responsible for his conduct is not a medical but a legal, social, or moral judgment. . . . it is society as a whole, represented by a judge or jury which decides whether a man with the characteristics described should or should not be held accountable for his acts (pp. 619–620).

Inherent in all of this is the fact that insanity is not a psychological/medical term, but is instead a legal term. Hence, the expert has the problem of transforming clinical data into an opinion as to whether or not the individual is insane. Although the judge and jury ultimately decide the issue, it is probable that the expert will be asked directly whether or not the individual is "insane." Also, even though a subsequent term, *incompetency*, refers to the person's mental status at the time of the examination, there is an extra difficulty in that insanity requires an inference to mental status at the time of the alleged act.

Until the Durham decision in 1954, there was fairly high correlation between the legal concept of insanity and the concept of psychosis. However, the Durham decision allowed the inclusion of the *Sociopathic Personality*, the DSM-I term in use at that time, as a mental disease included under insanity. The second clause in the ALI Rule noted earlier was directed at eliminating this exception.

At present, under the ALI standard, it seems reasonably clear that several conditions in DSM-III can be considered to fit with the concept of insanity. First, the presence of delusions, hallucinations, or other significant interference with cognitive functioning should be enough to warrant an assertion of insanity. Hence, most of the schizophrenic disorders and those dissociative disorders in which the behavior is relevant to the criminal act would be considered appropriate. Also, in most instances, the paranoid disorders and some of the severe affective disorders, such as manic episode and depressive episode, would fit these criteria. Appropriate sections in this text deal with the specific diagnostic criteria commonly associated with these categories.

Courts are particularly responsive to organic conditions that occur at the time of the alleged offense, even when there is little reason to argue cause rather than correlation. One case in which there was some evidence of a causal link is a case of hypothyroid psychosis, commonly referred to in the literature as myxedema psychosis, during which a young man allegedly committed a murder (Easson, 1980). He was held to be incompetent at the time of the trial. Later, after a two-month course of thyroid medication returned him to a status of competency, he stood trial and was found to be not guilty by reason of insanity, even though he was clearly sane at the time of his trial. Myxedema psychosis is rare, and it is marked by both paranoid symptoms and cognitive deficits. In this case, the person had referred himself for hospitalization because of his mental symptoms several months before the murder, and despite the fact that his scar for a prior thyroid operation had been noted, no effort was made to evaluate further for hypothyroidism.

There are two major exceptions to a judgment of insanity. The first are those conditions resulting from substance abuse, particularly if the substance was willingly ingested. As asserted in Barrett v. United States (377 A.2d 62, 1977):

Temporary insanity created by voluntary use of alcohol or drugs will not relieve an accused of criminal responsibility even if that mental condition would otherwise meet the applicable legal definition of insanity (p. 62).

However, there are occasions when this is not so clearly applicable. First, insanity may be argued if the substance abuse was caused by another without the victim's awareness. Second, as stated in State of New Jersey v. Stasio (78 N.J. 467, 1979):

Insanity is available when the voluntary use of the intoxicant or drug results in a fixed state of insanity after the influence of the intoxicant or drug has spent itself (p. 467).

The second exception to a judgment of insanity, as already noted, is that the secondary paragraph of the ALI Rule does not allow an insanity defense where there is an "abnormality manifested only by repeated criminal or otherwise antisocial contact." This would usually disallow the antisocial personality disorder syndrome.

Kurlychek and Jordan (1980) present an interesting study that compared the MMPI profiles of thirty male defendants who were found to be criminally responsible and those of twenty male defendants who were determined to be criminally not responsible. The modal code in the nonresponsible group was the 8–6 code. Six nonresponsibles obtained that code, and only two responsibles did. Three responsibles each obtained 2–3 and 2–7 codes, and no nonresponsibles scored in that pattern. The modal code for the responsible group was 8–7 (six subjects), though three nonresponsible subjects also obtained that pattern. The high incidence of the 8–6 code type in the nonresponsible clients suggested to the authors that highly delusional thought processes are a prevalent factor in nonresponsible defendants. The common scales in the responsible group (8–7, 2–3, 2–7, and 2–0) indicate that more neurotic and inhibitory effects on any psychotic tendencies are found in responsible individuals.

Since faking bad is particularly likely to be an issue in a decision about insanity, the reader is referred to the section on malingering. All reasonable precautions should be taken to prevent this. Also, to buttress the credibility of testimony, a number of clinicians have found it helpful to have protocols scored and interpreted by computer. Although this only offers part of the information a clinician needs to interpret the profile, it lends support and apparent credence to testimony.

As yet, effective tests specific to the assessment of insanity have not been developed, in contrast to those tests used to evaluate efficiently competency to stand trial. However, initial data suggest that a rating scale, the Rogers Criminal Responsibility Assessment Scale (RCRAS), could be worthwhile (Rogers et al., 1981). Twenty-three variables are rated to give scores on five discrete scales (the client's reliability, evidence of possible CNSI, psychopathology, cognitive control, and behavioral control). A hierarchical decision model, based on the ALI Rule, is then applied to these data. Persons interested in obtaining a copy of the RCRAS should contact Richard Rogers at Rush Medical College in Chicago.

## Civil Commitment

Psychologists are becoming increasingly involved in assessments of dangerousness to self or others as it relates to civil commitment cases. The requirements for civil commitment have been increasingly refined through such decisions as the celebrated Donaldson case (O'Connor v. Donaldson, 95 S. Ct. 2486, 1975).

At present, the basic requirements for civil commitment are 1) presence of mental illness or disorder, leading to 2) dangerousness. This dangerousness is further interpreted as being physically dangerous to others, or being unable to provide the basics of life for oneself. In addition (particularly following the Donaldson case), 3) some form of effective treatment must be available where the client is to be committed, and 4) the least restrictive alternative must be used.

The prediction of dangerousness is one of the most difficult assessment questions a clinician must face (Shah, 1981; Megargee, 1981). The decision has to focus on reasonably immediate dangerousness to self or others, and the clinician must come to a decision under the standard of "reasonable probability." On the first point, the clinician could act on the most accurate prediction of dangerousness available by simply collecting all persons who had committed a severe assault just as they left a penitentiary and then commit them, since in the long run it is reasonably certain that a high proportion of these individuals will endanger others. Of course, they do not provide an immediate threat of dangerousness—the issue here.

With regard to the clinician's prediction of dangerousness in an individual client, the reader is referred to the sections on aggression and suicide potential. Also, assessments for mental retardation are appropriate, since in some cases there is an inability to provide one's basic life care. Consideration of organic dysfunction (or CNSI) may also be relevant (Monroe, 1981), as in the senile individual who is a diabetic. Such persons would not be able to take medication as required, and in that sense would endanger their own life. The clinician must recall, however, that the ability to predict specific dangerousness in any reasonably circumscribed period of time is very low, and, in most cases, probably not at a level to warrant the cost, that is, the restriction of a person's freedom and civil liberties (Shah, 1981; Megargee, 1981).

## Incompetency

Incompetency refers to a variety of legal situations—handling an estate or making a will—and the criteria differ for each of these. With the exception of competency to stand trial, clinicians have seldom been involved. However, some attorneys are now asking psychologists or other clinicians to assess their clients at the time they write a will if the attorney thinks there might be any future contesting of the will on the basis of competency. The clinician's report, made at the time of the writing of the will, is then filed with the will, making any later challenge rather absurd since the original assessment will be based on far more data than will be available following the individual's death.

In general, competency to stand trial requires that these people have adequate memory function and intelligence and be reasonably oriented as to place and time. Insanity refers to the mental condition at the time they allegedly committed the crime, whereas incompetency to stand trial refers to their mental condition at the time of the trial. In addition, and more specifically, the Supreme Court has stipulated that "the test must be whether he has sufficient present ability to consult with his lawyer with a reasonable degree of rational understanding—and whether he has a rational as well as a factual understanding of the proceedings against him" (Dusky v. United States, 362 US 402, 1960). They have to understand the nature of the proceedings with which they are involved and the consequences of those proceedings and manifest an ability to cooperate with the attorney in the preparation of their defense.

These are clearly different criteria from any of the notions relating to insanity. These are much more specific and more related to actual behavior than to inferred mental status. Yet many clinicians who testify regarding incompetency do not realize this differentiation (Schwitzgebel & Schwitzgebel, 1980), and as a result often confuse the issue of competency with that of either "psychosis" or "responsibility."

One of the major ways an individual can be incompetent is as a result of inadequate intellectual ability; the reader is referred to the prior section on mental retardation. However, the clinician should not make a decision by using a strict transition from any particular IQ to an arbitrary cut-off point for competency. The IQ is a critical variable, but the clinician must also take into account other factors, such as history of adaptation, common sense, and any already observed ability to cooperate with the attorney and discuss the issues of law. Most individuals with mild mental retardation can cooperate effectively, although not always. As one proceeds through the levels of moderate, severe, and profound mental retardation, the proportion of those persons who cannot competently assist in their trial rises quickly.

If clinicians do any significant number of competency screenings, it is strongly recommended that they become familiar with and use the competency screening instruments devised by the Laboratory of Community Psychiatry (1973) at Harvard, particularly the Competency Assessment Instrument (CAI) and the Competency Screening Test (CST). That group also attempted to develop a projective test for competency, similar in design to the TAT, but so far have not found adequate reliability and validity.

The CAI attempts to standardize and structure the interview procedure. It is formulated as a set of thirteen areas of ego-awareness, covering virtually all of the legal grounds required of defendants if they are to cope effectively with such proceedings. Some of the areas assessed by the CAI are: awareness of available legal defenses, understanding of court procedures, appreciation of charges, range and nature of possible penalties, appraisal of possible outcome, capacity to inform the attorney adequately, and capacity to testify. The client is then evaluated on a scoring system of one (total incompetency) to six (totally competent) on the degree of ability in each area, based on an extensive interview as well as the history data. For example, in the ego function of "quality of relating to attorney," some of the suggested questions are: "Do you think your attorney is trying to do a good job for you?" or "Do you agree with his plans for handling your case?"

Interrater reliability on the scoring of responses to the items in the latest version of the CAI is .87, definitely an acceptable figure. The authors make the point that the efficacy and reliability of this instrument, as well as the Competency Screening Test, are directly correlated with experience with the instrument and with the competency process itself. Reliability increased dramatically from the point of the first experience with the CAI to its fourth or fifth use. Before using these instruments, a test use with some colleague consultation is advised. Persons can obtain a full report of this project, entitled *Competency to Stand Trial and Mental Illness*, from the National Institute of Mental Health, Center for Crime and Delinquency, 5600 Fishers Lane, Rockville, Maryland 20852, or can get in touch with the Laboratory of Community Psychiatry at Harvard University.

The CST is a sentence-completion technique that has been copyrighted by the project's psychologists, Paul Lipsitt and David Lelos. It consists of twenty-two sentence stems, such as "when Phil was accused of the crime, he . . . ," and the like. A handbook in the appendix of the report gives differently scored answers for each item, as they are scaled as either 0, 1, or 2, with higher scores indicating higher levels of competency.

The five items that were found to be particularly predictive of competency are:[1]

9. When the lawyer questioned his client in court, the client said . . .
13. When the witness testifying against Harry gave incorrect evidence, he . . .
14. When Bob disagreed with his lawyer on his defense . . .
19. When I think of being sent to prison . . .
22. If I had a chance to speak to the Judge . . .

The scoring emphasizes degrees of legal understanding and psychological integration. For example, on No. 9 above, answers such as "I am not guilty" or "I did not do anything" are assigned a 2, whereas an overspecific, vague, or hesitant response, such as "he had no knowledge of it," or "I don't know why—I guess I'm not guilty" brings the score down to 1. Irrelevant answers such as "he was too nervous to talk," or "the obvious thing"

1. P. Lipsitt and D. Lelos, *Competency Screening Test*, copyright 1970 by P. Lipsitt and D. Lelos, Used with permission.

are scored zero. Other similar scoring procedures are used with the other five items.

An impressive level of interrater reliability of .93 was obtained for the CST, using standard Z scores. Also, the overall predictive accuracy of the CST "in agreement with subsequent court determinations of competency," was 89.7 percent. By combining the CST predictive information with the validity scales of the MMPI and the female and male Draw-A-Person test, an accuracy rate above .90 is obtained.

There is some evidence that the CST screening was more valid than the highly structured and practiced judgments made by their trained raters. For example, some persons who were eventually designated as incompetent by the raters, based on overall data, actually showed clear evidence of competence throughout all the tests. However, these particular individuals had a history of markedly aggressive behavior and their crimes were repugnant to the community. Hence, the raters may have been swayed by those issues.

Shatin (1979) found that a brief form of the Competency Screening Test (again, items 9, 13, 14, 19, 22) correlated .92 with the full scale version in twenty-one female patients in a forensic psychiatric service examined for mental competence to stand trial, a result consistent with some data collected by the test's authors. This brief form also classified seventeen of the twenty-one patients in direct agreement with the results of a full clinical evaluation. Thus, there is good reason to believe that these five items will be useful and applicable to preliminary competency evaluations.

An excellent competency examination would include the Competency Assessment Instrument as a means of structuring the interview, the Competency Screening Test, a WAIS, an MMPI, and further assessments specific to potential malingering and personality functioning, such as the 16 PF and the Marlowe-Crowne Social Desirability Scale.

## Conclusion

From a general perspective, anyone who is called on to testify as an expert witness would do well to remember the following points on how to deal with the courtroom situation (Pacht et al., 1973):[1]

1. Prepare your inferences and opinions from the data ahead of time, as they will be better received by the court than simple data statements.
2. To the degree possible, be in contact with the attorney ahead of time so as to be aware, optimally through a dry run, of the questioning that will occur.

1. A. Pacht, J. Kuehn, H. Bassett, and M. Nash, "The Current Status of the Psychologist as an Expert Witness." *Professional Psychology*, 1973, 4, pp. 409–413. Used with permission.

3. Be accurate and honest to all parties involved in describing the limits of your expertise.

4. Be prepared to give a general overview of all examination devices used, being ready to explain their functioning, general degree of usage, and some idea of their validity in language the court will find acceptable and understandable.

5. Prepare testimony to avoid the use of jargon that is not easily understood by nonprofessionals.

6. Never testify from the perspective of being an advocate or an adversary. Simply give an honest and thorough account, and attempt to avoid any disservice to the court and client.

# Appendix A

# General Outline for Report Writing

The following general outline has been found to be useful in report writing. The clinician collects all relevant data and then goes through the sequence point by point as the report is dictated or written. Sequence, exclusion of subsections, or inclusion of other information sections is easily adjusted to the requirements of an individual case.

## Report Issues and Questions

A. *Level of Response:*
   Answer questions fully? Volunteer information? Protocols adequate? Attitude toward testing?

B. *General Characteristics:*
   Age, Education attained, Dress, Speech. Socioeconomic status?

C. *Historical Factors:*
   Level of adjustment—As child? As adolescent? Prior hospitalizations and diagnoses? Parental relationships? Then and now? Sibling relationships? Then and now?

D. *Other Present Situational Factors:*
   Marital relationship? Children? Job or School? Other maintaining factors?

E. *Affect and Level of Anxiety:*
   Amount? Appropriateness? In-session versus ongoing functioning? General mood? Effects on testing?

F. *IQ Level:*
   Subtest variability? Educational preparation versus inherent ability? Potential functioning? Personality inferences?

G. *Organic Involvement:*
   Degree? Specific or Global? Cause—alcoholism, birth, or prenatal factors, trauma? Cause of or coincidental to other disorder?

H. *Thought Processes:*
   Hallucinations? Delusions? Paranoid traits? Degree of insight? Adequate social judgments? Adequate abstracting ability? Orientation to environment?

I. *Overall Statement of Personality Functioning—Diagnosis*

J. *Treatment Recommendations:*
   Individual? Group therapy? Chemotherapy? Hospitalization? Predictions of dangerousness? To self? To others? Interest in change? Probability of maintenance in treatment?

K. *Prognosis, Summary Formulations, and Conclusions*

# Appendix B

## Meyer Information Battery

(When adapting this battery, more adequate space
for responses should be included.)

Name _____ Age _____ Sex _____ Date _____

Please finish each of the sentences and say as much as you can about how
you feel. Use your true feelings in your answers. Try to do every one and
say as much as possible about yourself. Thank you.

My favorite kind of job would be _____

_____

Men think I _____

_____

I could be a better worker if _____

_____

Women think I _____

_____

My school grades _____

_____

My father _____

_____

Failure _____

_____

Most bosses _____

_____

My blood boils when _____

_____

My biggest fear is _____

_____

My mother _____

_____

I like best the kind of work which _____

_____

My proudest time is _____

_____

I wish I could forget _____

_____

If things go badly for you, do you get angry or depressed? _____

_____

What do you then do about it? _____

_____

Do you feel it would help to talk to anyone about your problems? _____

_____

Why or why not? _____

_____

What do you think the future holds for you and why? _____

_____

At what time in your life were you closest to panic? _____

_____

 Why? _____

_____

When did you feel most guilty? _____

_____

 Why? _____

_____

What does marriage mean to you? _____

_____

Explain in some detail what death means to you. _____

_____

_____

If I could be anything that I wished, I would choose to be _____

_____ because _____

_____

If I could have any three wishes in the world, I would wish

 1. _____

 2. _____

 3. _____

If I could make any one change in other people, it would be _____

_____

because _____

The very earliest thing that I can remember as a child is _____

_____

_____

My most pleasant memory is _____

_____

_____

My most unpleasant memory is _____

_____

_____

Explain the four proverbs below. For example, the proverb *Large oaks from little acorns grow* means that great things may have small beginnings. Say as best you can what each of these proverbs means.

When the cat's away the mice will play _____

_____

_____

It never rains but it pours _____

_____

_____

Don't cry over spilt milk _____

_____

_____

The burnt child dreads the fire _____

_____

_____

If the following people were asked to describe you in one word, what word would each probably use?

Mother _____

Father _____

Brother(s) _____

Sister(s) _____

Your spouse, or most intimate opposite sex friend _____

Your best friend now _____

Your  boss  _____

Your son(s) _____

Your  daughter(s)  _____

## 2. Draw-A-Group

Now, please draw a picture of any group scene that involves you and at least two other people. I know that many people are not artists and may seldom draw anything—however, simply go ahead and do your best. Use first names or role names (e.g., Jack, Sue, Amy, friend, father, sister, me, etc.) to label each of the figures in your drawing. Remember, I understand that not everyone draws well or even likes to draw—all I want is your best effort. Thank you.

### 3. Drawing Explanation

Use the space below to describe what is happening in the drawing you made. Describe what is going on; whether someone is talking to someone; what they are saying; or anything else that is important. Give all the details you can. Thank you.

What is your most serious physical problem at this time? _____

_____

What treatment are you receiving? _____

_____

What is your most serious emotional problem at this time? _____

Why? _____

_____

How could other people help you change for the better?_____

_____

Do you prefer to live in the city, the suburbs, or the country? _____

Why? _____

_____

Which man of the past or present do you most admire? _____

Why? _____

Which woman of the past or present do you most admire? _____

Why? _____

Who has been more meaningful to you, your father or your mother? _____

Why? _____

Do you practice a religion? _____ Why and in what way, or why not? ____

_____

Has your sexual history been good or bad? _____ Describe it and say why
it has been good or bad for you _____

_____

Do you believe in God? _____ Why or why not? _____

_____

What has been the greatest injustice you have suffered? _____

_____ What did you do about it? _____

_____

*Thank you for your cooperation*

# Appendix C

## Neuropsychological Assessment Process

1. Behavior during Interview(s); Physical Appearance

2. Presenting problem
   A. Symptoms
      1. Self Report
      2. Observation
      3. Corollary Reports

   B. Dimensions of Problem
      1. Duration
      2. Pervasiveness
      3. Severity
      4. Frequency

3. Background
   A. Historical Setting
      1. Onset of symptoms (acute? gradual?)
      2. Circumstances surrounding onset
      3. Evidence of, data re premorbid functioning

   B. Relevant Organismic Variables
      1. Age
      2. Sex
      3. Educational background
      4. Socioeconomic status
      5. Occupational status, responsibilities

   C. Current Physical/Physiological Condition
      1. Medication; types and dosages
      2. Medical complications (e.g., metastasis)
      3. Other factors not directly related to presenting problem

D. Consequences and Implications of Presenting Problem
1. Functional aspects of impairment regarding:
   job
   family
   school
   social milieu
2. Legal status (e.g., pending litigation)
3. Necessary changes in habits, roles (especially if acute)
4. Adoption of coping skills, defense mechanisms, both healthy and unhealthy

4. Evaluation of Current Performance Capabilities Based on Results of Comprehensive Assessment Procedure
   A. Content of comprehensive assessment battery:
   1. Analysis of current intellectual functioning, using global instrument (e.g., WISC-R, WAIS)
   2. Assessment of language skills:
      Reading
      Writing
      Comprehension
      Speech and articulation
   3. Evaluation of reasoning and problem solving, both verbal and nonverbal
   4. Evaluation of motor speed and coordination both unilaterally and bilaterally
   5. Evaluation of somatoperceptual sensitivity, both unilaterally and bilaterally
   6. Assessment of memory functions:
      immediate
      short-term
      long-term
   7. Evaluation of ability to concentrate and attend reliably to instructions and tasks
   8. Evaluation of visuo-spatial, visuo-constructional skills
   9. Rough screening for evidence of primary sensory impairment

## Application of Data Obtained
## from Neuropsychological Evaluation

1. Detailed description of strengths/weaknesses based on an analysis of formal test data
   a. Identify current level of overall functioning
   b. Indicate consistency of current performance

    c. Estimate quality of present functioning vis-à-vis premorbid characteristics

    d. Estimate stability of current results

2. Evaluation of patient's current attitudes toward his/her situation:
    a. Expectancies regarding recovery
    b. Attitude toward disease
    c. Motivation for treatment
    d. Understanding of status/condition
    e. Coping skills, responses to stress and crisis

3. Identification of targets for modification, intervention

4. Priority of treatment recommendations (including reevaluation and follow-up), based on available resources

5. Judgment regarding prognosis, based on:
    a. Age at time of onset
    b. Phase of illness or disease
    c. Known morbidity rates
    d. Severity of affliction
    e. Accessibility of family, other social support systems
    f. Test results
    g. Patient's attitude

6. Arrangement for follow-up and continued monitoring

# Bibliography

Abel, G., Becker, J., Blanchard, E., and Flanagan, B. The behavioral assessment of rapists. In J. Hays, T. Roberts, and K. Solway (Eds.), *Violence and the violent individual*. New York: SP Books, 1981.

Abrams, D., and Wilson, T. Effects of alcohol on social anxiety in women: Cognitive versus physiological processes. *Journal of Abnormal Psychology*, 1979, *88*, 161–173.

Abramson, P., Perry, L., Seeley, T., Seeley, D., and Rothblatt, A. Thermographic measurement of sexual arousal: A discriminant validity analysis. *Archives of Sexual Behavior*, 1981, *10*, 171–176.

Adams, J. *Psychoanalysis of drug dependence*. New York: Grune & Stratton, 1978.

Adler, G. The borderline-narcissistic personality disorder continuum. *American Journal of Psychiatry*, 1981, *138*, 46–50.

Albert, S., Fox, H., and Kahn, M. Faking psychosis on the Rorschach: Can expert judges detect malingering? *Journal of Personality Assessment*, 1980, *44*, 115–119.

Altman, J., and Wittenborn, J. Depression-prone personality in women. *Journal of Abnormal Psychology*, 1980, *89*, 303–308.

American Psychiatric Association. *Diagnostic and statistical manual of mental disorders* (DSM-I) (1st ed.). Washington, D.C.: American Psychiatric Association, 1952.

———. *Diagnostic and statistical manual of mental disorders* (DSM-II) (2nd ed.). Washington, D.C.: American Psychiatric Association, 1968.

———. *Diagnostic and statistical manual of mental disorders* (DSM-III) (3rd ed.). Washington, D.C.: American Psychiatric Association, 1980.

Arkes, H. Impediments to accurate clinical judgement and possible ways to minimize their impact. *Journal of Consulting and Clinical Psychology*, 1981, *49*, 323–330.

Armentrout, J., and Hauer, A. MMPI's of rapists of adults, rapists of children and non-rapist sex offenders. *Journal of Clinical Psychology*, 1978, *34*, 330–332.

Aronow, E., and Reznikoff, M. *Rorschach content interpretation*. New York: Grune & Stratton, 1976.

Bagarrozzi, D., Jurich, A., and Jackson, R. *Marital and family therapy: New perspectives in theory, research, and practice*. New York: Human Sciences Press, 1982.

Balloun, K., and Holmes, D. Effects of repeated examinations on the ability to detect guilt with a polygraphic examination: A laboratory experiment with a real crime. *Journal of Applied Psychology*, 1979, *64*, 316–322.

Barbaree, H., Marshall, W., and Lanthier, R. Deviant sexual arousal in the rapist. *Behavior Research and Therapy*, 1979, *17*, 215–222.

Barlow, D., Abel, G., and Blanchard, E. Gender identity change in transsexuals. *Archives of General Psychiatry*. 1979, *36*, 1001–1007.

Barrett, C. Personality (character) disorders. In R. Woody (Ed.), *The encyclopedia of clinical assessment*. San Francisco, CA: Jossey-Bass, 1980.

——. Personal Communication, 1981.

Beck, A. *Cognitive therapy and the emotional disorders.* New York: International Universities Press, 1976.

Beck, S. The Rorschach test: A multi-dimensional test of personality. In H. Anderson, H. Harold, and G. Anderson, (Eds.), *An introduction to projective techniques.* Englewood Cliffs, NJ: Prentice-Hall, 1951.

Beck, S., and Beck, A. *Rorschach's test: II. 1 Gradients in mental disorder. Third edition of II. A variety of personality pictures.* New York: Grune & Stratton, 1978.

Beck, S., and Molish, H. *Rorschach's test: Advances in interpretation*, New York: Grune & Stratton, 1952.

Belkin, G. Introduction. In G. Belkin (Ed.), *Contemporary psychotherapies.* Chicago: Rand McNally, 1980.

Belli, M. Transsexual surgery: A new tort. *Journal of Family Law*, 1979, *17*, 487–504.

Bender, L. *A visual motor gestalt test and its clinical use.* New York: American Orthopsychiatric Association, 1938.

Benton, A. The neuropsychology of facial recognition. *American Psychologist*, 1980, *35*, 176–186.

Berger, P. Medical treatment of mental illness. *Science*, 1978, *200*, 974–981.

Berne, E. *Games people play.* New York: Grove, 1964.

Bernheim, K., and Lewine, R. *Schizophrenia.* New York: W.W. Norton, 1979.

Bertinetti, J. Substance abuse. In R. Woody (Ed.), *The encyclopedia of clinical assessment.* San Francisco, CA: Jossey-Bass 1980.

Beutler, L., Karacan, I., Anch, M., Salis, P., Scott, F., and Williams, R. MMPI and MIT discriminators of biogenic and psychogenic impotence. *Journal of Consulting and Clinical Psychology*, 1975, *43*, 899–908.

Blackwell, B. Benzodiazepines: Drug abuse and data abuse. *Psychiatric Opinion*, 1979, *16*, 10, 37.

Blair, J., and Justice, R. *The broken taboo.* New York: Human Science Press, 1979.

Blatt, S., and Allison, J. The intelligence test in personality assessment. In A. Rabin (Ed.), *Projective techniques in personality assessment.* New York: Springer, 1968.

——. The intelligence test in personality assessment. In A. Rabin (Ed.), *Assessment with projective techniques.* New York: Springer, 1981.

Blatt, S., Baker, B., and Weiss, J. Wechsler Object Assembly Subtest and bodily concern. *Journal of Consulting and Clinical Psychology*, 1970, *34*, 269–274.

Boerger, A., Graham, J., and Lilly, R. Behavioral correlates of single-scale MMPI types. *Journal of Consulting and Clinical Psychology*, 1974, *42*, 398–402.

Brandsma, J. *Outpatient treatment of alcoholism.* Baltimore: University Park Press, 1979.

Breggin, P. *Electroshock: Its brain-disabling effects.* New York: Springer, 1979.

Bruch, H. *The golden cage: The enigma of anorexia nervosa.* Cambridge, Mass.: Harvard University Press, 1978.

Budzynski, T., Stoyva, J., and Peffer, K. Biofeedback techniques in psychosomatic disorders. In A. Goldstein and E. Foa (Eds.), *Handbook of behavioral interventions.* New York: Wiley, 1980.

Bugental, J. Someone needs to worry: The existential anxiety of responsibility and decision. In G. Belkin (Ed.), *Contemporary psychotherapies.* Chicago: Rand McNally, 1980.

Burns, J., and Kintz, B. Eye contact while lying during an interview. *Bulletin of the Psychonomic Society,* 1976, 7, 87–89.

Butcher, J. (Ed.). *New developments in the use of the MMPI.* Minneapolis: University of Minnesota Press, 1979.

Carroll, B. A specific laboratory test for the diagnosis of melancholia. *Archives of General Psychiatry,* 1981, 38, 15–22.

Carson, R. Interpretative manual to the MMPI. In J. Butcher (Ed.), *MMPI: Research developments and clinical applications.* New York: McGraw-Hill, 1969.

Casper, R., Eckert, E., Halmi, K., Goldberg, S., and Davis, V. Bulimia. Its incidence and clinical importance in patients with anorexia nervosa. *Archives of General Psychiatry,* 1980, 37, 1030–1035.

Cattell, R. Personal communication, 1978.

———. *Personality and learning theory, Vol. 2: The structure of personality in its environment.* New York: Springer, 1979.

———. *Personality and mood by questionnaire.* San Francisco, CA: Jossey-Bass, 1973.

———. *The scientific analysis of personality.* Chicago: Aldine, 1965.

Cattell, R., Eber, H., and Tatsuoka, M. *Handbook for the Sixteen Personality Factors Questionnaire.* Champaign, IL: IPAT, 1970.

Cattell, R., and Warburton, F. *Objective personality and motivation tests.* Champaign, IL: University of Illinois Press, 1967.

Cautela, J., and Wall, C. Covert conditioning in clinical practice. In A. Goldstein and E. Foa (Eds.), *Handbook of behavioral interventions.* New York: Wiley, 1980.

Chambless, D., and Goldstein, A. The treatment of agoraphobia. In A. Goldstein and E. Foa (Eds.), *Handbook of behavioral interventions.* New York: Wiley, 1980.

Cheek, D. Emotional factors in persistent pain states. *The American Journal of Clinical Hypnosis,* 1965, 9, 100–101.

Cheek, F., and Miller, M. The use of behavior modification techniques in developing socially appropriate behaviors in substance abusers. In J. Lowinson and P. Ruiz (Eds.), *Substance Abuse; Clinical problems and perspectives.* Baltimore: Williams & Wilkins, 1981.

Cleckley, H. *The mask of sanity* (4th ed.). St. Louis, MO: Mosby, 1964.

Cofer, D., and Wittenborn, J. Personality characteristics of formerly depressed women. *Journal of Abnormal Psychology,* 1980, 89, 309–315.

Cohen, M., Seghorn, T., and Calmas, W. Sociometric study of sex offenders. *Journal of Abnormal Psychology,* 1969, 74, 249–255.

Conley, J. An MMPI typology of male alcoholics: Admission, discharge, and outcome date. *Journal of Personality Assessment,* 1981, 45, 33–39.

Costello, R. Empirical derivation of a partial personality typology of alcoholics. *Journal of Studies of Alcoholism*, 1978, *39*, 1258–1266.

Cox, D. Exhibitionism: An overview. In D. Cox and R. Daitzman (Eds.), *Exhibitionism*. New York: Garland STPM, 1980.

Cox, D., and Meyer, R. Behavioral treatment parameters with primary dysmenorrhea. *Journal of Behavioral Medicine*, 1978, *1*, 297–310.

Craigie, F., and Ross, S. The use of a videotape pre-treatment training program to encourage treatment-seeking among alcoholic detoxification patients. *Behavior Therapy*, 1980, *11*, 141–147.

Curran, J., Monti, P., and Corriveau, D. Treatment of schizophrenia. In A. Bellack, M. Hersen, and A. Kazdin (Eds.) *International handbook of behavior modification and therapy*. New York: Plenum, 1982.

Dahlstrom, W., and Dahlstrom, L. (Eds.) *Basic readings on the MMPI*. Minneapolis: University of Minnesota Press, 1980.

Dahlstrom, W., and Welsh, G. *An MMPI Handbook: A guide to clinical practice and research*. Minneapolis: University of Minnesota Press, 1980.

Dahlstrom, W., Welsh, G., and Dahlstrom, L. E. *An MMPI Handbook Vol. 1. Clinical Interpretation*. Minneapolis: University of Minnesota Press, 1972.

———. *An MMPI Handbook, Vol. 2: Research Applications*. Minneapolis: University of Minnesota Press, 1975.

Davis, K., and Sines, J. An antisocial behavior pattern associated with a specific MMPI profile. *Journal of Consulting and Clinical Psychology*, 1971, *36*, 229–234.

Davison, G. Homosexuality: The ethical challenge. *Journal of Consulting and Clinical Psychology*, 1976, *44*, 157–162.

———. Not can but ought: The treatment of homosexuality, *Journal of Consulting and Clinical Psychology*, 1978, *45*, 170–172.

Dell, L., Ruzickah, M., and Palisi, A. Personality and other factors associated with gambling addiction. *The International Journal of the Addictions*, 1981, *16*, 149–156.

Diaz-Buxo, J., Caudle, J., Chandler, J., Farmer, C., and Holbrook, W. Dialysis of schizophrenic patients: A double-blind study. *American Journal of Psychiatry*, 1980, *137*, 1220–1222.

Donnelly, E., Murphy, D., Waldaman, I., and Reynolds, T. MMPI differences between unipolar and bipolar depressed subjects: A replication. *Journal of Clinical Psychology*, 1976, *32*, 610–612.

Duckworth, J. *MMPI interpretation manual for counselors and clinicians*. Muncie, IN: Accelerated Development, 1979.

Duehn, W. Covert sensitization in group treatment of adolescent drug abusers. *International Journal of the Addictions*, 1978, *13*, 485–491.

Easson, W. Myxedema psychosis: Insanity defense in homicide. *The Journal of Clinical Psychiatry*, 1980, *41*, 316–318.

Eber, H. Personal Communication, 1972.

———. Personal Communication, 1975.

Edinger, J. Cross-validation of the Megargee MMPI typology for prisoners. *Journal of Consulting and Clinical Psychology*, 1979, *47*, 234–242.

Ellis, A. *Humanistic psychotherapy: The rational-emotive approach*. New York: McGraw-Hill, 1973.

————. A note on the treatment of agoraphobics with cognitive modification versus prolonged exposure "in vivo." *Behavior Research and Therapy*, 1979, *17*, 162–164.

————. A young male who is afraid of becoming a fixed homosexual. In G. Belkin (Ed.), *Contemporary psychotherapies*. Chicago: Rand McNally, 1980.

Ellsworth, R., Collins, J., Casey, N., Schoonover, R., Hickey, R., Hyer, L., Twenlow, S., and Nesselroade, J. Some characteristics of effective psychiatric treatment programs. *Journal of Consulting and Clinical Psychology*, 1979, *47*, 799–817.

Emmelkamp, P. Anxiety and fear. In A. Bellack, M. Hersen, and A. Kazdin (Eds.). *International handbook of behavior modification and therapy*. New York: Plenum, 1982.

Emmelkamp, P., VanDerHelm, M., VanZanten, B., and Plochg, I. Treatment of obsessive-compulsive patients: The contribution of self-instructional training to the effectiveness of exposure. *Behavior Research and Training*, 1980, *18*, 61–66.

Exner, J. *The Rorschach: A comprehensive system (Vol. 2)*. New York: Wiley, 1974.

————. *The Rorschach: A comprehensive system (Vol. 2) Current research and advanced interpretation*, New York: Wiley, 1978.

Fabry, J. Depression. In R. Woody (Ed.), *Encyclopedia of clinical assessment*. San Francisco, CA: Jossey-Bass, 1980.

Fersch, E. *Psychology and psychiatry and courts and corrections*. New York: Wiley, 1980.

Finkelhor, D. *Sexually victimized children*. New York: The Free Press, 1979.

Fischer, J., and Gochros, H. *Handbook of behavior therapy with sexual problems*. (Vols. 1 and 2). New York: Pergamon, 1977.

Fischer, J., Schiavi, R., Edwards, A., Davis, D., Reitman, M., and Fine, V. Evaluation of nocturnal penile tumescence in the differential diagnosis of sexual impotence: A quantitative study. *Archives of General Psychiatry*, 1979, *36*, 431–437.

Fleming, M., Cohen, D., Salt, P., Jones, D., and Jenkins, S. A study of pre- and postsurgical transsexuals: MMPI characteristics. *Archives of Sexual Behavior*, 1981, *10*, 161–170.

Foa, E., Steketee, G., and Ascher, L. Systematic desensitization. In A. Goldstein and E. Foa (Eds.), *Handbook of behavioral interventions*. New York: Wiley, 1980.

Foa, E., and Tillmanns, A. The treatment of obsessive-compulsive neurosis. In A. Goldstein and E. Foa (Eds.), *Handbook of behavioral interventions*. New York: Wiley, 1980.

Fordyce, W. Use of the MMPI in the assessment of chronic pain. In J. Butcher, G. Dahlstrom, M. Gynther, and W. Schofield (Eds.) *Clinical notes on the MMPI*. Nutley, NJ: Roche Psychiatric Service, 1979.

Forgione, A. Instrumentation and techniques. The use of mannequins in the behavioral assessment of child molesters: Two case reports. *Behavior Therapy*, 1976, *7*, 678–685.

Foust, L. The legal significance of formulations of fire-setting behavior. *International Journal of Law and Psychiatry*, 1979, *2*, 371–388.

Fowler, R. *Advanced interpretation of the MMPI*. Guadaloupe, French W.I.: SEPA Workshops, 1981.

———. *The clinical use of the automated MMPI*. Nutley, NJ: Roche Psychiatric Service, 1976.

Fulkerson, S., and Willage, D. Decisional ambiguity as a source of "cannot say" responses on personality questionnaires. *Journal of Personality Assessment*, 1980, *44*, 381–386.

Gardener, E. The role of the classification system in outpatient psychiatry. In M. Katz, J. Cole, and W. Barton (Eds.), *The role of methodology in psychiatry and psychopathology*. Washington, D.C.: U.S. Public Health Service, 1965.

Garfinkel, P., Noldsky, H., and Garner, D. The heterogeneity of anorexia nervosa. *Archives of General Psychiatry*, 1980, *37*, 1036–1040.

Garmezy, N. Never mind the psychologists; Is it good for the children? *The Clinical Psychologist*, 1978, *31*, 1, 4–6.

Gearing, M. The MMPI as a primary differentiator and predictor of behavior in prison: A methodological critique and review of the recent literature. *Psychological Bulletin*, 1979, *86*, 929–963.

Gilberstadt, H., and Duker, J. *A handbook for clinical and actuarial MMPI interpretation*. Philadelphia: Saunders, 1965.

Gilbert, J. *Interpreting psychological test data*. New York: Van Nostrand Reinhold, 1978.

———. *Interpreting Psychological Test Data—II*. New York: Van Nostrand Reinhold, 1980.

Gillis, J., and Blevins, K. Sources of judgmental impairment in paranoid and nonparanoid schizophrenics. *Journal of Abnormal Psychology*, 1978, *87*, 587–596.

Glasser, W. Two cases in reality therapy. In G. Belkin (Ed.), *Contemporary psychotherapies*. Chicago: Rand McNally, 1980.

Glasser, W., and Zunin, L. Reality therapy. In R. Corsini (Ed.), *Current psychotherapies*. Itasca, IL: Peacock, 1973.

Golden, C. *Clinical interpretation of objective psychological tests*. New York: Grune & Stratton, 1979.

Golden, R., and Meehl, P. Detection of the schizoid taxon with MMPI indicators. *Journal of Abnormal Psychology*, 1979, *88*, 217–233.

Goldfried, M., Stricker, G., and Weiner, I. *Rorschach handbook of clinical and research applications*. Englewood Cliffs, NJ: Prentice-Hall, 1971.

Goldstein, A., and Stein, N. *Prescriptive psychotherapies*. New York: Pergamon, 1976.

Graham, J. *The MMPI: A practical guide*. New York: Oxford University Press, 1977.

Gray, H., and Hutchinson, H. The psychopathic personality: A survey of Canadian psychiatrists' opinion. *Canadian Psychiatric Association Journal*, 1964, *9*, 450–461.

Greene, R. *The MMPI: An interpretive manual*. New York: Grune & Stratton, 1980.

Greist, J., Marks, I., Berlin, F., Gournay, K., and Noshirvani, H. Avoidance versus confrontation of fear. *Behavior Therapy*, 1980, *11*, 1–14.

Gross, W., and Carpenter, L. Alcoholic personality: Reality or fiction? *Psychological Reports*, 1971, *28*, 375–378.

Groth, A., and Birnbaum, J. *Men who rape*. New York: Plenum, 1979.

Gruenewald, D. Analogues of multiple personality in psychosis. *International Journal of Clinical and Experimental Hypnosis*, 1978, *26*, 1–8.

Guertin, W., Ladd, C., Frank, G., Rabin, A., and Hiester, D. Research with the WAIS: 1960–1965. *Psychological Bulletin*, 1966, *66*, 385–409.

——. Research with the WAIS: 1965–1970. *Psychological Record*, 1971, *21*, 289–339.

Guertin, W., Rabin, A., Frank, G., and Ladd, C. Research with the WAIS: 1955–1960. *Psychological Bulletin*, 1962, *59*, 1–26.

Gynther, M., Altman, H. and Slettin, I. (a) Replicated correlates of MMPI two-point types: the Missouri Actuarial System. *Journal of Clinical Psychology*, 1973. Monograph Supplement No. 39.

Gynther, M., Altman, H. and Warbin, W. (b) Interpretation of uninterpretable Minnesota Multiphasic Personality Inventory Profiles. *Journal of Consulting and Clinical Psychology*, 1973, *40*, 78–83.

Gynther, M., and Green, S. Accuracy may make a difference, but does a difference make for accuracy?: A response to Pritchard and Rosenblatt. *Journal of Consulting and Clinical Psychology*, 1980, *48*, 268–272.

Haier, R., Murphy, D., and Buchsbaum, M. Paranoia and platelet MAO in normals and nonschizophrenic psychiatric groups. *American Journal of Psychiatry*. 1979, *136*, 308–310.

Hanback, J., and Revelle, W. Arousal and perceptual sensitivity in hypochondriacs. *Journal of Abnormal Psychology*, 1978, *87*, 523–530.

Harmon, T., Nelson, R., and Hayes, S. Self-monitoring of mood versus activity by depressed clients. *Journal of Consulting and Clinical Psychology*, 1980, *48*, 30–38.

Hathaway, S. A coding system for MMPI profiles. *Journal of Consulting Psychology*, 1947, *11*, 334–337.

Hathaway, S., and McKinley, J. *The Minnesota Multiphasic Personality Inventory manual.* New York: Psychological Corporation, 1967.

Hayes, S. Single case experimental design and empirical clinical practice. *Journal of Consulting and Clinical Psychology*, 1981, *49*, 193–211.

Hays, J., Solway, K., and Schreiner, D. Intellectual characteristics of juvenile murderers vs. status offenders. *Psychological Reports*, 1978, *43*, 80–82.

Hedlund, J. MMPI clinical scale correlates. *Journal of Consulting and Clinical Psychology*, 1977, *45*, 739–750.

Heinrich, T., and Amolsch, T. A note on the situational interpretation of WAIS profile patterns. *Journal of Personality Assessment*, 1978, *42*, 418–420.

Heller, J. *Something Happened.* New York: Knopf, 1974, 435.

Helman, C. "Tonic," "Fuel," and "Food": Social and symbolic aspects of the long-term use of psychotropic drugs. *Social Science and Medicine*, 1981, *15B*, 521–533.

Hendrix, E., Thompson, L., and Rau, B. Behavioral treatment of an "hysterically" clenched fist. *Journal of Behavior Therapy and Experimental Psychiatry*, 1978, *9*, 273–276.

Hendrix, M., and Meyer, R. Applications of feedback electromyography. *Journal of Biofeedback*, 1974, *2*, 13–21.

——. Toward more comprehensive and durable client changes: A case report.

*Psychotherapy: Theory, Research, and Practice,* 1976, *13,* 263–266.

Hewett, B., and Martin, W. Psychometric comparisons of sociopathic and psycho-pathological behaviors of alcoholics and drug abusers versus a low drug use control population. *The International Journal of the Addictions,* 1980, *15,* 77–105.

Hogan, R. Implosive therapy in the short-term treatment of psychotics. In G. Belkin (Ed.), *Contemporary psychotherapies.* Chicago: Rand McNally, 1980.

Holland, T., Levi, M., and Watson, C. MMPI basic scales vs. two-point codes in the discrimination of psychopathological groups. *Journal of Clinical Psychology,* 1981, *37,* 394–396.

Holland, T., and Watson, C. Multivariate analysis of WAIS-MMPI relationships among brain-damaged, schizophrenic, neurotic, and alcoholic patients. *Journal of Clinical Psychology,* 1980, *36,* 352–359.

Hollon, S., and Beck, A. Psychotherapy and drug therapy: Comparison and com-binations. In S. Garfield and A. Bergin (Eds.), *Handbook of psychotherapy and behavior change.* New York: Wiley, 1978.

IPAT Staff. *Information Bulletin No. 8 to the 16 PF Handbook.* Champaign, IL: Institute for Personality and Ability Testing, 1963.

———. *Manual for the 16 PF.* Champaign, IL: Institute for Personality and Ability Testing, 1972.

Janov, A. The case of Gary. In G. Belkin (Ed.), *Contemporary psychotherapies.* Chicago: Rand McNally, 1980.

Jarvik, M. The psychopharmacological revolution. *Psychology Today,* 1967, *1,* 51–59.

Johnson, D., and Quinlan, D. Fluid and rigid boundaries of paranoid and non-paranoid schizophrenics on a role-playing task. *Journal of Personality Assessment,* 1980, *44,* 523–531.

Johnson, J., Klinger, D., and Gianetti, R. Band width in diagnostic classification using the MMPI as a predictor. *Journal of Consulting and Clinical Psychology,* 1980, *48,* 340–349.

Johnson, M. Verbal abstracting ability and schizophrenia. *Journal of Consulting Psychology,* 1966, *30,* 275–277.

Karon, B. The Thematic Apperception Test. In A. Rabin (Ed.), *Assessment with projective techniques.* New York: Springer, 1981.

———. The psychoanalysis of schizophrenia. In P. Magero (Ed.), *The construction of madness.* New York: Pergamon, 1976.

Karson, S. The Sixteen Personality Factor Test in clinical practice. *Journal of Clinical Psychology,* 1959, *15,* 174–176.

———. Validating clinical judgments with the 16 PF test. *Journal of Clinical Psychology,* 1960, *16,* 394–397.

Karson, S., and O'Dell, J. *Clinical use of the 16 PF.* Champaign, IL: IPAT, 1976.

Keiser, T., and Lowy, D. Heroin addiction and the Wechsler Digit Span Test. *Journal of Clinical Psychology,* 1980, *36,* 347–351.

Kellam, A. Shoplifting treated by aversion to a film. *Behavior Research and Therapy,* 1969, *7,* 125–127.

Kelley, C., and King, G. (a) Cross validation of the 2–8/8–2 MMPI Code type for young adult psychiatric outpatients. *Journal of Personality Assessment*, 1979, *43*, 143–149.

———. (b) Behavioral correlates of the 2-7-8 MMPI profile type in students at a university mental health center. *Journal of Consulting and Clinical Psychology*, 1979, *47*, 679–685.

———. (c) Behavioral correlates of infrequent 2-point MMPI code types at a university mental health center. *Journal of Clinical Psychology*, 1979, *35*, 576–585.

Kelly, G. *The psychology of personal constructs*. 2 vols. New York: W. W. Norton, 1955.

Kembler, K. The nosologic validity of paranoia (Simple Delusional Disorder). *Archives of General Psychiatry*, 1980, *37*, 695–706.

Kestenbaum, R., Resnick, R., Washton, A., and Lipton, J. *Cocaine effects on psychomotor performance*. Proceedings of the 40th Annual Scientific Meeting Committee on Problems of Drug Dependence. Baltimore, MD, 1978, 333–339.

King, G., and Kelley, C. Behavioral correlates for spike-4, spike-9, and 4-9/9-4 MMPI profiles in students at a university mental health center. *Journal of Clinical Psychology*, 1977, *33*, 718–724.

Kinsey, A., Pomeroy, W., and Martin, C. *Sexual behavior in the human male*. Philadelphia: Saunders, 1948.

———. *Sexual behavior in the human female*. Philadelphia: Saunders, 1953.

Kirman, W. The modern psychoanalytic treatment of depression. In G. Belkin (Ed.), *Contemporary psychotherapies*. Chicago: Rand McNally, 1980.

Kish, G., Hagen, J., Woody, M., and Harvey, H. Alcoholics' recovery from cerebral impairment as a function of duration of abstinence. *Journal of Clinical Psychology*, 1980, *36*, 584–589.

Klee, S., and Meyer, R. Alleviation of performance deficits of depression through thermal feedback training. *Journal of Clinical Psychology*, 1981, *37*, 515–518.

Klingler, D., and Saunders, D. A factor-analysis of the items for nine subtests of the WAIS. *Multivariate Behavioral Research*, 1975, *10*, 131–154.

Klopfer, B., and Davidson, H. *Rorschach's technique: An introductory manual*. New York: Harcourt Brace, 1962.

Klopfer, W., and Taulbee, E. Projective tests. *Annual Review of Psychology*, 1976, *27*, 543–576.

Kolata, G. New drugs and the brain. *Science*, 1979, *205*, 774–777.

Koss, M., and Butcher, J. A comparison of psychiatric patients' self-report with other sources of clinical information. *Journal of Research in Personality*, 1973, *7*, 225–236.

Krasegnor, N. Analysis and modification of substance abuse. *Behavior Modification*, 1980, *4*, 35–56.

Krug, S. *Clinical analysis questionnaire manual*. Champaign, IL: IPAT, 1980.

———. Further evidence on the 16 PF Distortion Scales. *Journal of Personality Assessment*, 1978, *42*, 513–518.

———. *Interpreting 16 PF profile patterns*. Champaign, IL: IPAT, 1981.

Kunce, J., Ryan, J., and Eckelman, C. Violent behavior and differential WAIS characteristics. *Journal of Consulting and Clinical Psychology*, 1976, *44*, 42–45.

Kupfer, D. Psychiatric history and mental status examination. In N. Freedman, H. Kaplan, and B. Sadock (Eds.), *Comprehensive textbook of psychiatry, II.* Baltimore: Williams & Wilkins, 1975.

Kurlychek, R., and Jordan, L. MMPI code types of responsible and nonresponsible criminal defendants. *Journal of Clinical Psychology*, 1980, *36*, 590–593.

Laboratory of Community Psychology. *Competency to stand trial and mental illness.* Rockville, MD: National Institute of Mental Health, 1973.

Lachar, D. *The MMPI: Clinical assessment and automated interpretation.* Los Angeles: Western Psychological Services, 1974.

Lachar, D., and Wrobel, T. Validation of clinicians' hunches: Construction of a new MMPI critical item set. *Journal of Consulting and Clinical Psychology*, 1979, *47*, 277–284.

Lane, J., and Lachar, D. Correlates of broad MMPI categories. *Journal of Clinical Psychology*, 1979, *35*, 560–566.

Lang, A., Goechner, D., Adesso, V., and Marlatt, A. Effects of alcohol on aggression in male social drinkers. *Journal of Abnormal Psychology*, 1975, *84*, 508–518.

Lasch, C. *The culture of narcissism.* New York: W. W. Norton, 1978.

La Torre, R. Devaluation of the human love object: Heterosexual rejection as a possible antecedent to fetishism. *Journal of Abnormal Psychology*, 1980, *89*, 295–298.

Lehmann, H. Schizophrenia: Clinical features. In A. Freedman, H. Kaplan, and B. Sadock (Eds.), *Comprehensive textbook of psychiatry II.* Baltimore: Williams & Wilkins, 1975.

Lerner, P. (Ed.) *Handbook of Rorschach scales.* New York: International Universities Press, 1975.

Levitt, E. *Primer on the Rorschach technique.* Springfield, IL: Charles C. Thomas, 1980.

Lewinsohn, P., and Hoberman, H. Depression. In A. Bellack, M. Hersen, and A. Kazdin (Eds.), *International handbook of behavior modification and therapy.* New York: Plenum, 1982.

Lezak, M. *Neuropsychological assessment.* New York: Oxford University Press, 1976.

Lipton, M. Lithium: Developments in basic and clinical research. *American Journal of Psychiatry*, 1978, *135*, 1059–1061.

Lovibond, S., and Caddy, G. Discriminated aversive control in the modification of alcoholics' drinking behavior. *Behavior Therapy*, 1970, *1*, 437–444.

Lykken, D. A study of anxiety in the sociopathic personality. *Journal of Abnormal and Social Psychology*, 1957, *55*, 6–10.

MacAndrew, C. The differentiation of male alcoholic outpatients from nonalcoholic psychiatric patients by means of the MMPI. *Quarterly Journal of Studies on Alcohol*, 1965, *26*, 238–46.

Macciocchi, S., and Meyer, R. Expectancy mediated behavior change in a detection situation. Unpublished manuscript. 1981.

McConaghy, N. Sexual deviations. In A. Bellack, M. Hersen, and A. Kazdin (Eds.) *International handbook of behavior modification and therapy.* New York: Plenum, 1982.

McPherson, F., Brougham, L., and McLaren, S. Maintenance of improvement in agoraphobic patients treated by behavioral methods—a four-year followup. *Behavior Research and Therapy*, 1980, *18*, 150–152.

Maletzky, B. Assisted covert sensitization. In D. Cox and R. Daitzman (Eds.), *Exhibitionism*. New York: Garland STPM, 1980.

Marks, P., Seeman, W., and Haller, D. *The actuarial use of the MMPI with adolescents and adults*. Baltimore: Williams & Wilkins, 1974.

Marlowe, D., and Crowne, D. *The approval motive*. New York: Wiley, 1964.

Masters, W., and Johnson, V. *Human sexual inadequacy*. Boston: Little, Brown, 1970.

Masters, W., Johnson, V., and Kolodny, R., *Human sexuality*. Boston: Little, Brown, 1982.

Matarazzo, J. *Wechsler's measurement and appraisal of adult intelligence*. Baltimore: Williams and Wilkins, 1972.

Mathew, R., Claghorn, J., and Largen, J. Craving for alcohol in sober alcoholics. *American Journal of Psychiatry*. 1979, *136*, 603–606.

May, W., Barlow, D., and Hay, L. Treatment of stereotypic cross-gender motor behavior using convert modeling in a boy with gender identity confusion. *Journal of Consulting and Clinical Psychology*, 1981, *49*, 388–394.

Meehl, P., and Hathaway, S. The K factor as a suppressor variable in the MMPI. In W. Dahlstrom and L. Dahlstrom (Eds.), *Basic readings on the MMPI*. Minneapolis: University of Minnesota Press, 1980.

Megargee, E. Methodological problems in the prediction of violence. In J. Hays, T. Roberts, and K. Solway (Eds.), *Violence and the violent individual*. New York: SP Books, 1981.

———. (Ed.) *Research in clinical assessment*. New York: Harper & Row, 1966.

Megargee, E., and Bohn, M. *Classifying criminal offenders*. Beverly Hills, CA: Sage, 1979.

Megargee, E., and Cook, P. Negative response bias and the MMPI O-H scale: A response to Deiker. *Journal of Consulting and Clinical Psychology*, 1975, *43*, 725, 729.

Megargee, E., Cook, P., and Mendelsohn, G. Development and validation of an MMPI scale of assaultiveness in overcontrolled individuals. *Journal of Abnormal Psychology*, 1967, *72*, 519–528.

Mehrabian, A. Nonverbal betrayal of feeling. *Journal of Experimental Research in Personality*, 1971, *5*, 64–73.

Meichenbaum, D. *Cognitive behavior modification*. New York: Plenum, 1977.

Meiselman, K. *Incest*. San Francisco, CA: Jossey-Bass, 1978.

Meister, R. *Hypochondria*. New York: Taplinger, 1980.

Merriam, K. The experience of schizophrenia. In P. Magaro (Ed.), *The construction of madness*. Oxford: Pergamon, 1976.

Meyer, R. A behavioral treatment approach to sleepwalking associated with test anxiety. *Journal of Behavior Therapy and Experimental Psychiatry*, 1975, *6*, 202–212.

———. The antisocial personality. In R. Woody (Ed.), *Encyclopedia of mental assessment*. San Francisco, CA: Jossey-Bass, 1980.

Meyer, R., and Freeman, W. A social episode model of human sexual behavior. *Journal of Homosexuality*, 1977, *2*, 123–131.

Meyer, R., and Osborne, Y. H. *Case studies in abnormal behavior.* Boston: Allyn and Bacon, 1982.

Meyer, R., and Salmon, P. *Abnormal psychology.* Boston: Allyn and Bacon, In press.

Millon, T. *Disorders of personality, DSM-III: Axis II.* New York: Wiley, 1981.

Mineka, S. The role of fear in theories of avoidance learning, flooding, and extinction. *Psychological Bulletin*, 1979, *86*, 985–1011.

Money, J., and Weideking, C. Gender identity/role normal differentiation and its transpositions. In B. Wolman (Ed.), *Handbook of human sexuality*. Englewood Cliffs, NJ: Prentice-Hall, 1980.

Monohan, J. *Predicting Violent Behavior.* Beverly Hills, CA: Sage, 1981.

Monroe, R. Brain dysfunction in prisoners. In J. Hays, T. Roberts, and K. Solway (Eds.), *Violence and the violent individual.* New York: SP Books, 1981.

Munjack, D., Oziel, L., Kanno, P., Whipple, K., and Leonard, M. Psychological characteristics of males with secondary erectile failure. *Archives of Sexual Behavior*, 1981, *10*, 123–132.

Murphy, G., and Wetzel, R. Suicide risk by birth cohort in U.S., 1949–1974. *Archives of General Psychiatry*, 1980, *37*, 519–525.

Nelson, J., and Charney, D. The symptoms of major depressive illness. *American Journal of Psychiatry*, 1981, *138*, 1–13.

Nemiah, J. Obsessive compulsive neurosis. In A. Freedman, H. Kaplan, and B. Sadock (Eds.), *Comprehensive textbook of psychiatry/II.* Baltimore: Williams & Wilkins, 1975.

Neuringer, C. Relationship between life and death among individuals of varying levels of suicidality. *Journal of Clinical and Consulting Psychology*, 1979, *47*, 407–408.

Newmark, C. (Ed.) *MMPI clinical and research trends.* New York: Praeger, 1979.

Newmark, C., and Hutchins, T. Age and MMPI indices of schizophrenia. *Journal of Clinical Psychology*, 1980, *36*, 768–769.

NIMH Staff. *Lithium in the treatment of mood disorders.* Rockville, MD: National Institute of Mental Health, 1977.

Ogdon, D. *Psychodiagnostics and personality assessment: A handbook.* Los Angeles: Western Psychological Services, 1977.

Olbrisch, M. Psychotherapeutic interventions in physical health. *American Psychologist*, 1977, *32*, 762–777.

Osgood, C., Luria, Z., Jeans, R., and Smith, A. The three faces of Evelyn: A case report. *Journal of Abnormal Psychology*, 1976, *85*, 247–286.

Ost, L., Verremalm, A., and Johansson, J. Individual response patterns and the effects of different behavioral methods in the treatment of social phobia. *Behavior Research and Therapy*, 1981, *19*, 1–16.

Pachman, J., Foy, D., and Van Erd, M. Goal choice of alcoholics: A comparison of those who choose total abstinence vs. those who choose responsible, controlled drinking. *Journal of Clinical Psychology*, 1978, *34*, 781–783.

Pacht, A., Kuehn, J., Bassett, H., and Nash, M. The current status of the psychologist as an expert witness. *Professional Psychology*, 1973, *4*, 409–413.

Palazzoli, M. *Self-starvation: From individual to family therapy in the treatment of anorexia nervosa.* New York: Jason Aronson, 1978.

Pallis, C., and Bamji, A. McIlroy was here. Or was he? *British Medical Journal,* 1979, *6169,* 973–975.

Pankratz, L. A review of the Munchausen Syndrome, *Clinical Psychology Review,* 1981, *1,* 65–78.

Patalano, F. Comparison of MMPI scores of drug abusers and Mayo Clinic normative groups, *Journal of Clinical Psychology,* 1980, *36,* 576–579.

Pauly, I. The current status of the change of sex operation. *Journal of Nervous and Mental Disease,* 1968, *147,* 460–471.

Penk, W., Woodward, W., Robinowitz, R., and Parr, W. An MMPI comparison of polydrug and heroin abusers. *Journal of Abnormal Psychology,* 1980, *89,* 299–302.

Pennington, B., Peterson, L., and Barker, H. The diagnostic use of the MMPI in organic brain dysfunction. *Journal of Clinical Psychology,* 1979, *35,* 484–492.

Perls, F., Hefferline, R., and Goodman, P. *Gestalt therapy.* New York: Julian, 1958.

Peterson, R. Review of the Rorschach. In O. Buros (Ed.), *The eighth mental measurements yearbook.* Highland Park, NJ: Gryphon Press, 1978.

Philips, J., and Ray, R. Behavioral approaches to childhood disorders: Review and critique. *Behavior Modification,* 1980, *4,* 3–34.

Phillips, L., and Smith, J. *Rorschach interpretation: Advanced technique.* New York: Grune & Stratton, 1953.

Pritchard, D., and Rosenblatt, A. Racial bias in the MMPI: A methodological review. *Journal of Consulting and Clinical Psychology,* 1980, *48,* 263–267.

Propkop, C., Bradley, L., Margolis, R., and Gentry, W. Multivariate analysis of the MMPI profiles of patients with multiple pain complaints. *Journal of Personality Assessment,* 1980, *44,* 246–252.

Rabin, A. Lectures and personal communication, 1964.

———. (Ed.) *Projective techniques in personality assessment.* New York: Springer, 1968.

———. Projective methods: A historical introduction. In A. Rabin (Ed.), *Assessment with projective techniques.* New York: Springer, 1981.

———. Review of the Rorschach. In O. Buros (Ed.), *The seventh mental measurements yearbook.* Highland Park, NJ: Gryphon Press, 1972.

Rachman, S. *Obsessions and compulsions.* Englewood Cliffs, NJ: Prentice-Hall, 1980.

Rada, R., Laws, D., and Kellner, R. Plasma testosterone levels in the rapist. *Psychomatic Medicine,* 1976, *38,* 257–268.

Rader, C. MMPI profile types of exposers, rapists and assaulters in a court services population. *Journal of Consulting and Clinical Psychology,* 1977, *45,* 61–69.

Rapaport, D., Gill, M., and Schafer, R. *Diagnostic psychological testing.* New York: International Universities Press, 1968 (rev. ed., Robert R. Holt [Ed.]).

Rickers-Ovsiankina, M. (Ed.). *Rorschach psychology.* New York: Wiley, 1960.

Ritzler, B., Zambianco, D., Harder, D., and Kaskey, M. Psychotic patterns of the concept of object on the Rorschach Test. *Journal of Abnormal Psychology,* 1980, *89,* 46–55.

Rogers, C. *Client-centered therapy.* Boston: Houghton Mifflin, 1951.

Rogers, R., Dolmetsch, R., and Cavanaugh, J. An empirical approach to insanity evaluations. *Journal of Clinical Psychology*, 1981, *37*, 683–687.

Rogers, T., Forehand, R., and Griest, D. The conduct disordered child: An analysis of family problems. *Clinical Psychology Review*, 1981, *1*, 139–147.

Rorschach, H. *Psychodiagnostics* (5th ed.). New York: Grune & Stratton, 1951.

Rosen, J. *Direct analysis.* New York: Grune & Stratton, 1953.

Rosenhan, D. On being sane in insane places. *Science*, 1973, *179*, 250–258.

Russell, E. Three patterns of brain damage on the WAIS. *Journal of Clinical Psychology*, 1979, *35*, 611–620.

Salmon, P. Personal communication, 1982.

Sanchez, V., and Lewinsohn, P. Assertive behavior and depression. *Journal of Consulting and Clinical Psychology*, 1980, *48*, 119–120.

Schmauk, F. Punishment, arousal, and avoidance learning in sociopaths. *Journal of Abnormal and Social Psychology*, 1970, *76*, 325–335.

Schneidman, E. An overview: Personality, motivation, and behavior theories. In L. Hankoff and B. Einsidler (Eds.), *Suicide.* Littleton, MA: PSG Publishing, 1979.

Schuckit, M., and Morrissey, E. Drug abuse among alcoholic women. *American Journal of Psychiatry*, 1979, *136*, 607–611.

Schwartz, M. *Clinical and psychometric assessment of brain dysfunction in the aged.* Los Angeles: APA Advanced Workshops, 1981.

Schwartz, M. and Graham, J. Construct validity of the MacAndrew Alcoholism Scale. *Journal of Consulting and Clinical Psychology*, 1979, *47*, 1090–1095.

Schwitzgebel, R., and Schwitzgebel, R. *Law and psychological practice.* New York: Wiley, 1980.

Scovern, A., and Kilmann, P. Status of electroconvulsive therapy: Review of the outcome literature. *Psychological Bulletin*, 1980, *87*, 260–303.

Seamons, D., Howell, R., Carlisle, A., and Roe, A. Rorschach simulation of mental illness and normality by psychotic and nonpsychotic legal offenders. *Journal of Personality Assessment*, 1981, *45*, 130–135.

Selye, H. *The stress of life.* New York: McGraw-Hill, 1956.

Seixas, F. Alcohol. In J. Lowinson and P. Ruiz (Eds.), *Substance abuse: Clinical problems and perspectives.* Baltimore: Williams & Wilkins, 1981.

Shacht, T., and Nathan, P. But is it good for psychologists? *American Psychologist*, 1977, *32*, 1017–1025.

Shafer, R. *Clinical application of psychological tests.* New York: International Universities Press, 1948.

———. *Psychoanalytic interpretation in Rorschach testing.* New York: Grune & Stratton, 1954.

Shah, S. Dangerousness: Conceptual, prediction, and public policy issues. In J. Hays, T. Roberts, and K. Solway (Eds.), *Violence and the violent individual.* New York: SP Books, 1981.

Shatin, L. Brief form of the Competency Screening Test for Mental Competence to Stand Trial. *Journal of Clinical Psychology*, 1979, *35*, 464–467.

Sherry, G., and Levine, B. An examination of procedural variables in flooding therapy. *Behavioral Therapy*, 1980, *11*, 148–155.

Silver, R., Isaacs, K., and Mansky, P. MMPI correlates of affective disorders. *Journal of Clinical Psychology*, 1981, *37*, 836–839.

Silverman, L. Psychoanalytic theory: The reports of my death are greatly exaggerated. *American Psychologist*, 1976, *31*, 621–637.

Sinnott, A., Jones, A., Scott-Fordham, A., and Woodward, R. Augmentation of in vivo exposure treatment for agoraphobia by the formation of neighborhood self-help groups. *Behaviour Research and Therapy*, 1981, *19*, 339–347.

Slavney, P., Breitner, J., and Rabins, P. Variability of mood and hysterical traits in women. *Journal of Psychiatric Research*, 1977, *13*, 155–160.

Small, A., Madero, J., Gross, H., Teagno, L., Leib, J., and Ebert, M. A comparative analysis of primary anorexics and schizophrenics on the MMPI. *Journal of Clinical Psychology*, 1981, *37*, 733–736.

Smith, C., and Graham, J. Behavioral correlates for the MMPI standard F scale and for a modified F scale for Black and White psychiatric populations. *Journal of Consulting and Clinical Psychology*, 1981, *49*, 455–459.

Smith, M., and Glass, G. Meta-analysis of psychotherapy outcome studies. *American Psychologist*, 1977, *32*, 955–1008.

Smith, R. Voyeurism: A review of the literature. *Archives of Sexual Behavior*, 1976, *5*, 585–609.

Smith, S., and Meyer, R. Working between the legal system and the therapist. In D. Cox and R. Daitzman (Eds.), *Exhibitionism*. New York: Garland STPM 1980.

Sneddon, J. Myasthenia gravis—The difficult diagnosis. *British Journal of Psychiatry*, 1980, *136*, 92–93.

Sobell, M., Sobell, L., Ersner-Hershfield, S., and Nirenberg, T. Alcohol and drug problems. In A. Bellack, M. Hersen, and A. Kazdin (Eds.) *International handbook of behavior modification and therapy*. New York: Plenum, 1982.

Spiegel, D. SPI and MMPI predictors of psychopathology. *Journal of Projective Techniques and Personality Assessment*, 1969, *33*, 265–273.

Spitzer, R., Cohen, J., Fliess, J., and Endicott, J. Quantification of agreement in psychiatric diagnosis: A new approach. *Archives of General Psychiatry*, 1967. *17*, 83–87.

Spitzer, R., Forman, J., and Nee, J. DSM-III field trials: Initial interrater diagnostic reliability. *American Journal of Psychiatry*, 1979, *136*, 815–817.

Spitzer, R., Skodol, A., Gibbon, M., and Williams, J. *DSM-III case book*. Washington, D.C.: American Psychiatric Association, 1981.

Squire, L., Slater, P., and Miller, P. Retrograde amnesia and bilateral ECT. *Archives of General Psychiatry*, 1981, *38*, 89–95.

Stern, G., Miller, C., Ewy, H., and Grant, P. Perceived control: Bogus rate feedback and reported symptom reduction for individuals with accumulated life stress events. *Biofeedback and Self-Regulation*, 1980, *5*, 37–50.

Strassberg, D., Reimherr, F., Ward, M., Russell, S., and Cole, A. The MMPI and chronic pain. *Journal of Consulting and Clinical Psychology*, 1981, *49*, 220–226.

Streiner, D., and Miller, H. Prorating incomplete Wiggins and MacAndrew Scales. *Journal of Personality Assessment*, 1981, *45*, 427–429.

————. A table for prorating Incomplete Form MMPI's. *Journal of Consulting and Clinical Psychology*, 1979, *47*, 474–477.

Svanum, S., and Dallas, C. Alcoholic MMPI types, and their relationship to patient characteristics, polydrug abuse, and abstinence following treatment. *Journal of Personality Assessment*, 1981, *45*, 278–287.

Tollison, C., and Adams, H. *Sexual disorders*. New York: Gardner, 1979.

Trethvithick, L., and Hosch, H. MMPI correlates of drug addiction based on drug of choice. *Journal of Consulting and Clinical Psychology*, 1978, *46*, 180.

Tripp, C. *The homosexual matrix*. New York: New American, 1976.

Trotter, S. Federal Commission OK's psychosurgery. *APA Monitor*, 1976, *7*, 4–5.

Tsushima, W., and Wedding, D. MMPI results of male candidates for transsexual surgery. *Journal of Personality Assessment*, 1979, *43*, 385–387.

Tucker, D. Lateral brain function, emotion, and conceptualization. *Psychological Bulletin*, 1981, *89*, 19–46.

Tullman, G., Gilner, F., Kolodny, R., Dorwbush, R., and Tullman, G. The pre- and post-therapy measurement of communication skills of couples undergoing sex therapy at the Masters and Johnson Institute. *Archives of Sexual Behavior*, 1981, *10*, 95–110.

Van Hasselt, V., Milliones, J., and Hersen, M. Behavioral assessment of drug addiction: Strategies and issues in research and treatment. *The International Journal of the Addictions*, 1981, *16*, 43–68.

Virkunen, M. Victim-precipitated pedophilia offenses. *British Journal of Criminology*, 1975, *15*, 175–179.

Vogel, G., Vogel, F., McAbee, R., and Thurmond, A. Improvement of depression by REM sleep deprivation. *Archives of General Psychiatry*, 1980, *37*, 247–253.

Wadsworth, R., and Checketts, K. Influence of religious affiliation on psychodiagnosis. *Journal of Consulting and Clinical Psychology*, 1980, *48*, 234–240.

Wagner, E., and Heise, M. Rorschach and Hand Test Data comparing bipolar patients in manic and depressive states. *Journal of Personality Assessment*, 1981, *45*, 240–249.

Wagner, E., and Wagner, C. Similar Rorschach patterning in three cases of anorexia nervosa. *Journal of Personality Assessment*. 1978, *42*, 426–429.

Walker, P. The role of antiandrogens in the treatment of sex offenders. In B. Qualls, J. Wincze, and D. Barlow (Eds.), *The prevention of sexual disorders*. New York: Plenum, 1978.

Walker, P., and Meyer, W. Medroxyprogesterone Acetate treatment for paraphiliac sex offenders. In J. Hays, T. Roberts, and K. Solway (Eds.), *Violence and the violent individual*. New York: SP Books, 1981.

Ward, L., and Selby, R. An abbreviation of the MMPI with increased comprehensibility and reliability. *Journal of Clinical Psychology*, 1980, *36*, 180–186.

Ward, L., and Ward, J. MMPI readability reconsidered. *Journal of Personality Assessment*, 1980, *44*, 387–389.

Warrington, E. Constructional apraxia. In P. Vinker and G. Bruyn (Eds.), *Handbook of Clinical Neurology*. Amsterdam: New Holland, 1969.

Watson, C., Plemel, D., and Jacobs, L. An MMPI sign to separate organic from functional psychiatric patients. *Journal of Clinical Psychology*, 1978, *34*, 398–432.

Weeks, D., Freeman, C., and Kendall, R. ECT: III. Enduring cognitive defects? *The British Journal of Psychiatry*, 1980, *137*, 26–37.

Welsh, G. An extension of Hathaway's MMPI Profile Coding System. *Journal of Consulting Psychology,* 1948, *12,* 343–344.

Wiggins, J. Content dimensions in the MMPI. In J. Butcher (Ed.), *MMPI: Research developments and clinical applications.* New York: McGraw-Hill, 1969.

Wiggins, J., Goldberg, L., and Applebaum, M. MMPI content scales: Interpretive norms and correlations with other scales. *Journal of Consulting and Clinical Psychology,* 1971, *37,* 403–410.

Winder, P., O'Dell, J., and Karson, S. New motivational distortion scales for the 16 PF. *Journal of Personality Assessment,* 1975, *39,* 532–537.

Winer, D. Anger and dissociation: A case study of multiple personality. *Journal of Abnormal Psychology,* 1978, *87,* 368–372.

Winters, K., Weintraub, S., and Neale, V. Validity of MMPI codetypes in identifying DSM-III schizophrenics, unipolars, and bipolars. *Journal of Consulting and Clinical Psychology,* 1981, *49,* 486–487.

Wolin, S., Bennett, L., and Noonan, D. Family rituals and the recurrence of alcoholism over generations. *American Journal of Psychiatry,* 1979, *136,* 589–593.

Wurtman, R., Growden, J., and Barbeau, A. *Choline and lecithin in neurologic and psychiatric diseases.* New York: Raven, 1979.

Yablonsky, L. *Psychodrama: Resolving emotional problems through role playing.* New York: Basic Books, 1976.

Yochelson, S., and Samenow, S. *The criminal mind.* New York: Jason Aronson, 1976.

Yudofsky, S., Williams, D., and Gorman, V. Propranolol in the treatment of rage and violent behavior in patients with chronic brain syndrome. *American Journal of Psychiatry,* 1981, *138,* 218–220.

Zimmerman, I., and Woo-Sam, J. *Clinical interpretation of the Wechsler Adult Intelligence Scale.* New York: Grune & Stratton, 1973.

Zubin, J. But is it good for science? *The Clinical Psychologist.* 1978, *31,* 1–7.

Zuckerman, M., Buchsbaum, M., and Murphy, D. Sensation seeking and its biological correlates. *Psychological Bulletin,* 1980, *88,* 187–214.

# Name Index

Abel, G., 155, 158, 230, 231
Abrams, D., 52
Abramson, P., 156, 231
Adams, H., 178
Adams, J., 191
Adesso, V., 52
Adler, G., 200
Albert, S., 239
Allison, J., 3, 70
Altman, J., 97
American Psychiatric Association, 7, 171
Amolsch, T., 196
Arkes, H., 6
Armentrout, J., 231
Aronow, E., 3
Ascher, L., 114

Bagarrozzi, D., 50, 56, 61, 73, 80, 126, 142, 200, 214, 232
Baker, B., 141
Balloun, K., 241
Bamji, A., 128
Barbaree, H., 230
Barbeau, A., 73
Barker, H., 253
Barlow, D., 155, 158
Barrett, C., 23, 87, 90, 142, 188, 208, 211
Beck, A., 76, 96, 102
Beck, S., 3, 89, 109, 245
Belkin, G., 50, 170, 205
Belli, M., 155
Bender, L., 252, 255, 256, 259
Benton, A., 251, 252, 256
Berger, P., 67
Berne, E., 148, 193
Bernheim, K., 83
Bertinetti, J., 61
Beutler, L., 175
Birnbaum, J., 231
Blackwell, B., 57
Blair, J., 162
Blanchard, E., 155, 158
Blatt, S., 3, 70, 141

Blevins, K., 83
Boerger, A., 3
Bohn, M., 3, 194, 195, 198, 215, 216, 220, 244
Brandsma, J., 56
Breggin, P., 93
Bruch, H., 233, 235
Budzynski, T., 131
Bugental, J., 58, 142
Burns, J., 241
Butcher, J., 3, 14

Caddy, G., 55
Calmas, W., 230
Carpenter, L., 53
Carroll, B., 99
Carson, R., 3, 30
Casper, R., 233, 234
Cattell, R., 3, 5, 38–47
Cautela, J., 50, 63, 160, 210
Chambless, D., 112
Charney, D., 99
Checketts, K., 15
Cheek, D., 139
Cheek, F., 61, 63, 66
Cleckley, H., 194
Cofer, D., 97
Cohen, M., 230
Conley, J., 52, 53
Cook, P., 228, 243
Costello, R., 54
Cox, D., 163, 164, 165, 178
Craigie, F., 55
Crowne, D., 241
Curran, J., 73, 75, 79

Dahlstrom, L., 3
Dahlstrom, W., 3, 45
Dallas, C., 52, 59, 60
Davis, K., 30, 228, 243
Davison, G., 173
Davison, H., 3
Dell, L., 222
Diaz-Buxo, J., 73
Donnelly, E., 103

300

# Subject Index